Libraries and Information Services in the United Kingdom and the Republic of Ireland 2015

Libraries and Information Services in the United Kingdom and the Republic of Ireland 2015

 facet publishing

© CILIP: the Chartered Institute of Library and Information Professionals 2015

Published by Facet Publishing
7 Ridgmount Street, London WC1E 7AE
www.facetpublishing.co.uk

Facet Publishing is wholly owned by CILIP: the Chartered Institute of Library and Information Professionals.

First published as *Libraries in the United Kingdom and the Republic of Ireland* by The Library Association, 1960 and thereafter annually.

Twenty-ninth edition published as *Libraries and Information Services in the United Kingdom and the Republic of Ireland* by Facet Publishing, 2002. This thirty-eighth edition 2015.

ISBN 978-1-85604-801-9
ISSN 1741-7120

This thirty-eighth edition has been compiled by Flagholme Publishing Services and Lin Franklin.

Text printed on FSC accredited material.

MIX
Paper from
responsible sources
FSC® C013604
www.fsc.org

Typeset in 9/11pt Humanist 521 by Flagholme Publishing Services.
Printed and bound in Great Britain by CPI Group (UK) Ltd, Croydon CR0 4YY.

CONTENTS

How this book is organized

Libraries and Information Services in the United Kingdom and the Republic of Ireland is published annually, and is a listing of organizations falling into the five categories below.

I Public library authorities

■ All public library authorities in the UK and the Republic of Ireland, arranged under home countries
  - Public Libraries in England, Northern Ireland, Scotland, Wales and Crown Dependencies
  - Public Libraries in the Republic of Ireland

Service managers and officers are listed, as supplied by the individual authorities.

It is clearly impossible to list here all branch libraries, mobile bases and so on, so each entry includes headquarters/central library details, together with major branches and area/regional/group libraries, as supplied by each individual library. Libraries in this section are arranged by name of authority.

A listing of the nine Government regions in England, indicating which public library authorities fall in their areas, is given on page 369.

2 Academic libraries (arranged by name of institution)

■ University libraries in the UK and the Republic of Ireland, together with major department and site/campus libraries
■ College libraries at the universities of Oxford, Cambridge and London
  Please note: potential users of the Oxford and Cambridge libraries should be aware that their use is restricted to members of the college, and to bona fide scholars on application to the Librarian; any additional information about their use is given with each entry.
■ The university-equivalent colleges in the Republic of Ireland
■ Other degree-awarding institutions in the UK
  All colleges of higher education funded by HEFCE, SHEFC and HEFCW are included.

3 Selected government, national and special libraries in the UK and the Republic of Ireland

■ Special libraries are included if they are one of the main libraries or organizations in their subject field. For example, the British Architectural Library at the Royal Institute of British Architects is included for architecture, the Institution of Civil Engineers for civil engineering.

Many of the libraries in this section require a prior appointment to be made before visiting.

4 Schools and departments of information and library studies

■ Each academic institution offering courses in information and library studies, with full contact details of the departments concerned.

5 Index

■ Organizations are fully indexed by name and place.

Updating Libraries and Information Services in the UK

The directory is compiled by mailing questionnaires or entries for updating to libraries already listed in this book, and to others that have been suggested for inclusion. We would like to thank libraries for taking the time to reply to yet another mailing. Every attempt was made to contact all the libraries, but where no reply was forthcoming after repeated reminders, information from the institution's website at the time of compilation was included and the publishers cannot accept responsiblity for any inaccurate information obtained in this way.

We are dependent upon libraries to keep us informed of changes throughout the year so that their information is as current as possible when we contact them for the preparation of the next edition.

Please help us to improve this directory

Any comments about additions or other changes to *Libraries and Information Services in the United Kingdom and the Republic of Ireland* will be welcomed. Please address them to:

The Editor, Libraries and Information Services in the UK, Facet Publishing, 7 Ridgmount Street, London WC1E 7AE

Tel: 020 7255 0590
e-mail: info@facetpublishing.co.uk

Public Libraries in the United Kingdom, the Channel Islands and the Isle of Man

England
Northern Ireland
Scotland
Wales
Crown Dependencies

Service managers and officers are listed as supplied by the individual authorities

BARKING AND DAGENHAM

Authority: London Borough of Barking and Dagenham
Barking Learning Centre, 2 Town Square, Barking, Essex IG11 7NB
☎020 8724 8530 (enquiries and administration)
e-mail: libraries@lbbd.gov.uk
url: www.lbbd.gov.uk/libraries
Group Manager – Libraries Zoinul Abidin (e-mail: zoinul.abidin@lbbd.gov.uk)
Customer Services Manager Ms Vashti Thorne BA MCLIP (e-mail: vashti.thorne@lbbd.gov.uk)

Central/largest library
Barking Library, Barking Learning Centre, 2 Town Square, Barking, Essex IG11 7NB
☎020 8724 8725

Community libraries
Dagenham Library, 1 Church Elm Lane, Dagenham, Essex RM10 9QS

Marks Gate Library, Marks Gate Childrens Centre, Rose Lane, Chadwell Heath, Essex RM6 5NJ
☎020 8270 4165

Robert Jeyes Community Library, Chadwell Heath Community Centre, High Road, Chadwell Heath, Essex RM6 6AS
☎020 8270 4305

Thames View Library, Bastable Avenue, Barking, Essex IG11 0LG
☎020 8270 4164

Valence Library, Becontree Avenue, Dagenham, Essex RM8 3HS
☎020 8270 6864

BARNET

Authority: London Borough of Barnet
Children's Service – Libraries & Local Studies, Building 4, North London Business Park, Oakleigh Road South, London N11 1NP
☎020 8359 7775
Fax 0870 889 6804
url: www.barnet.gov.uk/libraries
Head of Libraries & Local Studies Ms Hannah Richens BA(Hons) DipILM MCLIP
(e-mail: hannah.richens@barnet.gov.uk)
Operations and Customer Service Manager Ms Gill Harvey BSc(Hons) MCLIP (e-mail: gill.harvey@barnet.gov.uk)
Business Development Manager Mike Fahey (e-mail: mike.fahey@barnet.gov.uk)

Lending libraries

Burnt Oak Library, Watling Avenue, Edgware, Middlesex HA8 0UB
☎020 8359 3880
e-mail: burnt.oak.library@barnet.gov.uk
Library Customer Service Manager David Izzard (e-mail: david.izzard@barnet.gov.uk)

Childs Hill Library, 320 Cricklewood Lane, London NW2 2QE
☎020 8359 3900
e-mail: childshill.library@barnet.gov.uk
Assistant Library Customer Service Manager Irfan Iqbal (e-mail:
irfan.iqbal@barnet.gov.uk)

Chipping Barnet Library, 3 Stapylton Road, Barnet, Herts EN5 4QT
☎020 8359 4040
e-mail: chipping.barnet.library@barnet.gov.uk
Library Customer Service Manager Robert Prosser (e-mail:
robert.prosser@barnet.gov.uk)

Church End Library, 24 Hendon Lane, Finchley, London N3 1TR
☎020 8359 3800
e-mail: church.end.library@barnet.gov.uk
Library Customer Service Manager Steve Saunders (e-mail:
steve.saunders@barnet.gov.uk)

East Barnet Library, 85 Brookhill Road, East Barnet, Herts EN4 8SG
☎020 8359 3860
e-mail: east.barnet.library@barnet.gov.uk
Library Customer Service Manager Ms Claire Finnett (e-mail:
claire.finnett@barnet.gov.uk)

East Finchley Library, 226 High Road, London N2 9BB
☎020 8359 3815
e-mail: east.finchley.library@barnet.gov.uk
Library Customer Service Manager Sim Branaghan (e-mail:
sim.branaghan@barnet.gov.uk)

Edgware Library, Hale Lane, Edgware, Middlesex HA8 8NN
☎020 8359 2626
e-mail: edgware.library@barnet.gov.uk
Library Customer Service Manager Jon Killick (e-mail: jon.killick@barnet.gov.uk)

Golders Green Library, 156 Golders Green Road, London NW11 8HE
☎020 8359 2060
e-mail: golders.green.library@barnet.gov.uk
Library Customer Service Manager Dinul Ullah (e-mail: dinul.ullah@barnet.gov.uk)

Grahame Park Library, The Concourse, London NW9 5XL
☎020 8359 3930
e-mail: grahame.park.library@barnet.gov.uk
Assistant Library Customer Service Manager Ms Nalayini Indran (e-mail:
nalayini.indran@barnet.gov.uk)

Hendon Library, The Burroughs, London NW4 4BQ
☎020 8359 2628

e-mail: hendon.library@barnet.gov.uk
Library Customer Service Manager Ms Sarah Green (e-mail:
sarah.green@barnet.gov.uk)

Mill Hill Library, Hartley Avenue, London NW7 2HX
☎020 8359 3830
e-mail: mill.hill.library@barnet.gov.uk
Library Customer Service Manager Ms Nati Lamela (e-mail:
nati.lamela@barnet.gov.uk)

North Finchley Library, Ravensdale Avenue, North Finchley, London N12 9HP
☎020 8359 3845
e-mail: north.finchley.library@barnet.gov.uk
Library Customer Service Manager Ms Fiona Page-Roberts

Osidge Library, Brunswick Park Road, London N11 1EY
☎020 8359 3920
e-mail: osidge.library@barnet.gov.uk
Library Customer Service Manager Sumbal Bukhari (e-mail:
sumbal.bukhari@barnet.gov.uk)

South Friern Library, Colney Hatch Lane, London N10 1HD
☎020 8359 3946
e-mail: south.friern.library@barnet.gov.uk
Assistant Library Customer Service Manager Ms Lynn McMeechan (e-mail:
lynn.mcmeechan@barnet.gov.uk)

BARNSLEY

Authority: Barnsley Metropolitan Borough Council
Central Library, 36 Wellington Street, Barnsley, South Yorks S70 1WA
☎(01226) 773911
Fax (01226) 773955
e-mail: barnsleylibraryenquiries@barnsley.gov.uk
url: www.barnsley.gov.uk/libraries
Head of Barnsley Libraries & Information Service Mrs Kathryn Green BA(Hons)
MCLIP DMS
Management Support Officer Ms Rachel Sanderson (e-mail:
rachelsanderson@barnsley.gov.uk)

Central/largest library
Central Library, 36 Wellington Street, Barnsley, South Yorks S70 1WA
☎(01226) 773911
Fax (01226) 773955
Senior Information Librarian Ms Lesley Stables (e-mail: lesleystables@barnsley.gov.uk)

BATH AND NORTH EAST SOMERSET

Authority: Bath and North East Somerset Council
**HQ Resources: Customer Service, Bath Central Library, 19a The Podium, Northgate
Street, Bath BA1 5AN**
☎(01225) 394041

url: www.bathnes.gov.uk/libraries
Face to Face and Outreach Operations Manager Mrs June Brassington MCLIP
(01225 396424; e-mail: june_brassington@bathnes.gov.uk)

Central/largest library
Bath Library and Information Centre, 19a The Podium, Northgate Street, Bath BA1 5AN
☎(01225) 394041 (enquiries)
e-mail: libraries@bathnes.gov.uk
SMS (text): (07797) 806545
Libraries Development Manager Ms Julia Burton BLib MCLIP (01225 396078; e-mail:
julia_burton@bathnes.gov.uk)
Customer Services Team Leader – Libraries Mrs Helen Chamberlain BA MCLIP MCMI
(e-mail: helen_chamberlain@bathnes.gov.uk)

Group libraries
Keynsham Library, Riverside, Temple Street (opp Keynsham Leisure Centre), Keynsham,
Bristol BS31 1LA
☎(01225) 394041

Midsomer Norton Library, 119 High Street, Midsomer Norton, Bath BA3 2DA
☎(01225) 394041

BEDFORD

Authority: Bedford Borough Council
Libraries, Bedford Central Library, Harpur Street, Bedford MK40 1PG
☎(01234) 718178
Fax (01234) 315490
url: www.bedford.gov.uk
Head of Libraries Ms Jenny Poad BA DMS MCLIP (e-mail: jenny.poad@bedford.gov.uk)

Central/largest library
Central Library, Harpur Street, Bedford MK40 1PG
☎(01234) 718178
Fax (01234) 718053
e-mail: bedfordshire.libraries@bedford.gov.uk
Central Library & Service Development Manager Ms Kerry O'Neil BA(Hons) MCLIP

Area libraries
Kempston Library, Halsey Road, Kempston, Bedford MK42 8AU
☎(01234) 276453
Fax (01234) 841476
e-mail: bedfordshire.libraries@bedford.gov.uk
Library Manager Ms Jess Taylor

Putnoe Library, Library Walk, Putnoe, Bedford MK41 8HQ
☎(01234) 276462
Fax (01234) 272833
e-mail: bedfordshire.libraries@bedford.gov.uk
Library Manager Ms Coral Clarke

BEXLEY

Authority: London Borough of Bexley
Libraries, Heritage & Archive Service, Ground Floor, Footscray Offices, Maidstone Road, Sidcup, Kent DA14 5HS
☎020 8303 7777
Fax 020 3045 4542
e-mail: libraries@bexley.gov.uk
url: www.bexley.gov.uk
Head of Libraries, Heritage and Archives Ms Judith Mitlin BSc PLD DMS (020 8309 4131; e-mail: judith.mitlin@bexley.gov.uk)

Central/largest library
Central Library, Townley Road, Bexleyheath, Kent DA6 7HJ
☎020 8303 7777
Fax 020 3045 3783
Group Manager Vacant

BIRMINGHAM

Authority: Birmingham City Council
Library of Birmingham, Centenary Square, Broad Street, Birmingham B1 2ND
☎0121 242 4242 (enquiries), 0121 303 6674 (management)
e-mail: enquiries@libraryofbirmingham.gov.uk
url: www.libraryofbirmingham.com
Assistant Director (Library of Birmingham) Brian Gambles MBE MA(Oxon) (e-mail: brian.gambles@birmingham.gov.uk)
Head of Business Management Ms Rebecca Bostock (e-mail: rebecca.bostock@birmingham.gov.uk)
Head of Customer Experience Ms Dawn Beaumont MA MCLIP (e-mail: dawn.beaumont@birmingham.gov.uk)
Head of Learning Resources David Potts BA(Hons) (e-mail: david.potts@birmingham.gov.uk)
Senior Service Manager, Community Libraries Kevin Duffy BA(Hons) PGDipLib (e-mail: kevin.duffy@birmingham.gov.uk)

BLACKBURN WITH DARWEN

Authority: Blackburn with Darwen Borough Council
Central Library, Town Hall Street, Blackburn, Lancashire BB2 1AG
☎(01254) 661221 (enquiries), 01254 587902 (facilities)
Fax (01254) 678898
url: www.blackburn.gov.uk/libraries
Service Manager, Libraries, Heritage and Arts Mrs Kath Sutton BA MCLIP (01254 587907; e-mail: kath.sutton@blackburn.gov.uk)
Principal Librarian: Customer Services Ms Adele Karwat BA MCLIP (01254 587954; e-mail: adele.karwat@blackburn.gov.uk)
Principal Librarian: Literacy Development, Learning and Stock Miss Jean Gabbatt BLib MCLIP (01254 587937; e-mail: jean.gabbatt@blackburn.gov.uk)

Senior Librarian: Literacy Development Mrs Geraldine Wilson MCLIP (01254 587236; e-mail: geraldine.wilson@blackburn.gov.uk)

BLACKPOOL

Authority: Blackpool Borough Council
Cultural Services, Places Directorate, Central Library, Queen Street, Blackpool, Lancs FY1 1PX
☎(01253) 478106 (enquiries)
url: www.blackpool.gov.uk/libraries
Head of Cultural Services Ms Polly Hamilton (e-mail: polly.hamilton@blackpool.gov.uk)
Head of Arts Ms Carolyn Primett BA MA (e-mail: carolyn.primett@blackpool.gov.uk)
Head of Heritage Ms Heather Morrow (e-mail: heather.morrow@blackpool.gov.uk)

Central/largest library
Central Library, Queen Street, Blackpool, Lancs FY1 1PX
☎(01253) 478080

BOLTON

Authority: Bolton Metropolitan Borough Council
Central Library and Museum, Le Mans Crescent, Bolton, Lancs BL1 1SE
☎(01204) 333173
Fax (01204) 332225
e-mail: central.library@bolton.gov.uk; libraries@bolton.gov.uk
url: www.boltonlams.co.uk; www.bolton.gov.uk
Head of Library Service Mrs Julie Spencer MBE BA(Hons) MBA MCLIP (e-mail: julie.spencer@bolton.gov.uk)
Customer Services Manager Mrs Ann Melmoth BA MBA MCLIP (e-mail: ann.melmoth@bolton.gov.uk)
Collections Access Manager Ms Mary Keane BA(Hons) DipLib MCLIP (e-mail: mary.keane@bolton.gov.uk)

BOURNEMOUTH

Authority: Bournemouth Borough Council
Bournemouth Libraries, Information, Community and Culture, Town Hall, Bourne Avenue, Bournemouth BH2 6DY
☎(01202) 454848 (general enquiries)
e-mail: bournemouth@bournemouthlibraries.org.uk
url: www.bournemouth.gov.uk/libraries
Service Director Ms Sue Bickler (01202 454966; e-mail: sue.bickler@bournemouth.gov.uk)
Service and Strategy Manager: Bournemouth Libraries Ms Medi Bernard BA DipLib MCLIP (01202 454618; e-mail: medi.bernard@bournemouthlibraries.org.uk)

Central/largest library
The Bournemouth Library, 22 The Triangle, Bournemouth BH2 5RQ
☎(01202) 454848
Area Manager Ms Vicki Goldie BA(Hons) MCLIP (e-mail: vicki.goldie@bournemouthlibraries.org.uk)

BRACKNELL FOREST

Authority: Bracknell Forest Council
Environment, Culture and Communities, Time Square, Market Street, Bracknell, Berks RG12 IJD
☎(01344) 423149
Fax (01344) 411392
e-mail: bracknell.library@bracknell-forest.gov.uk
url: www.bracknell-forest.gov.uk/libraries
Head of Libraries, Arts and Heritage Ms Ruth Burgess BLib MCLIP (01344 351315;
e-mail: ruth.burgess@bracknell-forest.gov.uk)

Central/largest library

Bracknell Library, Town Square, Bracknell, Berks RG12 1BH
☎(01344) 423149
Fax (01344) 411392
e-mail: bracknell.library@bracknell-forest.gov.uk
url: www.bracknell-forest.gov.uk/libraries
Community Services Manager Mrs Fiona Atkinson BA(Hons) MA MCLIP (e-mail:
fiona.atkinson@bracknell-forest.gov.uk)

BRADFORD

Authority: City of Bradford Metropolitan District Council
City Library, Centenary Square, Bradford BD1 ISD
☎(01274) 433600
e-mail: public.libraries@bradford.gov.uk
url: www.bradford.gov.uk
Assistant Director, Culture and Tourism Tony Stephens (01274 431862; e-mail:
tony.stephens@bradford.gov.uk)

Branch libraries

Branch libraries, c/o Shipley Library, 2 Well Croft, Shipley, Bradford BD18 3QH
☎(01274) 437152
e-mail: public.libraries@bradford.gov.uk
Principal Libraries Officer: Operations North Ms Jackie Kitwood BA DipLib MCLIP
(01274 437152; e-mail: jackie.kitwood@bradford.gov.uk)

BRENT

Authority: London Borough of Brent
Environment and Neighbourhoods, Brent Civic Centre, 5th Floor North, Engineers Way, Wembley, Middlesex HA9 0FJ
☎020 8937 3144
url: www.brent.gov.uk
Strategic Director of Environment and Neighbourhoods Ms Sue Harper
Operational Director Neighbourhoods (Interim) Tom Jeffrey (020 8937 5001; e-mail:
tom.jeffrey@brent.gov.uk)
Head of Libraries, Arts and Heritage Ms Susan McKenzie BA DAA (020 8937 3142;
e-mail: susan.mckenzie@brent.gov.uk)

Area libraries

Ealing Road Library, Coronet Parade, Wembley, Middlesex HA0 4BA
☎020 8937 3560

Harlesden Library, Craven Park Road, Harlesden, London NW10 8SE
☎020 8937 3570

Kilburn Library, 42 Salusbury Road, Kilburn, London NW6 6NN
☎020 8937 3530

Kingsbury Library, 522–524 Kingsbury Road, Kingsbury, London NW9 9HE
☎020 8937 3520

Wembley Library, Brent Civic Centre, Engineers Way, Wembley, Middlesex HA9 0FJ
☎020 8937 3500

Willesden Green Library Centre, 95 High Road, Willesden, London NW10 2SF
(Closed for regeneration project – due to reopen 2015. Interim libraries in operation –
check website for details)

BRIGHTON AND HOVE

Authority: Brighton and Hove City Council
**Royal Pavilion Libraries and Museums Divisions, Cultural Services, Jubilee Library,
Jubilee Street, Brighton BN1 1GE**
☎(01273) 290800 (general); (01273) 296930 (administration)
Fax (01273) 296976
url: www.citylibraries.info
Head of Libraries and Information Services Ms Sally McMahon BA DipLib MCLIP
(e-mail: sally.mcmahon@brighton-hove.gov.uk)
Libraries Community & Development Manager Alan Issler BA MCLIP (e-mail:
alan.issler@brighton-hove.gov.uk)
Libraries Resources Manager Ms Kate Rouse MSc (e-mail:
kate.rouse@brighton-hove.gov.uk)

Central libraries

Jubilee Library, Jubilee Street, Brighton BN1 1GE
☎(01273) 290800

Hove Library, 182-186 Church Road, Hove, East Sussex BN3 2EG
☎(01273) 290700

BRISTOL

Authority: Bristol City Council
Central Library, College Green, Bristol BS1 5TL
☎0117 903 7200 (all enquiries)
Fax 0117 922 1081
e-mail: bristol.library.service@bristol.gov.uk
url: www.bristol.gov.uk
Head of Libraries Ms Kate Murray BA(Hons) (e-mail: K.M.murray@bristol.gov.uk)
Library Central Services Manager Ms Janet Bremner BA MCLIP (e-mail:
janet.bremner@bristol.gov.uk), Ms Emelli Doran BSc (e-mail: emelli.doran@bristol.gov.uk)
(job-share)

Library Asset Manager Ms Julie York BA MCLIP (e-mail: julie.york@bristol.gov.uk)
Reader Engagement Manager Mrs Julia E Ball BLib MCLIP (e-mail:
julia.ball@bristol.gov.uk)

BROMLEY

Authority: London Borough of Bromley
Central Library, High Street, Bromley, Kent BRI IEX
☎020 8460 9955 (enquiries and administration)
Fax 020 8466 7860
e-mail: central.library@bromley.gov.uk
url: www.bromley.gov.uk
Library Operations and Commissioning Manager Tim Woolgar MCLIP (e-mail:
tim.woolgar@bromley.gov.uk)

Central/largest library
Central Library, High Street, Bromley, Kent BRI IEX
☎Tel/fax etc. as HQ

District libraries
Beckenham Library, Beckenham Road, Beckenham, Kent BR3 4PE
☎020 8650 7292/3

Orpington Library, The Walnuts, Orpington, Kent BR3 0TW
☎(01689) 831551

BUCKINGHAMSHIRE

Authority: Buckinghamshire County Council
Culture and Learning, County Hall, Walton Street, Aylesbury, Bucks HP20 IUU
☎(0845) 370 8090; (0845) 230 3232
Fax (01296) 382405
e-mail: library@buckscc.gov.uk
url: www.buckscc.gov.uk/libraries
Head of Culture and Learning Services Mrs Paula Buck (01296 382986; e-mail:
pbuck@buckscc.gov.uk)
Library Service Manager David Jones (01296 382254; e-mail: c-dajones@buckscc.gov.uk)
Library Operations Manager Ms Janet Webb (01296 387881; e-mail:
jwebb@buckscc.gov.uk)
Library Development Manager Ms Julia King (01296 383125; e-mail:
jking@buckscc.gov.uk)
Library Support Manager Ms Hazel Edwards (01296 383623; e-mail:
haedwards@buckscc.gov.uk)

Main group libraries
Amersham/Chesham Group Libraries, Chiltern Avenue, Amersham, Bucks HP6 5AH
☎(0845) 370 8090
Library Manager Ms Glenys Brown (e-mail: gbrown@buckscc.gov.uk)

Aylesbury Group Libraries, Walton Street, Aylesbury, Bucks HP20 IUU
☎(0845) 370 8090

Group Library Manager Ms Deborah Evans (e-mail: dmevans@buckscc.gov.uk)

Hazlemere/Beaconsfield Group Libraries, Reynolds Road, Beaconsfield, Bucks HP9 2NJ
☎(0845) 370 8090
Group Library Manager Ms Helen Goreham BLib MCLIP (e-mail:
hgoreham@buckscc.gov.uk)

High Wycombe Group Libraries, 5 Eden Place, High Wycombe, Bucks HP11 2DH
☎(0845) 370 8090
Group Library Manager Ms Karen Hills (e-mail: khills@buckscc.gov.uk)

Marlow/Princes Risborough Group Libraries, Institute Road, Marlow, Bucks SL7 1BL
☎(0845) 370 8090
Group Library Manager Ms Sally Walters (e-mail: swalters@buckscc.gov.uk)

BURY

Authority: Bury Council
**Department of Children, Young People and Culture, 3 Knowsley Place, Duke Street,
Bury, Lancs BL9 0EJ**
e-mail: library.suggestions@bury.gov.uk
url: www.bury.gov.uk/libraries
Head of Libraries Revd Elizabeth A Binns MBE BA(Hons) DM RGN (0161 253 5973;
e-mail: e.binns@bury.gov.uk)

Central/largest library
Bury Library, Manchester Road, Bury, Lancs BL9 0DG
☎0161 253 5873
Fax 0161 253 5857
e-mail: bury.lib@bury.gov.uk
Community Library Supervisor Ms Carol McLoone

Branch libraries
Prestwich Library & Adult Learning Centre, Longfield Centre, Prestwich, Manchester
M25 1AY
☎0161 253 7214/7216
Fax 0161 798 9981
e-mail: prestwich.lib@bury.gov.uk
Library & Adult Learning Centre Supervisor David Galloway BA DipLib

Radcliffe Library, Stand Lane, Radcliffe, Manchester M26 1NW
☎0161 253 7161
Fax 0161 724 6087
e-mail: radcliffe.lib@bury.gov.uk
Community Library Supervisors Mrs Stephanie Lamb, David Kell

Ramsbottom Library & Adult Learning Centre, Carr Street, Ramsbottom, Bury, Lancs
BL0 9AE
☎0161 253 5352/5425
e-mail: ramsbottom.lib@bury.gov.uk
Library & Adult Learning Centre Supervisor Ms Deborah Smith

Tottington Library, Market Street, Tottington, Bury, Lancs BL8 3LN

☎0161 253 6652
Fax (01204) 886517
e-mail: tottington.lib@bury.gov.uk
Community Library Supervisor Mrs Stephanie Lamb

Unsworth Library, Sunnybank Road, Unsworth, Bury, Lancs BL9 8ED
☎0161 253 7560
Fax 0161 272 1931
e-mail: unsworth.lib@bury.gov.uk
Community Library Supervisor Ms Carol McLoone

Whitefield Library & Adult Learning Centre, Pinfold Lane, Whitefield, Manchester M45 7NY
☎0161 253 5548
Fax 0161 796 1780
e-mail: whitefield.lib@bury.gov.uk
Library & Adult Learning Centre Supervisor Ms Deborah Smith

Community centres and libraries
Brandlesholme Community Library, 375 Brandlesholme Road, Bury, Lancs BL8 1HS
☎0161 764 2731
e-mail: brandlesholme.lib@bury.gov.uk
Community Library Supervisor Mrs Stephanie Lamb

Coronation Road Community Centre and Library, Westminster Avenue, Radcliffe, Lancs
M26 3WD
☎0161 253 5443
e-mail: coronation.lib@bury.gov.uk
Community Library Supervisor David Kell

Dumers Lane Community Centre and Library, 245 Dumers Lane, Radcliffe, Bury, Lancs
M26 2GN
☎0161 253 5503
e-mail: dumers.lib@bury.gov.uk
Community Library Supervisor David Kell

Moorside Community Library, St John's Church Hall, Parkinson Street, Bury, Lancs BL9 6NY
☎0161 253 6471
e-mail: moorside.lib@bury.gov.uk
Community Library Supervisor Mrs Dawn Broadhurst BA

Topping Fold Library, Topping Fold Road, Bury, Lancs BL9 7NG
☎0161 253 6361
e-mail: topping.lib@bury.gov.uk
Community Library Supervisor Mrs Claire Bebbington

Community libraries
Ainsworth Library, Church Street, Ainsworth, Lancs BL2 5RP
☎0161 253 5886
e-mail: ainsworth.lib@bury.gov.uk

Castle Sport and Leisure Library, Castle Leisure Centre, Bolton Street, Bury, Lancs BL9 0EZ
☎0161 253 5560
e-mail: castle.lib@bury.gov.uk

New Kershaw Centre Library, New Kershaw Centre, Deal Street, Bury, Lancs BL9 7PZ
☎0161 253 6400
e-mail: kershaw.lib@bury.gov.uk

Sedgeley Park Community Library, St Gabriel's Community Rooms, Bishops Road,
Prestwich, Manchester M25 0HT
☎0161 798 9420

South Cross Street Community Library, 90 South Cross Street, Bury, Lancs BL9 0RS
☎0161 253 6079

Centre for cultural collections
Archives, Local and Family History, Bury Museum and Archives, Moss Street, Bury, Lancs
BL9 0DR
☎0161 253 6782
e-mail: archives@bury.gov.uk
Borough Archivist Ms Gillian Paxton
Information Services Librarian Adam Carter

CALDERDALE

Authority: Calderdale Metropolitan Borough Council
Central Library, Northgate, Halifax, Yorks HX1 1UN
☎(01422) 392630 (enquiries), 392605 (administration)
Fax (01422) 392615
e-mail: libraries@calderdale.gov.uk
url: www.calderdale.gov.uk
Library Services Manager Mrs Carole Knowles MA MCLIP (e-mail:
carole.knowles@calderdale.gov.uk)

CAMBRIDGESHIRE

Authority: Cambridgeshire County Council
**Cambridgeshire Libraries, Archives and Information, CC1218, Shire Hall, Cambridge
CB3 0AP**
☎(01223) 703520 (administration)
e-mail: your.library@cambridgeshire.gov.uk
url: www.cambridgeshire.gov.uk/library
Head of Community and Cultural Services Mrs Christine May BA MCLIP (01223
703521; e-mail: christine.may@cambridgeshire.gov.uk)
Support Services Manager Mrs Jill Terrell BSc DipLib MCLIP (01223 703298; e-mail:
jill.terrell@cambridgeshire.gov.uk)
Operations and Service Development Manager Ms Lynda Martin BA MCLIP DMS
MIMgt (01223 376273; e-mail: lynda.martin@cambridgeshire.gov.uk)

Central/largest library
Central Library, 7 Lion Yard, Cambridge CB2 3QD
☎0345 045 5225

Hub libraries
Ely Library, 6 The Cloisters, Ely, Cambs CB7 4ZH

☎0345 045 5225
Fax (01353) 616164

Huntingdon Library and Archive, Princes Street, Huntingdon, Cambs PE29 3PA
☎0345 045 5225
Fax (01480) 372729

March Library, City Road, March, Cambs PE15 9LT
☎0345 045 5225
Fax (01354) 754760

St Ives Library, Station Road, St Ives, Cambs PE27 5BW
☎0345 045 5225
Fax (01480) 375496

St Neots Library, Priory Lane, St Neots, Cambs PE19 2BH
☎0345 045 5225
Fax (01480) 396006

Wisbech Library, 5 Ely Place, Wisbech, Cambs PE13 1EU
☎0345 045 5225
Fax (01945) 589240

CAMDEN

Authority: Camden Council
Libraries, Information and Community Learning, Culture and Environment Directorate, 7th Floor, Town Hall Extension, Argyle Street, London WC1H 8EQ
☎020 7974 4001
url: www.camden.gov.uk

Central/largest library

Swiss Cottage Library, 88 Avenue Road, London NW3 3HA
☎020 7974 4001 (general enquiries)
e-mail: swisscottagelibrary@camden.gov.uk
Senior Officers Raheel Mapara, Ms Jenny Harman, Ms Pamela Butler

Libraries

(telephone numbers for the following libraries are the same as for HQ)
Camden Town Library, Crowndale Centre, 218 Eversholt Street, London NW1 1BD
e-mail: camdentownlibrary@camden.gov.uk
Senior Officers Ms Lesley Halliday, Ms Yasmin Hounsell

Highgate Library, Chester Road, London N19 5DH
e-mail: highgatelibrary@camden.gov.uk
Senior Officer Ms Caroline Spencer

Holborn Library, 32–38 Theobalds Road, London WC1X 8PA
e-mail: holbornlibrary@camden.gov.uk
Senior Officer Edward Berridge

Kentish Town Library, 262–266 Kentish Town Road, London NW5 2AA
e-mail: kentishtownlibrary@camden.gov.uk
Senior Officer Ms Caroline Spencer

Kilburn Library Centre, 12–22 Kilburn High Road, London NW6 5UH
e-mail: kilburnlibrarycentre@camden.gov.uk
Senior Officer Chris Davies

Queens Crescent Library, 165 Queens Crescent, London NW5 4HH
e-mail: queenscrescentlibrary@camden.gov.uk
Senior Officer Tony May

St Pancras Library, Camden Town Hall Extension, Argyle Street, London WC1H 8NN
e-mail: stpancraslibrary@camden.gov.uk
Senior Officer Abul Kashim

West Hampstead Library, Dennington Park Road, London NW6 1AU
e-mail: westhampsteadlibrary@camden.gov.uk
Senior Officers Saul Letourneau, Ms Jeanette Canziani

Other services
Camden Local Studies and Archives Centre, Holborn Library, 32–38 Theobalds Road,
London WC1X 8PA
e-mail: localstudies@camden.gov.uk
Senior Officer, Local Studies Tudor Allen

Schools Library Service, Swiss Cottage Central Library, 88 Avenue Road, London NW3 3HA
☎020 7474 6510
e-mail: sls@camden.gov.uk
Senior Officer Ms Jean Aston (e-mail: jean.aston@camden.gov.uk)

(Belsize, Chalk Farm and Heath Community Libraries are staffed by volunteers. See
website for contact details)

CENTRAL BEDFORDSHIRE
Authority: Central Bedfordshire Council

Libraries Operations, Dunstable Library, Vernon Place, Dunstable, Beds LU5 4HA
☎0300 300 8060
url: www.centralbedfordshire.gov.uk
Interim Library Services Manager Ms Nicola Avery BAHons) MCLIP

Largest libraries
Dunstable Library, Vernon Place, Dunstable, Beds LU5 4HA
☎0300 300 8056
e-mail: dunstable.library@centralbedfordshire.gov.uk
url: http://virtual-library.culturalservices.net
Library Manager John Booth (e-mail: john.booth@centralbedfordshire.gov.uk)

Leighton Buzzard Library, Lake Street, Leighton Buzzard, Beds LU7 1RX
☎0300 300 8059
e-mail: leightonbuzzard.library@centralbedfordshire.gov.uk
Library Manager Ms Hazel Kerr (e-mail: hazel.kerr@centralbedfordshire.gov.uk)

Area libraries
Ampthill Library, 1 Dunstable Street, Ampthill, Beds MK45 2NL
☎0300 300 6921

e-mail: ampthill.library@centralbedfordshire.gov.uk
Library Manager Ms Susan Morgan (e-mail: sue.morgan@centralbedfordshire.gov.uk)

Arlesey Resource Centre, High Street, Arlesey, Beds SG15 6SN
☎(01462) 731469
e-mail: enquiries@arleseyresourcecentre.org.uk
Library Manager Vacant

Barton Library, Bedford Road, Barton, Beds MK45 4PP
☎0300 300 8054
e-mail: barton.library@centralbedfordshire.gov.uk
Library Manager James Smiles (e-mail: james.smiles@centralbedfordshire.gov.uk)

Biggleswade Library, Chestnut Avenue, Biggleswade, Beds SG18 0LL
☎0300 300 6939
e-mail: biggleswade.library@centralbedfordshire.gov.uk
Library Manager Ms Kerry Matthews (e-mail:
kerry.matthews@centralbedfordshire.gov.uk)

Flitwick Library, Coniston Road, Flitwick, Beds MK45 1QJ
☎0300 300 8057
e-mail: flitwick.library@centralbedfordshire.gov.uk
Library Manager Ms Carly Levingstone (e-mail:
carly.levingstone@centralbedfordshire.gov.uk)

Houghton Regis Library, Bedford Square, Houghton Regis, Beds LU5 5ES
☎0300 300 8058
e-mail: houghtonregis.library@centralbedfordshire.gov.uk
Library Manager Ms Nicola Bell (e-mail: nicola.bell@centralbedfordshire.gov.uk)

Potton Library, Clock House, Potton, Beds SG19 2NP
☎0300 300 8063
e-mail: potton.library@centralbedfordshire.gov.uk
Library Manager Ms Gillian Studley (e-mail: gillian.studley@centralbedfordshire.gov.uk)

Sandy Library, Market Square, Sandy, Beds SG19 1EH
☎0300 300 8065
e-mail: sandy.library@centralbedfordshire.gov.uk
Library Manager Ms Madeline Phippen (e-mail:
madeline.phippen@centralbedfordshire.gov.uk)

Shefford Library, High Street, Shefford, Beds SG17 5DD
☎0300 300 8067
e-mail: shefford.library@centralbedfordshire.gov.uk
Library Manager Ms Jacqui Yeomans (e-mail:
jacqui.yeomans@centralbedfordshire.gov.uk)

Stotfold Library, Hitchin Road, Stotfold, Beds SG5 4HP
☎0300 300 8067
e-mail: stotfold.library@centralbedfordshire.gov.uk
Library Manager Ms Liz Durrant (e-mail: liz.durrant@centralbedfordshire.gov.uk)

Toddington Library, 9 Market Square, Toddington, Beds LU5 6BP
☎0300 300 8069
e-mail: toddington.library@centralbedfordshire.gov.uk
Library Manager Ms Elizabeth Morris (e-mail: lis.morris@centralbedfordshire.gov.uk)

CHESHIRE EAST

Authority: Cheshire East Council
Customer Services and Libraries, Local Community Services, Macclesfield Town Hall, Market Place, Macclesfield, Cheshire SK10 1EA
☎0300 123 5018
e-mail: libraries@cheshireeast.gov.uk
url: www.cheshireeast.gov.uk/libraries.aspx
Principal Manager Local Community Services Paul Bayley (01625 378029; e-mail: paul.bayley@cheshireeast.gov.uk)

Group HQs

Crewe Library, Prince Albert Street, Crewe, Cheshire CW1 2DH
☎(01270) 371203
Fax (01270) 375293
Area Librarian South Mrs Joanne Shannon (e-mail: joanne.shannon@cheshireeast.gov.uk)

Macclesfield Library, 2 Jordangate, Macclesfield, Cheshire SK10 1EE
☎(01625) 374013
Fax (01625) 612818
Area Librarian North Paul Everitt MCLIP (e-mail: paul.everitt@cheshireeast.gov.uk)

CHESHIRE WEST AND CHESTER

Authority: Cheshire West and Chester Council
Place (Operations) HQ, 58 Nicholas Street, Chester CH1 2NP
☎0300 123 8123
e-mail: librarynotifications@cheshirewestandchester.gov.uk
url: www.cheshirewestandchester.gov.uk/libraries
Senior Manager, Customer Services and Libraries Ms Julie Bellis (e-mail: julie.bellis@cheshirewestandchester.gov.uk)

Chester Library, Northgate Street, Chester CH1 2EF
☎(01244) 972612
Fax (01244) 315534
e-mail: chester.infopoint@cheshirewestandchester.gov.uk
Library Services Manager Mrs Rachel Foster BA(Hons) MCLIP (01244 972612; e-mail: rachel.foster@cheshirewestandchester.gov.uk)

Ellesmere Port Library, Civic Way, Ellesmere Port, Cheshire L65 0BG
☎0151 337 4689
e-mail: eport.infopoint@cheshirewestandchester.gov.uk
Lead Librarian Chester and Ellesmere Port Area Mrs Anne Ainsworth BA MCLIP (0151 337 4689; e-mail: anne.ainsworth@cheshirewestandchester.gov.uk)

Northwich Library, Witton Street, Northwich, Cheshire CW9 5DR
☎(01606) 44221
Fax (01606) 48396
e-mail: northwich.infopoint@cheshirewestandchester.gov.uk
Lead Librarian Northwich/Winsford and Rural Area Ms Sally Starkey BA MA (0151 337 4682; e-mail: sally.starkey@cheshirewestandchester.gov.uk)

☎024 7678 5181
Fax 024 7670 0329
e-mail: arenapark.library@coventry.gov.uk

Bell Green Community Library and Learning Centre, 17–23 Riley Square, Bell Green, Coventry CV2 1LS
☎024 7678 5819
Fax 024 7666 3468
e-mail: bellgreen.library@coventry.gov.uk

Caludon Castle School and Community Library, Axholme Road, Coventry CV2 5BD
☎024 7678 8300
Fax 024 7663 6282
e-mail: caludon.library@coventry.gov.uk

Canley Community Library, Prior Deram Walk, Canley, Coventry CV4 8FT
☎024 7678 6963
Fax 024 7671 7361
e-mail: canley.library@coventry.gov.uk

Cheylesmore Community Library, Poitiers Road, Cheylesmore, Coventry CV3 5JX
☎024 7678 6966
Fax 024 7650 5287
e-mail: cheylesmore.library@coventry.gov.uk

Coundon Community Library, Moseley Avenue, Radford, Coventry CV6 1HT
☎024 7678 6969
Fax 024 7659 8768
e-mail: coundon.library@coventry.gov.uk

Earlsdon Community Library, Earlsdon Avenue North, Earlsdon, Coventry CV5 6FZ
☎024 7678 6970
Fax 024 7671 7958
e-mail: earlsdon.library@coventry.gov.uk

Finham Community Library, Finham Green Road, Finham, Coventry CV3 6EP
☎024 7678 6974
Fax 024 7641 9524
e-mail: finham.library@coventry.gov.uk

Foleshill Community Library, Broad Street, Foleshill, Coventry CV6 5BG
☎024 7678 6977
Fax 024 7670 5640
e-mail: foleshill.library@coventry.gov.uk

Hillfields Community Library, St Peter's Centre, Charles Street, Hillfields, Coventry CV1 5NP
☎024 7678 6980
Fax 024 7623 1970
e-mail: library.hillfields@coventry.gov.uk

Jubilee Crescent Community Library, Jubilee Crescent, Radford, Coventry CV6 3EX
☎024 7678 6981
Fax 024 7659 5728
e-mail: jubileecrescent.library@coventry.gov.uk

Stoke Community Library, Kingsway, Stoke, Coventry CV2 4EA
☎024 7678 6990
Fax 024 7645 2567
e-mail: stoke.library@coventry.gov.uk

Tile Hill Community Library and Learning Centre, Jardine Crescent, Tile Hill, Coventry
CV4 9PL
☎024 7678 6785
Fax 024 7646 4021
e-mail: tilehill.library@coventry.gov.uk

Willenhall Community Library, 106 Remembrance Road, Willenhall, Coventry CV3 3DP
☎024 7678 6991
Fax 024 7630 2151
e-mail: willenhall.library@coventry.gov.uk

CROYDON

Authority: Croydon Council (in partnership with Cultural Community Solutions Limited)
Central Library, Croydon Clocktower, Katharine Street, Croydon CR9 IET
☎020 3700 1034
Fax 020 8253 1004
e-mail: croydon.centrallibrary@carillionservices.co.uk
url: www.croydon.gov.uk
Senior Operations Manager Mrs Elaine Collier (e-mail:
elaine.collier@carillionservices.co.uk)
Senior Library Manager Ms Klasiena Habibi (e-mail:
klasiena.habibi@carillionservices.co.uk)

Branch libraries
Ashburton Library, Ashburton Learning Village, Oasis Academy Shirley, Shirley Road,
Addiscombe, Croydon CR9 7AL
☎020 3700 1001
e-mail: croydon.ashburtonlibrary@carillionservices.co.uk

Bradmore Green Library, Bradmore Way, Coulsdon, Croydon CR5 1PE
☎020 3700 1003
e-mail: croydon.bradmoregreenlibrary@carillionservices.co.uk

Broad Green Library, 89 Canterbury Road, Croydon CR0 3HH
☎020 3700 1005
e-mail: croydon.broadgreenlibrary@carillionservices.co.uk

Coulsdon Library, Brighton Road, Coulsdon, Croydon CR5 2NH
☎020 3700 1007
e-mail: croydon.coulsdonlibrary@carillionservices.co.uk

New Addington Library, 61 Central Parade, New Addington, Croydon CR0 0JD
☎020 3700 1009
e-mail: croydon.newaddingtonlibrary@carillionservices.co.uk

Norbury Library, Beatrice Avenue, Norbury, Croydon SW16 4UW
☎020 3700 1011
e-mail: croydon.norburylibrary@carillionservices.co.uk

Purley Library, Banstead Road, Purley, Croydon CR8 3YH
☎020 3700 1013
e-mail: croydon.purleylibrary@carillionservices.co.uk

Sanderstead Library, Farm Fields, South Croydon, Croydon CR2 0HL
☎020 3700 1015
e-mail: croydon.sandersteadlibrary@carillionservices.co.uk

Selsdon Library, Addington Road, Selsdon, Croydon CR2 8LA
☎020 3700 1017
e-mail: croydon.selsdonlibrary@carillionservices.co.uk

Shirley Library, Wickham Road/Hartland Way, Shirley, Croydon CR0 8BH
☎020 3700 1019
e-mail: croydon.shirleylibrary@carillionservices.co.uk

South Norwood Library, Lawrence Road, South Norwood, Croydon SE25 5AA
☎020 3700 1021
e-mail: croydon.southnorwoodlibrary@carillionservices.co.uk

Thornton Heath Library, 190 Brigstock Road, Thornton Heath, Croydon CR7 7JE
☎020 3700 1023
e-mail: croydon.thorntonheathlibrary@carillionservices.co.uk

CUMBRIA

Authority: Cumbria County Council
Environment and Community Services, 1st Floor, The Lonsdale Building, The Courts, Carlisle CA3 8NA
Fax (01228) 227108
url: www.cumbria.gov.uk/libraries
Assistant Director, Local Services Jim Grisenthwaite (01228 221540; e-mail: jim.grisenthwaite@cumbria.gov.uk)
County Manager – Library Services Bruce Bennison
Principal Administrative Officer Vacant

Group libraries
Barrow-in-Furness Library, Ramsden Square, Barrow-in-Furness, Cumbria LA14 1LL
☎(01229) 407370
Fax (01229) 831446
e-mail: barrow.library@cumbria.gov.uk
Area Library Manager Tom Holliday MCLIP

Carlisle Library, 11 Globe Lane, Carlisle CA3 8NX
☎(01228) 227310
Fax (01228) 593479
e-mail: carlisle.library@cumbria.gov.uk
Area Library Manager Mike Lister MCLIP

Daniel Hay Library, Lowther Street, Whitehaven, Cumbria CA28 7QZ
☎(01946) 506400
Fax (01946) 690240
e-mail: whitehaven.library@cumbria.gov.uk
Area Library Manager Mrs Alayne Cowling MCLIP

Kendal Library, Stricklandgate, Kendal, Cumbria LA9 4PY
☎(01539) 713520
Fax (01539) 739847
e-mail: kendal.library@cumbria.gov.uk
Area Library Manager Tom Holliday MCLIP

Penrith Library, St Andrews Churchyard, Penrith, Cumbria CA11 7YA
☎(01768) 812100
Fax (01768) 867595
e-mail: penrith.library@cumbria.gov.uk
Area Library Manager Mike Lister MCLIP

Workington Library, Vulcans Lane, Workington, Cumbria CA14 2ND
☎(01900) 706170
Fax (01900) 601266
e-mail: workington.library@cumbria.gov.uk
Area Library Manager Mrs Alayne Cowling MCLIP

DARLINGTON

Authority: Darlington Borough Council
Central Library, Crown Street, Darlington DL1 1ND
☎(01325) 462034 (enquiries)
Fax (01325) 381556
e-mail: crown.street.library@darlington.gov.uk
url: www2.darlington.gov.uk
Events and Libraries Manager Ms Marion Ogle
Lending Services Manager Ms Carole Houghton MA MCLIP
Local Studies Librarian Miss Katherine Williamson
Stock Services Librarian Mrs Jean Longstaff

Branch library
Cockerton Library, Cockerton Green, Darlington DL3 9AA
☎(01325) 461320
Lending Services Manager Ms Carole Houghton MA MCLIP

DERBY

Authority: Derby City Council
Derby City Libraries, Ground Floor, Corporation Street, Derby DE1 2FS
☎(01332) 640761
e-mail: libraries@derby.gov.uk
url: www.derby.gov.uk/libraries
Head of Library Services David Potton MA DipLib MCLIP (01332 641719; e-mail:
david.potton@derby.gov.uk)
Assistant Head of Library Services (Resources and Learning) Mark Elliott BLib(Hons)
MCLIP PGC(Man) (01332 641725; e-mail: mark.elliott@derby.gov.uk)
Assistant Head of Library Services (Operations and Community) Ms Fran Renwick
MA MCLIP (01332 641726; e-mail: fran.renwick@derby.gov.uk)

Central/largest library

Central Library, The Wardwick, Derby DE1 1HS
☎(01332) 641701 (enquiries)
Fax (01332) 369570
Operations Manager (Central Library Services) Ms Julie Topham (01332 641703;
e-mail: julie.topham@derby.gov.uk)

DERBYSHIRE

Authority: Derbyshire County Council
Health and Communities Department, County Hall, Matlock, Derbyshire DE4 3AG
☎(01629) 536166 (enquiries and administration)
Fax (01629) 536522
e-mail: derbyshire.libraries@derbyshire.gov.uk
url: www.derbyshire.gov.uk
Strategic Director of Health and Communities David Lowe (e-mail:
david.lowe@derbyshire.gov.uk)
Assistant Director of Libraries and Heritage Don Gibbs BA MCLIP (e-mail:
don.gibbs@derbyshire.gov.uk)
Service Development Manager Martyn Shaw BA DipLib MCLIP (e-mail:
martyn.shaw@derbyshire.gov.uk)
Service Delivery Manager Ms Julie Powell (e-mail: julie.powell@derbyshire.gov.uk)

Central/largest library

Chesterfield Library, New Beetwell Street, Chesterfield, Derbyshire S40 1QN
☎(01629) 533400
Fax (01246) 209304
e-mail: chesterfield.library@derbyshire.gov.uk
Senior Librarian Ms Janet Scott BA MA MCLIP (e-mail: janet.scott@derbyshire.gov.uk)

Cluster libraries

Alfreton Library (Alfreton Cluster), Severn Square, Alfreton, Derbyshire DE55 7BQ
☎(01773) 833199
Fax (01773) 521020
e-mail: alfreton.library@derbyshire.gov.uk
Senior Library Manager Ms Julie Stirland (e-mail: julie.stirland@derbyshire.gov.uk)

Dronfield Library (Dronfield Cluster), Manor House, High Street, Dronfield, Derbyshire
S18 1PY
☎(01629) 533450
Fax (01246) 291489
e-mail: dronfield.library@derbyshire.gov.uk
Senior Library Managers Ms Sue Lee (e-mail: sue.lee@derbyshire.gov.uk), Ms Marie
Mann (e-mail: marie.mann@derbyshire.gov.uk)

Glossop Library (Glossop Cluster), Victoria Hall, Talbot Street, Glossop, High Peak,
Derbyshire SK13 7DQ
☎(01457) 852616
Fax (01457) 856329
e-mail: glossop.library@derbyshire.gov.uk
Senior Library Manager Ms Julia Bedford (e-mail: julia.bedford@derbyshire.gov.uk)

Matlock Library (Matlock Cluster), Steep Turnpike, Matlock, Derbyshire DE4 3DP
☎(01629) 533837
Fax (01629) 760749
e-mail: matlock.library@derbyshire.gov.uk
Senior Library Manager Ms Sue Jackson (e-mail: sue.jackson@derbyshire.gov.uk)

Swadlincote Library (Swadlincote Cluster), Civic Way, Swadlincote, Derbyshire DE11 0AD
☎(01629) 533013
Fax (01283) 216352
e-mail: swadlincote.library@derbyshire.gov.uk
Senior Library Manager Ms Angie Lomas (e-mail: angie.lomas@derbyshire.gov.uk)

DEVON

Authority: Devon County Council
Devon Libraries, Great Moor House, Bittern Road, Sowton, Exeter, Devon EX2 7NL
☎(01392) 384315
Fax (01392) 384316
e-mail: devlibs@devon.gov.uk
url: www.devon.gov.uk/libraries
Head of Libraries Ms Ciara Eastell BA(Hons) MA MCLIP (e-mail:
ciara.eastell@devon.gov.uk)
Service Support Manager Mike Skinner BLS DipHE (e-mail:
mike.skinner@devon.gov.uk)
Operations Manager Ms Liz Alexander MCLIP (e-mail: liz.alexander@devon.gov.uk)

Central/largest libraries
Barnstaple Library, Tuly Street, Barnstaple, Devon EX31 1EL
☎(01271) 388593
e-mail: barnstaple.library@devon.gov.uk
Librarian Manager Mrs Jude Jeal

Exeter Library, Castle Street, Exeter, Devon EX4 3PQ
☎(01392) 384218
Fax (01392) 384228
e-mail: exeter.library@devon.gov.uk
Library Manager Vacant

Larger branch libraries
Bideford Library, 6 New Road, Bideford, Devon EX39 2HR
☎(01237) 476075 (tel/fax)
Librarians i/c Ms L Grainger, M Chamings

Exmouth Library, 40 Exeter Road, Exmouth, Devon EX8 1PS
☎(01395) 272677
Fax (01395) 271426
Librarian i/c C Launder

Honiton Library, 48 New Street, Honiton, Devon EX14 1BS
☎(01404) 42818
Fax (01404) 45326
Librarian i/c Ms L Isaacson

Kingsbridge Library, Ilbert Road, Kingsbridge, Devon TQ7 1EB
☎(01548) 852315
Fax (01548) 857210
Librarian i/c Ms M Johnson

Newton Abbot Library, Passmore Edwards Centre, Market Street, Newton Abbot, Devon TQ12 2RJ
☎(01392) 384012
Librarian i/c Ms C Marshall

St Thomas Library, 35 Church Road, St Thomas, Exeter, Devon EX2 9AZ
☎(01392) 252783
Librarian i/c L Rawlings

Sidmouth Library, Blackmore Drive, Sidmouth, Devon EX10 8LA
☎(01395) 512192
Librarian i/c Ms C Pentecost

Tavistock Library, The Quay, Plymouth Road, Tavistock, Devon PL19 8AB
☎(01822) 612218
Fax (01822) 610690
Librarian i/c Ms H Cooper

Teignmouth Library, Fore Street, Teignmouth, Devon TQ14 8DY
☎(01626) 774646
Fax (01626) 870155
Librarian i/c Ms J Wilson

Tiverton Library, Phoenix House, Phoenix Lane, Tiverton, Devon EX16 6SA
☎(01884) 244644
Fax (01884) 244645
Librarian i/c Mrs W Humble

DONCASTER

Authority: Doncaster Metropolitan Borough Council
Central Library, Waterdale, Doncaster DN1 3JE
☎(01302) 734305
Fax (01302) 734302
e-mail: centrallibrary@doncaster.gov.uk
url: http://library.doncaster.gov.uk
Head of Libraries and Culture Nick Stopforth BSc FRSA MCLIP
Central Library Manager Ms Janis Robinson (e-mail: janis.robinson@doncaster.gov.uk)

DORSET

Authority: Dorset County Council
County Library HQ, Colliton Park, Dorchester, Dorset DT1 1XJ
☎(01305) 225000 (enquiries)
Fax (01305) 224344 (administration)
e-mail: dorsetlibraries@dorsetcc.gov.uk
url: www.dorsetforyou.com/libraries

Head of Community Services Paul Leivers BA MBA MCLIP (e-mail:
p.leivers@dorsetcc.gov.uk)
Dorset Library Services Manager Mrs Tracy Long BA(Hons) MCLIP (01305 224458;
e-mail: t.long@dorsetcc.gov.uk)
Senior Managers, Customer Services Ms Mary Yardley MA MCLIP (01305 224968;
e-mail: m.yardley@dorsetcc.gov.uk), Mrs Linda Constable BA(Hons) MCLIP PGDip(Res)
Senior Manager Ms Sharon Kirkpatrick BLS MCLIP (01305 228529; e-mail:
s.d.kirkpatrick@dorsetcc.gov.uk)
Business Support Manager Sam Porter (01305 224927; e-mail:
s.i.porter@dorsetcc.gov.uk)

DUDLEY

Authority: Dudley Metropolitan Borough Council
Dudley Library, St James's Road, Dudley, West Midlands DY1 1HR
☎(01384) 815568
Fax (01384) 815543
url: www.dudley.gov.uk/libraries
Head of Service – Library Strategy and Development Mrs Jayne Wilkins BA(Hons)
MCLIP (01384 812680; fax: 01384 815543; e-mail: jayne.wilkins@dudley.gov.uk)
Head of Service – Library Operations Mrs Jen Beardsmore BA MCLIP (01384 815551;
fax: 01384 815543; e-mail: jen.beardsmore@dudley.gov.uk)

Locality libraries

Brierley Hill Library, High Street, Brierley Hill, West Midlands DY5 3ET
☎(01384) 812865
Fax (01384) 812866
e-mail: brierleyhill.library@dudley.gov.uk
Locality Librarian Ms Sandra Francis

Dudley Library, St James's Road, West Midlands DY1 1HR
☎(01384) 815560
Fax (01384) 815543
e-mail: dudley.library@dudley.gov.uk
Locality Librarian Mrs Sharon Whitehouse BA MCLIP

Halesowen Library, Queensway Mall, The Cornbow, Halesowen, West Midlands B63 4AJ
☎(01384) 812982
Fax (01384) 812981
e-mail: halesowen.library@dudley.gov.uk
Locality Librarian Ms Sandra Francis

Sedgley Library, Ladies Walk Centre, Ladies Walk, Sedgley, West Midlands DY3 3UA
☎(01384) 812790
e-mail: sedgley.library@dudley.gov.uk
Locality Librarian Mrs Sharon Whitehouse BA MCLIP

Stourbridge Library, Crown Centre, Crown Lane, Stourbridge, West Midlands DY8 1YE
☎(01384) 812945
Fax (01384) 812946
e-mail: stourbridge.library@dudley.gov.uk
Locality Librarian Mrs Annette Templar BA(Hons)

Archives and Local History Centre

Archives and Local History Centre, Tipton Road, Dudley, West Midlands DY1 4SQ

☎(01384) 812770 (tel/fax)

e-mail: archives.centre@dudley.gov.uk

Archivists Ms Helen Donald (e-mail: helen.donald@dudley.gov.uk), Robert Bennett (e-mail: robert.bennett@dudley.gov.uk)

DURHAM

Authority: Durham County Council

Libraries, Learning and Culture, Adults, Wellbeing and Health, Sevenhills, Unit 1 Greenhills Business Park, Enterprise Way, Spennymoor, Co Durham DL16 6JB

☎0191 383 6543

Fax 0191 383 4182

url: www.durham.gov.uk

Strategic Manager – Libraries Ms Anne Davison BA MCLIP (e-mail: anne.davison@durham.gov.uk)

Strategic Manager – Heritage and Culture Neil Hillier (e-mail: neil.hillier@durham.gov.uk)

Team Manager – Library Support Ms Julia Cruddace (e-mail: julia.cruddace@durham.gov.uk)

Central/largest library

Durham Clayport Library, Millennium Place, Durham DH1 1WA

☎0191 386 4003

Fax 0191 386 0379

e-mail: durhamclayportlibrary@durham.gov.uk

Manager Vacant

EALING

Authority: Ealing Council (in partnership with Cultural Community Solutions Limited)

Library Administrative Office, 1st Floor SW, Perceval House, 14–16 Uxbridge Road, London W5 2HL

☎020 8825 7216

url: www.ealing.gov.uk/info/200460/libraries

Assistant Director, Arts, Heritage and Libraries Ms Carole Stewart (e-mail: cstewart@ealing.gov.uk)

Library Contract Manager Lee Stallard (e-mail: lee.stallard@carillionservices.co.uk)

Central/largest library

Ealing Central Library, 103 Ealing Broadway Centre, London W5 5JY

☎020 3700 1052

e-mail: ealing.centrallibrary@carillionservices.co.uk

Main libraries

Acton Town Hall Library, Everyone Active Acton Centre, High Street, Acton, London W3 6NE

☎020 3700 1056

e-mail: ealing.actonlibrary@carillionservices.co.uk

Greenford Library, Oldfield Lane South, Greenford, Middlesex UB6 9LG
☎020 3700 1062
e-mail: ealing.greenfordlibrary@carillionservices.co.uk

Northolt Library, Church Road, Northolt, Middlesex UB5 5AS
☎020 3700 1078
e-mail: ealing.northoltlibrary@carillionservices.co.uk

Southall Library at the Dominion Centre, Dominion Arts Centre, The Green, Southall,
Middlesex UB2 4BQ
☎020 3700 1059
e-mail: ealing.southalllibrary@carillionservices.co.uk

EAST RIDING OF YORKSHIRE

Authority: East Riding of Yorkshire Council
**East Riding Libraries, Council Offices, Main Road, Skirlaugh, East Riding of Yorks
HU11 5HN**
☎(01482) 392702
Fax (01482) 392711
url: www.eastriding.gov.uk
Libraries, Archives and Museums Service Manager Mrs Libby Herbert (01482
392701; e-mail: libby.herbert@eastriding.gov.uk)

EAST SUSSEX

Authority: East Sussex County Council
**Library and Information Service, West D, County Hall, St Anne's Crescent, Lewes, East
Sussex BN7 1UE**
☎(01273) 481870 (administration)
url: www.eastsussex.gov.uk
Assistant Director, Communities and Customer Services Dr Irene Campbell MA
DipLib MCLIP FRSA (01273 481347; e-mail: irene.campbell@eastsussex.gov.uk)
Assistant Head of Library and Information Services: Strategy and Performance
Ms Rhona Drever MA(Hons) DipLib MCLIP (01273 481329; e-mail:
rhona.drever@eastsussex.gov.uk)
Assistant Head of Library and Information Services: Customer Services
Mrs Valerie Wright MCLIP (01273 482129; e-mail: valerie.wright@eastsussex.gov.uk)

Area libraries
Eastbourne Library, Grove Road, Eastbourne, East Sussex BN21 4TL
Fax (01323) 649174
Area Manager Ms Laura Chrysostomou (e-mail: laura.chrysostomou@eastsussex.gov.uk)

Hastings Library, Brassey Institute, 13 Claremont, Hastings, East Sussex TN34 1HE
Fax (01424) 443289
Area Manager Mick Bacon MCLIP (01424 420501; e-mail: mick.bacon@eastsussex.co.uk)

Branch libraries
Battle Library, 7 Market Square, Battle, East Sussex TN33 0XA
e-mail: library.battle@eastsussex.gov.uk

Bexhill Library, Western Road, Bexhill-on-Sea, East Sussex TN40 1DY
e-mail: library.bexhill@eastsussex.gov.uk

Crowborough Library, Pine Grove, Crowborough, East Sussex TN6 1DH
e-mail: library.crowborough@eastsussex.gov.uk

Eastbourne Library, Grove Road, Eastbourne, East Sussex BN21 4TL
e-mail: library.eastbourne@eastsussex.gov.uk

Forest Row Library, The Community Centre, Hartfield Road, Forest Row, East Sussex
RH18 5DZ
e-mail: library.forestrow@eastsussex.gov.uk

Hailsham Library, Western Road, Hailsham, East Sussex BN27 3DN
e-mail: library.hailsham@eastsussex.gov.uk

Hampden Park Library, Brodrick Close, Hampden Park, Eastbourne, East Sussex
BN22 9NQ
e-mail: library.hampdenpark@eastsussex.gov.uk

Hastings Children's Library, Robertson Passage, off Robertson Street, Hastings, East Sussex
TN34 1HL
e-mail: hastings.children@eastsussex.gov.uk

Hastings Library, Brassey Institute, 13 Claremont, Hastings, East Sussex TN34 1HE
e-mail: library.hastings@eastsussex.gov.uk

Heathfield Library, 21 High Street, Heathfield, East Sussex TN21 8LU
e-mail: library.heathfield@eastsussex.gov.uk

Hollington Library, 96 Battle Road, St Leonards on Sea, East Sussex TN37 7AG
e-mail: library.hollington@eastsussex.gov.uk

Langney Library, Unit 3, The Shopping Centre, 110 Kingfisher Drive, Langney, Eastbourne,
East Sussex BN23 7RT
e-mail: library.langney@eastsussex.gov.uk

Lewes Library, Styles Field, Friars Walk, Lewes, East Sussex BN7 2LZ
e-mail: library.lewes@eastsussex.gov.uk

Mayfield Library, Mayfield CE School, Fletching Street, Mayfield, East Sussex TN20 6TA
e-mail: library.mayfield@eastsussex.gov.uk

Newhaven Library, 16 High Street, Newhaven, East Sussex BN9 9PD
e-mail: library.newhaven@eastsussex.gov.uk

Ore Library, Old London Road, Ore, Hastings, East Sussex TN35 5BP
e-mail: library.ore@eastsussex.gov.uk

Peacehaven Library, Meridian Centre, Peacehaven, East Sussex BN10 8BB
e-mail: library.peacehaven@eastsussex.gov.uk

Pevensey Bay Library, Wallsend House, Richmond Road, Pevensey Bay, East Sussex
BN24 6AU
e-mail: library.pevenseybay@eastsussex.gov.uk

Polegate Library, Windsor Way, Polegate, East Sussex BN26 6QF
e-mail: library.polegate@eastsussex.gov.uk

Ringmer Library, Cecil Gates Room, The Village Hall, Lewes Road, Ringmer, Lewes, East Sussex BN8 5QH
e-mail: library.ringmer@eastsussex.gov.uk

Rye Library, 30 High Street, Rye, East Sussex TN31 7JF
e-mail: library.rye@eastsussex.gov.uk

Seaford Library, 15–17 Sutton Park Road, Seaford, East Sussex BN25 1QX
e-mail: library.seaford@eastsussex.gov.uk

Uckfield Library, Library Way, High Street, Uckfield, East Sussex TN22 1AR
e-mail: library.uckfield@eastsussex.gov.uk

Wadhurst Library, High Street, Wadhurst, East Sussex TN5 6AP
e-mail: library.wadhurst@eastsussex.gov.uk

Willingdon Library, Coppice Avenue, Lower Willingdon, Eastbourne, East Sussex BN20 9PN
e-mail: library.willingdon@eastsussex.gov.uk

ENFIELD

Authority: London Borough of Enfield
Finance, Resources and Customer Services, PO Box 58, Civic Centre, Enfield, Middlesex EN1 3XJ
☎020 8379 3747 (enquiries and administration)
url: www.enfield.gov.uk
Head of Libraries and Museums Ms Julie Gibson MA MCLIP (020 8379 3749; e-mail: julie.gibson@enfield.gov.uk)
Library and Museum Service Business Manager Mrs Madeline Barratt BA MCLIP DipLaw (e-mail: madeline.barratt@enfield.gov.uk)

ESSEX

Authority: Essex County Council
Essex County Library, County Hall, Market Road, Chelmsford, Essex CM1 1QH
e-mail: essexlib@essexcc.gov.uk
url: www.essexcc.gov.uk/libraries
Head of Face to Face Services Ms Amy Donovan (e-mail: amy.donovan@essexcc.gov.uk)
Planning and Performance Manager Geoff Elgar DipLib BA(Hons) MCLIP (e-mail: geoff.elgar@essexcc.gov.uk) (based at Essex Record Office, Wharf Road, Chelmsford CM2 6YT)
Library Locality Manager – North Ms Jenny Salisbury BLib(Hons) MCLIP (e-mail: jenny.salisbury@essexcc.gov.uk) (based at Essex Record Office, Wharf Road, Chelmsford CM2 6YT)
Library Locality Manager – South Ms Liz Malone LLB(Hons) DipLIS MCLIP (e-mail: liz.malone@essex.gov.uk) (based at Essex Record Office, Wharf Road, Chelmsford CM2 6YT)

Major libraries
Chelmsford Library, PO Box 882, Market Road, Chelmsford, Essex CM1 1LH
☎(01245) 492758
Fax (01245) 492536
e-mail: chelmsford.library@essexcc.gov.uk

Colchester Library, Trinity Square, Colchester, Essex CO1 1JB
☎(01206) 245900
Fax (01206) 245901
e-mail: colchester.library@essexcc.gov.uk

GATESHEAD

Authority: Gateshead Metropolitan Borough Council
Libraries and Arts Service, Central Library, Prince Consort Road, Gateshead, Tyne and Wear NE8 4LN
☎0191 433 8400
Fax 0191 477 7454
e-mail: libraries@gateshead.gov.uk
url: www.gateshead.gov.uk/libraries
Principal Libraries Manager Stephen Walters BSc MCLIP (e-mail: stephenwalters@gateshead.gov.uk)
Libraries Operations Manager Ms Angela Lingwood MCLIP (e-mail: angelalingwood@gateshead.gov.uk)

GLOUCESTERSHIRE

Authority: Gloucestershire County Council
Libraries and Information, Quayside House, Shire Hall, Gloucester GL1 2HY
☎0845 230 5420 (library helpline), (01452) 425048 (management)
Fax (01452) 425042
e-mail: libraryhelp@gloucestershire.gov.uk
url: www.gloucestershire.gov.uk/libraries
Head of Library Services Ms Sue Laurence BA(Hons) DipLib MCLIP (e-mail: sue.laurence@gloucestershire.gov.uk)
Operations & Development Manager (Countywide) Mrs Jill Barker BA DipLib MCLIP (e-mail: jill.barker@gloucestershire.gov.uk)
Digital Library Services Manager Mrs Katie Smith BA(Hons) MA MCLIP (e-mail: katie.a.smith@gloucestershire.gov.uk)

Main libraries

Central locality
Cheltenham Library, Clarence Street, Cheltenham, Glos GL50 3JT
☎(01242) 532686/532687
Fax (01242) 532684

Gloucester Library, Brunswick Road, Gloucester GL1 1HT
☎(01452) 426973/426978
Fax (01452) 330523
Lead Localities Manager: Central Mrs Jane Everiss (e-mail: jane.everiss@gloucestershire.gov.uk)

East locality
Cirencester Library, The Waterloo, Cirencester, Glos GL7 2PZ
☎(01285) 659813

Dursley Library, May Lane, Dursley, Glos GL11 4JH
☎(01453) 543059
Fax (01453) 548230

Stow-on-the-Wold Library, St Edwards Hall, The Square, Stow-on-the-Wold, Glos GL54 1AF
☎(01451) 830352

Stroud Library, Lansdown, Stroud, Glos GL5 1BB
☎(01453) 751651
Fax (01453) 762060
Localities Manager: East Miss Anne Riley (e-mail: anne.riley@gloucestershire.gov.uk)

West locality
Coleford Library, The Main Place, Old Station Way, Coleford, Glos GL16 8RH
☎(01594) 833351

Newent Library, High Street, Newent, Glos GL18 1AN
☎(01531) 820447

Tewkesbury Library, Sun Street, Tewkesbury, Glos GL20 5NX
☎(01684) 293086
Fax (01684) 290125
Localities Manager: West Peter Clark (e-mail: peter.clark@gloucestershire.gov.uk)

GREENWICH

Authority: Royal Borough of Greenwich Council (Libraries managed by Greenwich Leisure Limited)
Greenwich Leisure Limited, Middlegate House, Royal Arsenal, Woolwich, London SE18 1JL
☎020 8317 5000
Fax 020 8317 5021
e-mail: greenwich.libraries@gll.org
url: www.gll.org
Head of Libraries, GLL Ms Diana Edmonds MBE BA DipLib FCLIP

District libraries
Blackheath Library, 17–23 Old Dover Road, London SE3 7BT
☎020 8858 1131

Eltham Centre Library, Archery Road, London SE9 1HA
☎020 8921 3452

Woolwich Centre Library, Wellington Street, London SE18 6HQ
☎020 8921 5750

HACKNEY

Authority: London Borough of Hackney
Strategic Leadership Team, Heritage and Culture, Health and Community Services, Hackney Service Centre, 2nd Floor – South Zone, 1 Hillman Street, London E8 1DY
☎020 8356 7578/7579
e-mail: info@hackney.gov.uk

url: www.hackney.gov.uk
Head of Libraries, Heritage and Culture Edward Rogers (020 8356 4782; e-mail:
edward.rogers@hackney.gov.uk)
Library Development & Support Manager Ms Sue Comitti MCLIP (020 8356 7572;
e-mail: sue.comitti@hackney.gov.uk)
Group Managers, Libraries Ms Eileen Cannon (020 8356 2562; e-mail:
eileen.cannon@hackney.gov.uk), Ms Margaret Sinn (020 8356 5387; e-mail:
margaret.sinn@hackney.gov.uk)
Heritage Manager Ms Tahlia Coombs (020 8356 5584; e-mail:
tahlia.coombs@hackney.gov.uk)
Principal Archivist Ms Libby Adams (020 8356 5912; e-mail:
libby.adams@hackney.gov.uk)

Stock Services Department
Homerton Library, Homerton High Street, London E9 6AS
☎020 8356 1694
Knowledge & Stock Services Manager Cyprian Marah BA(Hons) DipEd DipLib MA
(020 8356 2568; e-mail: cyprian.marah@hackney.gov.uk)

Central/largest library
Hackney Central Library, Technology and Learning Centre, 1 Reading Lane, London E8 1GQ
☎020 8356 5239
Duty Library Manager Robert Morgan (020 8356 2562; e-mail:
robert.morgan@hackney.gov.uk), Adrian Morris (020 8356 2574; e-mail:
adrian.morris@hackney.gov.uk)

Town centre libraries
Clapton Library, Northwold Road, London E5 8RA
☎020 8356 1620
Fax 020 8806 7849
Duty Library Manager Ms Marcia Charles (020 8356 7484; e-mail:
marcia.charles@hackney.gov.uk)

Community Library Service, c/o Stoke Newington Library, Church Street, London N16 0JS
☎020 8356 5238
Fax 020 8356 5234
e-mail: homevisitservice.library@hackney.gov.uk
Community Library Manager Christopher Garnsworthy (e-mail:
christopher.garnsworthy@hackney.gov.uk)

Dalston C L R James Library, Dalston Square, London E8 3BQ
☎020 8356 8947
Fax 020 7254 4655
Duty Library Managers Anthony Kane (e-mail: anthony.kane@hackney.gov.uk), Purvez
Chuhan (e-mail: purvez.chuhan@hackney.gov.uk)

Hackney Archives, 43 De Beauvoir Road, London N1 5SQ
☎020 7241 2886
Fax 020 7241 6688
e-mail: archives@hackney.gov.uk
url: www.hackney.gov.uk/archives

Principal Archivist Ms Libby Adams (020 8356 5912; e-mail:
libby.adams@hackney.gov.uk)

Homerton Library, Homerton High Street, London E9 6AS
☎020 8356 1963
Fax 020 8356 7945
Duty Library Manager Ms Sarah Fletcher (020 8356 1697; e-mail:
sarah.fletcher@hackney.gov.uk)

Shoreditch Library, 80 Hoxton Street, London N1 6LP
☎020 8356 5236/2542
Fax 020 8356 4353
Duty Library Managers David Nwankwo-Ntah (020 8356 5236; e-mail:
david.nwankwo-ntah@hackney.gov.uk), Ms Catherine De-Abaitua (e-mail:
catherine.de-abaitua@hackney.gov.uk)

Stamford Hill Library, Portland Avenue, London N16 6SB
☎020 8356 1964
Fax 020 8356 1709
Duty Library Manager Earl Bailey (020 8356 1748; e-mail: earl.bailey@hackney.gov.uk)

Stoke Newington Library, Church Street, London N16 0JS
☎020 8356 5235/5230
Fax 020 8356 5234
Duty Library Manager Callum Docherty (020 8356 5238; e-mail:
callum.docherty@hackney.gov.uk)

Woodberry Down Community Library, Robin Redmond Centre, 440 Seven Sisters Road,
London N4 2RD
☎020 8356 1965
(Woodberry Down Community Library is run by local volunteers)

HALTON

Authority: Halton Borough Council
Halton Lea Library, Halton Lea, Runcorn, Cheshire WA7 2PF
☎(0151) 511 7744
url: www.halton.gov.uk/libraries
Library Services Manager Mrs Paula Reilly-Cooper BSc DipLib MCLIP (0303 333 4300
ext 4096; e-mail: paula.reilly-cooper@halton.gov.uk) (Based at Select Security Stadium,
Lowerhouse Lane, Widnes WA8 7DZ)
Operational Manager Ms Julie Griffiths BA(Hons) MA MCLIP (e-mail:
julie.griffiths@halton.gov.uk)

Contacts for Central/Largest and Area Libraries
Stock Specialist Officer Mrs Trudy Jones BA(Hons) MCLIP (e-mail:
trudy.jones@halton.gov.uk)
Young Persons Officer Mrs Allyson Watt BA(Hons) MCLIP (e-mail:
allyson.watt@halton.gov.uk) (based at Widnes Library, Victoria Square, Widnes WA8 7QY)
Reader Development Officer Ms Janette Fleming (e-mail:
janette.fleming@halton.gov.uk)
Bibliographical Services Officer Mrs Geraldine Kane BA(Hons) MCLIP

Central/largest library

Halton Lea Library, Halton Lea, Runcorn, Cheshire WA7 2PF
☎0151 511 7744

Area libraries

Ditton Library, Queens Avenue, Ditton, Widnes, Cheshire WA8 8HR
☎0151 424 2459

Runcorn Library, Granville Street, Runcorn, Cheshire WA7 1NE
☎0151 511 7666

Widnes Library, Kingsway Learning Centre, Victoria Square, Widnes, Cheshire WA8 7QY
☎0151 907 8383

HAMMERSMITH AND FULHAM see TRI-BOROUGH LIBRARIES AND ARCHIVES

(LONDON BOROUGH OF HAMMERSMITH AND FULHAM; ROYAL BOROUGH OF KENSINGTON AND CHELSEA; WESTMINSTER CITY COUNCIL)

HAMPSHIRE

Authority: Hampshire County Council
Library and Information Service, Library HQ, Units 5/6 Moorside Place, Moorside Road, Winnall Industrial Estate, Winchester, Hants SO23 7RX
☎(01962) 826688
Fax (01962) 856615
url: www.hants.gov.uk/library
Head of Operations Alec Kennedy (01962 826681; e-mail: alec.kennedy@hants.gov.uk)
Group Managers Ms Julie Edyvean (01962 826618; e-mail: julie.edyvean@hants.gov.uk),
Ms Helen Bryant (07912 341075; e-mail: helen.bryant@hants.gov.uk) (based at
Waterlooville Library), Ms Jane Selby (07912 341072; e-mail: jane.selby@hants.gov.uk)
(based at Romsey Library)
Stock Manager Ms Carol Marshall (01962 826611; e-mail: carol.marshall@hants.gov.uk)
Planning and Performance Manager Ms Kathy Allen (01962 826607; e-mail:
kathy.allen@hants.gov.uk)

HARINGEY

Authority: London Borough of Haringey
Haringey Library Services, Central Library, High Road, Wood Green, London N22 6XD
☎020 8489 2780
url: www.haringey.gov.uk/libraries
Interim Head of Libraries and Culture David Murray (020 8489 4541; e-mail:
david.murray@haringey.gov.uk)

Central Library

Wood Green Central Library, High Road, Wood Green, London N22 6XD

☎020 8489 2780
Fax 020 8489 2555
Library Manager Tony Wilson

Area libraries

Hornsey Library, Haringey Park, London N8 9JA
☎020 8489 1118
Library Manager Ms Lucy Matheson

Marcus Garvey Library, Tottenham Green Leisure Centre, 1 Philip Lane, London N15 4JA
☎020 8489 5309
Library Manager Ms Bernadette Brewster

HARROW

Authority: Harrow Council (in partnership with Cultural Community Solutions Limited)
Civic Centre Library, Civic 7, Civic Centre, Station Road, Harrow, Middlesex HA1 2XY
☎020 3714 7747
e-mail: harrow.library@carillionservices.co.uk
url: www.harrowlibraries.com
Service Manager – Libraries, Sports and Leisure Tim Bryan BA DipLib MCLIP (e-mail:
tim.bryan@harrow.gov.uk)

Central/largest library

Gayton Library, 5 St John's Road, Harrow, Middlesex HA1 2EE
☎020 3714 7731/7732
e-mail: harrow.gaytonlibrary@carillionservices.co.uk
Senior Library Manager Ms Fiona Mehta (e-mail: fiona.mehta@carillionservices.co.uk)

HARTLEPOOL

Authority: Hartlepool Borough Council
Central Library, 124 York Road, Hartlepool TS26 9DE
☎(01429) 272905
Fax (01429) 283400
e-mail: infodesk@hartlepool.gov.uk
url: www.hartlepool.gov.uk/libraries
Library Services Manager Mrs Kay Tranter BA(Hons) (e-mail:
kay.tranter@hartlepool.gov.uk)

HAVERING

Authority: London Borough of Havering
Central Library, St Edwards Way, Romford, Essex RM1 3AR
☎(01708) 432389 (enquiries); (01708) 434924 (library marketing)
e-mail: libraryservices@havering.gov.uk
url: https://arena.yourlondonlibrary.net
Library Services Manager Ms Ann Rennie (01708 434922; e-mail:
ann.rennie@havering.gov.uk)
Frontline Services Manager Ms Nicky Dunne (01708 434930; e-mail:
nicky.dunne@havering.gov.uk)

HEREFORDSHIRE

Authority: Herefordshire Council
Herefordshire Libraries, The Nelson Building, Whitecross Road, Hereford HR4 0DG
☎(01432) 261556
url: www.herefordshire.gov.uk/libraries
Library Service Manager Jon Chedgzoy BA(Hons) DipLib MCLIP (01432 260557; e-mail: jchedgzoy@herefordshire.gov.uk)

Central library
Hereford Library, Broad Street, Hereford HR4 9AU
☎(01432) 383600

Largest libraries
Leominster Library, 8 Buttercross, Leominster, Herefordshire HR6 8BN
☎(01432) 383290

Ross-on-Wye Library, Cantilupe Road, Ross-on-Wye, Herefordshire HR9 7AN
☎(01432) 383280

HERTFORDSHIRE

Authority: Hertfordshire County Council
Libraries, Culture and Learning, CHO222 County Hall, Peggs Lane, Hertford, Herts SG13 8DQ
☎0300 123 4049
url: www.hertsdirect.org/libraries
Head of Libraries, Culture and Learning Andrew Bignell BA DipLib (e-mail: andrew.bignell@hertscc.gov.uk)
Principal Librarian: Information Services Ms Jean Holmes BA MCLIP (e-mail: jean.holmes@hertscc.gov.uk)
Principal Librarian: Resources Ms Sue Valentine BA(Hons) MCLIP (e-mail: sue.valentine@hertscc.gov.uk)
Principal Librarian: Customers and Communities Ms Michele Murphy BA(Hons) MCLIP (e-mail: michele.murphy@hertscc.gov.uk)
Area Librarian: East Ms Rachel Bilton BLib(Hons) MCLIP (e-mail: rachel.bilton@hertfordshire.gov.uk)
Area Librarian: Mid Ms Claire Barraclough BA MCLIP (e-mail: claire.barraclough@hertfordshire.gov.uk)
Area Librarian: West Russel Barrow BA(Hons) (e-mail: russel.barrow@hertfordshire.gov.uk)

Group libraries
(telephone numbers for the following libraries are the same as for HQ)
Bishop's Stortford Library, 6 The Causeway, Bishop's Stortford, Herts CM23 2EJ
e-mail: hertsdirect@hertfordshire.gov.uk

Hemel Hempstead Library, Combe Road, Hemel Hempstead, Hertfordshire HP1 1HJ

Hoddesdon Library, 98A High Street, Hoddesdon, Herts EN11 8HD

St Albans Library, The Maltings, St Albans, Herts AL1 3JQ
e-mail: hertsdirect@hertfordshire.gov.uk

Stevenage Library, Southgate, Stevenage, Herts SG1 1HD
e-mail: hertsdirect@hertfordshire.gov.uk

Watford Library, Hempstead Road, Watford, Herts WD1 3EU
e-mail: hertsdirect@hertfordshire.gov.uk

Welwyn Garden City Central Library & Information Service, Campus West, Welwyn
Garden City, Herts AL8 6AJ
e-mail: hertsdirect@hertfordshire.gov.uk

HILLINGDON

Authority: London Borough of Hillingdon
Central Library, 14 High Street, Uxbridge, Middlesex UB8 1HD
☎(01895) 250600 (enquiries), (01895) 250713 (administration)
Fax (01895) 811164
e-mail: librarycontact@hillingdon.gov.uk
url: www.hillingdon.gov.uk/libraries
Deputy Director – Residents Services Steve Palmer (e-mail:
spalmer@hillingdon.gov.uk)
Manager, Arts and Libraries Daniel Waller BA(Hons) (e-mail:
dwaller@hillingdon.gov.uk)

Central/largest library
Uxbridge Library, 14 High Street, Uxbridge, Middlesex UB8 1HD
☎(01895) 250600
Fax (01895) 811164
e-mail: librarycontact@hillingdon.gov.uk
Uxbridge Library Manager Ms Zoe Iggulden

HOUNSLOW

Authority: London Borough of Hounslow (in partnership with Cultural Community
Solutions Limited)
**Hounslow Libraries, CentreSpace, Treaty Centre, High Street, Hounslow, Middlesex
TW3 1ES**
☎0845 456 2800 (enquiries)
Fax 0845 456 2965
e-mail: hounslow-info@carillionservices.co.uk
url: www.hounslow.info
Senior Operations Manager Mrs Elaine Collier (e-mail:
elaine.collier@carillionservices.co.uk)
Libraries Development Manager Ms Fiona Tarn (e-mail:
fiona.tarn@carillionservices.co.uk)

Central/largest library
Hounslow Library, CentreSpace, Treaty Centre, High Street, Hounslow, Middlesex TW3 1ES
☎0845 456 2800
Fax 0845 456 2965

Branch libraries

Beavers Library @ The Hub, 103 Salisbury Road, Hounslow, Middlesex TW4 7NW
☎020 8572 6995

Bedfont Library, Staines Road, Bedfont, Middlesex TW14 8BD
☎020 8890 6173

Brentford Library, Boston Manor Road, Brentford, Middlesex TW8 8DW
☎020 8560 8801

Chiswick Library, Duke's Avenue, Chiswick, London W4 2AB
☎020 8994 1008

Cranford Library, Bath Road, Cranford, Middlesex TW5 9TL
☎020 8759 0641

Feltham Library, The Centre, High Street, Feltham, Middlesex TW13 4GU
☎020 8890 3506

Hanworth Air Park Leisure Centre and Library, Uxbridge Road, Hanworth, Middlesex
TW13 5EG
☎020 8898 0256

Heston Library, New Heston Road, Heston, Middlesex TW5 0LW
☎020 8570 1028

Isleworth Library, Twickenham Road, Isleworth, Middlesex TW7 7EU
☎020 8560 2934

Osterley Library, St Mary's Crescent, Osterley, Middlesex TW7 4NB
☎020 8560 4295

ISLE OF WIGHT

Authority: Isle of Wight Council
**Library Headquarters, 5 Mariners Way, Somerton Industrial Estate, Cowes, Isle of
Wight PO31 8PD**
☎(01983) 203880 (enquiries and administration)
Fax (01983) 203899
url: www.iwight.com/Residents/Libraries-Cultural-and-Heritage
Library Service Manager Rob Jones BA MCLIP CertEd (e-mail: rob.jones@iow.gov.uk)
Development Librarian – Operations Andrew Walker BA MCLIP (e-mail:
andrew.walker@iow.gov.uk)
Development Librarian – Stock and Information John English BLib DMS (e-mail:
john.english@iow.gov.uk)
Development Librarian – Young People and Lifelong Learning Mrs Elspeth Jackson
BA(Hons) DipLIS MCLIP (e-mail: elspeth.jackson@iow.gov.uk)

Central/largest libraries

Cowes Library, Beckford Road, Cowes, Isle of Wight PO31 7SG
☎(01983) 293341 (tel/fax)

Freshwater Library, School Green Road, Freshwater, Isle of Wight PO35 5NA
☎(01983) 752377 (tel/fax)

Lord Louis Library, Orchard Street, Newport, Isle of Wight PO30 1LL
☎(01983) 527655 (enquiries and administration)
Fax (01983) 825972

Ryde Library, George Street, Ryde, Isle of Wight PO33 2JE
☎(01983) 562170
Fax (01983) 615644

Sandown Library, High Street, Sandown, Isle of Wight PO36 8AF
☎(01983) 402748 (tel/fax)

Ventnor Library, High Street, Ventnor, Isle of Wight PO38 1LX
☎(01983) 852039 (tel/fax)

Community libraries
Bembridge Community Library, Church Road, Bembridge, Isle of Wight PO35 5NA
☎(01983) 873102 (tel/fax)

Brighstone Community Library, New Road, Brighstone, Newport, Isle of Wight PO30 4AX
☎(01983) 740446 (tel/fax)

East Cowes Community Library, The York Centre, 11 York Avenue, East Cowes, Isle of Wight PO32 6QY
☎(01983) 718662 (tel/fax)

Edward Edwards Library, High Street, Niton, Isle of Wight PO38 2AZ
☎(01983) 730863 (tel/fax)

Shanklin Library, Victoria Avenue, Shanklin, Isle of Wight PO37 6PG
☎(01983) 863126 (tel/fax)

ISLINGTON

Authority: London Borough of Islington
Library and Heritage Services, Central Library, 2 Fieldway Crescent, London N5 1PF
☎020 7527 6900 (enquiries), 020 7527 6905 (administration)
Fax 020 7527 6906
e-mail: hlcs@islington.gov.uk
url: www.islington.gov.uk/libraries
Head of Library and Heritage Services Ms Rosemary Doyle MCLIP MBA (020 7527 6903; e-mail: rosemary.doyle@islington.gov.uk)
Assistant Head of Library and Heritage Services Ms Michelle Gannon BSc(Hons) (020 7527 6907; e-mail: michelle.gannon@islington.gov.uk)
Children and Young People's Services Manager Geoff James BA(Hons) DipLib MCLIP (020 7527 6997; e-mail: geoff.james@islington.gov.uk)

Central/largest library
Central Library, 2 Fieldway Crescent, London N5 1PF
☎020 7527 6900
Fax 020 7527 6902
Customer Services Manager Ms Maureen Black (020 7527 6950; e-mail: maureen.black@islington.gov.uk)

Other libraries

Archway Library, Hamlyn House, Highgate Hill, London N19 5PH
☎020 7527 7820
Fax 020 7527 7833
e-mail: archway.library@islington.gov.uk
Person in charge Cuneyt Yilmaz

Finsbury Library, 245 St John Street, London EC1V 4NB
☎020 7527 7960
Fax 020 7527 7998
e-mail: finsbury.library@islington.gov.uk
Person in charge Chris Millington

John Barnes Library, 275 Camden Road, London N7 0JN
☎020 7527 7900
Fax 020 7527 7907
e-mail: johnbarnes.library@islington.gov.uk
Person in charge Cuneyt Yilmaz

Lewis Carroll Library, Copenhagen Street, London N1 0ST
☎020 7527 7936
Fax 020 7527 7935
e-mail: lewiscarroll.library@islington.gov.uk
Person in charge Ms Kate Tribe, Ms Pamela Quantrill

Mildmay Library, 21–23 Mildmay Park, London N1 4NA
☎020 7527 7880
Fax 020 7527 7898
e-mail: mildmay.library@islington.gov.uk
Person in charge Ms Marcia Ludlow

N4 Library, 26 Blackstock Road, London N4 2DW
☎020 7527 7800
Fax 020 527 7808
e-mail: n4.library@islington.gov.uk
Person in charge Nick Tranmer

North Library, Manor Gardens, London N7 6JX
☎020 7527 7840
Fax 020 7527 7854
e-mail: north.library@islington.gov.uk
Person in charge Nick Tranmer

South Library, 115–117 Essex Road, London N1 2SL
☎020 7527 7860
Fax 020 7527 7869
e-mail: south.library@islington.gov.uk
Persons in charge Ms Marcia Ludlow

West Library, Bridgeman Road, London N1 1BD
☎020 7527 7920
Fax 020 7527 7929
e-mail: west.library@islington.gov.uk
Persons in charge Ms Kate Tribe, Ms Pamela Quantrill

KENSINGTON AND CHELSEA see
TRI-BOROUGH LIBRARIES AND ARCHIVES
(LONDON BOROUGH OF HAMMERSMITH AND FULHAM; ROYAL BOROUGH OF KENSINGTON AND CHELSEA; WESTMINSTER CITY COUNCIL)

KENT

Authority: Kent County Council
Kent History and Library Centre, James Whatman Way, Maidstone, Kent ME14 ILQ
☎(01622) 696548
Fax (01622) 696445
e-mail: libraries@kent.gov.uk
url: www.kent.gov.uk/libs
Head of Libraries, Registration & Archives Ms Cath Anley
Business Manager Ms Diane Chilmaid
Operations Manager Ms Lynn Catt
Service Improvement Programme Manager Ms Susan Sparks, James Pearson
Registration & Nationality Manager Ms Sharon Birch
Stock Services Manager Ken Jarvis

Ask-a-Kent Librarian
Kent History and Library Centre, James Whatman Way, Maidstone, Kent ME14 ILQ
☎(01622) 696438
Fax (01622) 696445
e-mail: AKL@kent.gov.uk
url: www.kent.gov.uk/leisure-and-community/libraries/ask-a-kent-librarian
Service Improvement Manager (Information, Digital Inclusion and Active Citizenship) Ms Christel Pobgee

Main district libraries
Ashford Gateway Plus, Church Road, Ashford, Kent TN23 IAS
☎0300 041 3131
Fax (01233) 620295
e-mail: ashfordlibrary@kent.gov.uk
url: www.kent.gov.uk/libs
Area Manager Ms Sue Fordham

Canterbury Library, 18 High Street, Canterbury, Kent CT1 2RA
☎0300 041 3131
e-mail: canterburylibrary@kent.gov.uk
Area Manager Ms Barbara Bragg

Dartford Library, Central Park, Market Street, Dartford, Kent DA1 1EU
☎0300 041 3131
Fax (01322) 278271
e-mail: dartfordlibrary@kent.gov.uk
Area Manager Ms Avis Heppenstall

Dover Discovery Centre, Market Square, Dover, Kent CT16 1PH
☎0300 041 3131
Fax (01304) 225914
e-mail: doverlibrary@kent.gov.uk
Area Manager Ms Jackie Taylor-Smith

Gravesend Library, Windmill Street, Gravesend, Kent DA12 1BE
☎0300 041 3131
Fax (01474) 320284
e-mail: gravesendlibrary@kent.gov.uk
Area Manager Ms Avis Heppenstall

Kent History & Library Centre, James Whatman Way, Maidstone, Kent ME14 1LQ
☎(01622) 696548
Fax (01622) 696445
e-mail: historyandlibrarycentre@kent.gov.uk
Area Manager Ms Shirley Sheridan

Sevenoaks Library, Buckhurst Lane, Sevenoaks, Kent TN13 1LQ
☎0300 041 3131
Fax (01732) 459581
e-mail: sevenoakslibrary@kent.gov.uk
Area Manager Ms Donna-Marie Dunn

Shepway - Folkestone Library, 2 Grace Hill, Folkestone, Kent CT20 1HD
☎0300 041 3131
Fax (01303) 242907
e-mail: folkestonelibrary@kent.gov.uk
Area Manager Ms Sue Fordham

Swale – Sittingbourne Library, Central Avenue, Sittingbourne, Kent ME10 4AH
☎0300 041 3131
Fax (01795) 428376
e-mail: sittingbournelibrary@kent.gov.uk
Area Manager Ms Barbara Bragg

Thanet – Margate Library, Thanet Gateway Plus, Cecil Street, Margate, Kent CT9 1RE
☎0300 041 3131
Fax (01843) 293015
e-mail: margatelibrary@kent.gov.uk
Area Manager Ms Jackie Taylor-Smith

Tonbridge Library, 1 Avebury Avenue, Tonbridge, Kent TN9 1TG
☎0300 041 3131
Fax (01732) 358300
e-mail: tonbridgelibrary@kent.gov.uk
Area Manager Ms Amanda Forrest

Tunbridge Wells Library, Mount Pleasant Road, Tunbridge Wells, Kent TN1 1NS
☎0300 041 3131
Fax (01892) 514657
e-mail: tunbridgewellslibrary@kent.gov.uk
Area Manager Ms Donna-Marie Dunn

KINGSTON UPON HULL

Authority: Kingston upon Hull City Council
Central Library, Albion Street, Kingston upon Hull HU1 3TF
☎(01482) 210000 (enquiries), (01482) 616824 (administration)
Fax (01482) 616827
e-mail: reference.library@hullcc.gov.uk
url: www.hullcc.gov.uk/libraries
Assistant Head of Service – Libraries Ms Michelle Alford BA(Hons)

Area libraries

Avenues Library, 76 Chanterlands Avenue, Kingston upon Hull HU5 3TS
☎(01482) 331280
e-mail: avenues.library@hullcc.gov.uk

Bransholme Library, District Centre, Goodhart Road, Bransholme, Kingston upon Hull
HU7 4EF
☎(01482) 331234
e-mail: bransholme.library@hullcc.gov.uk

Fred Moore Library, Wold Road, Kingston upon Hull HU5 5UN
☎(01482) 331239
e-mail: fredmoore.library@hullcc.gov.uk

Freedom Centre Library, Freedom Centre, Preston Road, Kingston upon Hull HU9 3QB
☎(01482) 710100
e-mail: prestonroad.library@hullcc.gov.uk

Gipsyville Library, Gipsyville Multi Pupose Centre, North Road, Kingston upon Hull HU4 6JA
☎(01482) 616973
e-mail: gipsyville.library@hullcc.gov.uk

Greenwood Avenue Library, Greenwood Avenue, Kingston upon Hull HU6 9RU
☎(01482) 331257
e-mail: greenwood.library@hullcc.gov.uk

Holderness Road Customer Service Centre and Library, 1 The Mount, Holderness Road,
Kingston upon Hull HU9 2AH
☎(01482) 318830
e-mail: holderness.csc@hullcc.gov.uk

Ings Customer Service Centre and Library, Savoy Road, Kingston upon Hull HU8 0TY
☎(01482) 331250
e-mail: ingsroadlibrary@hullcc.gov.uk

Longhill Library, 162 Shannon Road, Kingston upon Hull HU8 9RW
☎(01482) 331530
e-mail: longhill.library@hullcc.gov.uk

Waudby Library (within the Waudby Centre), Hemswell Avenue, Kingston upon Hull
UP9 5LD
☎(01482) 331264
e-mail: waudby.library@hullcc.gov.uk

Western Library, 254 The Boulevard, Kingston upon Hull HU3 3ED

☎(01482) 331217
e-mail: western.library@hullcc.gov.uk

KINGSTON UPON THAMES

Authority: Royal Borough of Kingston upon Thames
Kingston Library, Fairfield Road, Kingston upon Thames, Surrey KT1 2PS
☎020 8547 6413 (administration)
Fax 020 8547 6426
url: www.kingston.gov.uk
Strategic Manager: Library and Heritage Service Ms Grace McElwee BA(Hons) DipLib MCLIP (020 8547 6423; e-mail: grace.mcelwee@kingston.gov.uk)
Lead Officer: Library Operations Geoff Boulton BA MCLIP (020 8547 6419; e-mail: geoff.boulton@kingston.gov.uk)
Team Leader: Adult Services Ms Alison Townsend BA MA MCLIP (020 8547 6494; e-mail: alison.townsend@kingston.gov.uk)
Team Leader: Children & Youth Services Michael Treacy (020 8547 6431; e-mail: michael.treacy@kingston.gov.uk)

Branch libraries

Community Library, Surbiton Library Annexe, Ewell Road, Surbiton, Surrey KT6 6AG
☎020 8547 6453
Fax 020 8339 9805
e-mail: comlib@kingston.gov.uk

Hook and Chessington Library, Hook Road, Chessington, Surrey KT9 1EJ
☎020 8547 5006
Fax 020 8547 6483
e-mail: hookandchessington.library@kingston.gov.uk
Team Leader: Operations – Hook, Surbiton & Tolworth Libraries Ms Michaela Newman (020 8547 6482; e-mail: michaela.newman@kingston.gov.uk)

Kingston Library, Fairfield Road, Kingston upon Thames, Surrey KT1 2PS
☎020 8547 5006
Fax 020 8547 6401
e-mail: kingston.library@kingston.gov.uk
Team Leader: Operations – Kingston and Malden & Coombe Neighbourhood Libraries Ms Carolyn Roberts (020 8547 6499; e-mail: carolyn.roberts@kingston.gov.uk)

New Malden Library, Kingston Road, New Malden, Surrey KT3 3LY
☎020 8547 5006
Fax 020 8547 6495
e-mail: newmalden.library@kingston.gov.uk
Team Leader: Operations – Kingston and Malden & Coombe Neighbourhood Libraries Ms Carolyn Roberts (020 8547 6499; e-mail: carolyn.roberts@kingston.gov.uk)

Old Malden Library, Church Road, Worcester Park, Surrey KT4 7RD
☎020 8547 5006
Fax 020 8547 6469
e-mail: oldmalden.library@kingston.gov.uk
Team Leader: Operations – Kingston and Malden & Coombe Neighbourhood Libraries Ms Carolyn Roberts (020 8547 6499; e-mail: carolyn.roberts@kingston.gov.uk)

Surbiton Library, Ewell Road, Surbiton, Surrey KT6 6AG
☎020 8547 5006
Fax 020 8547 6449
e-mail: surbiton.library@kingston.gov.uk
Team Leader: Operations – Hook, Surbiton & Tolworth Libraries Ms Michaela
Newman (020 8547 6482; e-mail: michaela.newman@kingston.gov.uk)

Tolworth Community Library and IT Learning Centre, The Broadway, Tolworth, Surbiton,
Surrey KT6 7DJ
☎020 8547 5006
Fax 020 8547 6471
e-mail: tolworth.library@kingston.gov.uk
Team Leader: Operations – Hook, Surbiton & Tolworth Libraries Ms Michaela
Newman (020 8547 6482; e-mail: michaela.newman@kingston.gov.uk)

Tudor Drive Library, Tudor Drive, Kingston upon Thames, Surrey KT2 5QH
☎020 8547 6457
Fax 020 8547 6459
e-mail: tudordrive.library@kingston.gov.uk
**Team Leader: Operations – Kingston and Malden & Coombe Neighbourhood
Libraries** Ms Carolyn Roberts (020 8547 6499; e-mail: carolyn.roberts@kingston.gov.uk)

KIRKLEES

Authority: Kirklees Council
**Kirklees Customer & Exchequer Services, Red Doles Lane, Huddersfield, West Yorks
HD2 IYF**
☎(01484) 226300
url: www.kirklees.gov.uk
Assistant Director, Customer & Exchequer Services Ms Jane Brady (01484 221193;
e-mail: jane.brady@kirklees.gov.uk) (based at 3rd Floor, Civic Centre 1, Huddersfield,
West Yorks HD1 2NF
Chief Librarian Ms Carol Stump (e-mail: carol.stump@kirklees.gov.uk)
Assistant Head of Service (Frontline Services) Dave Thompson (01484 226303;
e-mail: dave.thompson@kirklees.gov.uk)

Central/largest library
Huddersfield Library & Information Centre, Princess Alexandra Walk, Huddersfield, West
Yorks HD1 2SU
☎(01484) 221951
Fax (01484) 221952
Manager i/c Ms Kathryn Harrison BA(Hons) PGDipLib MCLIP (e-mail:
kathryn.harrison@kirklees.gov.uk)

Area libraries and information centres
Area Central. Shepley Library & Information Centre, Marsh Lane, Shepley, Huddersfield,
West Yorks HD8 8AE
☎(01484) 222728
Manager i/c Ms Kathryn Harrison BA(Hons) PGDipLib MCLIP (e-mail:
kathryn.harrison@kirklees.gov.uk)

Area North. Dewsbury Library & Information Centre, Railway Street, Dewsbury, West Yorks WF12 8EQ
☎(01924) 325080
Manager i/c Ms Alison Peaden BA MCLIP (e-mail: alison.peaden@kirklees.gov.uk)

Area South. Holmfirth Library & Information Centre, 47 Huddersfield Road, Holmfirth, West Yorks HD9 3JH
☎(01484) 222430

Mobiles and Home Service, Customer & Exchequer Services, Library and Information Centres HQ, Red Doles Lane, Huddersfield, West Yorks HD2 1YF
☎(01484) 226350
Manager i/c Ms Salma Dad (e-mail: salma.dad@kirklees.gov.uk)

KNOWSLEY

Authority: Knowsley Metropolitan Borough Council
Huyton Library, Civic Way, Huyton, Merseyside L36 9GD
☎0151 443 3738
Fax 0151 443 3739
url: www.knowsley.gov.uk/residents/libraries.aspx
Head of Libraries Peter Marchant MA BA(Hons) DipLib DM MCLIP (e-mail: peter.marchant@knowsley.gov.uk)

Central/largest library

Huyton Library, Civic Way, Huyton, Merseyside L36 9GD
☎0151 443 3734
Fax 0151 443 3739
e-mail: huyton.library@knowsley.gov.uk
Library Manager Paul Whitehouse

Branch libraries

Halewood Library, The Halewood Centre, Roseheath Drive, Halewood, Knowsley, Merseyside L26 0TS
☎0151 443 2086
e-mail: halewood.library@knowsley.gov.uk

Kirkby Library, The Kirkby Centre, Norwich Way, Kirkby, Merseyside L32 8RR
☎0151 443 4290
e-mail: kirkby.library@knowsley.gov.uk

Prescot Library, The Prescot Centre, Aspinall Street, Prescot, Merseyside L34 5GA
☎0151 443 5101
e-mail: prescot.library@knowsley.gov.uk

Stockbridge Village Library, The Withens, Stockbridge Village, Merseyside L26 1AB
☎0151 443 2501
e-mail: stockbridge.library@knowsley.gov.uk

LAMBETH

Authority: London Borough of Lambeth
Lambeth Libraries and Archives, Brixton Library, Brixton Oval, London SW2 1JQ

☎020 7926 0750 (enquiries); 020 7926 1000 (switchboard)
e-mail: lambethlibraries@lambeth.gov.uk
url: www.lambeth.gov.uk
Head of Libraries Ms Susanna Barnes (e-mail: sbarnes@lambeth.gov.uk)
Libraries Manager: Projects, Performance and Transition Michel Merson (e-mail: mmerson@lambeth.gov.uk)
Libraries Manager: Customer and Quality Service Oniel Williams (e-mail: owilliams@lambeth.gov.uk)
Development Librarian: Adult Reading and Health Tim O'Dell (e-mail: to'dell@lambeth.gov.uk)
Development Librarian: Early Years, Literacy, Skills and Business Abibat Olulode (e-mail: aolulode@lambeth.gov.uk)
Development Librarians: Information and Digital Ms Zoey Dixon (e-mail: ZCDixon@lambeth.gov.uk), Ms Katrina Tandoh (e-mail: ktandoh@lambeth.gov.uk)
Senior Children and Young People Librarian Ms Sandra Davidson (e-mail: sdavidson@lambeth.gov.uk) (based at Clapham Library)

Lambeth Archives and Local Studies Library
Lambeth Archives and Library, 52 Knatchbull Road, London SE5 9QY
☎020 7926 6076
Fax 020 7926 6080
e-mail: archives@lambeth.gov.uk
Managers Jon Newman MA DAA (e-mail: jnewman@lambeth.gov.uk), Len Reilly BA DipLib MCLIP (e-mail: ljreilly@lambeth.gov.uk)

Lambeth libraries
Brixton Tate Library, Brixton Oval, London SW2 1JQ
☎020 7926 1056
e-mail: brixtonlendinglibrary@lambeth.gov.uk
Library Manager Ms Liz Buchanan

Carnegie Library, 192 Herne Hill Road, London SE24 0AG
☎020 7926 6050
e-mail: carnegielibrary@lambeth.gov.uk
Library Manager Ms Caroline Mackie

Clapham Library, Mary Seacole Centre, 91 Clapham High Road, London SW4 7DB
☎020 7926 0717
e-mail: claphamlibrary@lambeth.gov.uk
Library Manager Ms Vincia Bennett

Durning Library, 167 Kennington Lane, London SE11 4HF
☎020 7926 8682
e-mail: durninglibrary@lambeth.gov.uk
Library Manager Dale Arndell

Minet Library, 52 Knatchbull Road, London SE5 9QY
☎020 7926 6073
Library Manager Ms Joanne Johnson

Streatham Tate Library, 63 Streatham High Road, London SW16 1PN
☎020 7926 6768

e-mail: streathamlibrary@lambeth.gov.uk
Library Manager Arthur Lech

Tate South Lambeth Library, 180 South Lambeth Road, London SW8 1QP
☎020 7926 0705
e-mail: southlambethlibrary@lambeth.gov.uk
Library Manager Ms Maria Kwofie

Waterloo Library, 114–118 Lower Marsh, London SE1 7AG
☎020 7926 8750
e-mail: waterloolibrary@lambeth.gov.uk
Library Manager Ms Pauline Edole

West Norwood Library, The Old Library, 14–16 Knights Hill, London SE27 0HY
☎020 7926 8092
e-mail: westnorwoodlibrary@lambeth.gov.uk
Library Manager Ms Rosanna Osborne

Stock Services, 188 Herne Hill Road, London SE24 0AG
☎020 7926 6069
Fax 020 7926 6072
e-mail: stocksupportservices@lambeth.gov.uk
Development Librarian: Children and Young People Ms Clare Stockbridge Bland BA MCLIP (e-mail: cstockbridgebland@lambeth.gov.uk)

LANCASHIRE

Authority: Lancashire County Council
Adult Services, Health and Wellbeing, 1st Floor, Christ Church Precinct, PO Box 78, County Hall, Fishergate, Preston, Lancs PR1 8XJ
e-mail: library@lancashire.gov.uk
url: www.lancashire.gov.uk/libraries
Head of Library Service Mrs Julie Bell BA(Hons) MCLIP (01772 534010; e-mail: julie.bell@lancashire.gov.uk)
Strategic Manager – Support David Blackett BA MCLIP (01772 534091; e-mail: david.blackett@lancashire.gov.uk)
Strategic Manager – Planning Ms Ann Marsh BLib MCLIP (01772 536727; e-mail: ann.marsh@lancashire.gov.uk)

District libraries
For all district libraries contact 0300 123 6703
Accrington Library, St James' Street, Accrington, Lancs BB5 1NQ
Burnley Library, Grimshaw Street, Burnley, Lancs BB11 2BD
Chorley Library, Union Street, Chorley, Lancs PR7 1EB
Clitheroe Library, Church Street, Clitheroe, Lancs BB7 2DG
Fleetwood Library, North Albert Street, Fleetwood, Lancs FY7 6AJ
Harris Library, Market Square, Preston, Lancs PR1 2PP
Lancaster Library, Market Square, Lancaster, Lancs LA1 1HY
Leyland Library, Lancastergate, Leyland, Preston, Lancs PR25 1EX
Nelson Library, Market Square, Nelson, Lancs BB9 7PU
Rawtenstall Library, Queen's Square, Rawtenstall, Lancs BB4 6QU
St Anne's Library, 254 Clifton Drive South, Lytham St Anne's, Lancs FY8 1NR
Skelmersdale Library, Southway, Skelmersdale, Lancs WN8 6NL

LEEDS

Authority: Leeds City Council
Library Headquarters, I Bowcliffe Road, Off Gibraltar Island Road, Hunslet, Leeds LS10 1HB
☎0113 395 2311/3 (general enquiries)
Fax 0113 395 2362/3

Central/largest library

Central Library, Municipal Buildings, Calverley Street, Leeds LS1 3AB
☎0113 247 8421
Fax 0113 395 1335
url: www.leeds.gov.uk
Head of Library and Information Service Mrs Bev Rice BA (e-mail: bev.rice@leeds.gov.uk)

LEICESTER

Authority: Leicester City Council
Leicester Libraries, 2nd Floor, Town Hall Square, Leicester LE1 9BG
☎0116 254 3540 (administration)
e-mail: libraries@leicester.gov.uk
url: www.leicester.gov.uk/libraries
Head of Libraries and Information Services Adrian Wills BA DMS MCLIP (0116 454 3541; e-mail: adrian.wills@leicester.gov.uk)
Libraries Development Manager Lee Warner BA(Hons) (0116 454 3542; e-mail: lee.warner@leicester.gov.uk), Ms Sally Mitchell (0116 454 3545; e-mail: sally.mitchell@leicester.gov.uk), Paul Gobey BA DipLib MCLIP (0116 454 0083; e-mail: paul.gobey@leicester.gov.uk)

Central/largest libraries

Leicester Central Library, Bishop Street, Leicester LE1 6AA
☎0116 299 5401
e-mail: central-library@leicester.gov.uk

LEICESTERSHIRE

Authority: Leicestershire County Council
Library Services, County Hall, Glenfield, Leicester LE3 8RL
☎0116 305 4699
Fax 0116 305 7440
e-mail: libraries@leics.gov.uk
url: www.leics.gov.uk/libraries
Head of Service Delivery Nigel Thomas BLib(Hons) MCLIP DPLM (e-mail: nthomas@leics.gov.uk)
Modernising Services Manager Steve Kettle (e-mail: steve.kettle@leics.gov.uk)

Main library group HQs

Coalville Library, High Street, Coalville, Leics LE67 3EA
☎0116 305 3565

Fax (01530) 832019
Principal Manager Ms Carol Cowley (e-mail: carol.cowley@leics.gov.uk)

Hinckley Library, Lancaster Road, Hinckley, Leics LE10 0AT
☎0116 305 2500
Fax 0116 305 2514
Principal Manager Ms Carol Cowley (e-mail: carol.cowley@leics.gov.uk)

Loughborough Library, Granby Street, Loughborough, Leics LE11 3DZ
☎0116 305 2420
Fax (01509) 610594
Principal Manager Ms Judith Neville (e-mail: judith.neville@leics.gov.uk)

Market Harborough Library, The Symington Building, Adam and Eve Street, Market Harborough, Leics LE16 7PQ
☎0116 305 3627
Fax 0116 305 0670
Principal Manager Ms Karen Cox (e-mail: karen.cox@leics.gov.uk)

Melton Mowbray Library, Wilton Road, Melton Mowbray, Leics LE13 0UJ
☎0116 305 3646
Fax 0116 305 0735
Principal Manager Ms Karen Cox (e-mail: karen.cox@leics.gov.uk)

Oadby Library, 10 The Parade, Oadby, Leicester LE2 5BF
☎0116 305 8763
Fax 0116 305 8163
Principal Manager Ms Jilly Cunnington (e-mail: jilly.cunnington@leics.gov.uk)

Wigston Library, Bull Head Street, Wigston, Leicester LE18 1PA
☎0116 305 3689
Fax 0116 281 2985
Principal Manager Ms Jilly Cunnington (e-mail: jilly.cunnington@leics.gov.uk)

LEWISHAM

Authority: London Borough of Lewisham
Community Services, Laurence House, 1 Catford Road, London SE6 4RU
☎020 8314 8024
Fax 020 8314 3229
e-mail: libraries@lewisham.gov.uk
url: www.lewisham.gov.uk/libraries
Head of Library and Information Services Antonio Rizzo BA(Hons) MA(ISM) (e-mail: antonio.rizzo@lewisham.gov.uk)

Central/largest library
Lewisham Library, 199-201 Lewisham High Street, London SE13 6LG
☎020 8314 9800
e-mail: libraries@lewisham.gov.uk
Area Manager Victor Chapman BLib(Hons) MCLIP, Christopher Moore

District libraries
Downham Library, Downham Health & Leisure Centre, Moorside Road, London BR1 5EP

☎020 8314 9705
e-mail: libraries@lewisham.gov.uk
Area Manager Ms Elizabeth Radford

The Library@Deptford Lounge, Deptford Lounge, Giffin Street, London SE8 4RJ
☎020 8314 7299
e-mail: libraries@lewisham.gov.uk
Area Managers Ms Christine Carl, Paulo Pisani

LINCOLNSHIRE

Authority: Lincolnshire County Council
Libraries and Heritage, Orchard House, Orchard Street, Lincoln LNI IBA
☎(01522) 550586
Fax (01522) 552811
url: www.lincolnshire.gov.uk
Head of Libraries and Heritage Jonathan Platt (e-mail:
jonathan.platt@lincolnshire.gov.uk)
Network Manager East Gary Porter (01522 552831; e-mail:
gary.porter@lincolnshire.gov.uk)
Network Manager West William Brown (01522 552839; e-mail:
william.brown@lincolnshire.gov.uk)

Central/largest libraries
Lincoln Central Library, Free School Lane, Lincoln LN2 1EZ
☎(01522) 782010
Fax (01522) 575011
e-mail: lincoln_library@lincolnshire.gov.uk

Mobile Library Services, Eastgate Centre, 105 Eastgate, Sleaford, Lincs NG34 7EN
☎(01522) 550361
Fax (01522) 550372

LIVERPOOL

Authority: Liverpool City Council
Liverpool Central Library and Archive, William Brown Street, Liverpool L3 8EW
☎Contact number for all Liverpool libraries: 0151 233 3069
url: www.liverpool.gov.uk
Divisional Manager John Keane BA(Hons) MCLIP (0151 233 5833; e-mail:
john.keane@liverpool.gov.uk)

Central/largest library
Central Library, William Brown Street, Liverpool L3 8EW
e-mail: central.library@liverpool.gov.uk

Other large libraries
Allerton Library, Liverpool L18 6HG
e-mail: allerton.library@liverpool.gov.uk

Childwall Fiveways Library, Liverpool L15 6QR
e-mail: childwall.library@liverpool.gov.uk

Norris Green Library, Townsend Avenue, Liverpool L11 5AF
e-mail: norrisgreen.library@liverpool.gov.uk

LONDON, CITY OF

Authority: City of London
Culture, Heritage & Libraries, Aldermanbury, London EC2V 7HH
☎020 7332 1850
e-mail: directorofculture@cityoflondon.gov.uk
url: www.cityoflondon.gov.uk
Director David Pearson MA FCLIP FSA (e-mail: david.pearson@cityoflondon.gov.uk)

Central/largest libraries
Barbican Library, Barbican Centre, Silk Street, London EC2Y 8DS
☎020 7638 0569
Fax 020 7638 2249
Head of Barbican and Community Libraries Ms Carol Boswarthack BA MCLIP (e-mail: carol.boswarthack@cityoflondon.gov.uk)

Guildhall Library, Aldermanbury, London EC2V 7HH
☎020 7332 1868 (Guildhall Library), 020 7332 1812 (City Business Library)
e-mail: guildhall.library@cityoflondon.gov.uk; cbl@cityoflongon.gov.uk
Head of Guildhall and City Business Libraries Ms Sara Pink (e-mail: sara.pink@cityoflondon.gov.uk)

Regional/district libraries
Artizan Street Library and Community Centre, Artizan Street, London E1 7AF
☎020 7332 3810
e-mail: artizanlib@cityoflondon.gov.uk
Centre Manager Stephen Berwick (e-mail: stephen.berwick@cityoflondon.gov.uk)

Shoe Lane Library, Hill House, Little New Street, London EC4A 3JR
☎020 7583 7178
e-mail: shoelane@cityoflondon.gov.uk
Librarian Leslie King BA MCLIP (e-mail: leslie.king@cityoflondon.gov.uk)

LUTON

Authority: Luton Culture (Luton Culture Services Trust for Luton Borough Council)
Libraries Service, Central Library, St George's Square, Luton, Beds LU1 2NG
☎(01582) 547418 (enquiries)
Fax (01582) 547461
e-mail: libraryinfo@lutonculture.com
url: www.lutonlibraries.co.uk
Director of Libraries Ms Narinder Bhourlay (01582 547422; e-mail: narinder.bhourlay@lutonculture.com)
Strategy and Development Manager Ms Fiona Marriott BA MCLIP (01582 547417; e-mail: fiona.marriott@lutonculture.com)

Central/largest library
Central Library, St George's Square, Luton, Beds LU1 2NG

☎(01582) 547418
Group Library Manager Mrs Clare Dimmock

Branch libraries

Bury Park Library, Bury Park Community Centre, 161 Dunstable Road, Luton, Beds LU1 1BW
☎(01582) 486569
Group Library Manager Mrs Clare Dimmock

Leagrave Library, Marsh Road, Luton, Beds LU3 2NL
☎(01582) 556650
Fax (01582) 556651
Group Library Manager Ms Sally Crosby

Lewsey Library, Landrace Road, Luton, Beds LU4 0SW
☎(01582) 696094
Group Library Manager Ms Sally Crosby

Marsh Farm Library and Luton Home Library Service, Lea Manor High School, Northwell Drive, Luton, Beds LU3 3TL
☎(01582) 574803/491428 (Home Library Service)
e-mail: homelibraryservice@lutonculture.com
Group Library Manager Ms Sally Crosby

Stopsley Library, Hitchin Road, Luton, Beds LU2 7UG
☎(01582) 706368
Group Library Manager Mrs Clare Dimmock

MANCHESTER

Authority: Manchester City Council
Manchester Libraries, Information and Archives, Community and Cultural Services: Growth and Neighbourhoods, PO Box 532, Town Hall, Albert Square, Manchester M60 2LA
☎0161 234 1902
Fax 0161 274 7056
e-mail: libraries@manchester.gov.uk
url: www.manchester.gov.uk/libraries
Strategic Lead – Head of Libraries, Information and Archives Neil MacInnes (e-mail: n.macinnes@manchester.gov.uk)
City Wide Services Managers Ms Jill Sharp BA DipLib MCLIP (e-mail: j.sharp@manchester.gov.uk), Ms Jane McKelvey (e-mail: j.mckelvey@manchester.gov.uk)
Archives+ Manager Kevin Bolton (e-mail: k.bolton@manchester.gov.uk)
Transformation Manager Paul Wright (e-mail: p.wright@manchester.gov.uk)

Central/largest library

Central Library, St Peter's Square, Manchester M2 5PD
☎0161 234 1983
Fax 0161 274 7053
e-mail: libraries@manchester.gov.uk
Central Library Customer Services Manager David Green (e-mail: d.green1@manchester.gov.uk)

Neighbourhood Libraries

Abraham Moss Library, Crescent Road, Crumpsall, Manchester M8 5UF
☎0161 227 3777

Avenue Library and Learning Centre, Victoria Avenue East, Blackley, Manchester M9 6HW
☎0161 219 2393

Beswick Library, 60 Grey Mare Lane, Manchester M11 3DS
☎0161 245 7241

Books to Go, Hammerstone Depot, Manchester M18 8EQ
☎0161 227 3800

Brooklands Library, Moor Road, Manchester M23 9BP
☎0161 245 7087

Chorlton Library, Manchester Road, Chorlton, Manchester M21 9PN
☎0161 227 3700

Didsbury Library, 692 Wilmslow Road, Didsbury, Manchester M20 2DN
☎0161 277 3755

Fallowfield Library, Platt Lane, Manchester M14 7FB
☎0161 227 3744

Forum Library, Forum Square, Manchester M22 5RX
☎0161 277 3700

Gorton Library, Garratt Way, Manchester M18 8HE
☎0161 227 3737

Hulme Library, Stretford Road, Manchester M15 5FQ
☎0161 227 3739

Levenshulme Library, Cromwell Grove, Manchester M19 3QE
☎0161 227 3725

Longsight Library, 519 Stockport Road, Manchester M12 4NE
☎0161 277 3706

Moss Side Powerhouse Library, 140 Raby Street, Manchester M14 1SL
☎0161 227 3758

Newton Heath Library, Old Church Street, Manchester M40 2JB
☎0161 234 4474

North City Library, Rochdale Road, Harpurhay, Manchester M9 4AF
☎0161 219 6442

Withington Library, 410 Wilmslow Road, Manchester M20 3BN
☎0161 227 3720

Community libraries

Barlow Moor Community Library, 23 Merseybank Avenue, Chorlton, Manchester M21 7NT
☎0161 227 3742

Burnage Library, Activity and Information Hub, Burnage Lane, Manchester M19 1EW
☎0161 227 3774

Miles Platting Community Library, Victoria Mill Community Centre, Lower Vickers Street, Manchester M40 7LJ
☎0161 227 3787

New Moston Community Library, Nuthurst Road, Manchester M40 3PJ
☎0161 219 6461

Northenden Community Library, Parkway Green House, 460 Palatine Road, Manchester M22 4DJ
☎0161 227 3747

MEDWAY

Authority: Medway Council
Chatham Library, Gun Wharf, Dock Road, Chatham, Kent ME4 4TX
☎(01634) 337799
Fax (01634) 337800
e-mail: chatham.library@medway.gov.uk/libraries
url: www.medway.gov.uk/libraries
Library Services Manager Duncan Mead BA MCLIP (01634 337282; e-mail: duncan.mead@medway.gov.uk)

Central/largest libraries

Chatham Library, Gun Wharf, Dock Road, Chatham, Kent ME4 4TX
☎(01634) 337799
Fax (01634) 337800
e-mail: chatham.library@medway.gov.uk

Gillingham Library, High Street, Gillingham, Kent ME7 1BG
☎(01634) 337799

Strood Library, 32 Bryant Road, Strood, Rochester, Kent ME2 3EP
☎(01634) 337799
Fax (01634) 297919

MERTON

Authority: London Borough of Merton
Libraries and Heritage Services, Merton Civic Centre, London Road, Morden, Surrey SM4 5DX
☎020 8545 3783
Fax 020 8545 3237
url: www.merton.gov.uk
Head of Libraries and Heritage Services Anthony Hopkins (020 8545 3770; e-mail: anthony.hopkins@merton.gov.uk)
Libraries Operations Manager Ms Lisa Mustoe (020 8545 3783; e-mail: lisa.mustoe@merton.gov.uk)
Services Manager Ms Annette Acquah (020 8545 4089; e-mail: annette.acquah@merton.gov.uk)

Main libraries

Mitcham Library, London Road, Mitcham, Surrey CR4 7YR

☎020 8274 5745
Fax 020 8646 6360
e-mail: mitcham.library@merton.gov.uk
Library Manager Ms Hannah Basing

Morden Library, Civic Centre, London Road, Morden, Surrey SM4 5DX
☎020 8545 4040
Fax 020 8545 4037
e-mail: morden.library@merton.gov.uk
Library Manager Ms Sarah Azhar

Wimbledon Library, Wimbledon Hill Road, London SW19 7NB
☎020 8274 5757
Fax 020 8944 6804
e-mail: wimbledon.library@merton.gov.uk
Library Manager Ms Chandra Kargupta

Branch libraries
Donald Hope Library (Colliers Wood), Cavendish House, High Street, London SW19 2HR
☎020 8274 5757
Fax 020 8543 9767
e-mail: donaldhope.library@merton.gov.uk
Library Manager Vacant

Pollards Hill Library, South Lodge Avenue, Mitcham, Surrey CR4 1LT
☎020 8274 5745
Fax 020 8765 0925
e-mail: pollardshill.library@merton.gov.uk
Library Manager Ms Chrysella Holder

Raynes Park Library, Approach Road, London SW20 8BA
☎020 8274 5718
Fax 020 8542 1893
e-mail: raynespark.library@merton.gov.uk
Library Manager Ms Hannah Basing

West Barnes Library, Station Road, New Malden, Surrey KT3 6JF
☎020 8274 5789
Fax 020 8336 0554
e-mail: westbarnes.library@merton.gov.uk
Library Manager Ms Karren McCarthy

MIDDLESBROUGH
Authority: Middlesbrough Borough Council
Libraries and Information, Central Library, Victoria Square, Middlesbrough TS1 2AY
☎(01642) 729416 (administration)
Fax (01642) 729953
url: www.middlesbrough.gov.uk
Library Services Manager Mrs Jen Brittain BA(Hons) (01642 729418; e-mail:
jen_brittain@middlesbrough.gov.uk)

Central/largest library
Central Library, Victoria Square, Middlesbrough TS1 2AY
☎(01642) 729002 (enquiries), (01642) 729416 (administration)
Fax (01642) 729953
Resources Manager Ms Julie Tweedy BA MCLIP (e-mail:
julie_tweedy@middlesbrough.gov.uk)
Development and Operations Manager Mrs Diane Fleet BA(Hons) (01642 729417;
e-mail: diane_fleet@middlesbrough.gov.uk)

MILTON KEYNES

Authority: Milton Keynes Council
Central Library, 555 Silbury Boulevard, Milton Keynes MK9 3HL
☎(01908) 254050
Fax (01908) 254089
e-mail: central.library@milton-keynes.gov.uk
url: www.milton-keynes.gov.uk/libraries
Library Manager Ms Helen Bowlt BA(Hons) MCLIP (01908 254078; e-mail:
helen.bowlt@milton-keynes.gov.uk)
Library Staff and Volunteer Officer Garry Mitchell BA(Hons) MCLIP (01908 254068;
e-mail: garry.mitchell@milton-keynes.gov.uk)
Library Stock Development Officer Ms Veronica Banting BA(Hons) MCLIP
(01908 254087; e-mail: veronica.banting@milton-keynes.gov.uk)
Library Development Officer Eric Wright BA(Hons) MCLIP (01908 254204; e-mail:
eric.wright@milton-keynes.gov.uk)

NEWCASTLE UPON TYNE

Authority: Newcastle upon Tyne City Council
**Newcastle Libraries and Information Services, The Charles Avison Building, 33
Newbridge Street West, PO Box 88, Newcastle upon Tyne NE1 8AX**
☎0191 277 4100 (enquiries), 0191 277 4140 (administration)
Fax 0191 277 4137
e-mail: info@newcastle.gov.uk
url: www.newcastle.gov.uk/libraries
Assistant Director, Customers, Culture and Skills Tony Durcan BLib MCLIP (e-mail:
tony.durcan@newcastle.gov.uk)
Service Manager, Libraries and Leisure David Fay BA MCLIP (e-mail:
david.fay@newcastle.gov.uk)
Area Manager, Libraries Ms Angela Forster (0191 277 4148; e-mail:
angela.forster@newcastle.gov.uk)
Facilities and Buildings Manager Mark Thurston (0191 277 4167; e-mail:
mark.thurston@newcastle.gov.uk)

NEWHAM

Authority: London Borough of Newham
Community Neighbourhoods, Newham Dockside, 1000 Dockside Road, London E16 2QU
☎020 8430 2000 (Council switchboard)
url: www.newham.gov.uk

Head of Community Neighbourhoods Damian Atkinson (020 3373 4371)
Community Neighbourhood Business Manager Paul Drumm BA(Hons) MA MSc
(ext 30815)
Community Neighbourhood Managers Harry Holmes (ext 34694), Ms Nicola Mackie
(ext 39733), Ian Martin (ext 31495), Ms Shabana Qadir (ext 31267), Mohamed
Hammoudan (ext 34695), Syed Haque (ext 31540), Ms Laura Beswick (ext 36045)

Largest library
East Ham Library, 328 Barking Road, London E6 2RT
☎020 3373 0827
Community Neighbourhood Manager Ms Nicola Mackie

Branch libraries
Beckton Globe Library, 1 Kingsford Way, London E6 5JQ
☎020 3373 0853
Community Neighbourhood Manager Harry Holmes

Canning Town Library, Barking Road, Canning Town, London E16 4HQ
☎020 3373 0854
Community Neighbourhood Manager Paul Drumm BA(Hons) MA MSc

Custom House Library, Prince Regent Lane, London E16 3JJ
☎020 3373 0855
Community Neighbourhood Manager Paul Drumm BA(Hons) MA MSc

Green Street Library, 337–341 Green Street, Upton Park, London E13 9AR
☎020 3373 0857
Community Neighbourhood Manager Mohamed Hammoudan

Manor Park Library, 985–693 Romford Road, Manor Park, London E12 5AD
☎020 3373 0858
Community Neighbourhood Manager Ms Shabana Qadir

North Woolwich Library, 5 Pier Parade, North Woolwich, London E16 2LJ
☎020 3373 0843
Community Neighbourhood Manager Harry Holmes

Plaistow Library, North Street, Plaistow, London E13 9HL
☎020 3373 0859
Community Neighbourhood Manager Syed Haque

Stratford Library, 3 The Grove, Stratford, London E15 1EL
☎020 3373 0826 (Main), 020 3373 6881 (Archives & Local Studies)
Community Neighbourhood Manager Ms Laura Beswick

The Gate Library, 4–20 Woodgrange Road, Forest Gate, London E7 0QH
☎020 3373 0856
Community Neighbourhood Manager Ian Martin (020 3373 0856)

NORFOLK
Authority: Norfolk County Council
Library and Information Service, County Hall, Martineau Lane, Norwich NR1 2UA
☎(01603) 222049

Fax (01603) 222422
e-mail: libraries@norfolk.gov.uk
url: www.library.norfolk.gov.uk
Head of Libraries and Assistant Director Community Services (Cultural Services)
Mrs Jennifer Holland BA(Hons) MCLIP (01603 222272; e-mail:
jennifer.holland@norfolk.gov.uk)
Assistant Heads of Service – Localities Ms Sarah Hassan BA(Hons) MA (01362 656976;
e-mail: sarah.hassan@norfolk.gov.uk), Ms Jan Holden BA(Hons) DipLib MA (01603 774701;
e-mail: janet.holden@norfolk.gov.uk)
Assistant Head of Service – Development Mrs Lorna Payne MA MCLIP (01603
222273; e-mail: lorna.payne@norfolk.gov.uk)

Central/largest libraries
Dereham Library, 59 High Street, Dereham, Norfolk NR19 1DZ
☎(01362) 693184
Fax (01362) 691891
e-mail: dereham.lib@norfolk.gov.uk
Assistant Head of Service Ms Sarah Hassan BA(Hons) MA (e-mail:
sarah.hassan@norfolk.gov.uk)

Gorleston Library, Lowestoft Road, Gorleston, Norfolk NR31 6SG
☎(01493) 662156
Fax (01493) 446010
e-mail: gorleston.lib@norfolk.gov.uk
Assistant Head of Service Ms Jan Holden BA(Hons) DipLib MA (e-mail:
janet.holden@norfolk.gov.uk)

Great Yarmouth Library, Tolhouse Street, Great Yarmouth, Norfolk NR30 2SH
☎(01493) 844551
Fax (01493) 857628
e-mail: yarmouth.lib@norfolk.gov.uk
Assistant Head of Service Ms Jan Holden BA(Hons) DipLib MA (e-mail:
janet.holden@norfolk.gov.uk)

King's Lynn Library, London Road, King's Lynn, Norfolk PE30 5EZ
☎(01553) 772568
Fax (01553) 769832
e-mail: kings.lynn.lib@norfolk.gov.uk
Assistant Head of Service Ms Sarah Hassan BA(Hons) MA (e-mail:
sarah.hassan@norfolk.gov.uk)

Norfolk and Norwich Millennium Library, The Forum, Millennium Plain, Norwich NR2 1AW
☎(01603) 774774
Fax (01603) 774705
e-mail: millennium.lib@norfolk.gov.uk
Assistant Head of Service Ms Jan Holden BA(Hons) DipLib MA (e-mail:
janet.holden@norfolk.gov.uk)

Thetford Library, Raymond Street, Thetford, Norfolk IP24 2EA
☎(01842) 752048
Fax (01842) 750125
e-mail: thetford.lib@norfolk.gov.uk

Assistant Head of Service Ms Sarah Hassan BA(Hons) MA (e-mail: sarah.hassan@norfolk.gov.uk)

Area library HQs
North, South and West Area HQ, Dereham Library, 59 High Street, Dereham, Norfolk NR19 1DZ
☎(01362) 693184
Fax (01362) 691891
e-mail: dereham.lib@norfolk.gov.uk
Assistant Head of Service Ms Sarah Hassan BA(Hons) MA (e-mail: sarah.hassan@norfolk.gov.uk)

Norwich and East Area HQ, Norfolk and Norwich Millennium Library, The Forum, Millennium Plain, Norwich NR2 1AW
☎(01603) 774774
Fax (01603) 774705
e-mail: millennium.lib@norfolk.gov.uk
Assistant Head of Service Ms Jan Holden BA(Hons) DipLib MA (e-mail: janet.holden@norfolk.gov.uk)

NORTH EAST LINCOLNSHIRE

Authority: North East Lincolnshire Council
Central Library, Town Hall Square, Grimsby, North East Lincs DN31 1HG
☎(01472) 323600 (enquiries), (01472) 323617 (administration)
Fax (01472) 323618
e-mail: librariesandmuseums@nelincs.gov.uk
url: www.nelincs.gov.uk
Head of Cultural Services Steve Hipkins BA(Hons) MA DipLib MCLIP (01472 323611; e-mail: steve.hipkins@nelincs.gov.uk)
Principal Librarian Ms Anna Worrall (01472 323612; e-mail: anna.worrall@nelincs.gov.uk)

Branch libraries
Cleethorpes Library, Alexandra Road, Cleethorpes, North East Lincs DN35 8LG
☎(01472) 323648/323650
Fax (01472) 323652

Grant Thorold Library, Durban Road, Grimsby, North East Lincs DN32 8BX
☎(01472) 323631
Fax (01472) 323816

Humberston Library, Church Lane, Humberston, North East Lincs DN36 4HT
☎(01472) 323682

Immingham Library, Civic Centre, Pelham Road, Immingham, North East Lincs DN40 1QF
☎(01469) 516050
Fax (01469) 516051

Laceby Library, The Stanford Centre, Cooper Lane, Laceby, North East Lincs DN37 7AX
☎(01472) 323684

Nunsthorpe Library, Grimsby Institute of Further and Higher Education, Nunsthorpe, Community Campus, Sutcliffe Avenue, Grimsby, North East Lincs DN33 1AW
☎(01472) 323636

Scartho Learning Centre and Library, St Giles Avenue, Grimsby, North East Lincs DN33 2HB
☎(01472) 323638

Waltham Library, High Street, Waltham, North East Lincs DN37 0LL
☎(01472) 323656

Willows Library, Binbrook Way, Grimsby, North East Lincs DN37 9AS
☎(01472) 323679

NORTH LINCOLNSHIRE

Authority: North Lincolnshire Council
North Lincolnshire Central Library, Carlton Street, Scunthorpe, North Lincs DN15 6TX
☎(01724) 860161 (tel/fax)
e-mail: library.enquiries@northlincs.gov.uk
url: www.northlincs.gov.uk/library
Library and Information Services Manager Colin Brabazon BA DipLib MCLIP (e-mail: colin.brabazon@northlincs.gov.uk)

NORTH SOMERSET

Authority: North Somerset Council
North Somerset Libraries, Floor 1, Post point 18, Town Hall, Walliscote Grove Road, Weston-super-Mare, Somerset BS23 1UJ
☎(01934) 426658
e-mail: weston.library@n-somerset.gov.uk
url: www.librarieswest.org.uk (online catalogue); www.n-somerset.gov.uk/leisure/libraries
Library and Information Service Manager Andy Brisley BLib MCLIP (e-mail: andy.brisley@n-somerset.gov.uk)

Largest library

Weston-super-Mare Library, Ground Floor, Town Hall, Walliscote Grove Road, Weston-super-Mare, Somerset BS23 1UJ
☎(01934) 426010
e-mail: weston.library@n-somerset.gov.uk
Deputy Libraries Manager Ms Mary Lamb MCLIP (e-mail: mary.lamb@n-somerset.gov.uk)

NORTH TYNESIDE

Authority: North Tyneside Council
North Shields Library, North Shields Customer First Centre, Northumberland Square, North Shields, Tyne and Wear NE30 1QU
☎0191 643 5270
Fax 0191 200 6118
e-mail: central.library@northtyneside.gov.uk
url: www.northtyneside.gov.uk/libraries

Group Manager, Libraries, Community Centres and Tourist Information Centres (East) Ms Andrea Stephenson BA MCLIP (e-mail: andrea.stephenson@northtyneside.gov.uk)
Group Manager, Libraries, Community Centres and Tourist Information Centres (West) Ms Yvonne Gorgon BA(Hons) PGCE (e-mail: yvonne.gorgon@northtyneside.gov.uk)

Main libraries

Killingworth Library, White Swan Customer First Centre, Citadel East, Killingworth, Tyne and Wear NE12 6SS
☎(0191) 643 2040
Fax (0191) 643 8536
e-mail: killingworth.library@northtyneside.gov.uk

Wallsend Library, Wallsend Customer First Centre, 16 The Forum, Wallsend, Tyne and Wear NE28 8JR
☎0191 643 2075
Fax 0191 643 5839
e-mail: wallsend.library@northtyneside.gov.uk

Whitley Bay Library, Whitley Bay Customer First Centre, York Road, Whitley Bay, Tyne and Wear NE26 1AB
☎0191 643 5390
Fax 0191 200 8536
e-mail: whitleybay.library@northtyneside.gov.uk

NORTH YORKSHIRE

Authority: North Yorkshire County Council
Adult and Community Services (Library and Community Services), Library HQ, 21 Grammar School Lane, Northallerton, North Yorks DL6 1DF
☎(01609) 533800 (enquiries and administration)
Fax (01609) 780793
e-mail: libraries@northyorks.gov.uk
url: www.northyorks.gov.uk/libraries
General Manager Library and Information Service Ms Chrys Mellor BSc(Econ) DipLib MCLIP (e-mail: chrys.mellor@northyorks.gov.uk)
Management Co-ordinator (East) Lee Taylor BA(Hons) MA MCLIP (e-mail: lee.taylor@northyorks.gov.uk)
Management Co-ordinator (West) Mrs Judith Walsh (e-mail: judith.walsh@northyorks.gov.uk)

Larger libraries

Harrogate Library and Information Centre, Victoria Avenue, Harrogate, North Yorks HG1 1EG
☎0845 034 9520 (Lending), 0845 034 9521 (Reference)
Fax (01423) 523158
e-mail: harrogate.library@northyorks.gov.uk
url: www.northyorks.gov.uk/libraries/branches/harrogate.shtm

Scarborough Library and Information Centre, Vernon Road, Scarborough, North Yorks YO11 2NN
☎0845 034 9516 (Lending), 0845 034 9517 (Reference)
Fax (01723) 353893
e-mail: scarborough.library@northyorks.gov.uk
url: www.northyorks.gov.uk/libraries/branches/scarborough.shtm

(Note: These do not represent the full list of Library and Information Centres. Please see website for more details: www.northyorks.gov.uk/libraries)

NORTHAMPTONSHIRE

Authority: Northamptonshire County Council
Libraries HQ, Customer and Cultural Services, PO Box 216, John Dryden House, 8–10 The Lakes, Northampton NN4 7DD
☎0300 126 1000
Fax (01604) 237937
e-mail: nlis@northamptonshire.gov.uk
url: www.northamptonshire.gov.uk
Customer and Library Service Manager Ms Grace Kempster OBE BA(Hons) MLib MCLIP FRSA (e-mail: gkempster@northamptonshire.gov.uk)

Area libraries
Central Library, Abington Street, Northampton NN1 2BA
☎0300 126 1000
Fax (01604) 462055
Principal Librarian Ms Barbara Leigh (e-mail: bleigh@northamptonshire.gov.uk)

Daventry Library, North Street, Daventry, Northants NN11 4GH
☎0300 126 1000
Fax (01327) 300501
Principal Librarian Ms Robyn Davison (e-mail: rdavison@northamptonshire.gov.uk)

Kettering Library, Sheep Street, Kettering, Northants NN16 0AY
☎0300 126 1000
Fax (01536) 411349
Principal Librarian Mrs Anne Lovely BA(Hons) MCLIP (e-mail: alovely@northamptonshire.gov.uk)

NORTHUMBERLAND

Authority: Northumberland County Council
County Hall, Morpeth, Northumberland NE61 2EF
☎0845 600 6400
e-mail: mylibrary@northumberland.gov.uk
url: www.mylibrary.gov.uk

Central/largest library
Morpeth Library, Gas House Lane, Morpeth, Northumberland NE61 1TA
☎(01670) 620390
Library Operations Manager Mrs Ann Blakeley BA MCLIP DMS (e-mail: ann.blakeley@northumberland.gov.uk)

Larger libraries

Alnwick Library, Green Batt, Alnwick, Northumberland NE66 1TU
☎(01670) 622154

Ashington Library, Kenilworth Road, Ashington, Northumberland NE63 8AA
☎(01670) 813245

Bedlington Library, Glebe Road, Bedlington, Northumberland NE22 6JX
☎(01670) 622201

Berwick Library, Walkergate, Berwick-upon-Tweed, Northumberland TD15 1DB
☎(01289) 334051

Blyth Library, Bridge Street, Blyth, Northumberland NE24 2DJ
☎(01670) 361352

Cramlington Library, Forum Way, Cramlington, Northumberland NE23 6QD
☎(01670) 620232

Hexham Library, Queen's Hall, Beaumont Street, Hexham, Northumberland NE46 3LS
☎(01670) 624525

Ponteland Library, Thornhill Road, Ponteland, Newcastle upon Tyne NE20 9PZ
☎(01661) 823594

Prudhoe Library, Front Street, Prudhoe, Northumberland NE42 5AA
☎(01661) 832540

NOTTINGHAM

Authority: City of Nottingham Council
Department of Sport, Culture and Parks, Libraries and Information Service, Loxley House, Station Street, Nottingham NG2 3NG
☎0115 915 2828
Fax 0115 915 8680
e-mail: enquiryline@nottinghamcity.gov.uk
url: www.mynottingham.gov.uk/libraries
Head of Culture and Libraries Nigel Hawkins (0115 876 4969; e-mail: nigel.hawkins@nottinghamcity.gov.uk)

Central/largest library

Nottingham Central Library, Angel Row, Nottingham NG1 6HP
☎0115 915 2828
Fax 0115 915 2850
e-mail: enquiryline@nottinghamcity.gov.uk
url: www.mynottingham.gov.uk/libraries

NOTTINGHAMSHIRE

Authority: Nottinghamshire County Council
County Library, Glaisdale Parkway, Bilborough, Nottingham NG8 4GP
☎0115 982 9036
Fax 0115 928 6400
url: www.nottinghamshire.gov.uk/libraries

Group Manager – Libraries, Archives, Arts, Information and Learning Peter Gaw BA MCLIP (0115 977 4201; e-mail: peter.gaw@nottscc.gov.uk)
Team Managers, Libraries Ms Carol Newman BA MCLIP (0115 982 9040; e-mail: carol.newman@nottscc.gov.uk), Mrs Linda Turner BA MCLIP (0115 980 9042; e-mail: linda.turner@nottscc.gov.uk), Ms Kirsty Blyth BA MCLIP (e-mail: kirsty.blyth@nottscc.gov.uk) (job-share)
Team Manager, Library Network Services Nick London BA MCLIP (0115 982 9029; e-mail: nick.london@nottscc.gov.uk)

Central/largest library

Mansfield Central Library, Four Seasons Centre, Westgate, Mansfield, Notts NG18 1NH
☎(01623) 651337
Fax (01623) 664940
e-mail: mansfield.library@nottscc.gov.uk

Other services

Library Support Services, Units 4-6, Glaisdale Parkway, Bilborough, Nottingham NG8 4GP
☎0115 985 4242
Fax 0115 928 6400

Main libraries

Arnold County Library, Front Street, Arnold, Nottingham NG5 7EE
☎0115 920 2247
Fax 0115 967 3378
e-mail: arnold.library@nottscc.gov.uk

Beeston County Library, Foster Avenue, Beeston, Nottingham NG9 1AE
☎0115 925 5168
Fax 0115 922 0841
e-mail: beeston.library@nottscc.gov.uk

Newark County Library, Beaumond Gardens, Baldertongate, Newark-on-Trent, Notts NG24 1UW
☎(01636) 703966/676367
Fax (01636) 610045
e-mail: newark.library@nottscc.gov.uk

Retford County Library, Churchgate, Retford, Notts DN22 6PE
☎(01777) 708724
Fax (01777) 710020
e-mail: retford.library@nottscc.gov.uk

Sutton in Ashfield Library, Idlewells Precinct, Sutton in Ashfield, Notts NG17 1BP
☎(01623) 556296
Fax (01623) 551962
e-mail: sutton.library@nottscc.gov.uk

West Bridgford Library, Bridgford Road, West Bridgford, Nottingham NG8 4GP
☎0115 981 6506
Fax 0115 981 2951
e-mail: westbridgford.library@nottscc.gov.uk

Worksop Library, Memorial Avenue, Worksop, Notts S80 2BP
☎(01909) 535353

Fax (01909) 535342
e-mail: worksop.library@nottscc.gov.uk

OLDHAM

Authority: Oldham Metropolitan Borough Council
Oldham Library, Cultural Quarter, Greaves Street, Oldham, Lancashire OL1 1AL
☎0161 770 8000 (general enquiries)
e-mail: oldham.library@oldham.gov.uk
url: www.oldham.gov.uk
Head of Heritage, Libraries and Arts Ms Sheena Macfarlane (0161 770 4664; fax: 0161
770 4855; e-mail: sheena.macfarlane@oldham.gov.uk)

OXFORDSHIRE

Authority: Oxfordshire County Council
Oxford Central Library, Westgate, Oxford OX1 1DJ
☎(01865) 815509
e-mail: oxfordcentral.library@oxfordshire.gov.uk
url: www.oxfordshire.gov.uk/libraries
Library Service Manager Ms Jillian Southwell BA(Hons) DipLib MCLIP (01865 810203;
e-mail: jillian.southwell@oxfordshire.gov.uk)
Area Manager Mrs Shirley Toase BA MCLIP (e-mail: shirley.toase@oxfordshire.gov.uk)

Additional services

Library Support Services, Cultural Services, Holton, Oxford OX33 1QQ
☎(01865) 810200
Stock Support Services Librarian David Reed BA(Hons) MCLIP (01865 810235; e-mail:
david.reed@oxfordshire.gov.uk)

PETERBOROUGH

Authority: Peterborough Cultural and Leisure Trust (trading as Vivacity)
Central Library, Broadway, Peterborough PE1 1RX
☎(01733) 864280
Fax (01733) 319140
e-mail: libraries@vivacity-peterborough.com
url: www.vivacity-peterborough.com
Head of Museums, Libraries and Archives Ms Heather Walton BLS (e-mail:
heather.walton@vivacity-peterborough.com)

District libraries

Bretton Library, Bretton Centre, Bretton, Peterborough PE3 8DS
☎(01733) 864291
e-mail: brettonlibrary@vivacity-peterborough.com

Orton Library, Orton Centre, Orton, Peterborough PE2 0RQ
☎(01733) 864296
e-mail: ortonlibrary@vivacity-peterborough.com

Werrington Library, Staniland Way, Werrington, Peterborough PE4 6JT

☎(01733) 864282
e-mail: werringtonlibrary@vivacity-peterborough.com

Community libraries
Dogsthorpe Library, Central Avenue, Dogsthorpe, Peterborough PE1 4LH
☎(01733) 864300
e-mail: dogsthorpelibrary@vivacity-peterborough.com

Eye Library, Crowland Road, Eye, Peterborough PE6 7TN
☎(01733) 864142
e-mail: eyelibrary@vivacity-peterborough.com

Hampton Library, Clayburn Road, Hampton, Peterborough PE7 8HG
☎(01733) 864538
e-mail: hamptonlibrary@vivacity-peterborough.com

Stanground Library, Southfields Avenue, Stanground, Peterborough PE2 8RZ
☎(01733) 864302
e-mail: stangroundlibrary@vivacity-peterborough.com

Thorney Library, Church Street, Thorney, Peterborough PE6 0QB
☎(01733) 864542
e-mail: thorneylibrary@vivacity-peterborough.com

Woodston Library, Orchard Street, Woodston, Peterborough PE2 9AL
☎(01733) 864304
e-mail: woodstonlibrary@vivacity-peterborough.com

PLYMOUTH

Authority: Plymouth City Council
Plymouth Libraries, Central Library, Drake Circus, Plymouth PL4 8AL
☎(01752) 305900
e-mail: library@plymouth.gov.uk
url: www.plymouth.gov.uk/libraries
Library Service Manager Chris Goddard BMus(Hons) DipLib MCLIP (01752 305916;
e-mail: chris.goddard@plymouth.gov.uk)
Service Manager (Delivery) Ms Sandra Pentney BSc(Econ) MCLIP (01752 305939;
e-mail: sandra.pentney@plymouth.gov.uk)
Service Manager (Support and Development) Ms Sharon Shaw MCLIP (01752
305924; e-mail: sharon.shaw@plymouth.gov.uk)

POOLE

Authority: Borough of Poole
**Culture and Community Learning, 30–32 Northmead Drive, Creekmoor, Poole, Dorset
BH17 7RP**
☎(01202) 262432
url: www.poole.gov.uk
Head of Culture and Community Learning Kevin McErlane BA(Hons) DipLib MBA
(e-mail: k.mcerlane@poole.gov.uk)
Library Services Manager Ms Susan Wills (e-mail: sue.wills@poole.gov.uk)

Central/largest library
Central Library, Dolphin Centre, Poole, Dorset BH15 1QE
☎(01202) 262424
e-mail: centrallibrary@poole.gov.uk

PORTSMOUTH

Authority: Portsmouth City Council
Library Service, Central Library, Guildhall Square, Portsmouth PO1 2DX
☎023 9268 8058
e-mail: library.admin@portsmouthcc.gov.uk
url: www.portsmouth.gov.uk
Library and Archive Services Manager Mrs Lindy Elliott BA MCLIP (e-mail:
lindy.elliott@portsmouthcc.gov.uk)

School Library Service Centre, Cheltenham Road, Paulsgrove, Portsmouth PO6 3PL
☎023 9232 6612
e-mail: school.library@portsmouthcc.gov.uk
url: www.portsmouth.gov.uk
School Library Service Manager Peter Bone BA MCLIP (e-mail:
peter.bone@portsmouthcc.gov.uk)

Branch libraries
Alderman Lacey Library, Tangier Road, Copnor, Portsmouth PO3 6HU
☎023 9282 3991 (tel/fax)
e-mail: alderman.library@portsmouthcc.gov.uk

Beddow Library, Milton Road, Milton, Portsmouth PO4 8PR
☎023 9273 1848 (tel/fax)
e-mail: beddow.library@portsmouthcc.gov.uk

Carnegie Library, Fratton Road, Fratton, Portsmouth PO1 5EZ
☎023 9282 2581
Fax 023 9273 9244
e-mail: carnegie.library@portsmouthcc.gov.uk

Cosham Library, Spur Road, Cosham, Portsmouth PO6 3ED
☎023 9237 6023
Fax 023 9237 1877
e-mail: cosham.library@portsmouthcc.gov.uk

North End Library, Gladys Avenue, North End, Portsmouth PO2 9AX
☎023 9266 2651
Fax 023 9266 8151
e-mail: northend.library@portsmouthcc.gov.uk

Paulsgrove Library, Marsden Road, Paulsgrove, Portsmouth PO6 4JB
☎023 9237 7818 (tel/fax)
e-mail: paulsgrove.library@portsmouth.gov.uk

Portsea Library, St James Street, Portsea, Portsmouth PO1 3AP
☎023 9229 7072
e-mail: johnpounds.library@portsmouthcc.gov.uk

Southsea Library, 19–21 Palmerston Road, Southsea, Portsmouth PO5 3QQ
☎023 9268 8999
e-mail: southsea.library@portsmouthcc.gov.uk

READING

Authority: Reading Borough Council
Reading Central Library, Abbey Square, Reading RG1 3BQ
☎0118 901 5905
Fax 0118 901 5954
e-mail: info@readinglibraries.org.uk
url: www.readinglibraries.org.uk
Libraries and Resources Manager Ms Alison England BA(Hons) DipLib MCLIP
(0118 901 5970)
Branch Manager Mrs Caroline Lakeman
Support Staff Manager Mrs Karen Eccles

Branch libraries

Battle Library, 420 Oxford Road, Reading RG3 1EE
☎0118 901 5100
Fax 0118 901 5101
Branch Manager Mrs Karen Eccles

Caversham Library, Church Street, Caversham, Reading RG4 8AU
☎0118 901 5103
Fax 0118 901 5104
Branch Manager Ms Virginia Hobbs

Mobile Services, c/o Tilehurst Library, School Road, Tilehurst, Reading RG1 5AS
☎0118 901 5118
Manager Ms Dawn Littlefield

Palmer Park Library, St Bartholomew's Road, Reading RG1 3QB
☎0118 901 5106
Fax 0118 901 5107
Branch Manager Miss Christine Gosling

Southcote Library, Southcote Lane, Reading RG3 3BA
☎0118 901 5109
Fax 0118 901 5110
Branch Manager Mrs Elizabeth Long

Tilehurst Library, School Road, Tilehurst, Reading RG3 5AS
☎0118 901 5112
Fax 0118 901 5113
Branch Manager Andrew Mitchell

Whitley Library, Northumberland Avenue, Reading RG2 7PX
☎0118 901 5115
Fax 0118 901 5116
Branch Manager Mrs Karen Eccles

REDBRIDGE

Authority: London Borough of Redbridge
Vision – Redbridge Culture & Leisure, Central Library, Clements Road, Ilford, Essex IG1 1EA

☎020 8708 2414
Fax 020 8708 2431
e-mail: central.library@visionrcl.org.uk
url: www.redbridge.gov.uk/libraries
Head of Culture and Libraries Gareth Morley (e-mail: gareth.morley@visionrcl.org.uk)
Library Operations Manager Ms Anne Annison (e-mail:
anne.annison@@visionrcl.org.uk)
Library and Culture Development Manager Ms Anita Luby (e-mail:
anita.luby@visionrcl.org.uk)
Development Librarians, Library Development Team Ms Rhonda Brooks BA(Hons)
MA PGDipInfStud PGCE(FE) CELTA (e-mail: rhonda.brooks@@visionrcl.org.uk), Ms Rose
Meredith BA DipInfMgmt (e-mail: rose.meredith@visionrcl.org.uk), Jonathan Woolf
BA(Hons) MA DipLaw (e-mail: jonathan.woolf@visionrcl.org.uk), Ms Mina Rehman (e-mail:
mina.rehman@visionrcl.org.uk), Mrs Susan Page BSc(Econ) (e-mail:
sue.page@visionrcl.org.uk), Ms Rosemary Kennedy BA(Hons) MCLIP (e-mail:
rosemary.kennedy@visionrcl.org.uk)

Central/largest library
Redbridge Central Library, Clements Road, Ilford, Essex IG1 1EA
☎020 8708 2414
e-mail: central.library@visionrcl.org.uk
Principal Librarian: Customer Services and Staff Development Mrs Rosamund
Willis-Fear BA(Hons) MCLIP (e-mail: ros.willis-fear@@visionrcl.org.uk)

Branch libraries
Aldersbrook Library, 2a Park Road, London E12 5HQ
☎020 8496 0006
e-mail: aldersbrook.library@visionrcl.org.uk

Clayhall Library, 1 Claybury Broadway, Clayhall, Ilford, Essex IG5 0LQ
☎020 8708 9340
e-mail: clayhall.library@visionrcl.org.uk

Fullwell Cross Library, 140 High Street, Barkingside, Ilford, Essex IG6 2EA
☎020 8708 9281
e-mail: fulwellcross.library@visionrcl.org.uk

Gants Hill Library, 490 Cranbrook Road, Gants Hill, Ilford, Essex IG2 6LA
☎020 8708 9274
e-mail: gantshill.library@visionrcl.org.uk

Goodmayes Library, 76 Goodmayes Lane, Goodmayes, Ilford, Essex IG3 9QB
☎020 8708 7750
e-mail: goodmayes.library@visionrcl.org.uk

Hainault Library, 100 Manford Way, Chigwell, Essex IG7 4DD
☎020 8708 9206
e-mail: hainault.library@visionrcl.org.uk

Keith Axon Centre, 160–170 Grove Road, Chadwell Heath, Essex RM6 4XB
☎020 8708 0790
e-mail: keithaxon.centre@visionrcl.org.uk

South Woodford Library, 116 High Road, London E18 2QS
☎020 8708 9067
e-mail: southwoodford.library@visionrcl.org.uk

Wanstead Library, Spratt Hall Road, London E11 2RQ
☎020 8708 7400
e-mail: wanstead.library@visionrcl.org.uk

Woodford Green Library, Snakes Lane, Woodford Green, Essex IG8 0DX
☎020 8708 9055
e-mail: woodfordgreen.library@visionrcl.org.uk

Schools library service
Schools Library Service, Central Library, Clements Road, Ilford, Essex IC1 1EA
☎020 8708 2424
Fax 020 8708 2571
Schools Library Service Manager Mrs Nina Simon (e-mail: nina.simon@visionrcl.org.uk)

REDCAR AND CLEVELAND
Authority: Redcar and Cleveland Borough Council
Area Management Services, Redcar and Cleveland House, Kirkleatham Street, Redcar, Redcar and Cleveland TS10 1RT
☎(01642) 444141
url: www.redcar-cleveland.gov.uk
Library Officer Ian Wilson (e-mail: ian.wilson@redcar-cleveland.gov.uk)

Central/largest library
Redcar Central Library, Redcar and Cleveland House, Kirkleatham Street, Redcar, Redcar and Cleveland TS10 1RT
☎(01642) 444141
e-mail: redcar_library@redcar-cleveland.gov.uk

RICHMOND UPON THAMES
Authority: London Borough of Richmond upon Thames
Library Headquarters, The Cottage, Little Green, Richmond, Surrey TW9 1QH
☎020 8734 3308
e-mail: information@richmond.gov.uk
url: www.richmond.gov.uk/libraries
Library Operations Manager Ms Amanda Stirrup BA(Hons) MCLIP (e-mail: amanda.stirrup@richmond.gov.uk)
Library Strategy and Performance Manager Steve Liddle BA(Hons) DipLib (e-mail: steven.liddle@richmond.gov.uk)

Central/largest library
Richmond Lending Library, Little Green, Richmond, Surrey TW9 1QL
☎020 8734 3330
e-mail: richmond.library@richmond.gov.uk

Branch libraries

Castelnau Library, 75 Castelnau, Barnes, Middlesex SW13 9RT
☎020 8734 3350
e-mail: castelnau.library@richmond.gov.uk

East Sheen Library, Sheen Lane, London SW14 8LP
☎020 8734 3337
e-mail: eastsheen.library@richmond.gov.uk

Ham Library, Ham Street, Ham, Middlesex TW10 7HR
☎020 8734 3354
e-mail: ham.library@richmond.gov.uk

Hampton Hill Library, 68 High Street, Hampton Hill, Middlesex TW12 1NY
☎020 8734 3320
e-mail: hamptonhill.library@richmond.gov.uk

Hampton Library, Rosehill, Hampton, Middlesex TW12 2AB
☎020 8734 3347
e-mail: hampton.library@richmond.gov.uk

Hampton Wick Library, Bennet Close, Hampton Wick, Middlesex KT1 4AT
☎020 8734 3358
e-mail: hamptonwick.library@richmond.gov.uk

Kew Library, 106 North Road, Kew, Surrey TW9 4HJ
☎020 8734 3352
e-mail: kew.library@richmond.gov.uk

Reference Library, Old Town Hall, Whitaker Avenue, Richmond, Surrey TW9 1TP
☎020 8734 3308
e-mail: information@richmond.gov.uk

Richmond Local Studies Library & Archive, Old Town Hall, Whittaker Avenue, Richmond, Surrey TW9 1TP
☎020 8734 3309
e-mail: localstudies@richmond.gov.uk

Teddington Library, Waldegrave Road, Teddington, Middlesex TW11 8NY
☎020 8734 3304
e-mail: teddington.library@richmond.gov.uk

Twickenham Library, Garfield Road, Twickenham, Middlesex TW1 3JT
☎020 8734 3340
e-mail: twickenham.library@richmond.gov.uk

Whitton Library, 141 Nelson Road, Whitton, Middlesex TW2 7BB
☎020 8734 3343
e-mail: whitton.library@richmond.gov.uk

ROCHDALE

Authority: Rochdale Metropolitan Borough Council
Rochdale Centre Library, Number One Riverside, Smith Street, Rochdale, Greater Manchester OL16 1XU

☎0300 303 8876
url: www.rochdale.gov.uk/libraries
Operations Manager: Customer Access Philip Cooke BA(Hons) MA (01706 924889;
e-mail: philip.cooke@rochdale.gov.uk)
Libraries Team Leader (Rochdale and Middleton) Mrs Alison Copple (01706 924930;
e-mail: alison.copple@rochdale.gov.uk)
Libraries Team Leader (Heywood and Pennines) Mrs Helen Bingham (01706 924946;
e-mail: helen.bingham@rochdale.gov.uk)
Stock and Reader Development Manager Ms Joanne Eaves BA(Hons) MA (01706
924941; e-mail: joanne.eaves@rochdale.gov.uk)

Main libraries
Heywood Library, Lance Corporal Stephen Shaw MC Way, Heywood, Greater Manchester
OL10 1LL
☎0300 303 8876

Middleton Library, Long Street, Middleton, Greater Manchester M24 6DU
☎0300 303 8876

ROTHERHAM

Authority: Rotherham Metropolitan Borough Council
Library at Riverside, Riverside House, Main Street, Rotherham, South Yorks S60 1AE
☎(01709) 823606 (enquiries), (01709) 823623 (management)
Fax (01709) 823650 (enquiries)
e-mail: central.library@rotherham.gov.uk
url: www.rotherham.gov.uk
Customer & Cultural Services Manager Ms Elenore Fisher BA(Hons) DipLib MCLIP
(e-mail: elenore.fisher@rotherham.gov.uk)
Manager, Customer and Library Services Vacant

RUTLAND

Authority: Rutland County Council
Rutland County Library, Catmose Street, Oakham, Rutland LE15 6HW
☎(01572) 722918 (enquiries)
Fax (01572) 724906 (enquiries)
e-mail: libraries@rutland.gov.uk
url: www.rutland.gov.uk/libraries
Senior Culture & Leisure Manager Robert Clayton BA MA MCLIP (e-mail:
rclayton@rutland.gov.uk)

Community libraries
Ketton Library, High Street, Ketton, Rutland PE9 3TE
☎(01780) 720580

Ryhall Library, Coppice Road, Ryhall, Rutland PE9 4HY
☎(01780) 751726

Uppingham Library, Queen Street, Uppingham, Rutland LE15 9QR
☎(01572) 823218

ST HELENS

Authority: St Helens Council
Urban Regeneration Department, Libraries Management Team, Chester Lane Library, Four Acre Lane, St Helens, Merseyside WA9 4DE
☎(01744) 677486
Fax (01744) 677114
url: www.sthelens.gov.uk/libraries
Head of Library Services Mrs Sue Williamson MA(Oxon) MCLIP (01744 677496; e-mail: susanwilliamson@sthelens.gov.uk)
Service Development Manager (responsible for Children and Youth) Mrs Kathryn Boothroyd BA(Hons) MCLIP (01744 677486; e-mail: kathrynboothroyd@sthelens.gov.uk)

Central/largest library

Central Library, The Gamble Building, Victoria Square, St Helens, Merseyside WA10 1DY
☎(01744) 676954
e-mail: centrallibrary@sthelens.gov.uk
Manager Bill Renshaw (01744 676995; e-mail: williamrenshaw@sthelens.gov.uk)

SALFORD

Authority: Salford Community Leisure
Salford Community Leisure, Civic Centre, Chorley Road, Swinton, Salford M27 5DA
☎0161 778 0770
e-mail: libraries@salford.gov.uk
url: www.salford.gov.uk/libraries
Libraries and Information Service Manager Ms Sarah Spence BA(Hons) MCLIP (0161 778 0840; e-mail: sarah.spence@salford.scll.co.uk)
Library Manager with Responsibility for Services to Children and Young People Ms Jennifer Abbott (0161 778 0842; e-mail: jennifer.abbot@scll.co.uk)

Main libraries

Eccles Library, Eccles Gateway, 28 Barton Lane, Eccles, Manchester M30 0TU
☎0161 909 6528
Fax 0161 211 7002
Neighbourhood Library Manager Mrs Hannah Quinlan BA(Hons) MA MCLIP (e-mail: hannah.quinlan@scll.co.uk)

Pendleton Library, Pendleton Gateway, 1 Broadwalk, Salford M6 5FX
☎0161 909 6538
Fax 0161 211 7301
Neighbourhood Library Manager Ms Teresa Butler (e-mail: teresa.butler@scll.co.uk)

Swinton Library, Chorley Road, Swinton, Salford M27 4AE
☎0161 921 2360
Fax 0161 727 7071
Neighbourhood Library Manager Ms Sarah Hall (e-mail: sarah.hall@scll.co.uk)

Walkden Library, Walkden Gateway, 2 Smith Street, Walkden, Manchester M28 3EZ
☎0161 909 6518
Fax 0161 211 7114

Neighbourhood Library Manager Chris Carson BA DMS MCLIP (e-mail:
chris.carson@scll.co.uk)

SANDWELL

Authority: Sandwell Metropolitan Borough Council
**Library Headquarters, Central Library, High Street, West Bromwich, West Midlands
B70 8DZ**
☎0121 569 4904
Fax 0121 525 9465
e-mail: information.service@sandwell.gov.uk
url: www.libraries.sandwell.gov.uk
Chief Librarian Barry Clark BLib MCLIP (e-mail: barry_clark@sandwell.gov.uk)

Additional services

Library Services North (including Stock Support, Admin Support), Central Library, High
Street, West Bromwich, West Midlands B70 8DZ
☎0121 569 4904
Fax 0121 525 9465
Principal Libraries Officer (Operations) Ms Dawn Winter BA(Hons) (0121 569 4922;
e-mail: dawn_winter@sandwell.gov.uk)

Library Services South (including Community History & Archives Service), Smethwick
Library, High Street, Smethwick, West Midlands B66 1AA
Principal Libraries Officer (Strategy and Resources) Ms Heather Vickerman
BA(Hons) MCLIP (0121 558 0497; e-mail: heather_vickerman@sandwell.gov.uk)

SEFTON

Authority: Sefton Council
Recreation & Culture, 2nd Floor, Merton House, Stanley Road, Bootle, Liverpool L20 3JA
☎0151 934 4741
Fax 0151 934 2359
e-mail: library.service@sefton.gov.uk
url: www.sefton.gov.uk
Principal Library Manager David Eddy (e-mail: david.eddy@sefton.gov.uk), Andrew
Farthing (e-mail: andrew.farthing@sefton.gov.uk), Ms Angela Worth (e-mail:
angela.worth@sefton.gov.uk)

Central/largest libraries

Atkinson Library, Lord Street, Southport PR8 1DJ
☎0151 934 2118
Fax 0151 934 2115

Crosby Library, Crosby Road North, Waterloo, Liverpool L22 0LQ
☎0151 257 6400
Fax 0151 330 5770

SHEFFIELD

Authority: Sheffield City Council
Sheffield Libraries, Archives and Information, Central Library, Surrey Street, Sheffield SI IXZ
☎0114 273 4712 (enquiries)
Fax 0114 273 5009
e-mail: libraries@sheffield.gov.uk
url: www.sheffield.gov.uk/libraries
Head of Libraries and Community Services Ms Dawn Shaw (0114 273 4486; e-mail: dawn.shaw@sheffield.gov.uk)
Service Manager Nick Partridge BSc(Hons) (0114 273 4751; e-mail: nick.partridge@sheffield.gov.uk)
Service Development Manager John Murphy BSc(Hons) MA (0114 273 6645; e-mail: john.murphy@sheffield.gov.uk)
Heritage and Archives Manager Pete Evans (0114 203 9397; e-mail: pete.evans@sheffield.gov.uk)
Central and Collections Manager Ms Alison Jobey BA(Hons) MCLIP (0114 273 6499; e-mail: alison.jobey@sheffield.gov.uk)
Community Services Manager Ms Lynne Richardson BA (0114 205 3149; e-mail: lynne.richardson@sheffield.gov.uk)

District libraries

Chapeltown Library, Nether Ley Avenue, Sheffield S35 IAE
☎0114 203 7000/1
e-mail: chapeltown.library@sheffield.gov.uk

Crystal Peaks Library, 1–3 Peak Square, Crystal Peaks Complex, Waterthorpe, Sheffield S20 7PH
☎0114 293 0612
e-mail: crystalpeaks.library@sheffield.gov.uk

Darnall Library, Britannia Road, Sheffield S9 5JG
☎0114 203 7429
Fax 0114 293 0332
e-mail: darnall.library@sheffield.gov.uk

Ecclesall Library, Weetwood Gardens, Ecclesall Road South, Sheffield S11 9PL
☎0114 203 7222
e-mail: ecclesall.library@sheffield.gov.uk

Firth Park Library, 443 Firth Park Road, Sheffield S5 6QQ
☎0114 203 7433
Fax 0114 293 0009
e-mail: firthpark.library@sheffield.gov.uk

Highfield Library & Children's Centre, London Road, Sheffield S2 4NF
☎0114 203 7204
Fax 0114 293 0018 (Childrens Lib)
e-mail: highfield.library@sheffield.gov.uk

Hillsborough Library, Middlewood Road, Sheffield S6 4HD
☎0114 203 9529

Fax 0114 203 9530 (Children's Lib)
e-mail: hillsborough.library@sheffield.gov.uk

Manor Library, Ridgeway Road, Sheffield S12 2SS
☎0114 203 7805
Fax 0114 293 0410
e-mail: manor.library@sheffield.gov.uk

Parson Cross Library @ The Learning Zone, 320 Wordsworth Avenue, Sheffield S5 8NL
☎0114 203 9533
Fax 0114 293 0305
e-mail: parsoncross.library@sheffield.gov.uk

Stocksbridge Library, Manchester Road, Stocksbridge, Sheffield S36 1DH
☎0114 273 4205
e-mail: stocksbridge.library@sheffield.gov.uk

Tinsley Library, Tinsley Shopping Centre, Bawtry Road, Sheffield S9 1UY
☎0114 203 7432
Fax 0114 293 0029
e-mail: tinsley.library@sheffield.gov.uk

Woodseats Library, Chesterfield Road, Sheffield S8 0SH
☎0114 293 0411
Fax 0114 293 0413
e-mail: woodseats.library@sheffield.gov.uk

Archives
52 Shoreham Street, Sheffield S1 4SP
☎0114 203 9395
Fax 0114 203 9398
e-mail: archives@sheffield.gov.uk

SHROPSHIRE

Authority: Shropshire County Council
Library and Information Services, Community Services Directorate, The Shirehall, Abbey Foregate, Shrewsbury, Shropshire SY2 6ND
☎(01743) 255024
Fax (01743) 255001
e-mail: library.support@shropshire.gov.uk
url: www.shropshire.gov.uk/libraries
Library Service Manager Michael Lewis (e-mail: michael.lewis@shropshire.gov.uk)

Central/largest libraries
Shrewsbury Library, Castle Gates, Shrewsbury, Shropshire SY1 2AS
☎(01743) 255308
Fax (01743) 255309
e-mail: shrewsbury.library@shropshire.gov.uk
Library Area Manager, Central Rawden Parslow (e-mail: rawden.parslow@shropshire.gov.uk)

Area libraries

North Area. Oswestry Library, Arthur Street, Oswestry, Shropshire SY11 1JN
☎(01691) 677388
Fax (01691) 677399
e-mail: oswestry.library@shropshire.gov.uk
Library Area Manager, North Mrs Teresa Eccleston (e-mail:
teresa.eccleston@shropshire.gov.uk)

South Area. Ludlow Library, 7/9 Parkway, Ludlow, Shropshire SY8 2PG
☎(01584) 813600
Fax (01584) 813601
e-mail: ludlow.library@shropshire.gov.uk
Library Area Manager, South Ms Elaine Moss MCLIP (e-mail:
elaine.moss@shropshire.gov.uk)

SLOUGH

Authority: Slough Borough Council
Slough Library, 85 High Street, Slough SL1 1EA
☎(01753) 535166
Fax (01753) 825050
e-mail: library@slough.gov.uk
Head of Library Services Ms Liz McMillan MCLIP (e-mail: liz.mcmillan@slough.gov.uk)

SOLIHULL

Authority: Solihull Metropolitan Borough Council
Central Library, Homer Road, Solihull, West Midlands B91 3RG
☎0121 704 6965 (public enquiries), 0121 704 6941 (administration)
Fax 0121 704 6991
e-mail: libraryarts@solihull.gov.uk
url: www.solihull.gov.uk
Head of Libraries Mrs Tracey Cox BLS(Hons) MCLIP (0121 704 6945; e-mail:
tcox@solihull.gov.uk)
Service Manager – Quality and Support Ms Hilary Halliday BA MCLIP (0121 704 8227;
e-mail: hhalliday@solihull.gov.uk)
Operations and Community Engagement Manager Ms Kate Bunting (e-mail:
kate.bunting@solihull.gov.uk), David Gill (e-mail: dagill@solihull.gov.uk)

Main area libraries

Central Library, Homer Road, Solihull, West Midlands B91 3RG
☎0121 704 6965
Fax 0121 704 6991
Head of Libraries Mrs Tracey Cox BLS(Hons) MCLIP (e-mail: tcox@solihull.gov.uk)

Chelmsley Wood Library, Stephenson Drive, Chelmsley Wood, Solihull, West Midlands
B37 5TA
☎0121 788 4380
Fax 0121 788 4381
Operations and Community Engagement Manager Ms Kate Bunting (e-mail:
kate.bunting@solihull.gov.uk)

SOMERSET

Authority: Somerset County Council
Library Centre, Mount Street, Bridgwater, Somerset TA6 3ES
☎(01278) 451201
Fax (01278) 452787
url: www.somerset.gov.uk/libraries; www.librarieswest.org.uk
Contact Centre to speak to customer adviser: 0845 345 9177
Strategic Manager, Library Services Mrs Sue Crowley BLib MCLIP (01278 446677;
e-mail: sacrowley@somerset.gov.uk)
Service Manager, Performance and IT Ms Kate Turner MA BLib MCLIP
Stock Development Manager Nigel J Humphrey BLib MA MCLIP (01278 451021;
e-mail: nhumphrey@somerset.gov.uk)
Information and Skills Development Manager Mrs Maggie Harris MCLIP (01823
340303; e-mail: maharris@somerset.gov.uk)
Service Design and Development Manager Ms Janet Blake BA MCLIP (01823 340309;
e-mail: jblake@somerset.gov.uk)
Customer Services Manager Ms Sue Sheppard (07919 540889; e-mail:
SMSheppard@somerset.gov.uk)
Bibliographic Services Manager Miss Carol Gold (01278 451201; e-mail:
cgold2@somerset.gov.uk)
Manager, Resources for Learning Mrs Karen Horsfield BEd MSc MCLIP (01278 421015;
e-mail: kahorsfield@somerset.gov.uk)

Group libraries

Mendip & Sedgemoor Group, Bridgwater Library, Binford Place, Bridgwater, Somerset
TA6 3LF
☎(01278) 458373
Fax (01278) 451027

South Somerset Group, Yeovil Library, King George Street, Yeovil, Somerset BA20 1PY
☎(01935) 423144
Fax (01935) 431847

Taunton Deane & West Somerset Group, Taunton Library, Paul Street, Taunton, Somerset
TA1 3XZ
☎(01823) 336334
Fax (01823) 340302

SOUTH GLOUCESTERSHIRE

Authority: South Gloucestershire Council
**Library Service, Department for Environment and Community Services, PO Box 299,
Civic Centre, High Street, Kingsmead, Bristol BS15 0DR**
☎(01454) 865782
e-mail: libraries@southglos.gov.uk
url: www.southglos.gov.uk/libraries
Community Cultural Services Manager Martin Burton BA MCLIP
Operations Manager John Abraham MCLIP (01454 865664)

Central/largest library

Yate Library, 44 West Walk, Yate, South Glos BS37 4AX
☎(01454) 868006
Fax (01454) 865665
Group Librarian Neil Weston BA MCLIP

Group libraries

Bradley Stoke Library, Fiddlers Wood Lane, Bradley Stoke, South Glos BS32 9BS
☎(01454) 868006
Librarian Ms Gabrielle Suddell

Downend Library, Buckingham Gardens, Downend, South Glos BS16 5TW
☎(01454) 868006
Librarian Mrs Helen Egarr MCLIP

Kingswood Library, High Street, Kingswood, South Glos BS15 4AR
☎(01454) 868006
Librarian Ms Julie Barker

Thornbury Library, St Mary Street, Thornbury, South Glos BS35 2AA
☎(01454) 868006
Librarian Ms Rebecca Furness

SOUTH TYNESIDE

Authority: South Tyneside Council
South Tyneside Libraries, Central Library, Prince George Square, South Shields, Tyne and Wear NE33 2PE
☎0191 427 1818
Fax 0191 455 8085
e-mail: reference.library@southtyneside.gov.uk
url: www.southtyneside.info
Libraries Manager Ms Kathryn Armstrong MA MCLIP (e-mail:
kathryn.armstrong@southtyneside.gov.uk)
Senior Librarian: Support Russell Hall MA LLB (e-mail:
russell.hall@southtyneside.gov.uk)
Senior Librarian: Service Delivery Ms Julia Robinson MA (e-mail:
julia.robinson@southtyneside.gov.uk)

SOUTHAMPTON

Authority: Southampton City Council
City Libraries Service, Administration Office, Central Library, Civic Centre, Southampton SO14 7LW
☎023 8083 3007
Fax 023 8083 4483
e-mail: library@southampton.gov.uk
url: www.southampton.gov.uk/libraries
Libraries Manager David Baldwin MCLIP (023 8083 2219; e-mail:
david.baldwin@southampton.gov.uk)

Central/largest library
Central Library, Civic Centre, Southampton SO14 7LW
☎023 8083 3007; mobile libraries 07768 541797
Fax 023 8033 6305
e-mail: library@southampton.gov.uk
Supervisor Ms Kate Swindells (e-mail: kate.swindells@southampton.gov.uk)

Branch libraries
(telephone numbers and e-mail addresses same as for Central Library)
Bitterne Library, Bitterne Road East, Southampton SO18 5EG
Supervisor Ms Barbara McCaffrey (e-mail: barbara.mccaffrey@southampton.gov.uk)

Burgess Road Library, Burgess Road, Southampton SO16 3HF
Supervisor Ms Catherine Brear (e-mail: catherine.brear@southampton.gov.uk)

Cobbett Road Library, Cobbett Road, Southampton SO18 1HL
Supervisor Ms Selina Francis (e-mail: selina.francis@southampton.gov.uk)

Lordshill Library, District Centre, Lordshill, Southampton SO16 8HY
Supervisor Ms Lisa Dawbney (e-mail: lisa.dawbney@southampton.gov.uk)

Millbrook Library, Mansel Park Pavilion, Evenlode Road, Southampton SO16 9RS
Supervisor Vacant

Portswood Library, Portswood Road, Southampton SO17 2NG
Supervisor Ms Sara Goddard (e-mail: sara.goddard@southampton.gov.uk)

Shirley Library, Redcar Street, Southampton SO15 5LL
Supervisor Ms Josie Stradling (e-mail: josie.stradling@southampton.gov.uk)

Thornhill Library, 328 Hinkler Road, Southampton SO19 6DF
Supervisor Vacant

Weston Library, Chamberlayne Leisure Centre Cark Park, Weston, Southampton SO19 9GX
Supervisor Mrs Carolyn Taplin (e-mail: carolyn.taplin@southampton.gov.uk)

Woolston Library, Portsmouth Road, Southampton SO19 9AF
Supervisor Ms Jo Harley (e-mail: jo.harley@southampton.gov.uk)

SOUTHEND-ON-SEA
Authority: Southend-on-Sea Borough Council
The Southend Forum, Elmer Square, Southend-on-Sea, Essex SS1 1NS
☎(01702) 215011
e-mail: library@southend.gov.uk
url: www.southend.gov.uk/libraries
Group Manager: Libraries & Museum Simon May BSc MSc

SOUTHWARK
Authority: London Borough of Southwark
Environment and Leisure Department, Culture, Libraries, Learning and Leisure, PO Box 64529, London SE1 5LX
☎020 7525 3918

Fax 020 7525 1568
e-mail: southwark.libraries@southwark.gov.uk
url: www.southwark.gov.uk
Head of Culture, Libraries, Leisure and Learning Adrian Whittle BA (020 7525 1577;
e-mail: adrian.whittle@southwark.gov.uk)
Libraries, Arts and Heritage Manager Ms Pam Usher BA(Hons) DMS MCLIP
(020 7525 3918; e-mail: pam.usher@southwark.gov.uk)

Branch libraries
**(The following Branch Libraries may be contacted on 020 7525 2000 with the
exception of the Home Library Service)**
Blue Anchor Library, Market Place, Southwark Park Road, London SE16 3UQ
Brandon Library, Maddock Way, Cooks Road, London SE17 3NH
Camberwell Library, 17-21 Camberwell Church Street, London SE5 8TR
Canada Water Library, 21 Surrey Quays Road, London SE16 7AR
Dulwich Library, 368 Lordship Lane, London SE22 8NB
East Street/Old Kent Road Library, 168-170 Old Kent Road, London SE1 5TY
Grove Vale Library, 25-27 Grove Vale, London SE22 8EQ
Home Library Service, Wilson Road, Camberwell, London SE5 8PD
☎020 7525 2833
John Harvard Library, 211 Borough High Street, London SE1 1JA
Kingswood Library, Seeley Drive, London SE21 8QR
Local History Library, 211 Borough High Street, London SE1 1JA
Newington Library, 155 Walworth Road, London SE17 1RS
(temp library due to open Autumn 2014 following fire. Check website for details)
Nunhead Library, Gordon Road, London SE15 3RW
Peckham Library, 122 Peckham Hill Street, London SE15 5JR

STAFFORDSHIRE
Authority: Staffordshire County Council
Libraries and Arts, Places Directorate, Tipping Street, Stafford ST16 2LP
☎0300 111 8000
url: www.staffordshire.gov.uk
Commissioner for Tourism and the Cultural County Ms Janene Cox BLib MCLIP
(01785 278368; e-mail: janene.cox@staffordshire.gov.uk)
Libraries and Arts Manager Mrs Catherine Mann BA(Hons) MCLIP (01785 278320;
e-mail: catherine.mann@staffordshire.gov.uk)
Libraries Service Delivery Manager Mrs Elizabeth Rees-Jones BA(Hons) MCLIP
(01785 278344; e-mail: elizabeth.rees-jones@staffordshire.gov.uk)
Libraries Service Development Manager – Learning & Resources Alan Medway BLib
MCLIP (01785 278388; e-mail: alan.medway@staffordshire.gov.uk)
Libraries Service Development Manager – Support Services Mrs Helen Farr
(01785 278328; e-mail: helen.farr@staffordshire.gov.uk)
Libraries Service Development Manager – Children & Young People Mrs Sue Ball
BA MCLIP (01785 854170; e-mail: sue.ball@staffordshire.gov.uk)

Districts
Burton Library, Riverside, High Street, Burton-on-Trent, Staffs DE14 1AH
☎(01283) 239556

Fax (01283) 239571
e-mail: burton.library@staffordshire.gov.uk
District Manager Ms Dianne Wheeler (01283 239559; e-mail:
dianne.wheeler@staffordshire.gov.uk)

Cannock Library, Manor Avenue, Cannock, Staffs WS11 1AA
☎(01543) 510365
Fax (01543) 510373
e-mail: cannock.library@staffordshire.gov.uk
District Manager Mrs Karen Yeomans BA(Hons) MCLIP (01543 510368; e-mail:
karen.yeomans@staffordshire.gov.uk)

Leek Library, Nicholson Institute, Stockwell Street, Leek, Staffs ST13 6DW
☎(01538) 483209
e-mail: leek.library@staffordshire.gov.uk
District Manager Mrs Cathy Braddock BLib(Hons) MCLIP (01538 483206; e-mail:
cathy.braddock@staffordshire.gov.uk)

Lichfield Library, The Friary, Lichfield, Staffs WS13 6QG
☎(01543) 510700
Fax (01543) 510716
e-mail: lichfield.library@staffordshire.gov.uk
District Manager Paul Tovell (01543 510702; e-mail: paul.tovell@staffordshire.gov.uk)

Newcastle Library, Ironmarket, Newcastle, Staffs ST5 1AT
☎(01782) 297300
Fax (01782) 297323
e-mail: newcastle.library@staffordshire.gov.uk
District Manager Mrs Sam Mellenchip BA(Hons) PGDipLIS (01782 297305; e-mail:
samantha.mellenchip@staffordshire.gov.uk)

Perton Library, Severn Drive, Perton, Staffs WV6 7QU
☎(01902) 755794
Fax (01902) 754980
e-mail: perton.library@staffordshire.gov.uk
District Manager Graham Riley MCLIP (01902 756123; e-mail:
graham.riley@staffordshire.gov.uk)

Stafford Library, Market Street, Stafford ST16 2LQ
☎(01785) 278585
Fax (01785) 278599
District Manager Andrew Baker BA(Hons) MCLIP TSSF (01785 278335; e-mail:
andrew.baker@staffordshire.gov.uk), Mrs Charlotte Hernandez (e-mail:
charlotte.hernandez@staffordshire.gov.uk)

Tamworth Library, Corporation Street, Tamworth, Staffs B79 7DN
☎(01827) 475645
Fax (01827) 475658
e-mail: tamworth.library@staffordshire.gov.uk
District Manager Mrs Cathy Attwood MCLIP (01827 475651; e-mail:
cathy.attwood@staffordshire.gov.uk)

Prison Library Service

Library and Information Services, Unit 4A & 4C, Drummond Road, Astonfields Industrial Estate, Stafford, Staffs ST16 3HJ
Prison Library Service Development Manager Ms Lindsay Lorenz MCLIP (01785 278412; e-mail: lindsay.lorenz@staffordshire.gov.uk), Mrs Jean Reed (e-mail: jean.reed@staffordshire.gov.uk)

STOCKPORT

Authority: Stockport Metropolitan Borough Council
Office of the Chief Executive, Stockport Town Hall, Edward Street, Stockport SK1 3DJ
☎0161 217 6009 (enquiries and administration)
e-mail: libraries@stockport.gov.uk
url: www.stockport.gov.uk/libraries
Head of Service: Customer Engagement Ms Janet Wood (e-mail: janet.wood@stockport.gov.uk)

Central/largest library

Central Library, Wellington Road South, Stockport SK1 3RS
☎0161 474 4530 (Local Heritage Library), 0161 217 6009 (all other library enquiries)
e-mail: lending.library@stockport.gov.uk; libraries@stockport.gov.uk

Library Operations and Support Services, Phoenix House, Bird Hall Lane, Stockport SK3 0RA
☎0161 474 5604

STOCKTON-ON-TEES

Authority: Stockton-on-Tees Borough Council
Development and Neighbourhood Services, Municipal Buildings, Church Road, Stockton-on-Tees TS18 1LD
☎(01642) 393939
Fax (01642) 528078
url: www.stockton.gov.uk
Head of Culture and Leisure Reuben Kench (01642 527039; e-mail: reuben.kench@stockton.gov.uk)
Libraries and Heritage Services Manager Mark C E Freeman BA(Hons) MCLIP (01642 526481; e-mail: mark.freeman@stockton.gov.uk)
Library Development Officer Ms Emma Tennant MSc (01642 526520; e-mail: emma.tennant@stockton.gov.uk) (also responsible for children's services)
Community Libraries Officer Ms Deb McDonagh (01642 528484; e-mail: debbie.mcdonagh@stockton.gov.uk)
Digital Library Services Officer Steve Wild (01642 526501; e-mail: steve.wild@stockton.gov.uk)
Improvement Co-ordinator Mrs Sue Sneyd (01642 526472; e-mail: sue.sneyd@stockton.gov.uk)
Librarian, Stockton Central Library Ms Janet Dobson (01642 526521; e-mail: janet.dobson@stockton.gov.uk)
Reading Resources Librarian Mrs Claire Pratt BA MCLIP (01642 528044; e-mail: claire.pratt@stockton.gov.uk)

Information Services Officer Ms Carole Wood (01642 528079; e-mail: carole.wood@stockton.gov.uk)
Children's Librarian Ms Lucy Carlton-Walker (01642 528501; e-mail: lucy.carlton-walker@stockton.gov.uk)
Health and Wellbeing Librarian Ms Karen Morris (01642 526518; e-mail: karen.morris@stockton.gov.uk)
Bibliographic Service Librarian Ms Pam Sugden (01642 526104; e-mail: pam.sugden@stockton.gov.uk)

Branch libraries

Billingham Library, Bedale Avenue, Billingham, Stockton-on-Tees TS23 1AJ
☎(01642) 527895
e-mail: billingham.library@stockton.gov.uk
Branch Librarian Mrs Lucie Kirton

Egglescliffe Library, Butterfield Drive, Orchard Estate, Egglescliffe, Stockton-on-Tees TS16 0EL
☎(01642) 527958
e-mail: egglescliffe.library@stockton.gov.uk
Branch Librarian Ivan Limon

Fairfield Library, Fairfield Road, Stockton-on-Tees TS19 7AJ
☎(01642) 527962
e-mail: fairfield.library@stockton.gov.uk
Branch Librarian Ms Penny Slee

Ingleby Barwick Library, Ingleby Barwick Community Campus, Blair Avenue, Ingleby Barwick, Stockton-on-Tees TS17 5BL
☎(01642) 528528
e-mail: inglebybarwick.library@stockton.gov.uk
Branch Librarian Mrs Cath Watkins

Norton Library, 87 High Street, Norton, Stockton-on-Tees TS20 1AE
☎(01642) 528019
e-mail: norton.library@stockton.gov.uk
Branch Librarian Ms Debbie Branson

Roseberry Billingham Library, The Causeway, Billingham, Stockton-on-Tees TS23 2LB
☎(01642) 528084
e-mail: roseberry.library@stockton.gov.uk
Branch Librarian Mrs Lucie Kirton

Roseworth Library, Redhill Children's Centre, Redhill Road, Stockton-on-Tees TS19 9BX
☎(01642) 528098
e-mail: roseworth.library@stockton.gov.uk
Branch Librarian Mrs Jackie Fraser

Thornaby Central Library, Wrightson House, Pavillion Shopping Centre, Thornaby, Stockton-on-Tees TS17 9EW
☎(01642) 528117
e-mail: thornabycentral.library@stockton.gov.uk
Branch Librarian Mrs Shelagh Freeman MCLIP

Thornaby Riverbank Library, Riverbank Children's Centre, Gilmour Street, Thornaby, Stockton-on-Tees TS17 6PF
☎(01642) 528150
e-mail: thornaby.library@stockton.gov.uk
Branch Librarian Mrs Shelagh Freeman MCLIP

Yarm Library, 41 High Street, Yarm, Stockton-on-Tees TS15 9BH
☎(01642) 528152
e-mail: yarm.library@stockton.gov.uk
Branch Librarian Ivan Limon

STOKE-ON-TRENT

Authority: Stoke-on-Trent City Council
Libraries and Archives, Directorate of Assistant Chief Executive, City Central Library, Bethesda Street, Hanley, Stoke-on-Trent ST1 3RS
☎(01782) 238455 (enquiries); (01782) 238405 (administration)
Fax (01782) 238499
e-mail: stoke.libraries@stoke.gov.uk
url: www.stoke.gov.uk
Strategic Manager: Libraries Ms Janet Thursfield MCLIP (e-mail: janet.thursfield@stoke.gov.uk)
City Archivist Chris Latimer MA DAA (e-mail: chris.latimer@stoke.gov.uk)

SUFFOLK

Authority: Suffolk's Libraries Industrial & Provident Society
Ipswich County Library, Northgate Street, Ipswich IP1 3DE
☎(01473) 263811
Fax (01473) 263843
e-mail: help@suffolklibraries.co.uk
url: www.suffolklibraries.co.uk
General Manager Ms Alison Wheeler (e-mail: alison.wheeler@suffolklibraries.co.uk)

Central/largest library

Ipswich County Library, Northgate Street, Ipswich, Suffolk IP1 3DE
☎(01473) 263810
Fax (01473) 263843
e-mail: ipswich.library@suffolklibraries.co.uk
Library Manager Ms Marion Harvey (e-mail: marion.harvey@suffolklibraries.co.uk)

Larger libraries

Beccles Library, Blyburgate, Beccles, Suffolk NR34 9TB
☎(01502) 714073/716471
e-mail: beccles.library@suffolklibraries.co.uk
Library Manager Ms Maggie Ross (e-mail: maggie.ross@suffolklibraries.co.uk)

Bury St Edmunds Library, Sergeant's Walk, St Andrew's Street North, Bury St Edmunds, Suffolk IP33 1TZ
☎(01284) 732255
e-mail: bury.library@suffolklibraries.co.uk

Library Manager Neil Holmes (e-mail: neil.holmes@suffolklibraries.co.uk)

Felixstowe Library, Crescent Road, Felixstowe, Suffolk IP11 7BY
☎(01394) 694880
e-mail: felixstowe.library@suffolklibraries.co.uk
Library Manager Ms Steph Merrett (e-mail: steph.merrett@suffolklibraries.co.uk)

Haverhill Library, Camps Road, Haverhill, Suffolk CB9 8HB
☎(01440) 702638
e-mail: haverhill.library@suffolklibraries.co.uk
Library Manager Ms Sanphra Willmott (e-mail: sanphra.willmott@suffolklibraries.co.uk)

Lowestoft Library, Clapham Road South, Lowestoft, Suffolk NR32 1DR
☎(01502) 674660
Fax (01502) 674679
e-mail: lowestoft.library@suffolklibraries.co.uk
Library Manager Ms Tracy Etheridge (e-mail: tracy.etheridge@suffolklibraries.co.uk)

Newmarket Library, 1a The Rookery, Newmarket, Suffolk CB8 8EQ
☎(01638) 661216
e-mail: newmarket.library@suffolklibraries.co.uk
Library Manager Mrs Grace Myers-Crump (e-mail: grace.myers-crump@suffolklibraries.co.uk)

Stowmarket Library, Milton Road North, Stowmarket, Suffolk IP14 1EX
☎(01449) 613143
e-mail: stowmarket.library@suffolklibraries.co.uk
Library Manager Ms Ursula Scott (e-mail: ursula.scott@suffolklibraries.co.uk)

Sudbury Library, Market Hill, Sudbury, Suffolk CO10 2EN
☎(01787) 242570
e-mail: sudbury.library@suffolklibraries.co.uk
Library Manager Gareth Lewry (e-mail: gareth.lewry@suffolklibraries.co.uk)

Woodbridge Library, New Street, Woodbridge, Suffolk IP12 1DT
☎(01394) 446510
e-mail: woodbridge.library@suffolklibraries.co.uk
Library Manager Ms Helen Scrivener (e-mail: helen.scrivener@suffolklibraries.co.uk)

SUNDERLAND

Authority: Sunderland City Council
City Library and Arts Centre, Fawcett Street, Sunderland SR1 1RE
☎0191 561 1235 (enquiries and administration)
Fax 0191 565 5950
e-mail: libraries@sunderland.gov.uk
url: www.sunderland.gov.uk
Assistant Head of Community Services (Library Services) Mrs Marie Brett (e-mail: marie.brett@sunderland.gov.uk)
Library Outreach and Development Manager Mrs Allison Clarke BA (e-mail: allison.clarke@sunderland.gov.uk)
Library Services Delivery Manager Ms Julie McCann BA(Hons) MCLIP (e-mail: julie.mccann@sunderland.gov.uk)

Area library

Washington Town Centre Library and Customer Service Centre, Independence Square, Washington, Tyne and Wear NE38 7RZ
☎0191 219 5611

SURREY

Authority: Surrey County Council
Libraries and Culture, Room 353, County Hall, Penrhyn Road, Kingston upon Thames, Surrey KTI 2DW
☎03456 009009
Fax 020 8541 9447
url: www.surreycc.gov.uk/libraries
Head of Cultural Services Peter Milton (020 8541 7679; e-mail: peter.milton@surreycc.gov.uk)

Senior Management Team

Weybridge Library, Church Street, Weybridge, Surrey KT13 8DE
☎0300 200 1001
Library Operations Manager Mrs Rose Wilson BA(Hons) (07976 290762; e-mail: rose.wilson@surreycc.gov.uk)

The Drill Hall, Drill Hall Road, Off West Street, Dorking, Surrey RH4 1DD
☎(01306) 881499
Acting Virtual Content Manager Ms Helen Leech (07792 225915; e-mail: helen.leech@surreycc.gov.uk)
Service Enabling Officer Mrs Christine Ganderton (07792 225891; e-mail: christine.ganderton@surreycc.gov.uk)

Banstead Library, The Horseshoe, Bolters Lane, Banstead, Surrey SM7 2AW
☎0300 200 1001
Library Sectors Manager Mrs Kelly Saini-Badwal (07968 832372; e-mail: kelly.sainibadwal@surreycc.gov.uk)

Camberley Library, Knoll Road, Camberley, Surrey GU15 3SY
☎0300 200 1001
Property, Environment and Stock Manager John Case (07837 113140; e-mail: john.case@surreycc.gov.uk)

Surrey County Council Libraries, Gloucester Chambers, Jubilee Square, Woking, Surrey GU21 6GA
☎(01483) 541518
Programme Manager Ms Janet Thomas BA(Hons) MCLIP (07968 832420; e-mail: janet.thomas@surreycc.gov.uk)

Enquiries Direct

Enquiries Direct, c/o Guildford Library, 77 North Street, Guildford, Surrey GU1 4AL
☎(01483) 543599
Fax (01483) 543597
e-mail: libraries@surreycc.gov.uk

Library Sector Leads

Woking Library, Gloucester Walk, Woking, Surrey GU21 6EP
☎0300 200 1001
Library Sector Lead West (Acting) Simon Harding (07792 225786; e-mail: simon.harding@surreycc.gov.uk)

Dorking Library, St Martin's Walk, Dorking, Surrey RH4 1UT
☎0300 200 1001
Library Sector Lead East (Acting) Mark Spiller (07968 834658; e-mail: mark.spiller@surreycc.gov.uk)

Weybridge Library, Church Street, Weybridge, Surrey KT13 8DE
☎0300 200 1001
Library Sector Lead North Ms Crishna Simmons (07792 225746; e-mail: chrishna.simmons@surreycc.gov.uk)

Main libraries

(All libraries in this section can be contacted on 0300 200 1001)
Addlestone Library, Runnymede Civic Centre, Station Road, Addlestone, Surrey K15 2AF
Ashford Library, Church Road, Ashford, Middlesex TW15 2XB
Banstead Library, The Horseshoe, Bolters Lane, Banstead, Surrey SM7 2AW
Camberley Library, Knoll Road, Camberley, Surrey GU15 3SY
Caterham Valley Library, Stafford Road, Caterham, Surrey CR3 6JG
Cranleigh Library, High Street, Cranleigh, Surrey GU6 8AE
Dittons Library, Mercer Close, Thames Ditton, Surrey KT7 0BS
Dorking Library, St Martin's Walk, Dorking, Surrey RH4 1UT
Egham Library, High Street, Egham, Surrey TW20 9EA
Epsom Library, The Ebbisham Centre, 6 The Derby Square, Epsom, Surrey KT19 8AG
Esher Library, Old Church Path, Esher, Surrey KT10 9NS
Ewell Library, Bourne Hall, Spring Street, Ewell, Epsom, Surrey KT17 1UF
Farnham Library, Vernon House, 28 West Street, Farnham, Surrey GU9 7DR
Godalming Library, Bridge Street, Godalming, Surrey GU7 1HT
Guildford Library, 77 North Street, Guildford, Surrey GU1 4AL
Haslemere Library, 91 Wey Hill, Haslemere, Surrey GU27 1HP
Horley Library, Victoria Road, Horley, Surrey RH6 7AG
Leatherhead Library, The Mansion, Church Street, Leatherhead, Surrey KT22 8DP
Molesey Library, The Forum, Walton Road, West Molesey, Surrey KT8 2HZ
Oxted Library, 12 Gresham Road, Oxted, Surrey RH8 0BQ
Redhill Library, Warwick Quadrant, Redhill, Surrey RH1 1NN
Staines Library, Friends Walk, Staines, Middlesex TW18 4PG
Walton Library, 54 The Heart (off Hepworth Way), Walton on Thames, Surrey KT12 1GH
Weybridge Library, Church Street, Weybridge, Surrey KT13 8DE
Woking Library, Gloucester Walk, Woking, Surrey GU21 6EP

SUTTON

Authority: London Borough of Sutton
Sutton Central Library, St Nicholas Way, Sutton, Surrey SM1 1EA
☎020 8770 4700 (enquiries), 020 8770 4602 (administration)
Fax 020 8770 4777
e-mail: sutton.library@sutton.gov.uk

url: www.sutton.gov.uk
Executive Head of Neighbourhood and Communities Mrs Stephanie Crossley BA(Hons) DipLIS MCLIP (020 8770 4642; e-mail: stephanie.crossley@sutton.gov.uk)
Head of Libraries and Heritage Service Mrs Angela Fletcher BA(Hons) PGCE (020 8770 4755; e-mail: angela.fletcher@sutton.gov.uk)
Assistant Head of Libraries Jon Ward (020 8770 4708; e-mail: jon.ward@sutton.gov.uk)
Service Manager Customer Care and Policy Mrs Pauline Deakin BA MCLIP (020 8770 4772; e-mail: pauline.deakin@sutton.gov.uk)
Service Manager Reading and Information Ms Rachel Levy BA(Hons) MA (020 8770 4763; e-mail: rachel.levy@sutton.gov.uk)
Service Manager Operations Praveen Manghani (020 8770 4761; e-mail: praveen.manghani@sutton.gov.uk)

Main libraries
Carshalton Library@Westcroft, The Square, Carshalton, Surrey SM5 3BN
☎020 8647 1151
Library Manager Ms Tracey Parker, Ms Clare Canavan (job share)

Cheam Library, Church Road, Cheam, Surrey SM3 8QH
☎020 8644 9377
Library Manager Ms Sarah Withers, Ms Hannah Bell (job share)

Wallington Library, Shotfield, Wallington, Surrey SM6 0HY
☎020 8770 4900
Library Manager Ms Debbie Rumbles

Worcester Park Library, Windsor Road, Worcester Park, Surrey KT4 8ES
☎020 8337 1609
Library Manager Ms Kathy English

SWINDON

Authority: Swindon Borough Council
Libraries, Leisure, Culture and Traded Services, Wat Tyler House East, Swindon SN1 2JH
☎(01793) 466035
url: www.swindon.gov.uk
Head of Libraries Ms Allyson Jordan MCLIP (e-mail: ajordan@swindon.gov.uk)

Central/largest library
Swindon Central Library, Regent Circus, Swindon SN1 1QG
☎(01793) 463238
Fax (01793) 541319
e-mail: central.library@swindon.gov.uk

Group library
Acquisitions, Central Library, Regent Circus, Liden, Swindon SN3 1QG
☎(01793) 463510
Fax (01793) 463508
Acquisitions and Interlending Manager Adrian Peace (e-mail: apeace@swindon.gov.uk)
Strategic Managers, Libraries and Delivery Shaun Smith MCLIP (07467 440706; e-mail: s.smith@swindon.gov.uk), Leon Bolton (07884 270448; e-mail: l.bolton@swindon.gov.uk) (job share)

TAMESIDE

Authority: Tameside Metropolitan Borough Council
**Community Services, Council Offices, Wellington Road, Ashton-under-Lyne, Tameside
OL6 6DL**
url: www.tameside.gov.uk/libraries
Service Unit Manager Mrs Mandy Kinder (0161 342 2061; e-mail:
mandy.kinder@tameside.gov.uk)
Service Delivery Manager Ms Karen Heathcote BA DipLIS MCLIP (e-mail:
karen.heathcote@tameside.gov.uk)
Service Operations Manager Mrs Denise Lockyer (0161 342 2849; e-mail:
denise.lockyer@tameside.gov.uk)

Central/largest library
Tameside Central Library, Old Street, Ashton-under-Lyne, Tameside OL6 7SG
☎0161 342 2029 (lending/enquiries), 0161 342 2037 (bibliographical enquiries), 0161 342
2031 (information)
Fax 0161 330 4762
e-mail: information.direct@tameside.gov.uk; central.library@tameside.gov.uk
Information Services Librarian Imran Khan MA

Other large library
Hyde Library, Union Street, Hyde, Cheshire SK14 1ND
☎0161 342 4450
Fax 0161 368 0909
e-mail: hyde.library@tameside.gov.uk

TELFORD AND WREKIN

Authority: Telford and Wrekin Council
**Telford and Wrekin Libraries, Customer Services, Addenbrooke House, Ironmasters
Way, Telford, Shropshire TF3 4NT**
☎(01952) 382881
url: www.telford.gov.uk
Library Service Delivery Manager Ms Sharon Smith BA MCLIP (e-mail:
sharon.smith@telford.gov.uk)
Senior Librarian, Digital & Information Services Mrs Helen Nahal BLib MCLIP

THURROCK

Authority: Thurrock Council
Thurrock Libraries, Thameside Complex, Orsett Road, Grays, Essex RM17 5DX
☎(01375) 413976 (enquiries)
Fax (01375) 392666
e-mail: grays.library@thurrock.gov.uk
url: www.thurrock.gov.uk
Strategic Lead for Operational Resources and Libraries Unit Ms Janet Clarke
(e-mail: jclarke@thurrock.gov.uk)
Operations and Data Manager Ms Jenny Meads (e-mail: jmeads@thurrock.gov.uk)

Strategy and Development Manager Miss Rosalyn Jones BA(Hons) DipLib (e-mail: rjones@thurrock.gov.uk)

Central/largest library
Grays Library, Thameside Complex, Orsett Road, Grays, Essex RM17 5DX
☎(01375) 413976
e-mail: grays.library@thurrock.gov.uk
Library Manager Ms Annette Berry (e-mail: axberry@thurrock.gov.uk)

TORBAY

Authority: Torbay Council
Torquay Library, Lymington Road, Torquay, Devon TQI 3DT
☎(01803) 208300 (enquiries), (01803) 208310 (administration)
Fax (01803) 208314
url: www.torbay.gov.uk/libraries
Head of Library Services Mrs Sue Cheriton (01803 207972; e-mail: sue.cheriton@torbay.gov.uk) (Executive Head, Resident and Visitor Services)
Resources and Technical Services Librarian Miss Liz Kent BSc MCLIP (01803 208287; e-mail: liz.kent@torbay.gov.uk)
Community and Performance Librarian Nick Niles BA DipLib (01803 208288; e-mail: nick.niles@torbay.gov.uk)

Branch libraries
Brixham Library, Market Street, Brixham, Devon TQ5 8EU
☎(01803) 853870
Branch Librarian Mrs Eleanor Moss MA

Churston Library, Broadsands Road, Paignton, Devon TQ4 6LL
☎(01803) 843757
Branch Librarian Mrs Susie Murr MCLIP

Paignton Library, Great Western Road, Paignton, Devon TQ4 5AG
☎(01803) 208321
Branch Librarian Mrs Jo Gale

Torquay Library, Lymington Road, Torquay, Devon TQI 3DT
☎(01803) 208300

TOWER HAMLETS

Authority: London Borough of Tower Hamlets
Idea Stores, John Onslow House, I Ewart Place, Bow, London E3 5EQ
☎020 7364 4322
url: www.ideastore.co.uk
Head of Idea Stores Ms Judith St John (020 7364 5630; e-mail: judith.st.john@towerhamlets.gov.uk)
Deputy Head of Idea Stores Sergio Dogliani (020 7364 2649; e-mail: sergio.dogliani@towerhamlets.gov.uk)
Idea Store Development Manager Ms Kate Pitman BA MCLIP (020 7364 5740; e-mail: kate.pitman@towerhamlets.gov.uk)

Stock Development Manager Stephen Clarke BA MCLIP (020 7364 6794; e-mail: steve.j.clarke@towerhamlets.gov.uk)

Largest idea store/library

Idea Store Whitechapel, 321 Whitechapel Road, London E1 1BU
☎020 7364 4332
e-mail: ideastore@towerhamlets.gov.uk
Idea Store Manager Asab Ali (020 7364 1742; e-mail: asab.ali@towerhamlets.gov.uk)

Full-time idea stores/libraries

Bethnal Green Library, Cambridge Heath Road, London E2 0HL
☎020 7364 3492/3493
e-mail: ideastore@towerhamlets.gov.uk
Idea Store Manager Ms Barbara Stretch (e-mail: barbara.stretch@towerhamlets.gov.uk)

Cubitt Town Library, Strattondale Street, London E14 3HG
☎020 7987 3152
e-mail: ideastore@towerhamlets.gov.uk
Idea Store Manager Ms Lisa Randall (020 7364 1260; e-mail: lisa.randall@towerhamlets.gov.uk)

Idea Store Bow, 1 Gladstone Place, Roman Road, London E3 5ES
☎020 7364 4332
e-mail: ideastore@towerhamlets.gov.uk
Idea Store Manager Ms Barbara Stretch (020 7364 5775; e-mail: barbara.stretch@towerhamlets.gov.uk)

Idea Store Canary Wharf, Churchill Place, Canary Wharf, London E14 5RB
☎020 7364 4332
e-mail: ideastore@towerhamlets.gov.uk
Idea Store Manager Ms Lisa Randall (020 7364 1260; e-mail: lisa.randall@towerhamlets.gov.uk)

Idea Store Chrisp Street, 1 Vesey Path, East India Dock Road, London E14 6BT
☎020 8364 4332
e-mail: ideastore@towerhamlets.gov.uk
Idea Store Manager Shaw Rahman (020 7364 1502; e-mail: shaw.rahman@towerhamlets.gov.uk)

Idea Store Watney Market, 260 Commercial Road, London E1 2FB
☎010 7364 4332
e-mail: ideastore@towerhamlets.gov.uk
Idea Store Manager Shaw Rahman (020 7364 1502; e-mail: shaw.rahman@towerhamlets.gov.uk)

Local Studies and Archives

Bancroft Library, 277 Bancroft Road, London E1 4DQ
e-mail: localhistorylibrary@towerhamlets.gov.uk
Heritage Manager Ms Tamsin Bookey (020 7364 1293; e-mail: tamsin.bookey@towerhamlets.gov.uk)
Borough Archivist Malcolm Barr-Hamilton BA DAS (020 7364 1289)

TRAFFORD

Authority: Trafford Metropolitan Borough Council
**Transformation and Resources, Access Trafford, Sale Library, Sale Waterside, Sale,
Cheshire M33 7ZF**
☎0161 912 3189 (enquiries and administration)
Fax 0161 912 3019
e-mail: libraries@trafford.gov.uk
url: www.trafford.gov.uk/libraries
Head of Customer Service Ms Sarah Curran (0161 912 2823; e-mail:
sarah.curran@trafford.gov.uk)

Main branch libraries

Altrincham Library, 20 Stamford New Road, Altrincham, Cheshire WA14 1EJ
☎0161 912 3189
Fax 0161 941 6452

Sale Library, Sale Waterside, Sale, Cheshire M33 7ZF
☎0161 912 3189
Fax 0161 912 3019

Stretford Library, Kingsway, Stretford, Manchester M32 8AP
☎0161 912 3189
Fax 0161 865 3835

Urmston Library, Unit 34, Golden Way, Urmston, Manchester M41 0NA
☎0161 912 3189
Fax 0161 912 2947

TRI-BOROUGH LIBRARIES AND ARCHIVES

Authority: Tri-borough Libraries and Archives (London Borough of Hammersmith and
Fulham; Royal Borough of Kensington and Chelsea; Westminster City Council)

Hammersmith and Fulham HQ
Hammersmith Library, Shepherds Bush Road, London W6 7AT
☎020 7361 3610
e-mail: libcomments@lbhf.gov.uk
url: www.lbhf.gov.uk
Tri-borough Director of Libraries and Archives Mike Clarke

Area libraries
Fulham Library, 598 Fulham Road, London SW6 5NX
☎020 8753 3877
Site Manager Richard Grant

Hammersmith Library, Shepherds Bush Road, London W6 7AT
☎020 8753 3823
Site Manager Ms Ann Cooper

Shepherd's Bush Library, 6 Wood Lane, London W12 7BF
☎020 8753 3842
Site Manager Ms Mandy Charles

Branch library
Askew Road Library, 87–91 Askew Road, London W12 9AS
☎020 8753 3863
Site Manager Zedh Foley

Kensington and Chelsea HQ
Kensington Town Hall, Hornton Street, London W8 7NX
☎020 7361 3010
Fax 020 7361 2976
e-mail: libcomments@rbkc.gov.uk
url: www.rbkc.gov.uk
Tri-borough Director of Libraries and Archives Mike Clarke

Central/largest library
Kensington Central Library, Phillimore Walk, London W8 7RX
☎020 7631 3010
Fax 020 7361 2976

Main libraries
Brompton Library, 210 Old Brompton Road, London SW5 0BS
☎020 7631 3010

Chelsea Library, The Old Town Hall, Kings Road, London SW3 5EZ
☎020 7631 3010

North Kensington Library, 108 Ladbroke Grove, London W11 1PZ
☎020 7631 3010

Westminster HQ
Westminster Libraries, Management Suite, 3rd Floor, Westminster Reference Library, 35 St Martin's Street, London WC2H 7HP
☎020 7641 2496 (administration); 020 7641 1300 (library enquiries); 020 7641 1400 (renewals)
url: www.westminster.gov.uk
Tri-borough Director of Libraries and Archives Mike Clarke

Largest libraries
Charing Cross Library, 6 Charing Cross Road, London WC2H 0HF
☎020 7641 4625
e-mail: charingcrosslibrary@westminster.gov.uk
Site Manager Ms Helen Rogers

Marylebone Library, Macintosh House, 54 Beaumont Street, London W1G 6DG
e-mail: marylebonelibrary@westminster.gov.uk
Site Manager Ms Anabel Lopez

Paddington Library, Porchester Road, London W2 5DU
e-mail: paddingtonlibrary@westminster.gov.uk
Site Manager Ms Elizabeth Williams BA MCLIP

Victoria Library, 160 Buckingham Palace Road, London SW1W 9UD
e-mail: victorialibrary@westminster.gov.uk
Site Manager Ms Ann Farrell

Westminster Reference Library, 35 St Martin's Street, London WC2H 7HP
e-mail: referencelibrarywc2@westminster.gov.uk
Site Manager Ms Alexandra Buchholz

Community libraries
Church Street Library, Church Street, London NW8 8EW
e-mail: churchstreetlibrary@westminster.gov.uk
Site Manager Vic Stewart

Maida Vale Library, Sutherland Avenue, London W9 2QT
e-mail: maidavalelibrary@westminster.gov.uk
Site Manager Ben Walsh

Mayfair library, 25 South Audley Street, London W1K 2PB
e-mail: mayfairlibrary@westminster.gov.uk
Site Managers Frederic Jardin, Ms Gillian Nunns

Pimlico Library, Rampayne Street, London SW1V 2PU
e-mail: pimlicolibrary@westminster.gov.uk

Queen's Park Library, 666 Harrow Road, London W10 4NE
e-mail: queensparklibrary@westminster.gov.uk
Site Manager Hugh Thomas

St John's Wood Library, 20 Circus Road, London NW8 6PD
e-mail: stjohnswoodlibrary@westminster.gov.uk
Site Manager Ms Amy Houtenbos

UPPER NORWOOD JOINT LIBRARY

Authority: Upper Norwood Joint Library (jointly funded by the London Borough of
Lambeth and the London Borough of Croydon)
Upper Norwood Joint Library, 39–41 Westow Hill, Upper Norwood, London SE19 1TJ
☎020 8670 2551
Fax 020 8670 5468
e-mail: info@uppernorwoodlibrary.org
url: www.uppernorwoodlibrary.org
Principal Librarian Ms Carol Lewis
Assistant Librarian – Learning and Development Mrs Fiona Byers (e-mail:
fbyers@uppernorwood.akhter.com)
Assistant Librarian – Support and Resources Miss Rita Chakraborty (e-mail:
rchakraborty@uppernorwoodlibrary.org)

WAKEFIELD

Authority: Wakefield Metropolitan Council
**Libraries and Information Services, Wakefield One, Burton Street, Wakefield, West
Yorks WF2 0DQ**
☎(01924) 302261 (enquiries and administration)
e-mail: lib.admin@wakefield.gov.uk
url: www.wakefield.gov.uk/libraries
Library and Information Services Manager Andrew Wright BMus(Hons) DipLib

Library Managers Ms Sue Eustace, John Rushforth
Support Services Manager Ms Claire Pickering

WALSALL

Authority: Walsall Council
Libraries, Heritage and Arts, Zone 2L, Civic Centre, Darwall Street, Walsall, West Midlands WSI ITP
☎(01922) 650338
Fax (01922) 623234
e-mail: librarian@walsall.gov.uk
url: www.walsall.gov.uk/libraries
Head of Libraries, Heritage and Arts Mrs Sue Grainger MCLIP (e-mail: graingers@walsall.gov.uk)

Central/largest library

Central Library, Lichfield Street, Walsall, West Midlands WS1 1TR
☎(01922) 653121 (lending), (01922) 653110 (reference)
Fax (01922) 722687 (lending), (01922) 654013 (reference)
e-mail: centrallendinglibrary@walsall.gov.uk; reference@walsall.gov.uk
Central Library Manager Ms Denise Gold BA(Hons) (e-mail: goldd@walsall.gov.uk)
Strategic Library Manager – Operations Chris Cordes
Strategic Library Manager – Development Ms Rita Mills
SLSS Manager Ms Christine White

Area libraries

Aldridge Library, Rookery Lane, Aldridge, Walsall, West Midlands WS9 8NN
☎(01922) 655569
e-mail: aldridgelibrary@walsall.gov.uk

Beechdale Library, Beechdale Centre, Stephenson Square, Walsall, West Midlands WS2 7DX
☎(01922) 655890
e-mail: beechdalelibrary@walsall.gov.uk

Blakenall Library, Blakenall Village Centre, Thames Road, Blakenall, Walsall, West Midlands WS3 1LZ
☎(01922) 714967
e-mail: blakenalllibrary@walsall.gov.uk

Bloxwich Library, Elmore Row, Bloxwich, Walsall, West Midlands WS3 2HR
☎(01922) 655900
e-mail: bloxwichlibrary@walsall.gov.uk

Brownhills Library, Park View Centre, Chester Road North, Walsall, West Midlands WS8 7JB
☎(01922) 650730
e-mail: brownhillslibrary@walsall.gov.uk

Darlaston Library, 1 King Street, Darlaston, Walsall, West Midlands WS10 8DD
☎0121 654777
e-mail: darlastonlibrary@walsall.gov.uk

Local History Centre, Essex Street, Walsall, West Midlands WS2 7AS
☎(01922) 721305

Fax (01922) 634954
e-mail: localhistorycentre@walsall.gov.uk

Mobile and Home Library Service, Mobile Library Depot, Willenhall Lane, Bloxwich, Walsall, West Midlands WS3 2XN
☎(01922) 654333
e-mail: mobilelibrary@walsall.gov.uk

New Invention Library, The Square, Lichfield Road, Willenhall, Walsall, West Midlands WV12 5EA
☎(01922) 655570
e-mail: newinventionlibrary@walsall.gov.uk

Pelsall Library, High Street, Pelsall, Walsall, West Midlands WS3 4LX
☎(01922) 650455
e-mail: pelsalllibrary@walsall.gov.uk

Pheasey Library, Collingwood Centre, Collingwood Drive, Great Barr, Pheasey, Birmingham B43 7NE
☎(01922) 654865
e-mail: pheaseylibrary@walsall.gov.uk

Pleck Library, Darlaston Road, Pleck, Walsall, West Midlands WS2 9RE
☎(01922) 654860
e-mail: plecklibrary@walsall.gov.uk

Rushall Library, Pelsall Lane, Walsall, West Midlands WS4 1NL
☎(01922) 721310
e-mail: rushalllibrary@walsall.gov.uk

South Walsall Library, West Bromwich Road, Walsall, West Midlands WS5 4NW
☎(01922) 721347
e-mail: southwalsalllibrary@walsall.gov.uk

Streetly Library, Blackwood Road, Streetly, Birmingham B74 3PL
☎(01922) 654864
e-mail: streetlylibrary@walsall.gov.uk

Walsall Wood Library, Coppice Road, Walsall Wood, Walsall, West Midlands WS9 9BL
☎(01922) 655572
e-mail: walsallwoodlibrary@walsall.gov.uk

Willenhall Library, Walsall Street, Willenhall, Walsall, West Midlands WV13 2EX
☎(01922) 650777
e-mail: willenhalllibrary@walsall.gov.uk

WALTHAM FOREST

Authority: London Borough of Waltham Forest
Waltham Forest Town Hall, Forest Road, Walthamstow, London E17 4JF
☎020 8496 3000
e-mail: wfdirect@walthamforest.gov.uk; librarypromotions@walthamforest.gov.uk
url: www.walthamforest.gov.uk
Head, Culture and Community Services Ms Lorna Lee BA(Hons) MA MSc (e-mail: lorna.lee@walthamforest.gov.uk)

Head of Customer Services Edward Meyrick (e-mail:
edward.meyrick@walthamforest.gov.uk)
Group Manager Ms Jackie Staples (e-mail: jacqueline.staples@walthamforest.gov.uk)

Libraries

Hale End Library, Castle Avenue, Chingford, London E4 9QD
☎020 8496 3000
e-mail: wfdirect@walthamforest.gov.uk

Higham Hill Library, North Countess Road, Walthamstow, London E17 5HS
☎020 8496 3000
e-mail: wfdirect@walthamforest.gov.uk

Lea Bridge Library, Lea Bridge Road, Leyton, London E10 7HU
☎020 8496 3000
e-mail: wfdirect@walthamforest.gov.uk

Leyton Library, High Road, Leyton, London E10 5QH
☎020 8496 3000
e-mail: wfdirect@walthamforest.gov.uk

Leytonstone Library, Church Lane, Leytonstone, London E11 1HG
☎020 8496 3000
e-mail: wfdirect@walthamforest.gov.uk

North Chingford Library, The Green, Chingford, London E4 7EN
☎020 8496 3000
e-mail: wfdirect@walthamforest.gov.uk

Walthamstow Library, High Street, Walthamstow, London E17 7JN
☎020 8496 3000
e-mail: wfdirect@walthamforest.gov.uk

Wood Street Library, Forest Road, Walthamstow, London E17 4AA
☎020 8496 3000
e-mail: wfdirect@walthamforest.gov.uk

WANDSWORTH

Authority: Wandsworth Council (Greenwich Leisure Limited)
GLL Libraries, Middlegate House, The Royal Arsenal, London SE18 6SX
e-mail: wandsworth.libraries@gll.org
url: www.better.org.uk
Head of GLL Libraries Ms Diana Edmonds MBE BA DipLib FCLIP
Operations Manager Daniel Andrews BSc MA MCLIP

Largest libraries

Balham Library, 16 Ramsden Road, London SW12 8QY
☎020 8673 1129
e-mail: balham.library@gll.org

Battersea Library, 265 Lavender Hill, London SW11 1JB
☎020 7223 2334
e-mail: battersea.library@gll.org

Putney Library, 5/7 Disraeli Road, London SW15 2DR
☎020 8780 3085
e-mail: putney.library@gll.org

Tooting Library, 75 Mitcham Road, London SW17 9PD
☎020 8767 0543
e-mail: tooting.library@gll.org

WARRINGTON

Authority: Warrington Borough Council (LiveWire Warrington Community Interest Company)
Orford Jubilee Park, Jubilee Way, Warrington, Cheshire WA2 8HE
e-mail: library@livewirewarrington.org
url: www.livewirewarrington.co.uk
Area Neighbourhood & Wellbeing Manager (Libraries & Learning) Ms Tina Redford
(01925 442733)
Assistant Neighbourhood & Wellbeing Manager (Libraries & Learning)
Ms Jo Unsworth (01925 442733)

Branch libraries

Birchwood Library, Brock Road, Warrington, Cheshire WA3 7PT
☎(01925) 827491 (tel/fax)

Burtonwood Library, Chapel Lane, Burtonwood, Warrington, Cheshire WA5 4PS
☎(01925) 226563 (tel/fax)

Culcheth Library, Warrington Road, Culcheth, Warrington, Cheshire WA3 5SL
☎(01925) 763293 (tel/fax)

Lymm Library, Davies Way, Off Brookfield Road, Lymm, Warrington, Cheshire WA13 0QW
☎(01925) 754367
Fax (01925) 759367

Orford Library, Orford Jubilee Neighbourhood Hub, Jubilee Way, Orford, Warrington,
Cheshire WA2 8HE
☎(01925) 572504
Fax (01925) 624955

Padgate Library, Insall Road, Padgate, Warrington, Cheshire WA2 0HD
☎(01925) 818096 (tel/fax)

Penketh Library, Honiton Way, Penketh, Warrington, Cheshire WA5 2EY
☎(01925) 723730
Fax (01925) 791264

Stockton Heath Library, Alexandra Park, Stockton Heath, Warrington, Cheshire WA4 2AN
☎(01925) 261148
Fax (01925) 267787

Warrington Library, Museum Street, Warrington, Cheshire WA1 1JB
☎(01925) 442889
Fax (01925) 443257

Westbrook Library, Westbrook Centre, Westbrook Crescent, Warrington, Cheshire
WA5 5UG

☎(01925) 416561
Fax (01925) 230462

Woolston Library, Hall Road, Woolston, Warrington, Cheshire WA1 4PN
☎(01925) 813939
Fax (01925) 816146

WARWICKSHIRE

Authority: Warwickshire County Council
Customer Services (Face to Face), Resources Group, Shire Hall, Warwick CV34 4RR
☎(01926) 412867 (enquiries and administration)
e-mail: libraryenquiryteam@warwickshire.gov.uk
url: www.warwickshire.gov.uk/libraries
Customer Service Manager (Face to Face) Ayub Khan BA(Hons) FCLIP (01926 412657; e-mail: ayubkhan@warwickshire.gov.uk)

Network

Resources Group, Shire Hall, Warwick CV34 4RR
Customer Services Manager (Face to Face): Communities Ms Tanya Butchers BA(Hons) MA MCLIP (01926 476970; e-mail: tanyabutchers@warwickshire.gov.uk)

Leamington Library, Royal Pump Rooms, The Parade, Leamington Spa, Warwicks CV32 4AA
Customer Services Manager (Face to Face): South Ms Tracey Baker (01926 742741; e-mail: traceybaker@warwickshire.gov.uk)

Rugby Library, Little Elborow Street, Rugby, Warwicks CV21 3BZ
Customer Services Manager (Face to Face): North Ms Jayney Faulknall-Mills (01788 533270; e-mail: jayneyfaulknall-mills@warwickshire.gov.uk)

WEST BERKSHIRE

Authority: West Berkshire District Council
Cultural & Environmental Protection, Council Offices, Market Street, Newbury, Berks RG14 5LD
☎(01635) 519551
e-mail: library@westberks.gov.uk
url: www.westberks.gov.uk
Head of Libraries Mike Brook BA(Hons) DipLib MCLIP (e-mail: mbrook@westberks.gov.uk)

Central/largest library

Newbury Central Library, The Wharf, Newbury, Berks RG14 5AU
☎(01635) 519900
e-mail: newburylibrary@westberks.gov.uk

WEST SUSSEX

Authority: West Sussex County Council
Information Services, First Floor, Unit 6 Willow Park, 4B Terminus Road, West Sussex PO19 8EQ
☎(033022) 24786
url: www.westsussex.gov.uk
Information Services Manager Mrs Lesley Sim BA(Hons) MCLIP (e-mail: lesley.sim@westsussex.gov.uk)
(For management enquiries contact headquarters; for services contact one of the principal libraries)

Principal libraries

Crawley Library, Southgate Avenue, Crawley, West Sussex RH10 6HG
☎(01293) 651751
Area Librarian Ms Gill Burch (01293 651751; e-mail: gill.burch@westsussex.gov.uk)

Worthing Library, Richmond Road, Worthing, West Sussex BN11 1HD
☎(01903) 704809
Area Manager Justin Burns (01903 704809; e-mail: justin.burns@westsussex.gov.uk)

WESTMINSTER see TRI-BOROUGH LIBRARIES AND ARCHIVES (LONDON BOROUGH OF HAMMERSMITH AND FULHAM; ROYAL BOROUGH OF KENSINGTON AND CHELSEA; WESTMINSTER CITY COUNCIL)

WIGAN

Authority: Wigan Leisure and Culture Trust (on behalf of Wigan Council)
Culture, Wigan Library, The Wiend, Wigan WN1 1NH
☎(01942) 489791
e-mail: wiglib@wlct.org
url: www.wlct.gov.uk
Head of Culture Richard Bealing
Service Manager – Operations Ms Wendy Heaton MCLIP
Service Manager – Development Rob Sanderson

Central/largest libraries

Leigh Library, Turnpike Centre, Civic Square, Leigh, Lancs WN7 1EB
☎(01942) 404556 (lending), (01942) 404557 (information)
Fax (01942) 404567

Wigan Library, The Wiend, Wigan WN1 1NH
☎(01942) 827621 (lending), (01942) 827619 (information)
Fax (01942) 827640

WILTSHIRE

Authority: Wiltshire County Council
Library HQ, Bythesea Road, Trowbridge, Wilts BA14 8BS
☎(01225) 713707
Fax (01225) 713704
e-mail: libraryenquiries@wiltshire.gov.uk
url: www.wiltshire.gov.uk/libraries/
Head of Libraries Ms Joan Davis BALib MCLIP (e-mail: joan.davis@wiltshire.gov.uk)
Library Operations Manager Chris Moore BA(Hons) MSc MCLIP (e-mail:
chris.moore@wiltshire.gov.uk)
Library Development Manager Chris S Harling BA(Hons) MCLIP (e-mail:
chris.harling@wiltshire.gov.uk)
Library Systems Manager Nick Goddard MCMI (e-mail: nick.goddard@wiltshire.gov.uk)

Community group libraries

Chippenham Library, Timber Street, Chippenham, Wilts SN15 3EJ
☎(01249) 650536
Fax (01249) 443793
Community Librarian, Chippenham Group Ms Jessica Phillips BA(Hons) MSc MCLIP
(e-mail: jessica.phillips@wiltshire.gov.uk)

Devizes Library, Sheep Street, Devizes, Wilts SN10 1DL
☎(01380) 726878
Fax (01380) 722161
Community Librarian, Devizes Group Ms Wendy Beaver BLib MCLIP (e-mail:
wendy.beaver@wiltshire.gov.uk)

Royal Wootton Bassett Library, Borough Fields, Royal Wootton Bassett, Swindon, Wilts
SN4 7AX
☎(01793) 853249
Community Librarian, Royal Wootton Bassett Group Ms Carolyn Kennedy BA(Hons)
MCLIP (e-mail: carolyn.kennedy@wiltshire.gov.uk)

Salisbury Library, Market Place, Salisbury, Wiltshire SP1 1BL
☎(01722) 324145
Fax (01722) 413214
Community Librarian, Salisbury Group Philip Tomes BLib(Hons) MCLIP (e-mail:
philip.tomes@wiltshire.gov.uk)

Trowbridge Library, Ground Floor, Bythesea Road, Trowbridge, Wilts BA14 8JN
☎(01225) 716700
Fax (01225) 713715
Community Librarian, Trowbridge Group Basil Nankivell BSc(Hons) MCLIP (e-mail:
basil.nankivell@wiltshire.gov.uk)

Warminster Library, Three Horseshoes Walk, Warminster, Wilts BA12 9BT
☎(01985) 216022
Fax (01985) 846332
Community Librarian, Warminster Group Ms Sabina Edwards BA DipLib MLS MCLIP
(e-mail: sabina.edwards@wiltshire.gov.uk)

WINDSOR AND MAIDENHEAD

Authority: Royal Borough of Windsor and Maidenhead
Libraries, Arts and Heritage Service, Maidenhead Library, St Ives Road, Maidenhead, Berks SL6 1QU
☎(01628) 796969
Fax (01628) 796971
e-mail: maidenhead.library@rbwm.gov.uk
url: www.rbwm.gov.uk/web/onlinelibrary.htm
Head of Libraries, Arts & Heritage Mark Taylor BA MCLIP (01628 796989; fax: 01628 796986; e-mail: mark.taylor@rbwm.gov.uk)
Service Manager: Libraries Mrs Angela Gallacher BA(Hons) AUDIS (01628 795641; e-mail: angela.gallacher@rbwm.gov.uk)
Service Manager: Heritage & Arts Mrs Margaret Kirby BA(Hons) DipLib (01628 685811)

Central/largest library

Maidenhead Library, St Ives Road, Maidenhead, Berks SL6 1QU
☎(01628) 796968 (1st floor), 796969 (issue desk), 796985 (administration)
Fax (01628) 796971
e-mail: maidenhead.library@rbwm.gov.uk
Administration and Information Systems Officer Mrs Lisa Poole (01628 796985)

Other libraries

Ascot Durning Library, Ascot Racecourse, High Street, Ascot, Berks SL5 7JF
☎(01344) 630140

Boyn Grove Library, 11 Courthouse Road, Maidenhead, Berks SL6 6JE
☎(01628) 685617

Cookham Library, High Road, Cookham Rise, Maidenhead, Berks SL6 9JF
☎(01626) 526147

Cox Green Library, Highfield Lane, Cox Green, Maidenhead, Berks SL6 3AX
☎(01628) 673942

Datchet Library, Village Hall, Horton Road, Datchet, Berks SL3 9HR
☎(01753) 545310

Dedworth Library, Dedworth County School, Smith's Lane, Windsor, Berks SL4 5PE
☎(01753) 868733

Eton Library, 136 High Street, Eton, Berks SL4 6LT
☎(01753) 860506

Eton Wick Library, Village Hall, Eton Wick, Berks SL4 6LT
☎(01753) 857933

Old Windsor Library, Memorial Hall, Straight Road, Windsor, Berks SL4 2JL
☎(01753) 852098

Sunninghill Library, Reading Room, School Road, Sunninghill, Berks SL5 7AD
☎(01344) 621493

Windsor Library, Bachelors Acre, Windsor, Berks SL4 1ER
☎(01753) 743940

Container Library operating at five sites. Contact number (01628 796555):
Holyport
Shifford Crescent
Sunningdale
Woodlands Park
Wraysbury

Mobile and Home Library Service operating through one vehicle (01628 796314)

WIRRAL

Authority: Metropolitan Borough of Wirral
Transformation and Resources Department, Municipal Building, Birkenhead, Wirral, Cheshire CH41 6BU
☎0151 666 4717
url: www.wirral-libraries.net
Library Services Manager Mrs Julie Barkway BA DipLib MCLIP (e-mail:
julie.barkway@wirral.gov.uk)
Principal Librarian Peter Aspinall BA DipLib MCLIP

Central/largest library

Birkenhead Central Library, Borough Road, Birkenhead, Wirral, Cheshire CH41 2XB
☎0151 652 6106 (enquiries), 0151 653 4700 (administration)
Fax 0151 653 7320
e-mail: co-ord@wirral.libraries.net

Regional/district libraries

Bebington Central Library, Civic Way, Bebington, Wirral, Cheshire CH63 7PN
☎0151 643 7217
Fax 0151 643 7231
e-mail: bebington@wirral-library.net
Strategic Area Librarian Ms Claire Oxley

Wallasey Central Library, Earlston Road, Wallasey, Wirral, Cheshire CH45 5DX
☎0151 639 2334
Fax 0151 691 2040
e-mail: wallasey@wirral-library.net
Strategic Librarian Ms Elaine Wilson

West Kirby Library, The Concourse, West Kirby, Wirral, Cheshire CH48 4HX
☎0151 929 7808
Fax 0151 625 2558
e-mail: west.kirby@wirral-library.net
Strategic Librarian Ms Laura Pringle

WOKINGHAM

Authority: Wokingham Borough Council
Libraries and Lifelong Learning, Wokingham Library, Denmark Street, Wokingham, Berks RG40 2BB
☎0118 978 1368

Fax 0118 929 1214
e-mail: libraries@wokingham.gov.uk
url: www.wokingham.gov.uk/libraries
Libraries Manager Richard Alexander (0118 974 6278; e-mail:
richard.alexander@wokingham.gov.uk)
Reader Development Officer, Young People and Families Ms Elizabeth McDonald
(e-mail: elizabeth.mcdonald@wokingham.gov.uk)
Reader Development Officer, Adults Ms Heather Dyson (e-mail:
heather.dyson@wokingham.gov.uk)
Branch Supervisor Ms Gill Cheale

WOLVERHAMPTON

Authority: Wolverhampton City Council
**Community, Older People and Personalisation, Libraries and Information Services,
Central Library, Snow Hill, Wolverhampton WV1 3AX**
☎(01902) 552025 (enquiries and administration)
Fax (01902) 552024
e-mail: libraries@wolverhampton.gov.uk
url: www.wolverhampton.gov.uk/libraries
Acting City Librarian Robert Johnson BA(Hons) (01902 552186; e-mail:
robert.johnson@wolverhampton.gov.uk)

Branch Libraries (East)

Ashmore Park Library, Griffiths Drive, Wednesfield, Wolverhampton WV11 2JW
☎(01902) 556296
e-mail: libraries@wolverhampton.gov.uk

Collingwood Community Library, Broadway Gardens, Bushbury, Wolverhampton WV10 8EA
☎(01902) 556302
e-mail: libraries@wolverhampton.gov.uk

East Park Library, Hurstbourne Crescent, Eastfield, Wolverhampton WV1 2EE
☎(01902) 556257
e-mail: libraries@wolverhampton.gov.uk

Long Knowle Library, Wood End Road, Wednesfield, Wolverhampton WV11 1YG
☎(01902) 556290
e-mail: libraries@wolverhampton.gov.uk

Low Hill Library, Showell Circus, Low Hill, Wolverhampton WV10 9JJ
☎(01902) 556293
e-mail: libraries@wolverhampton.gov.uk

Pendeford Library, Whitburn Close, Pendeford, Wolverhampton WV9 5NJ
☎(01902) 556250
e-mail: libraries@wolverhampton.gov.uk

Wednesfield Library, 2 Well Lane, Wednesfield, Wolverhampton WV11 1XT
☎(01902) 556278
e-mail: libraries@wolverhampton.gov.uk

Branch Libraries (West)

Bilston Library, Mount Pleasant, Bilston, Wolverhampton WV14 7LU
☎(01902) 556253
e-mail: libraries@wolverhampton.gov.uk

Finchfield Library, White Oak Drive, Finchfield, Wolverhampton WV3 9AF
☎(01902) 556260
e-mail: libraries@wolverhampton.gov.uk

Penn Library, Coalway Avenue, Penn, Wolverhampton WV3 7LT
☎(01902) 556281
e-mail: libraries@wolverhampton.gov.uk

Spring Vale Library, Bevan Avenue, Wolverhampton WV4 6SG
☎(01902) 556284
e-mail: libraries@wolverhampton.gov.uk

Tettenhall Library, Upper Street, Tettenhall, Wolverhampton WV6 8QF
☎(01902) 556308
e-mail: libraries@wolverhampton.gov.uk

Warstones Library, Pinfold Grove, Warstone, Wolverhampton WV4 9PT
☎(01902) 556275
e-mail: libraries@wolverhampton.gov.uk

Whitmore Reans Library, Bargate Drive, Whitmore Reans, Wolverhampton WV6 0QW
☎(01902) 556269
e-mail: libraries@wolverhampton.gov.uk

WORCESTERSHIRE

Authority: Worcestershire County Council
Libraries and Learning, Culture and Community Services, County Hall, Spetchley Road, Worcester WR5 2NP
☎(01905) 822819
Fax (01905) 766899
e-mail: librarieshq@worcestershire.gov.uk
url: www.worcestershire.gov.uk/librariesandlearning
Strategic Libraries and Learning Manager Ms Kathy Kirk (e-mail: kkirk@worcestershire.gov.uk)
Change and Improvement Manager Ms Carol Brown (01905 766232; e-mail: cbrown@worcestershire.gov.uk)
Quality and Systems Manager Steve Mobley (01905 766940; e-mail: smobley@worcestershire.gov.uk)
Adult Learning Manager Colin Barnett (01905 766264; e-mail: cbarnett@worcestershire.gov.uk)
Literacy and Reading Manager Mrs Ruth Foster BA MCLIP MCMI (01905 427428; e-mail: rfoster@worcestershire.gov.uk)
Outreach and Mobile Services Manager Ms Nicki Hitchcock BA DipILS MCLIP (e-mail: nhitchcock1@worcestershire.gov.uk)

Countywide Information Service (Intranet and Website), Information and Business Systems Division, County Hall, Spetchley Road, Worcester WR5 2NP

☎(01905) 766927
url: www.worcestershire.gov.uk
Digital Delivery Team Manager Ms Jo Hilditch (e-mail: jhilditch@worcestershire.gov.uk)

Main libraries

Bromsgrove Library, Stratford Road, Bromsgrove, Worcs B60 1AP
☎(01905) 822722
Fax (01572) 765025
e-mail: bromsgrovelib@worcestershire.gov.uk
Bromsgrove Library Managers Ms Abigail Williams, Ms Janine Payne

Droitwich Library, Victoria Square, Droitwich, Worcs WR9 8DQ
☎(01905) 822722
Fax (01905) 797401
e-mail: droitwichlib@worcestershire.gov.uk
Droitwich Library Manager Ms Jacqueline Passey

Evesham Library, Oat Street, Evesham, Worcs WR11 4JP
☎(01905) 822722
Fax (01386) 765855
e-mail: eveshamlib@worcestershire.gov.uk
Evesham Library Manager Ms Beverley Orlowsky

Kidderminster Library, Market Street, Kidderminster, Worcs DY10 1PE
☎(01905) 822722
Fax (01562) 512907
e-mail: kidderminsterlib@worcestershire.gov.uk
Kidderminster Library Manager Ms Caroline Faulkner

Malvern Library, Graham Road, Malvern, Worcs WR14 2HU
☎(01905) 822722
Fax (01684) 892999
e-mail: malvernlib@worcestershire.gov.uk
Malvern Library Manager Ms Delphine Telfer

Redditch Library, 15 Market Place, Redditch, Worcs B98 8AR
☎(01905) 822722
Fax (01527) 68571
e-mail: redditchlib@worcestershire.gov.uk
Redditch Library Manager Ms Jodie Ford

The Hive, Sawmill Walk, The Butts, Worcester WR1 2PB
☎(01905) 822866
e-mail: worcesterlib@worcesteshire.gov.uk
Hive Library Services Manager Ms Janine Downes
(Note: Joint academic/public library of the University of Worcester and Worcestershire
County Council)

YORK

Authority: City of York Council (Explore York Libraries and Archive Mutual Limited)
Public Library and Archive Service, West Offices, 6 Station Rose, York YO1 6GA
☎(01904) 552828

e-mail: york@exploreyork.org.uk
url: www.exploreyork.org.uk
Chief Executive Ms Fiona Williams BA(Hons) DipLib MCLIP (e-mail:
fiona.williams@exploreyork.org.uk)

Central/largest library

Explore York Library Learning Centre, Museum Street, York YO1 7DS
☎(01904) 552828
e-mail: york@exploreyork.org.uk
url: www.exploreyork.org.uk
Explore Leaders Team Ms Janet Edge, Ms Gillian Holmes BSc PGDip (e-mail:
gillian.holmes@sruc.ac.uk), Andrew Stanton, Ms Allison Freeman

NORTHERN IRELAND

LIBRARIES NI (NORTHERN IRELAND LIBRARY AUTHORITY)

Authority: Libraries NI (Northern Ireland Library Authority)
Libraries NI, Business Support, 2nd Floor Portadown Library, 24–26 Church Street, Portadown, Co Armagh BT62 3LQ
☎(028) 3752 0738
e-mail: enquiries@librariesni.org.uk
url: www.librariesni.org.uk
Chief Executive Ms Irene Knox BA(Hons) MBA DipLib (e-mail: irene.knox@librariesni.org.uk)
Director of Library Services Ms Helen Osborn MLib MCLIP (e-mail: helen.osborn@librariesni.org.uk)
Director of Business Support Terry Heron BSc(Econ) HonsFCA (e-mail: terry.heron@librariesni.org.uk)

SCOTLAND

ABERDEEN

Authority: Aberdeen City Council
Aberdeen City Library and Information Services, Central Library, Rosemount Viaduct, Aberdeen AB25 1GW
☎(01224) 652500 (enquiries and administration)
Fax (01224) 641985
e-mail: CentralLibrary@aberdeencity.gov.uk
url: www.aberdeencity.gov.uk/libraries
Library and Information Services Manager Mrs Fiona Clark BA MCLIP (e-mail: fclark@aberdeencity.gov.uk)
Library Operations Manager John Grant BA MCLIP (01224 652521; e-mail: Jogrant@aberdeencity.gov.uk)
Service Development Manager Ms Susan Bell BA MCLIP (01224 652533; e-mail: sbell@aberdeencity.gov.uk)
Learning Development Manager Ms Helen Adair BA(Hons) MCLIP (e-mail: HAdair@aberdeencity.gov.uk)

ABERDEENSHIRE

Authority: Aberdeenshire Council
Libraries, Meldrum Meg Way, Oldmeldrum, Aberdeenshire AB51 0GN
☎(01651) 872707 (enquiries and administration)
Fax (01651) 872142
e-mail: libraries@aberdeenshire.gov.uk
url: www.aberdeenshire.gov.uk/libraries
Principal Libraries Officer Ms Sharon Jamieson BA(Hons) MSc DipLIS MCLIP (01651 871210; e-mail: sharon.jamieson@aberdeenshire.gov.uk)
Cultural Service Team Leader Ms Geraldine Downie BA MCLIP (e-mail: geraldine.downie@aberdeenshire.gov.uk)
Senior Librarians Ms Sue Cromar BA DipLib MCLIP (01651 871226; e-mail: sue.cromar@aberdeenshire.gov.uk), Mrs Fiona Gillies BA MCLIP (01651 871205; e-mail: fiona.gillies@aberdeenshire.gov.uk)

ANGUS

Authority: Angus Council
Services to Communities, The Yard, Queenswell Road, Forfar, Angus DD8 3JA
☎(01307) 475368
e-mail: communities@angus.gov.uk
url: www.angus.gov.uk
Interim Head of Services to Communities Alastair Wilson
Libraries Manager Ms Fiona Dakers BA DipIM MCLIP

Central/largest library

Library Support Services, 50 West High Street, Forfar, Angus DD8 1BA
☎(01307) 476477
e-mail: librarysupport.services@angus.gov.uk
Support Services Librarian Ms Vicky Fraser BA MCLIP

Area libraries

Arbroath Library, Hill Terrace, Arbroath, Angus DD11 1AH
☎(01241) 435605
e-mail: arbroath.library@angus.gov.uk
Librarian Henry Logan BA DipLib MCLIP

Brechin Library, 10 St Ninian's Square, Brechin, Angus DD9 7AA
☎(01356) 622687
e-mail: brechin.library@angus.gov.uk
Librarian Ms Christine Sharp BA MCLIP

Carnoustie Library, 21 High Street, Carnoustie, Angus DD7 6AN
☎(01241) 859620
e-mail: carnoustie.library@angus.gov.uk
Librarian Ms Hazel Cook BA MCLIP

Forfar Library, 50-56 West High Street, Forfar, Angus DD8 1BA
☎(01307) 476476
e-mail: forfar.library@angus.gov.uk
Librarian Gavin Hunter MA MCLIP

Kirriemuir Library, Town Hall, 28/30 Reform Street, Kirriemuir, Angus DD8 4BS
☎(01575) 577109
e-mail: kirriemuir.library@angus.gov.uk
Librarian Gavin Hunter MA MCLIP

Monifieth Library, High Street, Monifieth, Angus DD5 4AE
☎(01382) 533819
e-mail: monifieth.library@angus.gov.uk
Librarian Ms Hazel Cook BA MCLIP

Montrose Library, 214 High Street, Montrose, Angus DD10 8PH
☎(01674) 673256
e-mail: montrose.library@angus.gov.uk
Librarian Ms Christine Sharp BA MCLIP

ARGYLL AND BUTE

Authority: Argyll and Bute Council
Library and Information Service HQ, Highland Avenue, Sandbank, Dunoon, Argyll PA23 8QZ
☎(01369) 708664
Fax (01369) 705797
e-mail: libraryhq@argyll-bute.gov.uk
url: www.argyll-bute.gov.uk
Culture and Libraries Manager Patrick McCann BA MCLIP (e-mail:
pat.mccann@argyll-bute.gov.uk)

Library Operations Manager Ms Katherine MacLeod (01436 658808)
Culture and Library Development Officer Kevin Baker BA DipLib MCLIP (01631 567978)
Information and Local Studies Librarian Ms Eleanor McKay (01369 708663)
Reader Services Librarian Ms Pauline Flynn BA MCLIP (01369 708691)

Area libraries

Campbeltown Library, Aqualibrium, Kinloch Road, Campbeltown, Argyll PA28 6EG
☎(01586) 555435
Fax (01586) 555438
Library Supervisor Ms Barbara Mansell

Dunoon Library, 248 Argyll Street, Dunoon, Argyll PA23 7LT
☎(01369) 708682
Fax (01369) 701323
Library Supervisor Ms Pamela Horton

Helensburgh Library, West King Street, Helensburgh, Dunbartonshire G84 8EB
☎(01436) 658833
Fax (01436) 679567
Library Supervisor Ms Fiona Sharkey

Oban Library, 77 Albany Street, Oban, Argyll PA34 4AL
☎(01631) 571444
Fax (01631) 571372
Library Supervisor Ms Suzanne Nicholson

Rothesay Library, Moat Centre, Stuart Street, Rothesay, Bute PA20 0BX
☎(01700) 503266
Fax (01700) 500511
Library Supervisor Ms Patricia McArthur

CLACKMANNANSHIRE

Authority: Clackmannanshire Council
Clackmannanshire Libraries, Alloa Library, Room 9, Lime Tree House, North Castle Street, Alloa, Clackmannanshire FK10 1EX
☎(01259) 452262
Fax (01259) 216349
e-mail: libraries@clacks.gov.uk
url: www.clacksweb.org.uk/dyna/library
Team Leader, Library Service Ms Tracy Docherty MCLIP
Librarians Ian Keane, Ms Caroline Gunn
Information Librarian and Archivist Vacant

Branches within community access points

Alva Community Access Point, 153 West Stirling Street, Alva, Clackmannanshire FK12 2EL
☎(01259) 760652
Fax (01259) 760354

Clackmannan Community Access Point, Main Street, Clackmannan FK10 4JA
☎(01259) 721579

Fax (01259) 212493
Senior Community Access Officer Ms J Laird (e-mail: jlaird@clacks.gov.uk)

Dollar Community Access Point, Dollar Civic Centre, Park Place, Dollar, Clackmannanshire
FK14 7AA
☎(01259) 743253
Fax (01259) 743328

Menstrie Community Access Point, The Dumyat Leisure Centre, Main Street East,
Menstrie, Clackmannanshire FK11 7BJ
☎(01259) 769439
Fax (01259) 762941

Sauchie Community Access Point, 42-48 Main Street, Sauchie, Clackmannanshire FL10 3JY
☎(01259) 721679
Fax (01259) 218750
Senior Community Access Officer Mrs Kate Waddell (e-mail: kwaddell@clacks.gov.uk)

Tillicoultry Branch Library, Ben Cleuch Centre, Park Street, Tillicoultry, Clackmannanshire
FK13 6AG
☎(01259) 452202 (tel/fax)

Tullibody Library, Leisure Centre, Abercromby Place, Tullibody, Clackmannanshire FK10 2RS
☎(01259) 218725

COMHAIRLE NAN EILEAN SIAR

Authority: Comhairle nan Eilean Siar
Public Library, 19 Cromwell Street, Stornoway, Isle of Lewis, Hebrides HS1 2DA
☎(01851) 822744
Fax (01851) 704188
e-mail: library.enquiries@cne-siar.gov.uk
url: www.cne-siar.gov.uk
Principal Officer, Cultural and Information Services Ms Trish Botten BA(Hons)
(e-mail: trish.botten@cne-siar.gov.uk)
Team Leader, Youth Services Ms Kathleen Milne BSocSci PGDipLIS MA MCLIP

Area libraries
Castlebay Community Library, Castlebay Community School, Castlebay, Isle of Barra,
Hebrides HS9 5XD
☎(01871) 817200
Fax (01871) 810125
e-mail: castlebaylibrary@gnes.net
Senior Library Assistant Mrs Linda Mackinnon

Daliburgh Community Library, Daliburgh School, Daliburgh, Isle of South Uist, Hebrides
HS8 5SS
☎(01878) 700882 (Library), (01878) 700276 (School)
Library Assistant Mrs Joan Macinnes

Lionacleit Community Library, Sgoil Lionacleit, Liniclate, Isle of Benbecula, Hebrides HS7 5PJ
☎(01870) 603691 (tel/fax)

e-mail: lionacleitlibrary@gnes.net
Community Librarian Vacant

Shawbost Community Library, Sgoil Shiaboist, Shawbost, Isle of Lewis, Hebrides HS2 9BQ
☎(01851) 822880
e-mail: shawlib@gnes.net
Library Assistant Mrs Catherine Campbell

Tarbert Community Library, Sir E Scott School, Tarbert, Isle of Harris, Hebrides HS3 3BG
☎(01859) 502971
e-mail: fmmorrison1b@gnes.net
Library Assistant Mrs Fiona Morrison MA MCLIP (e-mail: fmmorrison1b@gnes.net)

DUMFRIES AND GALLOWAY

Authority: Dumfries and Galloway Council
Libraries, Information and Archives, Central Support Unit, Catherine Street, Dumfries DG1 1JB
☎(01387) 253820 (enquiries), 01387 252070 (administration)
Fax (01387) 260294
e-mail: yourlibrary@dumgal.gov.uk
url: www.dumgal.gov.uk
Service Manager Ms C Freeman
Library Support Officer Ms A Rinaldi BA(Hons) PGDip MSc MCLIP

District libraries

Annan Library, Charles Street, Annan, Dumfries and Galloway DG12 5AG
☎(01461) 202809 (tel/fax)

Archive Centre, Ewart Library, Catherine Street, Dumfries DG1 1JB
☎(01387) 253820
Fax (01387) 260294
e-mail: libarchive@dumgal.gov.uk

Castle Douglas Library, Market Hill, King Street, Castle Douglas, Dumfries and Galloway DG7 1AE
☎(01556) 502643 (tel/fax)

Dalbeattie Library, 23 High Street, Dalbeattie, Dumfries and Galloway DG5 4AD
☎(01556) 610898 (tel/fax)

Dalry Library, Main Street, Dalry, Castle Douglas, Dumfries and Galloway DG7 3UP
☎(01644) 430234 (tel/fax)

Eastriggs Library, Eastriggs Community School, Eastriggs, Annan, Dumfries and Galloway DG12 6PZ
☎(01461) 40844 (tel/fax)

Ewart Library, Catherine Street, Dumfries DG1 1JB
☎(01387) 253820
Fax (01387) 260294

Gatehouse Library, 63 High Street, Gatehouse of Fleet, Dumfries and Galloway DG7 2HS
☎(01557) 814646 (tel/fax)

Georgetown Library, Gillbrae Road, Georgetown, Dumfries DG1 4EJ
☎(01387) 256059 (tel/fax)

Gretna Library, Central Avenue, Gretna, Dumfries and Galloway DG16 5AQ
☎(01461) 338000 (tel/fax)

Kirkconnel Library, Greystone Avenue, Kelloholm, Dumfries and Galloway DG4 6RA
☎(01659) 67191 (tel/fax)

Kirkcudbright Library, Sheriff Court House, High Street, Kirkcudbright, Dumfries and
Galloway DG6 4JW
☎(01557) 331240 (tel/fax)

Langholm Library, Charles Street, Old Langholm, Dumfries and Galloway DG13 0AA
☎(01387) 380040 (tel/fax)

Lochmaben Library, Town Hall, High Street, Lochmaben, Lockerbie, Dumfries and
Galloway DG11 1NQ
☎(01387) 811865 (tel/fax)

Lochside Library, Lochside Road, Dumfries DG2 0LW
☎(01387) 268751 (tel/fax)

Lochthorn Library, Lochthorn, Dumfries DG1 1UF
☎(01387) 265780
Fax (01387) 266424

Lockerbie Library, 31–33 High Street, Lockerbie, Dumfries and Galloway DG11 2JL
☎(01576) 203380 (tel/fax)

Moffat Library, Town Hall, High Street, Moffat, Dumfries and Galloway DG10 9HF
☎(01683) 220952 (tel/fax)

Newton Stewart Library, Chuch Street, Newton Stewart, Dumfries and Galloway DG8 6ER
☎(01671) 403450 (tel/fax)

Port William Library, Church Street, Port William, Newton Stewart, Dumfries and
Galloway DG8 9QJ
☎(01988) 700406 (tel/fax)

Sanquhar Library, 106 High Street, Sanquhar, Dumfries and Galloway DG4 6DZ
☎(01659) 50626 (tel/fax)

Stranraer Library, North Strand Street, Stranraer, Dumfries and Galloway DG9 7LD
☎(01776) 707400
Fax (01776) 703565

Thornhill Library, Townhead Street, Thornhill, Dumfries and Galloway DG3 5NW
☎(01848) 330654 (tel/fax)

Whithorn Library, St John's Street, Whithorn, Dumfries and Galloway DG8 8PF
☎(01988) 500406 (tel/fax)

Wigtown Library, County Buildings, Wigtown, Dumfries and Galloway DG8 9JH
☎(01988) 403329 (tel/fax)

DUNDEE

Authority: Leisure and Culture Dundee
Head Office, Central Library, The Wellgate, Dundee DD1 1DB
☎(01382) 307462
Fax (01382) 307487
url: www.leisureandculturedundee.com
Managing Director of Leisure and Culture Dundee Stewart Murdoch MSc DPSE
DipYCW (e-mail: stewart.murdoch@leisureandculturedundee.com)
Library and Information Services Manager Mrs Judy Dobbie MA MCLIP (e-mail:
judy.dobbie@leisureandculturedundee.com)

Central/largest library

Central Library, The Wellgate, Dundee DD1 1DB
☎(01382) 431500 (enquiries), (01382) 431501 (administration)
Fax (01382) 431558
url: www.leisureandculturedundee.com
Adult Library and Information Services Section Leader Ms Shona Donaldson
BA(Hons) MCLIP (01382 451533; e-mail: shona.donaldson@leisureandculturedundee.com)
Library Performance and Resources Section Leader Ms Jayne Gair BA MCLIP (01382
431563; e-mail: jayne.gair@leisureandculturedundee.com)
Children's Library and Information Services Section Leader Ms Fiona Macpherson
MA MCLIP (01382 431549; e-mail: fiona.macpherson@leisureandculturedundee.com)
Information Services Section Leader Vacant
Senior Library and Information Officer (Schools) Ms Elaine Hallyburton MA(Hons)
DipLib (01382 431546; e-mail: elaine.hallyburton@leisureandculturedundee.com)
Senior Library and Information Officer (Staffing) Mrs Frances Scott BA MCLIP
(01382 431542; e-mail: frances.scott@leisureandculturedundee.com)
Senior Library and Information Officer (Stock Management) Vacant

Community libraries

Ardler Community Library, Ardler Complex, Turnberry Avenue, Ardler, Dundee DD2 3TP
☎(01382) 436366
Fax (01382) 436446
e-mail: ardler.library@leisureandculturedundee.com
Library and Information Worker Mrs Ann Smith

Arthurstone Community Library, Arthurstone Terrace, Dundee DD4 6RT
☎(01382) 438882
Fax (01382) 438886
e-mail: arthurstone.library@leisureandculturedundee.com
Library and Information Worker Vacant

Blackness Community Library, 225 Perth Road, Dundee DD2 1EJ
☎(01382) 435936
Fax (01382) 435942
e-mail: blackness.library@leisureandculturedundee.com
Library and Information Worker Ms Lorraine Andrews

Broughty Ferry Community Library, Queen Street, Broughty Ferry, Dundee DD5 2HN
☎(01382) 436919

Fax (01382) 436913
e-mail: broughty.library@leisureandculturedundee.com
Library and Information Officer Mrs Sandra Westgate
Library and Information Worker Mrs Lorraine Kell

Charleston Community Library, 60 Craigowan Road, Dundee DD2 4NL
☎(01382) 436639
Fax (01382) 436640
e-mail: charleston.library@leisureandculturedundee.com
Library and Community Centre Officer Ms Ailsa Caldwell

Coldside Community Library, 150 Strathmartine Road, Dundee DD3 7SE
☎(01382) 432849
Fax (01382) 432850
e-mail: coldside.library@leisureandculturedundee.com
Library and Information Officer Ms Susan Ferguson

Douglas Community Library, Balmoral Place, Douglas, Dundee DD4 8SH
☎(01382) 436915
Fax (01382) 436922
e-mail: douglas.library@leisureandculturedundee.com
Library and Information Officer Ms Barbara Cook

Fintry Community Library, Finmill Centre, Findcastle Street, Dundee DD4 9EW
☎(01382) 432560
Fax (01382) 432559
e-mail: fintry.library@leisureandculturedundee.com
Library and Information Officer Mrs Ruth McDowall

Hub Community Library and Learning Centre, Pitkerro Road, Dundee DD4 8ES
☎(01382) 438648
Fax (01382) 438627
e-mail: hub.library@leisureandculturedundee.com
Library and Information Officer Ms Barbara Cook

Kirkton Community Library, Derwent Avenue, Dundee DD3 0BW
☎(01382) 436326
Fax (01382) 436321
e-mail: kirkton.library@leisureandculturedundee.com
Library and Information Worker Mrs Ann Smith

Lochee Community Library, High Street, Lochee, Dundee DD2 3AU
☎(01382) 431835
Fax (01382) 431837
e-mail: lochee.library@leisureandculturedundee.com
Library and Information Worker Mrs Joan Rodger

Menzieshill Community Library, Orleans Place, Menzieshill, Dundee DD2 4BH
☎(01382) 432945
Fax (01382) 432948
e-mail: menzieshill.library@leisureandculturedundee.com
Library and Information Worker Mrs Lesley Agnew

Whitfield Community Library, The Crescent, 71 Lothian Crescent, Dundee DD4 0HU

☎(01382) 432561
Fax (01382) 432562
e-mail: whitfield.library@leisureandculturedundee.com
Library and Information Officer Mrs Ruth McDowall

EAST AYRSHIRE

Authority: East Ayrshire Leisure
East Ayrshire Leisure, Dick Institute, 14 Elmbank Avenue, Kilmarnock, Ayrshire KA1 3BU
☎(01563) 554300 (general enquiries)
Fax (01563) 554311
e-mail: libraries@east-ayrshire.gov.uk
url: www.eastayrshire.com
Digital and Information Officer Mrs Julia A Harvey MA(Hons) DipLib MCLIP (e-mail: julia.harvey@east-ayrshire.gov.uk)
Community Librarian Mrs Lynn Mee BA(Hons) MCLIP (e-mail: lynn.mee@east-ayrshire.gov.uk)
Library Programme Officer Mrs Margaret Patterson BA MCLIP (e-mail: margaret.patterson@east-ayrshire.gov.uk)

EAST DUNBARTONSHIRE

Authority: East Dunbartonshire Leisure & Culture Trust
East Dunbartonshire Libraries, EDLC-HQ, William Patrick Library, 2–4 West High Street, Kirkintilloch, East Dunbartonshire G66 1AD
☎0141 777 3143
Fax 0141 777 3040
e-mail: libraries@eastdunbarton.gov.uk
url: www.edlc.co.uk
General Manager Mark Grant (e-mail: mark.grant@eastdunbarton.gov.uk)

Central/largest library

William Patrick Library, 2-4 West High Street, Kirkintilloch, East Dunbartonshire G66 1AD
☎0141 777 3141/3142
Fax 0141 777 3140
e-mail: wpl@eastdunbarton.gov.uk
Team Leaders Ms Joan Hill (e-mail: joan.hill@eastdunbarton.gov.uk), Ms Maureen Fraser (e-mail: maureen.fraser@eastdunbarton.gov.uk) (William Patrick Team Leaders are also responsible for Craighead Library)

Community libraries

Bishopbriggs Library, 170 Kirkintilloch Road, Bishopbriggs, East Dunbartonshire G64 2LX
☎0141 772 4513
Fax 0141 762 5363
e-mail: bishopbriggs@eastdunbarton.gov.uk
Team Leaders Ms Brenda Gardiner (e-mail: brenda.gardiner@eastdunbarton.gov.uk), Ms Margaret Shearer (e-mail: margaret.shearer@eastdunbarton.gov.uk), Ms Naomi Niven (e-mail: naomi.niven@eastdunbarton.gov.uk) (job share) (Bishopbriggs Team Leaders are also responsible for Lenzie Library)

Brookwood Library, 166 Drymen Road, Bearsden, Glasgow G61 3RJ
☎0141 777 3021
Fax 0141 777 3022
e-mail: brookwood@eastdunbarton.gov.uk
Team Leaders Peter Brannan (e-mail: peter.brannan@eastdunbarton.gov.uk),
Ms Elizabeth Murray (e-mail: elizabeth.murray@eastdunbarton.gov.uk) (Brookwood
Library Team Leaders are also responsible for Westerton Library)

Craighead Library, Craighead Road, Milton of Campsie, East Dunbartonshire G66 8DL
☎(01360) 311925
e-mail: craighead@eastdunbarton.gov.uk
Team Leaders Ms Joan Hill (e-mail: joan.hill@eastdunbarton.gov.uk), Ms Maureen Fraser
(e-mail: maureen.fraser@eastdunbarton.gov.uk)

Lennoxtown Library, Main Street, Lennoxtown, East Dunbartonshire G66 7DG
☎(01360) 311436 (tel/fax)
e-mail: lennoxtown@eastdunbarton.gov.uk

Lenzie Library, 13 Alexandra Avenue, Lenzie, East Dunbartonshire G66 5BG
☎0141 776 3021
e-mail: lenzie@eastdunbarton.gov.uk

Milngavie Library, Allander Way, Milngavie, Glasgow G62 8PN
☎0141 956 2776 (tel/fax)
e-mail: milngavie@eastdunbarton.gov.uk
Team Leaders Ms Brenda Paton (e-mail: brenda.paton@eastdunbarton.gov.uk), Ms Tricia
Carr (e-mail: tricia.carr@eastdunbarton.gov.uk) (Milngavie Team Leaders are also
responsible for Lennoxtown Library)

Westerton Library, 82 Maxwell Avenue, Bearsden, Glasgow G61 1NZ
☎0141 943 0780 (tel/fax)
e-mail: westerton@eastdunbarton.gov.uk

EAST LOTHIAN

Authority: East Lothian Council
Library and Museum Headquarters, Dunbar Road, Haddington, East Lothian EH41 3PJ
☎(01620) 820605 (enquiries), (01620) 820600 (administration)
Fax (01620) 828201
e-mail: libraries@eastlothian.gov.uk (for general enquiries)
url: www.eastlothian.gov.uk
Service Manager - Customer Services Ms Eileen Morrison
Senior Librarian - Adult Services Mrs Donna Duff BA(Hons) MCLIP
Senior Librarian - Young People's Services Ms Agnès Guyon MSc MCLIP
Area Librarian (East) Mrs Trina Gavan MCLIP
Area Librarian (West) Mrs Dorothy Elliott MA DipLib

Largest library

Haddington Library, The John Gray Centre, Lodge Street, Haddington, East Lothian
EH41 3DX
☎(01620) 820680
e-mail: haddington.library@eastlothian.gov.uk
Assistant i/c Mrs Claire Johnston

Branch libraries

Dunbar Library, Bleachingfield Centre, Dunbar, East Lothian EH42 1DX
☎(01368) 866060
e-mail: dunbar.library@eastlothian.gov.uk
Assistant i/c Mrs Anne Hampshire

East Linton Library, 60A High Street, East Linton, East Lothian EH40 3BX
☎(01620) 820635
e-mail: eastlinton.library@eastlothian.gov.uk
Assistant i/c Mrs Carol Hastie

Gullane Library, East Links Road, Gullane, East Lothian EH31 2AF
☎(01620) 820645
e-mail: gullane.library@eastlothian.gov.uk
Assistant i/c Mrs Avril Sutherland

Longniddry Library, Church Way, Longniddry, East Lothian EH32 0LW
☎(01875) 818160
e-mail: longniddry.library@eastlothian.gov.uk
Assistant i/c Ms Ann Sturgeon

Musselburgh Library, 10 Bridge Street, Musselburgh, East Lothian EH21 6AG
☎0131 653 5130
e-mail: musselburgh.library@eastlothian.gov.uk
Branch Librarian Mrs Caroline Messer BA(Hons) MSc

North Berwick Library, The Old School, School Road, North Berwick, East Lothian
EH39 4JU
☎(01620) 820700
e-mail: northberwick.library@eastlothian.gov.uk
Assistant i/c Ms Dionne Howie

Ormiston Library, 5A Meadowbank, Ormiston, East Lothian EH35 5LQ
☎(01875) 616675
e-mail: ormiston.library@eastlothian.gov.uk

Port Seton Library, Community Centre, South Seton Park, Port Seton, East Lothian
EH32 0BG
☎(01875) 818170
e-mail: portseton.library@eastlothian.gov.uk
Assistant i/c Mrs Irene Muir

Prestonpans Library, West Loan, Prestonpans, East Lothian EH32 9NX
☎(01875) 818150
e-mail: prestonpans.library@eastlothian.gov.uk

Tranent Library, The George Johnstone Centre, 35 Winton Place, Tranent, East Lothian
EH33 1AE
☎(01875) 824150
e-mail: tranent.library@eastlothian.gov.uk

Wallyford Library, 3 Fa'side Buildings, Wallyford, East Lothian EH21 8BA
☎0131 653 5140
e-mail: wallyford.library@eastlothian.gov.uk
Assistant i/c Ms Wilma Porteous

EAST RENFREWSHIRE

Authority: East Renfrewshire Council
Library and Information Services, Education Department, 2II Main Street, Barrhead, East Renfrewshire G78 ISY
☎0141 577 3500 (enquiries)
Fax 0141 577 3501
url: www.eastrenfrewshire.gov.uk/libraries
Head of Education Services (Culture, Sport and Continuing Education) Ken McKinlay MA(Hons) PGDipLib MCLIP (0141 577 3103; e-mail: ken.mckinlay@eastrenfrewshire.gov.uk)
Cultural Strategy and Development Manager Ms Claire Scott (0141 577 3531; e-mail: claire.scott@eastrenfrewshire.gov.uk)
Learning Services Manager Ms Janice Weir BA MCLIP (0141 577 3516; e-mail: janice.weir@eastrenfrewshire.gov.uk)
Projects and Systems Manager Scott Simpson BA PGDipIT MCLIP (0141 577 3509; e-mail: scott.simpson@eastrenfrewshire.gov.uk)

Community libraries

Barrhead Community Library, 14 Lowndes Street, Barrhead, East Renfrewshire G78 IFA
☎0141 577 3518
e-mail: barrhead.library@eastrenfrewshire.gov.uk

Busby Community Library, Duff Memorial Hall, Main Street, Busby, East Renfrewshire G76 8DX
☎0141 577 4971
Fax 0141 577 3768
e-mail: busby.library@eastrenfrewshire.gov.uk

Clarkston Community Library, Clarkston Road, Clarkston, East Renfrewshire G76 8NE
☎0141 577 4972
e-mail: clarkston.library@eastrenfrewshire.gov.uk

Eaglesham Community Library, Montgomerie Hall, Eaglesham, East Renfrewshire G76 0LH
☎0141 577 3932
e-mail: eaglesham.library@eastrenfrewshire.gov.uk

Giffnock Community Library, Station Road, Giffnock, East Renfrewshire G46 6JF
☎0141 577 4976
e-mail: giffnock.library@eastrenfrewshire.gov.uk

Mearns Community Library, MacKinlay Place, Newton Mearns, East Renfrewshire G77 6EZ
☎0141 577 4979
e-mail: mearns.library@eastrenfrewshire.gov.uk

Neilston Community Library, Main Street, Neilston, East Renfrewshire G78 3NN
☎0141 577 4981
Fax 0141 577 4982
e-mail: neilston.library@eastrenfrewshire.gov.uk

Netherlee Community Library, Netherlee Pavilion, Linn Park Avenue, East Renfrewshire G44 3PG
☎0141 637 5102
e-mail: netherlee.library@eastrenfrewshire.gov.uk

Thornliebank Community Library, 1 Spiersbridge Road, Thornliebank, East Renfrewshire G46 7SJ
☎0141 577 4983
Fax 0141 577 4816
e-mail: thornliebank.library@eastrenfrewshire.gov.uk

Uplawmoor Community Library, Mure Hall, Tannoch Road, Uplawmoor, East Renfrewshire G78 4AD
☎(01505) 850564
e-mail: uplawmoor.library@eastrenfrewshire.gov.uk

EDINBURGH

Authority: City of Edinburgh Council
Headquarters, C2 Waverley Court, Level C3, 4 East Market Street, Edinburgh EH8 8BG
☎0131 529 7894
e-mail: eclis@edinburgh.gov.uk
url: http://yourlibrary.edinburgh.gov.uk
Head of Libraries and Information Services Ms M McChrystal BLib MCLIP (e-mail: martina.mcchyrstal@edinburgh.gov.uk)
Business Development Manager Ms Sarah Forteath (0131 529 3961; e-mail: sarah.forteath@edinburgh.gov.uk)
Information and Digital Services Manager Jim Thompson (0131 529 7790; e-mail: jim.thompson@edinburgh.gov.uk)
Customer Services Manager Paul McCloskey (0131 529 6156; e-mail: paul.mccloskey@edinburgh.gov.uk)

Central/largest library
Central Library, George IV Bridge, Edinburgh EH1 1EG
Central Library and Information Services Managers Ms Karen O'Brien (e-mail: karen.obrien@edinburgh.gov.uk), Ms Fiona Myles (e-mail: fiona.myles@edinburgh.gov.uk)

Community libraries
Balerno Library, 1 Main Street, Balerno, Edinburgh EH14 7EQ
☎0131 529 5500
Fax 0131 529 5502

Balgreen Library, 173 Balgreen Road, Edinburgh EH11 3AT
☎0131 529 5585
Fax 0131 529 5583
e-mail: balgreen.library@edinburgh.gov.uk

Blackhall Library, 56 Hillhouse Road, Edinburgh EH4 5EG
☎0131 529 5595
Fax 0131 336 5419
e-mail: blackhall.library@edinburgh.gov.uk

Colinton Library, 14 Thorburn Road, Edinburgh EH13 0BQ
☎0131 529 5603
Fax 0131 529 5607
e-mail: colinton.library@edinburgh.gov.uk

Corstorphine Library, 12 Kirk Loan, Edinburgh EH12 7HD
☎0131 529 5506
Fax 0131 529 5508
e-mail: corstorphine.library@edinburgh.gov.uk

Craigmillar Library, 101 Niddrie Mains Road, Edinburgh EH16 4DS
☎0131 529 5597
Fax 0131 529 5601
e-mail: craigmillar.library@edinburgh.gov.uk

Currie Library, 210 Lanark Road, Edinburgh EH14 5NN
☎0131 529 5609
Fax 0131 529 5613
e-mail: currie.library@edinburgh.gov.uk

Drumbrae Library Hub, 81 Drum Brae Drive, Edinburgh EH4 7FE
☎0131 529 5244
e-mail: drumbrae.library@edinburgh.gov.uk

Fountainbridge Library, 137 Dundee Street, Edinburgh EH11 1BG
☎0131 529 5616
Fax 0131 529 5621
e-mail: fountainbridge.library@edinburgh.gov.uk

Gilmerton Library, 13 Newtoft Street, Edinburgh EH17 8RG
☎0131 529 5628
Fax 0131 529 5627
e-mail: gilmerton.library@edinburgh.gov.uk

Granton Library, Wardieburn Terrace, Edinburgh EH5 1DD
☎0131 529 5630
Fax 0131 529 5634
e-mail: granton.library@edinburgh.gov.uk

Kirkliston Library, 16 Station Road, Edinburgh EH29 9BE
☎0131 529 5510
Fax 0131 529 5514
e-mail: kirkliston.library@edinburgh.gov.uk

Leith Library, 28–30 Ferry Road, Edinburgh EH6 5AE
☎0131 529 5517
Fax 0131 554 2720
e-mail: leith.library@edinburgh.gov.uk

McDonald Road Library, 2 McDonald Road, Edinburgh EH7 4LU
☎0131 529 5652
Fax 0131 529 5646
e-mail: mcdonald.library@edinburgh.gov.uk

Moredun Library, 92 Moredun Park Road, Edinburgh EH17 7HL
☎0131 529 5652
Fax 0131 529 5651
e-mail: moredun.library@edinburgh.gov.uk

Morningside Library, 184 Morningside Road, Edinburgh EH10 4PU

☎0131 529 5654
Fax 0131 447 4685
e-mail: morningside.library@edinburgh.gov.uk

Muirhouse Library, 15 Pennywell Court, Edinburgh EH4 4TZ
☎0131 529 5528
Fax 0131 529 5532
e-mail: muirhouse.library@edinburgh.gov.uk

Newington Library, 17–21 Fountainhall Road, Edinburgh EH9 2LN
☎0131 529 5536
Fax 0131 667 5491
e-mail: newington.library@edinburgh.gov.uk

Oxgangs Library, 343 Oxgangs Road, Edinburgh EH13 9LY
☎0131 529 5549
Fax 0131 529 5554
e-mail: oxgangs.library@edinburgh.gov.uk

Piershill Library, 30 Piersfield Terrace, Edinburgh EH8 7BQ
☎0131 529 5685
Fax 0131 529 5691
e-mail: piershill.library@edinburgh.gov.uk

Portobello Library, 14 Rosefield Avenue, Edinburgh EH15 1AU
☎0131 529 5558
Fax 0131 669 2344
e-mail: portobello.library@edinburgh.gov.uk

Ratho Library, 6 School Wynd, Ratho, Edinburgh EH28 8TT
☎0131 333 5297 (tel/fax)
e-mail: ratho.library@edinburgh.gov.uk

Sighthill Library, Gate 55, 55 Sighthill Road, Edinburgh EH11 4PB
☎0131 529 5569
Fax 0131 529 5572
e-mail: sighthill.library@edinburgh.gov.uk

South Queensferry Library, 9 Shore Road, South Queensferry, Edinburgh EH30 9RD
☎0131 529 5576
Fax 0131 529 5578
e-mail: southqueensferry.library@edinburgh.gov.uk

Stockbridge Library, 11 Hamilton Place, Edinburgh EH3 5BA
☎0131 529 5665
Fax 0131 529 5681
e-mail: stockbridge.library@edinburgh.gov.uk

Wester Hailes Library, 1 Westside Plaza, Wester Hailes, Edinburgh EH14 2FT
☎0131 529 5667
Fax 0131 529 5671
e-mail: westerhailes.library@edinburgh.gov.uk

Access Services/Mobiles
Direct Services, 343 Oxgangs Road North, Edinburgh EH13 9LY

☎0131 529 5683
Contact Ian Kirkby

FALKIRK

Authority: Falkirk Community Trust
Library Services, Falkirk Library Basement, Hope Street, Falkirk FK1 5AU
☎(01324) 506800
Fax (01324) 506801
url: www.falkirkcommunitytrust.org
Libraries Manager Vacant

Central/largest library
Falkirk Library, Hope Street, Falkirk FK1 5AU
☎(01324) 503605
Fax (01324) 503606
e-mail: falkirk.library@falkirkcommunitytrust.org
Principal Librarian Ms Anna Herron MA DipLib MCLIP

Other libraries
Bo'ness Library, Scotland's Close, Bo'ness, Falkirk EH51 0AH
☎(01506) 778520
Fax (01506) 778521
e-mail: bo'ness.library@falkirkcommunitytrust.org

Bonnybridge Library, Bridge Street, Bonnybridge, Falkirk FK4 1AA
☎(01324) 503295
e-mail: bonnybridge.library@falkirkcommunitytrust.org
Librarian Ms Naomi Kenny MA LPC LLB MSc MCLIP

Denny Library, 49 Church Walk, Denny, Falkirk FK6 6DF
☎(01324) 504242
Fax (01324) 504240
e-mail: denny.library@falkirkcommunitytrust.org
Librarian Ms Vikki Ring BA MCLIP

Grangemouth Library, Bo'ness Road, Grangemouth, Falkirk FK3 8AG
☎(01324) 504690
Fax (01324) 504691
e-mail: grangemouth.library@falkirkcommunitytrust.org
Senior Librarian Mrs Sharon Woodforde MCLIP

Larbert Library, 22 Hallam Road, Stenhousemuir, Larbert, Falkirk FK5 3JX
☎(01324) 503590
Fax (01324) 503592
e-mail: larbert.library@falkirkcommunitytrust.org
Senior Librarians Mrs Karyn Jaffray BA MCLIP, Miss Tanya Milligan MA MCLIP, Ms Fiona Fraser BA MCLIP

Meadowbank Library, 2A Stevenson Avenue, Polmont, Falkirk FK2 0GU
☎(01324) 503870
Fax (01324) 503871
e-mail: meadowbank.library@falkirkcommunitytrust.org

Slamannan Library, The Cross, Slamannan, Falkirk FK1 3EX
☎(01324) 851373
Fax (01324) 851862
e-mail: slamannan.library@falkirkcommunitytrust.org

FIFE

Authority: Fife Cultural Trust
Head Office, 16 East Fergus Place, Kirkcaldy, Fife KY1 1XT
☎(01592) 583204
e-mail: fife.libraries@onfife.com
url: www.onfife.com
Chief Executive Officer Ms Heather Stuart (e-mail: heather.stuart@onfife.com)

Group libraries

Cupar Library, 33-35 Crossgate, Cupar, Fife KY15 5AS
☎(01334) 659367

Dunfermline Carnegie Library, Abbot Street, Dunfermline, Fife KY12 7NL
☎(01383) 602365

Glenwood Library, Glenwood Shopping Centre, Glenrothes, Fife KY6 1PA
☎(01592) 583205

Kirkcaldy Galleries, War Memorial Gardens, Kirkcaldy, Fife KY1 1YG
☎(01592) 583206

St Andrews Library, Church Square, St Andrews, Fife KY16 9NN
☎(01334) 659378

GLASGOW

Authority: Glasgow Life
Culture and Sport Glasgow Life, The Mitchell Library, North Street, Glasgow G3 7DN
☎0141 287 2999 (enquiries), 0141 287 2870 (service development)
Fax 0141 287 2815
e-mail: lil@csglasgow.org
url: www.csglasgow.org
Head of Libraries Ms Karen Cunningham MA DipLib MCLIP (0141 287 5114; fax: 0141 287 5151; e-mail: karen.cunningham@csglasgow.gov.uk) (located at 20 Trongate, Glasgow G1 1LX)
Senior Library Managers Gordon Anderson BA MCLIP (0141 287 2949; e-mail: gordon.anderson@csglasgow.gov.uk), Ms Pamela Tulloch MA MBA DipLib MCLIP (0141 287 2862; e-mail: pamela.tulloch@csglasgow.gov.uk)

Community libraries

Anniesland Library and Learning Centre, 833 Crow Road, Glasgow G13 1LE
☎0141 276 1622
Fax 0141 276 1623

Baillieston Library and Learning Centre, 141 Main Street, Glasgow G69 6AA
☎0141 276 0706
Fax 0141 276 0707

Barmulloch Library and Learning Centre, 46 Wallacewell Quadrant, Glasgow G21 3PX
☎0141 276 0875
Fax 0141 276 0876

Bridgeton Library and Learning Centre, The Olympia Building, 2-16 Orr Street, Glasgow
G40 2HQ
☎0141 276 0870
Fax 0141 276 0871

Cardonald Library and Learning Centre, 1113 Mosspark Drive, Glasgow G52 3BU
☎0141 276 0880
Fax 0141 276 0881

Castlemilk Library and Learning Centre, 100 Castlemilk Drive, Glasgow G45 9TN
☎0141 276 0731
Fax 0141 276 0732

Couper Institute Library and Learning Centre, 84 Clarkston Road, Glasgow G44 3DA
☎0141 276 0771
Fax 0141 276 0772

Dennistoun Library and Learning Centre, 2a Craigpark, Glasgow G31 2NA
☎0141 276 0768
Fax 0141 276 0769

Drumchapel Library and Learning Centre, 65 Hecla Avenue, Glasgow G15 8LX
☎0141 276 1545
Fax 0141 276 1546

Elder Park Library and Learning Centre, 228a Langlands Road, Glasgow G51 3TZ
☎0141 276 1540
Fax 0141 276 1541

Gorbals Library and Cybercafé and Learning Centre, 180 Crown Street, Glasgow G5 4XD
☎0141 429 0949
Fax 0141 429 0167

Govanhill Library and Learning Centre, Govanhill Neighbourhood Centre, 6 Daisy Street,
Glasgow G42 8JL
☎0141 276 1550
Fax 0141 276 1551

Hillhead Library and Learning Centre, 348 Byres Road, Glasgow G12 8AP
☎0141 276 1617
Fax 0141 276 1618

Ibrox Library and Learning Centre, 1 Midlock Street, Glasgow G51 1SL
☎0141 276 0712
Fax 0141 276 0713

Knightswood Library and Learning Centre, 27 Dunterlie Avenue, Glasgow G13 3BB
☎0141 276 1555
Fax 0141 276 1556

Langside Library and Learning Centre, 2 Sinclair Drive, Glasgow G42 9QE
☎0141 276 0777
Fax 0141 276 0778

Leisure and Lifestyle at the Mitchell and Learning Centre, Granville Street, Glasgow G3 7DN
☎0141 287 2872

Library at the Bridge and Learning Centre, 1000 Westerhouse Road, Glasgow G34 9JW
☎0141 276 9712
Fax 0141 276 9711

Library@Goma and Learning Centre, Gallery of Modern Art, Queen Street, Glasgow
G1 3AZ
☎0141 287 3010
Fax 0141 249 9943

Maryhill Library and Learning Centre, 1508 Maryhill Road, Glasgow G20 9AD
☎0141 276 0715
Fax 0141 276 0716

Milton Library and Learning Centre, Milton Community Campus, 204 Liddesdale Road,
Glasgow G22 7AR
☎0141 276 0885
Fax 0141 276 0886

Parkhead Library and Learning Centre, 64 Tollcross Road, Glasgow G31 4XA
☎0141 276 1530
Fax 0141 276 1531

Partick Library and Learning Centre, 305 Dumbarton Road, Glasgow G11 6AB
☎0141 276 1560
Fax 0141 276 1561

Pollok Library and Leisure Centre, 27 Cowglen Road, Glasgow G53 2EN
☎0141 276 6877

Pollokshaws Library and Learning Centre, 50-60 Shawbridge Street, Glasgow G43 1RW
☎0141 276 1535
Fax 0141 276 1536

Pollokshields Library and Learning Centre, 30 Leslie Street, Glasgow G41 2LF
☎0141 276 1685
Fax 0141 276 1686

Possilpark Library and Learning Centre, 127 Allander Street, Glasgow G22 5JJ
☎0141 276 0928
Fax 0141 276 0929

Riddrie Library and Learning Centre, 1020 Cumbernauld Road, Glasgow G33 2QS
☎0141 276 0690
Fax 0141 276 0691

Royston Library and Learning Centre, 67 Royston Road, Glasgow G21 2QW
☎0141 276 0890
Fax 0141 276 0891

Service Development and Learning Centre, The Mitchell Library, North Street, Glasgow
G3 7DN
☎0141 287 2870
Fax 0141 287 2815

Shettleston Library, 154 Wellshot Road, Glasgow G32 7AX
☎0141 276 1643
Fax 0141 276 1645

Springburn Library and Learning Centre, Kay Street, Glasgow G21 1JY
☎0141 276 1690
Fax 0141 276 1691

Whiteinch Library and Learning Centre, 14 Victoria Park Drive South, Glasgow G14 9RL
☎0141 276 0695
Fax 0141 276 0696

Woodside Library and Learning Centre, 343 St George's Road, Glasgow G3 6JQ
☎0141 276 1609
Fax 0141 276 1610

HIGHLAND

(operated by High Life Highland Libraries, wholly owned by The Highland Council)

Authority: The Highland Council
12-13 Ardross Street, Inverness IV3 5NS
☎(01463) 663800
Chief Executive Ian Murray (01463 663800; e-mail: ian.murray@highlifehighland.com)

Library Service HQ
Library Support Unit, High Life Highland, 31A Harbour Road, Inverness IV1 1UA
☎(01463) 235713
Fax (01463) 236986
e-mail: libraries@highlifehighland.com
Principal Libraries Manager John West BA(Hons) PGDipLib MCLIP (01463 251250;
e-mail: john.west@highlifehighland.com)

Branch libraries
Achiltibuie Library, Coigach Community Hall, Achiltibuie, Ross & Cromarty, IV26 2YG
☎(01854) 622305 (tel/fax)
e-mail: achiltibuie.library@highlifehighland.com

Alness Library, Averon Centre, High Street, Alness, Ross & Cromarty, IV17 0QB
☎(01349) 882674
Fax (01349) 883587
e-mail: alness.library@@highlifehighland.com

Ardersier Library, Old School, Station Road, Ardersier, Inverness IV2 7SU
☎(01667) 460397 (tel/fax)
e-mail: ardersier.library@highlifehighland.com

Ardnamurchan Library, Sunart Centre (Àrainn Shuaineirt), Strontian, Acharacle, PH36 4JA
☎(01397) 709226 (tel/fax)
e-mail: ardnamurchan.library@highlifehighland.com

Aviemore Library, Aviemore Primary School & Community Centre, Muirton Aviemore,
PH22 1SF
☎(01479) 813141

e-mail: aviemore.library@highlifehighland.com

Badenoch Library, Badenoch Centre, Spey Street, Kingussie, Badenoch & Strathspey, PH21 1EH
☎(01540) 661596
e-mail: badenoch.library@highlifehighland.com

Beauly Library, Phipps Institute, Station Road, Beauly, Inverness IV4 7EH
☎(01463) 782930 (tel/fax)
e-mail: beauly.library@highlifehighland.com

Bettyhill Library & Service Point, Naver Teleservice Centre, Bettyhill, Sutherland KW14 7SS
☎(01349) 886606
e-mail: bettyhill.library@highlifehighland.com

Bonar Bridge Library, Carnegie Library, West End, Bonar Bridge, Sutherland IV24 3EA
☎(01862) 760083
e-mail: bonarbridge.library@highlifehighland.com

Broadford Library & Service Point, Old Quarry Industrial Estate, Broadford, Isle of Skye IV49 9AB
☎(01471) 820522
Fax (01471) 820076
e-mail: broadfordlibrary@highlifehighland.com

Brora Library & Cultural Centre, Gower Street, Brora, Sutherland KW9 6PD
☎(01408) 621128
Fax (01408) 622064
e-mail: brora.library@highlifehighland.com

Caol Library, Glenkingie Street, Caol, Fort William, PH33 7DP
☎(01397) 702829 (tel/fax)
e-mail: caol.library@highlifehighland.com

Cromarty Library, Hugh Miller Institute, Church Street, Cromarty, Ross & Cromarty, IV11 8XA
☎(01381) 600318 (tel/fax)
e-mail: cromarty.library@highlifehighland.com

Culloden Library, Keppoch Road, Culloden, Inverness IV2 7LL
☎(01463) 792531
Fax (01463) 793162
e-mail: culloden.library@highlifehighland.com

Dingwall Community Library, Dingwall Academy, Dingwall, Ross-shire IV15 9LT
☎(01349) 869869
Fax (01349) 869868
e-mail: dingwall.library@highlifehighland.com

Dornoch Library, Carnegie Buildings, High Street, Dornoch, Sutherland IV25 3SH
☎(01862) 811079 (tel/fax)
e-mail: dornoch.library@highlifehighland.com

Fort William Library, Airds Crossing, High Street, Fort William, Lochaber, PH33 6EU
☎(01397) 703552
Fax (01397) 703538

e-mail: fortwilliam.library@highlifehighland.com

Fortrose Community Library, Fortrose Academy, Academy Street, Fortrose, Ross & Cromarty, IV10 8TW
☎(01381) 622235 (tel/fax)
e-mail: fortrose.library@highlifehighland.com

Gairloch Community Library, Gairloch High School, Gairloch, Ross & Cromarty, IV21 2BP
☎(01445) 712469
e-mail: gairloch.library@highlifehighland.com

Glen Urquhart Library & Learning Centre, Drumnadrochit, Inverness-shire IV63 6XA
☎(01456) 459223
e-mail: glenurquhart.library@highlifehighland.com

Golspie Library, Community Centre, Golspie High School, Sutherland KW10 6RA
☎(01408) 634084
e-mail: golspie.library@highlifehighland.com

Grantown on Spey Library, YMCA Building, 80 High Street, Grantown-on-Spey, Badenoch & Strathspey, PH26 3HB
☎(01479) 873175 (tel/fax)
e-mail: grantown.library@highlifehighland.com

Helmsdale Library & Service Point, Community Centre, Dunrobin Street, Helmsdale, Sutherland KW8 6JX
☎(01431) 821690
e-mail: helmsdale.library@highlifehighland.com

Inshes Library, Inshes Road, Inverness IV2 3RF
☎(01463) 725928 (tel/fax)
e-mail: inshes.library@highlifehighland.com

Invergordon Library, High Street, Invergordon, Ross & Cromarty, IV18 0DG
☎(01349) 852698 (tel/fax)
e-mail: invergordon.library@highlifehighland.com

Inverness Library, Farraline Park, Inverness IV1 1NH
☎(01463) 236463
Fax (01463) 237001
e-mail: inverness.library@highlifehighland.com

Kinlochleven Community Library, Riverside Road, Kinlochleven, PH50 4QH
☎(01855) 832047
Fax (01855) 832048
e-mail: kinlochleven.library@highlifehighland.com

Knoydart Library, The Store, Inverie, Knoydart, by Mallaig, PH41 4PL
☎(01687) 460253
e-mail: knoydart.library@highlifehighland.com

Kyle of Lochalsh Service Point & Library, Main Street, Kyle of Lochalsh, Skye & Lochalsh, IV40 8AB
☎(01599) 534956
Fax (01599) 534562
e-mail: kyle.library@highlifehighland.com

Lairg Library, Community Centre, Main Street, Lairg, Sutherland IV27 4DD
☎(01549) 402577
e-mail: lairg.library@highlifehighland.com

Lochcarron Library, The Howard Doris Centre, Lochcarron, Ross & Cromarty, IV54 8UD
☎(01520) 722679 (tel/fax)
e-mail: lochcarron.library@highlifehighland.com

Mallaig Library, Mallaig and Morar Community Centre, West Bay, Mallaig, PH41 4PY
☎(01687) 460097
e-mail: mallaig.library@highlifehighland.com

Muir of Ord Library, Tarradale School, Great Northern Road, Muir of Ord, Ross & Cromarty, IV6 7SU
☎(01463) 870196 (tel/fax)
e-mail: muiroford.library@highlifehighland.com

Nairn Library, 68 High Street, Nairn IV12 4AU
☎(01667) 458506 (tel/fax)
e-mail: nairn.library@highlifehighland.com

Plockton Library, Village Hall, Harbour Street, Plockton, Ross & Cromarty, IV52 8TG
☎(01599) 544718 (tel/fax)
e-mail: plockton.library@highlifehighland.com

Portree Community Library, Viewfield Road, Portree, Isle of Skye IV51 9ET
☎(01478) 614823
Fax (01478) 614824
e-mail: portree.library@highlifehighland.com

Tain Library, Stafford Street, Tain, Ross & Cromarty, IV19 1AZ
☎(01862) 892391 (tel/fax)
e-mail: tain.library@highlifehighland.com

Thurso Library, Davidson's Lane, Thurso, Caithness KW14 7AF
☎(01862) 892391 (tel/fax)
e-mail: thurso.library@highlifehighland.com

Ullapool Library, Community High School, Mill Street, Ullapool, Ross & Cromarty, IV26 2UN
☎(01854) 612543 (tel/fax)
e-mail: ullapool.library@highlifehighland.com

Wick Library, Carnegie Public Library, Sinclair Terrace, Wick, Caithness KW1 5AB
☎(01955) 602864
Fax (01955) 603000
e-mail: wick.library@highlifehighland.com

INVERCLYDE

Authority: Inverclyde Council
49 Belville Street, Greenock, Renfrewshire PA15 4UN
☎(01475) 712330
e-mail: library.central@inverclyde.gov.uk
url: www.inverclyde.gov.uk/libraries
Libraries Manager Ms Alana Ward MA(Hons) (e-mail: alana.ward@inverclyde.gov.uk)

MIDLOTHIAN

Authority: Midlothian Council
Library HQ, 2 Clerk Street, Loanhead, Midlothian EH20 9DR
☎0131 271 3980
Fax 0131 440 4635
e-mail: library.hq@midlothian.gov.uk
url: www.midlothian.gov.uk/library/
Library Services Manager Philip Wark MCLIP
Administrator Ms Karen Cummings

Largest library

Penicuik Library, The Penicuik Centre, Carlops Road, Penicuik, Midlothian EH26 9EP
☎(01968) 664050
Fax (01968) 679408
e-mail: penicuik.library@midlothian.gov.uk
Senior Librarian Stephen Harris MA MSc

Branch libraries

Dalkeith Library, White Hart Street, Dalkeith, Midlothian EH22 1AE
☎0131 663 2083
Fax 0131 654 9029
e-mail: dalkeith.library@midlothian.gov.uk
Senior Librarian Thomas Regan BA MCLIP

Danderhall Library, 1A Campview, Danderhall, Midlothian EH22 1QD
☎0131 663 9293
e-mail: danderhall.library@midlothian.gov.uk
Library Manager Ms Rachel Archibald

Gorebridge Library, Hunterfield Road, Gorebridge, Midlothian EH23 4TT
☎(01875) 820630
Fax (01875) 823657
e-mail: gorebridge.library@midlothian.gov.uk
Library Manager Ms Elaine Robertson

Lasswade Library, Lasswade Centre, 19 Eskdale Drive, Bonnyrigg, Midlothian EH19 2LA
☎0131 271 4534
e-mail: lasswade.library@midlothian.gov.uk
Senior Librarian David Stevenson BA MCLIP

Loanhead Library, George Avenue, Loanhead, Midlothian EH20 9HD
☎0131 440 0824
e-mail: loanhead.library@midlothian.gov.uk
Library Manager Ms Annabel Cavaroli

Local and Family History Library, 2 Clerk Street, Loanhead, Midlothian EH20 9DR
☎0131 271 3976
Fax 0131 440 4635
e-mail: local.studies@midlothian.gov.uk
Local Studies Officer Dr Kenneth Bogle MA MCLIP PhD

Mayfield Library, Stone Avenue, Mayfield, Dalkeith, Midlothian EH22 5PB

☎0131 663 2126
e-mail: mayfield.library@midlothian.gov.uk
Library Manager Ms Isobel Allen

Newtongrange Library, St Davids, Newtongrange, Midlothian EH22 4LG
☎0131 663 1816
Fax 0131 654 1990
e-mail: newtongrange.library@midlothian.gov.uk
Library Manager Ms Jacqueline Elliot

Roslin Library, 9 Main Street, Roslin, Midlothian EH25 9LD
☎0131 448 2781
e-mail: roslin.library@midlothian.gov.uk
Library Manager Vacant

MORAY

Authority: The Moray Council
Educational & Social Care, Council Office, High Street, Elgin, Moray IV30 1BX
☎(01343) 562600 (enquiries), 01343 563391 (administration)
Fax (01343) 562630
url: www.moray.gov.uk/libraries
Head of Lifelong Learning, Culture and Sport Graham Jarvis (e-mail: graham.jarvis@moray.gov.uk)

Central/largest library

Elgin Library, Cooper Park, Elgin, Moray IV30 1HS
☎(01343) 562600
Fax (01343) 562630
e-mail: elgin.library@moray.gov.uk
Principal Librarian Mrs Sheila Campbell MCLIP (e-mail: sheila.campbell@moray.gov.uk)

Area libraries

Buckie Library, Cluny Place, Buckie, Banffshire AB56 1HB
☎(01542) 832121
Fax (01542) 835237
e-mail: buckie.library@moray.gov.uk
Senior Librarian (Communities) Ms Susan Butts MA(Hons) MCLIP

Forres Library, Forres House, High Street, Forres, Moray IV36 1BU
☎(01309) 672834
Fax (01309) 675084
e-mail: forres.library@moray.gov.uk
Senior Librarian (Communities) Ms Susan Butts MA(Hons) MCLIP

Keith Library, Union Street, Keith, Banffshire AB55 5DP
☎(01542) 882223
Fax (01542) 882177
e-mail: keith.library@moray.gov.uk
Senior Librarian (Communities) Ms Susan Butts MA(Hons) MCLIP

NORTH AYRSHIRE

Authority: North Ayrshire Council
Library Support, Dunlop Centre, Main Street, Dreghorn, Ayrshire KA11 4AQ
☎(01294) 215547
Fax (01294) 219605
e-mail: libraryhq@north-ayrshire.gov.uk
url: www.north-ayrshire.gov.uk
Senior Manager (Information and Culture) Ms Rhona Arthur BA FCLIP (01294
324415; fax: 01294 324444; e-mail: RhonaArthur@north-ayrshire.gov.uk)
Cultural Development Manager Ms Lesley Forsyth (01294 324407; fax: 01294 324444;
e-mail: lforsyth@north-ayrshire.gov.uk)
Information and Culture Officer Paul Cowan BEd(Hons) DipLib MCLIP (01294 212716;
fax: 01294 222509; e-mail: pcowan@north-ayrshire.gov.uk)
Systems Support Officer Ms Alison McAllister BA(Hons) MCLIP (01294 212716; fax:
01294 222509; e-mail: amcallister@north-ayrshire.gov.uk)
Children and Families Officer Ms Melanie Nolan BA DipLib MCLIP (01294 465591; fax:
01294 466841; e-mail: mnolan@north-ayrshire.gov.uk)

Central/largest library

Irvine Library, 168 High Street, Irvine, Ayrshire KA12 8AN
☎(01294) 271295
Fax (01294) 313051
e-mail: irvinelibrary@north-ayrshire.gov.uk

Area libraries

Largs Library, Allanpark Street, Largs, Ayrshire KA30 9AS
☎(01475) 673309 (tel/fax)
e-mail: largslibrary@north-ayrshire.gov.uk
Area Librarian Ms Eileen Vernon MA(Hons) DipLib MCLIP

Saltcoats Library, Springvale Place, Saltcoats, Ayrshire KA21 5LS
☎(01294) 469546 (tel/fax)
e-mail: saltcoatslibrary@north-ayrshire.gov.uk
Area Librarian Jim Macaulay MCLIP DipLib

NORTH LANARKSHIRE

Authority: CultureNL Limited
**CultureNL Limited, Summerlee Museum of Scottish Industrial Life, Heritage Way,
Coatbridge, North Lanarkshire ML5 1QD**
☎(01698) 332606
Fax (01698) 332624
url: www.culturenl.co.uk
Bibliographic and Outside Services Manager James Lindsay BA MCLIP (01698 332618;
e-mail: lindsayj@culturenl.co.uk)
Children's Library Services and Performance Manager Russell Brown BA(Hons)
MCLIP (e-mail: brownru@culturenl.co.uk)
Lending Services Manager (South) Mrs Catriona Wales BA MCLIP (e-mail:
walesc@culturenl.co.uk)

Lending Services Manager (North) Mrs Wendy Bennett BA MCLIP (e-mail: bennettw@culturenl.co.uk)

South Area

Motherwell Library, 35 Hamilton Road, Motherwell, North Lanarkshire ML1 3BZ
☎(01698) 332626
Fax (01698) 332625

North Area

Coatbridge Library, Buchanan Centre, 126 Main Street, Coatbridge, North Lanarkshire ML5 3BG
☎(01236) 856444

ORKNEY

Authority: Orkney Islands Council
The Orkney Library and Archive, 44 Junction Road, Kirkwall, Orkney KW15 IAG
☎(01856) 873166 (enquiries and administration)
Fax (01856) 875260
e-mail: general.enquiries@orkneylibrary.org.uk
url: www.orkneylibrary.org.uk
Library and Archive Manager Gary Amos (e-mail: gary.amos@orkneylibrary.org.uk)
Principal Librarian Ms Karen Walker BA (e-mail: karen.walker@orkneylibrary.org.uk)
Senior Archivist David Mackie (e-mail: david.mackie@orkneylibrary.org.uk)

PERTH AND KINROSS

Authority: Perth and Kinross Council
The A K Bell Library, York Place, Perth, Perthshire PH2 8EP
☎(01738) 444949
Fax (01738) 477010
e-mail: library@pkc.gov.uk
url: www.pkc.gov.uk/library
Libraries and Information Services Manager Ms Morag Kelly MA DipLib MCLIP
Operations Co-ordinator Mrs Jill MacKintosh

Area libraries

Auchterarder Library, Aytoun Hall, Chapel Wynd, Auchterarder, Perthshire PH3 1BL
☎(01764) 663850 (tel/fax)
e-mail: auchterarderlibrary@pkc.gov.uk
Senior Library Assistant Mrs Jane Gerrard

Blairgowrie Library, 46 Leslie Street, Blairgowrie, Perthshire PH10 6AW
☎(01250) 871305
Fax (01250) 872905
e-mail: blairgowrielibrary@pkc.gov.uk
Senior Library Assistant Craig Dennis

Breadalbane Community Library, Crieff Road, Aberfeldy, PH15 2FJ
☎(01887) 822405

e-mail: breadalbanelibrary@pkc.gov.uk
Library Supervisor Ms Karen MacKay

Loch Leven Community Library, Muirs, Kinross, Kinross-shire KY13 8FQ
☎(01577) 867205
e-mail: lochlevenlibrary@pkc.gov.uk
Library Supervisor Mrs Mary Jack

North Inch Community Library, North Inch Campus, Gowans Terrace, Perth PH1 5BF
☎(01738) 454406
e-mail: northinchlibrary@pkc.gov.uk
Library Supervisor Vince Davidson

Scone Library, Sandy Road, Scone, Perth, Perthshire PH2 6LJ
☎(01738) 553029 (tel/fax)
e-mail: sconelibrary@pkc.gov.uk
Senior Library Assistant Mrs Eileen MacDonald

Strathearn Community Library, Strathearn Community Campus, Pittenzie Road, Crieff,
Perthshire PH7 3RS
☎(01764) 657705
e-mail: strathearnlibrary@pkc.gov.uk
Library Supervisor Ms Janice Bourelle

Community libraries

Alyth Library, Airlie Street, Alyth, Blairgowrie, Perthshire PH11 8AH
☎(01828) 632731
e-mail: alythlibrary@pkc.gov.uk
Senior Library Assistant Mrs Gillian Murray

Birnam Library, The Institute, Station Road, Birnam, Dunkeld, Perthshire PH8 0DS
☎(01350) 727971
e-mail: birnamlibrary@pkc.gov.uk
Senior Library Assistant Mrs Margaret Quigley

Comrie Library, Drummond Street, Comrie, Perthshire PH6 2DS
☎(01764) 670273
e-mail: comrielibrary@pkc.gov.uk
Senior Library Assistant Mrs Deanna Shrieves

Coupar Angus Library, Town Hall, Union Street, Coupar Angus, Blairgowrie, Perthshire
PH13 9AE
☎(01828) 627090
e-mail: couparanguslibrary@pkc.gov.uk
Senior Library Assistant Mrs Shona Smith

Pitlochry Library, 26 Atholl Road, Pitlochry, Perthshire PH16 5BX
☎(01796) 474635
e-mail: pitlochrylibrary@pkc.gov.uk
Senior Library Assistant Mrs Grace Grant

RENFREWSHIRE

Authority: Renfrewshire Council
Library Services, Library Support Service, Netherhill Road, Gallowhill, Paisley, Renfrewshire PA3 4SF
☎0300 300 1188
Fax 0141 887 9557
e-mail: libraries@renfrewshire.gov.uk
url: www.renfrewshire.gov.uk
Libraries Manager Ms Jenifer McFarlane BA MCLIP (located at Paisley Museum, High Street, Paisley PA3 4SF)

Central/largest library

Central Library (Heritage Services), 68 High Street, Paisley, Renfrewshire PA1 2BB
☎0300 300 1188
Fax 0141 618 5351
Heritage Assistants Ms Claire Cabrie, Ms Pauline McDougall, Ms Denise Williams, Ms Pamela Logue

Central Library (Lending), 68 High Street, Paisley, Renfrewshire PA1 2BB
☎0300 300 1188
Fax 0141 618 5351
Senior Library Supervisor Ms Gill Robinson

Community libraries

Bishopton Library, 11 Greenock Road, Bishopton, Renfrewshire PA7 5JW
☎0300 300 1188
Fax 0141 618 5358
Senior Library Supervisors Ms Margaret Winters BA MCLIP, Ms Moira Reid BA MCLIP

Bridge of Weir Library, Cargill Hall, Lintwhite Crescent, Bridge of Weir, Renfrewshire PA11 3LJ
☎0300 300 1188
Fax 0141 618 5359
Senior Library Supervisor Ms Jacqui Gillaney

Erskine Library, Bridgewater Place, Erskine, Renfrewshire PA8 7AA
☎0300 300 1188
Fax 0141 618 5359
Senior Library Supervisor Ms Janet Clasper

Ferguslie Library, Tannahill Centre, Blackstoun Road, Paisley, Renfrewshire PA3 1NT
☎0300 300 1188
Fax 0141 618 5353
Senior Library Supervisor Ms Debbie McBride

Foxbar Library/Toy Library, Ivanhoe Road, Paisley, Renfrewshire PA2 0JZ
☎0300 300 1188
Fax 0141 618 5353
Senior Library Supervisors Ms Evelyn Gilchrist, Ms Fiona Richardson (e-mail: fiona.richardson@linacre.ox.ac.uk)

Glenburn Library, Fairway Avenue, Paisley, Renfrewshire PA2 8DX
☎0300 300 1188
Fax 0141 618 5355
Senior Library Supervisor Ms Pauline Simpson

Johnstone Library, 17 Collier Street, Johnstone, Renfrewshire PA5 8AR
☎0300 300 1188
Fax 0141 618 5356
Senior Library Supervisors Ms Kay Wright, Ms Pauline Chisholm

Linwood Library, 15 Bridge Street, Linwood, Renfrewshire PA3 3DB
☎0300 300 1188
Fax 0141 618 5350
Senior Library Supervisor Ms Margaret Sweenie

Lochwinnoch Library, Old School, High Street, Lochwinnoch, Renfrewshire PA12 4AB
☎0300 300 1188
Fax 0141 618 5360
Senior Library Supervisor Bryan Smith

Ralston Library, Community Centre, Allanton Avenue, Paisley, Renfrewshire PA1 3BL
☎0300 300 1188
Fax 0141 618 5348
Senior Library Supervisor Ms Moira Reid BA MCLIP

Renfrew Library, Paisley Road, Renfrew, Renfrewshire PA4 8LJ
☎0300 300 1188
Fax 0141 618 5349
Senior Library Supervisor James McGrath

SCOTTISH BORDERS

Authority: Scottish Borders Council
Scottish Borders Library Service, St Mary's Mill, Selkirk TD7 5EW
☎(01750) 20842
Fax (01750) 22875
url: www.scotborders.gov.uk
Cultural Services Manager Ian Brown
Library and Information Services Manager Ms Margaret Menzies BA MLib MCLIP
Senior Librarian - Adult Services Keith Nairn MSc MCLIP (e-mail:
knairn@scotborders.gov.uk)
Senior Librarian - Information and Digital Services Ms Sheena Milne MA MCLIP
DipLib
Senior Librarian - Children and Young People's Services Ms Gill Swales BA MCLIP
DipLib (e-mail: gswales@scotborders.gov.uk)
Librarian - Communities Mrs Ruth Holmes MSc MCLIP, Ms Christine Johnston
MA(Hons) PGDip(Inf)

Community libraries

Coldstream Library, Contact Centre, Gateway Centre, Coldstream, Scottish Borders
TD12 4AE
☎(01890) 883314 (tel/fax)
e-mail: libcoldstream@scotborders.gov.uk

Library and Information Services Manager Ms Margaret Menzies BA MLib MCLIP
Assistant Librarian Ms Joan B Sanderson BA MCLIP

Duns Library, Contact Centre, 49 Newtown Street, Duns, Berwickshire TD11 3AU
☎(01361) 882622
Fax (01361) 884104
e-mail: libduns@scotborders.gov.uk
Assistant Librarian Ms Joan B Sanderson BA MCLIP

Earlston Library, High School, Earlston, Scottish Borders TD4 6ED
☎(01896) 849282
Fax (01896) 848918
e-mail: libearlston@scotborders.gov.uk
Library Supervisor Mrs Anne Taitt

Eyemouth Library, Manse Road, Eyemouth, Scottish Borders TD14 5JE
☎(01890) 750300
Fax (01890) 751633
e-mail: libeyemouth@scotborders.gov.uk
Branch Librarian Nick Overfield

Galashiels Library, Lawyer's Brae, Galashiels, Selkirkshire TD1 3JQ
☎(01896) 752512
Fax (01896) 753575
e-mail: libgalashiels@scotborders.gov.uk
Assistant Librarian Ms Debbie McGill

Hawick Library, North Bridge Street, Hawick, Roxburghshire TD9 9QT
☎(01450) 372637
Fax (01450) 370991
e-mail: libhawick@scotborders.gov.uk
Assistant Librarian Mrs Julia Cawthorne

Innerleithen Library, Contact Centre, Buccleuch Street, Innerleithen, Scottish Borders
EH44 6LA
☎(01896) 830789 (tel/fax)
e-mail: libinnerleithen@scotborders.gov.uk
Assistant Librarian Ms Alison Tait

Jedburgh Library, Contact Centre, Castlegate, Jedburgh, Scottish Borders TD8 6AS
☎(01835) 863592 (tel/fax)
e-mail: libjedburgh@scotborders.gov.uk
Assistant Librarian Mrs Julia Cawthorne

Kelso Library, Contact Centre, Bowmont Street, Kelso, Roxburghshire TD5 7JH
☎(01573) 223171
Fax (01573) 226618
e-mail: libkelso@scotborders.gov.uk
Assistant Librarian Mrs Julia Cawthorne

Local Studies, St Mary's Mill, Selkirk TD7 5EW
☎(01750) 20842
Fax (01750) 22875
Librarian Mrs Jennifer Lauder BSc(Hons)MSc

Melrose Library, 18 Market Square, Melrose, Scottish Borders TD6 9PN
☎(01896) 823052 (tel/fax)
e-mail: libmelrose@scotborders.gov.uk
Branch Librarian Mrs Mairi Wight

Peebles Library, Chambers Institute, High Street, Peebles, Peeblesshire EH45 8AG
☎(01721) 720123
Fax (01721) 724424
e-mail: libpeebles@scotborders.gov.uk
Area Librarian Ms Alison Tait

Selkirk Library, Ettrick Terrace, Selkirk TD7 4LE
☎(01750) 20267 (tel/fax)
e-mail: libselkirk@scotborders.gov.uk
Acting Library Supervisor Ms Morag Cockburn

SHETLAND ISLANDS

Authority: Shetland Islands Council
Shetland Library, Lower Hillhead, Lerwick, Shetland ZE1 0EL
☎(01595) 743868 (enquiries and administration)
Fax (01595) 694430
e-mail: shetlandlibrary@shetland.gov.uk
url: www.shetland-library.gov.uk
Online catalogue: http://capitaldiscovery.co.uk/shetland
Executive Manager, Library Services Ms Karen Fraser (e-mail:
karen.fraser@shetland.gov.uk)
Support Services Librarian Douglas Garden (e-mail: douglas.garden@shetland.gov.uk)
Adult Services Librarian Ms Marghie West (e-mail: marghie.west@shetland.gov.uk)
Secretary/Administration Assistant Mrs Katrina Nicolson (e-mail:
katrina.nicolson@shetland.gov.uk)
Administration Assistant Ms Pat Leask (e-mail: pat.leask@shetland.gov.uk)
Systems Officer David Thomson (e-mail: david.thomson@shetland.gov.uk)
Young People's Services Librarian Mrs Morag Nicolson (e-mail:
morag.nicolson@shetland.gov.uk)

SOUTH AYRSHIRE

Authority: South Ayrshire Council
Library HQ, John Pollock Centre, Main Holm Road, Ayr KA8 0QD
☎(01292) 559316
Fax (01292) 619019
url: www.south-ayrshire.gov.uk
Libraries and Museums Co-ordinator Ms Jean Inness MA(Hons) DipLib MCLIP (e-mail:
jean.inness@south-ayrshire.gov.uk)

Central/largest library
Carnegie Library, 12 Main Street, Ayr KA8 8ED
☎(01292) 286385
Fax (01292) 611593
e-mail: carnegie.library@south-ayrshire.gov.uk

SOUTH LANARKSHIRE

Authority: South Lanarkshire Leisure and Culture
South Lanarkshire Leisure and Culture, North Stand, Cadzow Avenue, Hamilton, South Lanarkshire ML3 0LX
☎(01698) 476262
Fax (01698) 476198
e-mail: customer.services@southlanarkshireleisure.co.uk
url: www.slleisureandculture.co.uk
Libraries and Museums Manager Ms Diana Barr BA MCLIP MIMgt (e-mail: diana.barr@southlanarkshireleisure.co.uk)

Central/largest library

East Kilbride Central Library, 40 The Olympia, East Kilbride, South Lanarkshire G74 1PG
☎(01355) 220046
Fax (01355) 229365
e-mail: eastkilbride@library.s-lanark.org.uk
Librarian John Barr (e-mail: john.barr@library.s-lanark.org.uk)

STIRLING

Authority: Stirling Council
Library HQ, Springkerse Industrial Estate, Borrowmeadow Road, Stirling FK7 7TN
☎(01786) 237535 (enquiries/administration)
Fax (01786) 448548
e-mail: libraryheadquarters@stirling.gov.uk
url: www.stirling.gov.uk/community/libraries.htm
Libraries, Archives and Customer Services Manager Richard Aird (01786 237534)

Central/largest library

Central Library, Corn Exchange Road, Stirling FK8 2HX
☎(01786) 432106 (reference), (01786) 432107 (lending), (01786) 432108 (administration)
Fax (01786) 473094
e-mail: centrallibrary@stirling.gov.uk
Community Librarian Ms Lindsay McKrell BA MSc PhD MCLIP

WEST DUNBARTONSHIRE

Authority: West Dunbartonshire Council
West Dunbartonshire Libraries, 19 Poplar Road, Dumbarton G82 2RJ
☎(01389) 608041 (enquiries and administration)
Fax (01389) 608044
url: www.wdcweb.info
Executive Director, Educational Services Terry Lanagan (based at Council Offices, Garshake Road, Dumbarton G82 3PU)
Manager of Libraries and Culture Ms Gill Graham
Section Head, Libraries John Rushton

Area libraries

Clydebank Library, Dumbarton Road, Clydebank, Dumbarton G81 1XH

☎0141 962 2440 (enquiries)
Fax 0141 951 8275
Area Librarian Ms Laura Wilson BA(Hons) MCLIP (based at HQ)

Dumbarton Library, Strathleven Place, Dumbarton G82 1BD
☎(01389) 608992 (enquiries), (01389) 608038 (administration)
Fax (01389) 607302
Area Librarian Ms Laura Wilson BA(Hons) MCLIP (based at HQ)

WEST LOTHIAN

Authority: West Lothian Council
Library HQ, West Lothian Civic Centre, 2nd Floor North, Howden Road South, Livingston, West Lothian EH54 6FF
☎(01506) 281273
Fax (01506) 776345
e-mail: library.info@westlothian.gov.uk
url: www.westlothian.gov.uk/libraries
Central Support Co-ordinator Mrs Jeanette Castle MA(Hons) DipILS MCLIP (e-mail: jeanette.castle@westlothian.gov.uk)
Branch Libraries Co-ordinator Mrs Hilda Gibson ACLIP (01506 282901; e-mail: hilda.gibson@westlothian.gov.uk)

Central/largest library
Carmondean Library, Carmondean Centre, Livingston, West Lothian EH54 8PT
☎(01506) 777602 (enquiries)
e-mail: carmondean.lib@westlothian.gov.uk

Branch libraries
Almondbank Library, The Mall, Craigshill, Livingston, West Lothian EH54 5EJ
☎(01506) 777500
e-mail: almondbank.lib@westlothian.gov.uk

Armadale Library, West Main Street, Armadale, West Lothian EH48 3JB
☎(01501) 678400
e-mail: armadale.lib@westlothian.gov.uk

Bathgate Library, Bathgate Partnership Centre, South Bridge Street, Bathgate, West Lothian EH48 4PD
☎(01506) 776400
e-mail: bathgate.lib@westlothian.gov.uk

Blackburn Connected, Mill Centre, Blackburn, West Lothian EH47 7LQ
☎(01506) 776500
e-mail: blackburn.lib@westlothian.gov.uk

Blackridge Library, Craig Inn Centre, Blackridge, West Lothian EH48 3SP
☎(01501) 752396
e-mail: blackridge.lib@westlothian.gov.uk

Broxburn Library, West Main Street, Broxburn, West Lothian EH52 5RH
☎(01506) 775600
e-mail: broxburn.lib@westlothian.gov.uk

East Calder Library, Main Street, East Calder, West Lothian EH53 0EJ
☎(01506) 883633
e-mail: eastcalder.lib@westlothian.gov.uk

Fauldhouse Library, Lanrigg Road, Fauldhouse, West Lothian EH47 9JA
☎(01501) 770358
e-mail: fauldhouse.lib@westlothian.gov.uk
Supervisor Mrs Ann Beattie BA(Hons)

Lanthorn Library, Lanthorn Centre, Kenilworth Rise, Dedridge, Livingston, West Lothian
EH54 6NY
☎(01506) 777700
e-mail: lanthorn.lib@westlothian.gov.uk

Linlithgow Library, The Vennel, Linlithgow, West Lothian EH49 7EX
☎(01506) 775490
e-mail: linlithgow.lib@westlothian.gov.uk

Pumpherston Library, Pumpherston Primary School, 18 Uphall Station Road, Pumpherston,
West Lothian EH53 0LP
☎(01506) 435837
e-mail: pumpherston.lib@westlothian.gov.uk

West Calder Library, Main Street, West Calder, West Lothian EH55 8BJ
☎(01506) 771631
e-mail: westcalder.lib@westlothian.gov.uk

Whitburn Library, Union Road, Whitburn, West Lothian EH47 0AR
☎(01501) 678050
e-mail: whitburn.lib@westlothian.gov.uk

WESTERN ISLES see COMHAIRLE NAN EILEAN SIAR

ANGLESEY, ISLE OF

Authority: Isle of Anglesey County Council
Department of Lifelong Learning, Parc Mownt, Fford Glanhwfa, Llangefni, Ynys Môn LL77 7EY
☎(01248) 752095 (enquiries); (01248) 752900 (administration)
e-mail: libraries@anglesey.gov.uk
url: www.ynysmon.gov.uk
Director of Lifelong Learning Dr Gwynne Jones (e-mail: GwynneJones@anglesey.gov.uk)

Central/largest library

Llangefni Central Library, Lôn-y-Felin, Llangefni, Ynys Môn LL77 7RT
☎(01248) 752095
Fax (01248) 750197
e-mail: libraries@anglesey.gov.uk
Principal Librarian Ms Rachel Rowlands

Branch libraries

Amlwch Library, Lôn Parys, Amlwch, Ynys Môn LL68 9EA
☎(01407) 830145 (tel/fax)
e-mail: libraries@anglesey.gov.uk

Anglesey Archives, Industrial Estate Road, Bryn Cefni Industrial Estate, Llangefni, Ynys Môn LL77 7JA
☎(01248) 751930
e-mail: archives@ynysmon.gov.uk
Senior Archivist Hayden Burns

Holyhead Library, Newry Fields, Holyhead, Ynys Môn LL65 1LA
☎(01407) 762917
Fax (01407) 769616
e-mail: libraries@anglesey.gov.uk

Menai Bridge Library, Ffordd y Ffair, Menai Bridge, Ynys Môn LL59 5AS
☎(01248) 712706 (tel/fax)
e-mail: libraries@anglesey.gov.uk

BLAENAU GWENT

Authority: Life Leisure Trust (Blaenau Gwent)
Library Headquarters, The Regain Building, Mill Lane, Ebbw Vale, Blaenau Gwent NP23 6GR
url: www.blaenau-gwent.gov.uk
Principal Librarian Ms Tracy Jones (01495 355950; e-mail:
tracy.jones1@blaenau-gwent.gov.uk)

Central/largest library

Ebbw Vale Library, 21 Bethcar Street, Ebbw Vale, Blaenau Gwent NP23 6HH
☎(01495) 303069
Fax (01495) 350547
e-mail: ebbw.vale.library@blaenau-gwent.gov.uk

Area libraries

Abertillery Library, Station Hill, Abertillery, Blaenau Gwent NP13 1TE
☎(01495) 355646
e-mail: abertillery.library@blaenau-gwent.gov.uk

Blaina Library, Reading Institute, High Street, Blaina, Blaenau Gwent NP13 3BN
☎(01495) 355609 (tel/fax)
e-mail: blaina.library@blaenau-gwent.gov.uk

Brynmawr Library, Market Square, Brynmawr, Blaenau Gwent NP23 4AJ
☎(01495) 357743
Fax (01495) 357796
e-mail: brynmawr.library@blaenau-gwent.gov.uk

Cwm Library, Canning Street, Cwm, Blaenau Gwent NP23 7RW
☎(01495) 370454 (tel/fax)
e-mail: cwm.library@blaenau-gwent.gov.uk

Tredegar Library, The Circle, Tredegar, Blaenau Gwent NP22 3PS
☎(01495) 357869
Fax (01495) 355682
e-mail: tredegar.library@blaenau-gwent.gov.uk

BRIDGEND

Authority: Bridgend County Borough Council
Library and Information Service, Ravens Court, Brewery Lane, Bridgend CF31 4AP
☎(01656) 754800
Fax (01656) 642431
e-mail: blis@bridgend.gov.uk
url: www.bridgend.gov.uk/libraries
Group Manager (Cultural Services) Richard Hughes (e-mail:
richard.hughes@bridgend.gov.uk)
Interim Principal Officer: Libraries Richard Bellinger MSc MCLIP (e-mail:
richard.bellinger@bridgend.gov.uk)
Community Development Librarian Ms Helen Pridham BA DipIS MCLIP (e-mail:
helen.pridham@bridgend.gov.uk)
Children's Development Librarian Mrs Diana Apperley MA (e-mail:
diana.apperley@bridgend.gov.uk)

Central/largest libraries

Bridgend Library, Bridgend Recreation Centre, Bridgend CF31 4AH
☎(01656) 754830
Fax (01656) 754829
e-mail: bridgendlib@bridgend.gov.uk
Library Manager Mrs Pamela Grainger BA (e-mail: pamela.grainger@bridgend.gov.uk)

Maesteg Library, North's Lane, Maesteg, Glamorgan CF34 9AA
☎(01656) 754835
Fax (01656) 754834
e-mail: maestlib@bridgend.gov.uk
Library Manager Martyn Jones (e-mail: martyn.jones@bridgend.gov.uk)

Pencoed Library, Penybont Road, Pencoed, Glamorgan CF35 5RA
☎(01656) 754840
Fax (01656) 754842
e-mail: penclib@bridgend.gov.uk
Library Manager Ms Adele Parry (e-mail: adele.parry@bridgend.gov.uk)

Porthcawl Library, Church Place, Porthcawl, Glamorgan CF36 3AG
☎(01656) 754845
Fax (01656) 754847
e-mail: porthcawllib@bridgend.gov.uk
Library Manager Mrs Elaine Winstanley BSc (e-mail: elaine.winstanley@bridgend.gov.uk)

Pyle Library, Pyle Life Centre, Helig Fan, Pyle, Glamorgan CF33 6BS
☎(01656) 754850
Fax (01656) 754852
e-mail: pylelib@bridgend.gov.uk
Life Centre Manager Mrs Janet Arbery (e-mail: janet.arbery@bridgend.gov.uk)

CAERPHILLY

Authority: Caerphilly County Borough Council
Education and Leisure, Penalta House, Tredomen Park, Ystrad Mynach, Hengoed, Caerphilly CF82 7PG
☎(01443) 864033
Fax (01443) 866655
e-mail: libraries@caerphilly.gov.uk
url: www.caerphilly.gov.uk/libraries
Senior Manager, Libraries Gareth Evans MCLIP (01443 864033)
Operations Manager Mrs Jayne Lee MCLIP (01443 864060)
Group Specialist: Adult Services Manager Ms Karen E Pugh BA(Hons) MCLIP (01443 864059)
Group Specialist: Digital and E-services Manager Ms Lisa Thomas MCLIP (01443 864830)
Group Specialist: Children and Young People's Manager Mrs Karen John MCLIP (01443 864065)
Group Specialist: Audience Development and Engagement Manager Mrs Dianne Madhavan MCLIP (01443 864842)

CARDIFF

Authority: Cardiff Council
Cardiff Libraries, Wilcox House, Dunleavy Drive, Cardiff CF11 0BA
☎029 2038 2116 (Central Library)
e-mail: centrallibrary@cardiff.gov.uk
url: www.cardiff.gov.uk/libraries

Lead Libraries Officer Ms Nicola Richards BA(Hons) DipLib MCLIP (e-mail: nrichards@cardiff.gov.uk)
Branch Libraries Manager Ms Fiona Bailey (e-mail: fiona.bailey@cardiff.gov.uk)

CARMARTHENSHIRE

Authority: Carmarthenshire County Council
Llanelli Area Library, Vaughan Street, Llanelli, Carmarthenshire SA15 3AS
☎(01554) 773538
Fax (01554) 750125
Library Service Manager Mark Jewell BSc(Econ) (e-mail: mjewell@sirgar.gov.uk)

CEREDIGION

Authority: Ceredigion County Council
Public Library, Canolfan Alun R. Edwards, Queen's Square, Aberystwyth, Ceredigion SY23 2ED
☎(01970) 633703; 633716
Fax (01970) 625059
e-mail: llyfrgell.library@ceredigion.gov.uk
url: www.ceredigion.gov.uk
Head of Service (ICT & Customer Care) Ms Arwyn Morris
Library Service Manager Gareth Griffiths BA DipLib MCLIP (e-mail: gareth.griffiths@ceredigion.gov.uk)

Branch library

Branch Library, Canolfan Teifi, Pendre, Ceredigion SA43 1JL
☎(01239) 612578
Fax (01239) 612285
e-mail: teifillb@ceredigion.gov.uk
Branch Librarian Vacant

CONWY

Authority: Conwy County Borough Council
Culture and Information - Community Development Service, 2nd Floor, Library Buildings, Mostyn Street, Llandudno, Conwy LL30 2RP
☎(01492) 576139
Fax (01492) 575552
e-mail: library@conwy.gov.uk
url: www.conwy.gov.uk/library
Head of Community Service Ms Marianne Jackson
Section Head, Culture and Information Ms Ann Lloyd Williams PGCE AMA
(01492 575571; e-mail: ann.lloyd.williams@conwy.gov.uk)

Regional/community libraries

Abergele Library, Market Street, Abergele, Conwy LL22 7BP
☎(01492) 577505
e-mail: abergele.library@conwy.gov.uk

Colwyn Bay Library, Woodland Road West, Colwyn Bay, Conwy LL29 7DH
☎(01492) 577510
e-mail: colwynbay.library@conwy.gov.uk

Conwy Library, Civic Hall, Castle Street, Conwy LL32 6AY
☎(01492) 576089
e-mail: conwy.library@conwy.gov.uk

Llandudno Library, Mostyn Street, Llandudno, Conwy LL30 2RP
☎(01492) 574010
e-mail: llandudno.library@conwy.gov.uk

Llanrwst Library, Plas yn Dre, Station Road, Llanrwst, Conwy LL26 0DF
☎(01492) 577545
e-mail: llanrwst.library@conwy.gov.uk

DENBIGHSHIRE

Authority: Denbighshire County Council
Library Service, Yr Hen Garchar, Clwyd Street, Ruthin, Denbighshire LL15 1HP
☎(01824) 708204 (enquiries)
Fax (01824) 708202
url: www.denbighshire.gov.uk/libraries
Lead Officer: Libraries and Arts Robat Arwyn Jones BMus MCLIP DipLib
(01824 708203; e-mail: arwyn.jones@denbighshire.gov.uk)

Central/largest library
Rhyl Library, Museum and Arts Centre, Church Street, Rhyl, Denbighshire LL18 3AA
☎(01745) 353814
Fax (01745) 331438
e-mail: rhyl.library@denbighshire.gov.uk
Principal Community Librarian Ms Lucy Williams (e-mail:
lucy.williams@denbighshire.gov.uk)

FLINTSHIRE

Authority: Flintshire County Council
Library and Information Service, Library Headquarters, County Hall, Mold, Flintshire CH7 6NW
☎(01352) 704400
Fax (01352) 753662
e-mail: libraries@flintshire.gov.uk
url: www.flintshire.gov.uk
Principal Libraries and Arts Officer Mrs Pennie Corbett MLib MCLIP (01352 704402)

Group libraries
Broughton Library, Broughton Hall Road, Broughton, Nr Chester, Flintshire CH4 0QQ
☎(01244) 533727
Library Service Manager Gareth Edwards MCLIP

Buckley Library, Museum and Gallery, The Precinct, Buckley, Flintshire CH7 2EF
☎(01244) 549210

Fax (01244) 548850
Library Service Manager Ms Mandy Glendinning BEd

Connah's Quay Library, c/o County Hall, Mold, Flintshire CH7 6NW
☎(01352) 704400
Library Service Manager Mrs Carol A Guy BA MCLIP

Flint Library Learners Centre, Church Street, Flint, Flintshire CH6 5AP
☎(01352) 703737
Fax (01352) 731010
Library Service Manager Ms Kate Leonard BLib MCLIP

Holywell Library Learners Centre, North Road, Holywell, Flintshire CH8 7TQ
☎(01352) 713157
Fax (01352) 710744
Library Service Manager Mrs Catherine E Barber MCLIP

Mold Library and Museum, Earl Road, Mold, Flintshire CH7 1AP
☎(01352) 754791
Fax (01352) 754655
Library Service Manager Miss Nia W Jones BLib MCLIP

GWYNEDD

Authority: Gwynedd Council
Council Offices, Caernarfon, Gwynedd LL55 1SH
☎(01286) 679504
Fax (01286) 677347
e-mail: llyfrgell@gwynedd.gov.uk
url: www.gwynedd.gov.uk/library
Principal Librarian Hywel James BA DipLib MCLIP

Central/largest library
Caernarfon Library, Pavilion Hill, Caernarfon, Gwynedd LL55 1AS
☎(01286) 679463
Fax (01286) 671137
e-mail: llyfrgellcaernarfon@gwynedd.gov.uk
Community Services Librarian Mrs Eirlys Thomas MCLIP
User Services Manager Ms Nia Gruffydd MLib MCLIP (e-mail:
NiaGruffydd@gwynedd.gov.uk)

Largest libraries
Bangor Library, Ffordd Gwynedd, Bangor, Gwynedd LL57 1DT
☎(01248) 353479
Fax (01248) 370149
e-mail: llbangor@gwynedd.gov.uk
Library Services Promoter Gwawr Williams BA

Dolgellau Library, Ffordd y Bala, Dolgellau, Gwynedd LL40 2YF
☎(01341) 422771
Fax (01341) 423560
e-mail: lldolgellau@gwynedd.gov.uk
Information Librarian Aled Wyn Jones BA DipLib

Porthmadog Library, Stryd Wesla, Porthmadog, Gwynedd LL49 9BT
☎(01766) 514091
Fax (01766) 513821
e-mail: llporthmadog@gwynedd.gov.uk
South Gwynedd Community Librarian Ms Anna Yardley Jones BA DipLib MCLIP

MERTHYR TYDFIL

Authority: Merthyr Tydfil County Borough Council
Central Library, High Street, Merthyr Tydfil CF47 8AF
☎(01685) 353480
e-mail: library.services@merthyr.gov.uk
url: www.merthyr.gov.uk
Principal Librarian Ms Jane Sellwood

Area libraries

Aberfan Community Library, Aberfan and Merthyr Vale Community Centre, Pantglas Road, Aberfan, Merthyr Tydfil CF48 4QE

Dowlais Library, Church Street, Merthyr Tydfil CF48 3HS
☎(01685) 723051
Fax (01685) 723051
(Enquiries to Central Library)

Treharris Library, Perrott Street, Treharris, Merthyr Tydfil CF46 5ET
☎(01685) 353483
(Enquiries to Central Library)

MONMOUTHSHIRE

Authority: Monmouthshire County Council
Libraries and Information Service, PO Box 106, Manor Way, Caldicot, Monmouthshire NP26 9AN
☎(01291) 636390 (administration)
Fax (01291) 635736
url: www.libraries.monmouthshire.gov.uk
Head of Library and Information Services Ms Ann Jones MLib MCLIP (e-mail: annjones@monmouthshire.gov.uk)

Area libraries

Bryn-a-Cwm Area

Abergavenny Library, Baker Street, Abergavenny, Monmouthshire NP7 5BD
☎(01873) 735980
Fax (01873) 735985
e-mail: abergavennylibrary@monmouthshire.gov.uk
Library Manager Ms Vivienne Thomas BA BD MCLIP (e-mail: viviennethomas@monmouthshire.gov.uk)

Central Monmouthshire Area

Monmouth Library, Rolls Hall, Whitecross Street, Monmouth NP25 3BY

☎(01600) 775215
Fax (01600) 775218
e-mail: monmouthlibrary@monmouthshire.gov.uk
Library Managers Ms Julia Greenway MCLIP (e-mail:
juliagreenway@monmouthshire.gov.uk), Ms Sue Wallbank (e-mail:
suewallbank@monmouthshire.gov.uk) (job share)

Lower Wye Area

Chepstow Library, Manor Way, Chepstow, Monmouthshire NP16 5HZ
☎(01291) 635730
Fax (01291) 635736
e-mail: chepstowlibrary@monmouthshire.gov.uk
Library Managers Ms Sue Wallbank (e-mail: suewallbank@monmouthshire.gov.uk),
Ms Sally Bradford (e-mail: sallybradford@monmouthshire.gov.uk) (job share)

Severnside Area

Caldicot Library, Woodstock Way, Caldicot, Monmouthshire NP26 4DB
☎(01291) 426425
Fax (01291) 426426
e-mail: caldicotlibrary@monmouthshire.gov.uk
Library Manager Ms Fiona Ashley BLib MCLIP (e-mail:
fionaashley@monmouthshire.gov.uk)

NEATH PORT TALBOT

Authority: Neath Port Talbot County Borough Council
Library and Information Services, Reginald Street, Velindre, Port Talbot SA13 1YY
☎(01639) 899829
Fax (01639) 899152
e-mail: npt.libhq@npt.gov.uk
url: www.npt.gov.uk
County Librarian Wayne John MCLIP (e-mail: w.john@npt.gov.uk)

Central/largest libraries

Neath Library, Victoria Gardens, Neath, Neath Port Talbot SA11 3BA
☎(01639) 644604/635017
Fax (01639) 641912
e-mail: neath.library@npt.gov.uk

Port Talbot Library, Aberavon Shopping Centre (1st Floor), Port Talbot SA13 1PB
☎(01639) 763490/1
Fax (01639) 763489
e-mail: porttalbot.library@npt.gov.uk

NEWPORT

Authority: Newport City Council
**Community Learning and Libraries Service, Central Library, John Frost Square,
Newport, Gwent NP20 1PA**
☎(01633) 656656 (enquiries and administration)
Fax (01633) 222615

e-mail: central.library@newport.gov.uk
url: www.newport.gov.uk/libraries
Community Learning and Libraries Manager Mrs Gill John MBA MCLIP
Operations Manager Alun Prescott BA(Hons) DipILS

PEMBROKESHIRE

Authority: Pembrokeshire County Council
County Library, Dew Street, Haverfordwest, Pembrokeshire SA61 ISU
☎(01437) 775241 (administration, enquiries); (01437) 775244 (Lending Library)
url: www.pembrokeshire.gov.uk
Head of Cultural Services Mike Cavanagh (e-mail: mike.cavanagh@pembrokeshire.gov.uk)
Libraries Manager Mrs Anita Thomas BLib MCLIP (01437 776059; e-mail:
anita.thomas@pembrokeshire.gov.uk)
Collections Manager Ms Gill Gilliland DipLIS MCLIP (01437 774692; e-mail:
gill.gilliland@pembrokeshire.gov.uk)
Operations Manager South Ms Pamela Anthony (01437 776089; e-mail:
pamela.anthony@pembrokeshire.gov.uk)
Operations Manager North George Edwards BA MSc MCLIP (01437 776126; e-mail:
george.edwards@pembrokeshire.gov.uk)
Children and Families Librarian Ms Wendy Davies MCLIP (01437 776639; e-mail:
wendy.davies@pembrokeshire.gov.uk), Ms Fiona Bailey (e-mail:
fiona.bailey@cardiff.gov.uk)
Economy Librarian Ms Kath Woolcock MSc(Econ) (01437 776098; e-mail:
kath.woolcock@pembrokeshire.gov.uk)
Health and Wellbeing Librarian Vacant
Marketing and Performance Officer Shaun Raymond DipLIS (01437 776129; e-mail:
shaun.raymond@pembrokeshire.gov.uk)

Community libraries
County Library, Dew Street, Haverfordwest, Pembrokeshire SA61 ISU
☎(01437) 775244
Site Co-ordinator Ms Annabel Thomas

Fishguard Library, Fishguard Town Hall, Market Square, Fishguard, Pembrokeshire SA65 9HA
☎(01437) 776638
Fax (01348) 874990
Site Co-ordinator Vacant

Milford Haven Library, Suite 19, Cedar Court, Milford Haven, Pembrokeshire SA73 3LS
☎(01437) 771888
Senior Library Assistant Ms Tracy Collins

Pembroke Dock Library, Water Street, Pembroke Dock, Pembrokeshire SA72 6DW
☎(01437) 775825
Site Co-ordinator Stuart Croxford

Tenby Library, Greenhill Avenue, Tenby, Pembrokeshire SA70 7LB
☎(01834) 843934 (tel/fax)
Site Co-ordinator Vacant

POWYS

Authority: Powys County Council
County Library HQ, Cefnllys Lane, Llandrindod Wells, Powys LDI 5LD
☎(01597) 826860 (general enquiries)
Fax (01597) 826872
url: www.powys.gov.uk/libraries
Principal Librarian Mrs Kay Thomas BLib MCLIP

Main libraries
Brecon Library, Ship Street, Brecon, Powys LD3 9AE
☎(01874) 623346
Fax (01874) 622818
Group Librarian (South) Ms Vicki Workman

Llandrindod Wells Library, Cefnllys Lane, Llandrindod Wells, Powys LDI 5LD
☎(01597) 826870
Fax (01597) 826872

Newtown Library, Park Lane, Newtown, Powys SY16 IEJ
☎(01686) 626934
Fax (01686) 624935
Group Librarian (North) Mrs Mair Dafydd BA MCLIP

RHONDDA CYNON TAF

Authority: Rhondda Cynon Taf County Borough Council
Education and Lifelong Learning, Ty Trevithick, Abercynon, Mountain Ash, Rhondda Cynon Taf CF45 4UQ
☎(01443) 744000
Fax (01443) 744023
url: www.rhondda-cynon-taf.gov.uk
Head of Community Learning (Adult Education, Libraries and Welsh Language Services) Ms Wendy Edwards BA PGCE LLDip MPhil (e-mail: wendy.edwards@rctcbc.gov.uk)
Principal Librarian Nick E. Kelland BSc(Econ) MCLIP (01443 778952; e-mail: nick.e.kelland@rhondda-cynon-taff.gov.uk) (based at Treorchy Library)
Area Manager Richard Reed (01443 492138; e-mail: richard.reed@rhondda-cynon-taf.gov.uk) (based at Pontypridd Library)
Information Services Librarian Ms Menna James BSc(Econ) (01658 880054; e-mail: menna.james@rhondda-cynon-taf.gov.uk) (based at Aberdare Library)
Senior Librarian, Children and Youth Services Ms Wendy Cole BA MCLIP (01443 425419; e-mail: schools.library@rhondda-cynon-taf.gov.uk) (based at Ty Elai, Williamstown)
Senior Librarian, Mobiles and Special Services Ms Erika Neck BSc PGDip MCLIP (01685 880061; e-mail: erika.neck@rhondda-cynon-taf.gov.uk) (based at Aberdare Library)

Largest library
Aberdare Library, Green Street, Aberdare, Rhondda Cynon Taf CF44 7AG
☎(01685) 880050
Fax (01685) 881181

e-mail: Aberdare.Library@rhondda-cynon-taff.gov.uk
Senior Branch Librarian Ms Judith George (e-mail: judith.george@rctcbc.gov.uk)

Regional libraries
Pontypridd Library, Library Road, Pontypridd, Rhondda Cynon Taf CF37 2DY
☎(01443) 486850
Fax (01443) 493258
e-mail: Pontypridd.Library@rhondda-cynon-taff.gov.uk
Senior Branch Librarian Mrs Edwina Smart BA

Treorchy Library, Station Road, Treorchy, Rhondda Cynon Taf CF42 6NN
☎(01443) 773204
Fax (01443) 777047
e-mail: Treorchy.Library@rhondda-cynon-taff.gov.uk
Senior Branch Librarian Dean Price BSc(Econ) MCLIP

SWANSEA

Authority: City and County of Swansea
Library HQ, The Civic Centre, Oystermouth Road, Swansea SAI 3SN
☎(01792) 636430
Fax (01792) 636235
e-mail: swansea.libraries@swansea.gov.uk
url: www.swansea.gov.uk/libraries
Strategic Manager: Libraries and Culture Vacant
Library Services Manager Steve Hardman BSc(Econ) (01792 636610; e-mail:
steve.hardman@swansea.gov.uk)
Assistant Heads of Libraries Ms Karen Bewen-Chappell MCLIP (01792 636809; e-mail:
karen.bewen-chappell@swansea.gov.uk), Ms Caroline Tomlin BA DipLib MCLIP (01792
636809; e-mail: caroline.tomlin@swansea.gov.uk) (job share)
Principal Librarian: Resources and Reader Services Mrs Julie Clement BLib MCLIP
(01792 636628; e-mail: julie.clement@swansea.gov.uk)
Principal Librarian: Customer Services and Operations Mrs Jayne Trumper BA DipLib
MCLIP (01792 636938; e-mail: jayne.trumper@swansea.gov.uk)
Principal Librarian: Information and Learning Ms Karen Gibbins (01792 636329;
e-mail: karen.gibbins@swansea.gov.uk)

Central/largest library
Swansea Library, The Civic Centre, Oystermouth Road, Swansea SAI 3SN
☎(01792) 636464
Fax (01792) 637193
e-mail: libraryline@swansea.gov.uk
Library Manager Ms Kerry Pillai

Branch libraries
Gorseinon Library, 15 West Street, Gorseinon, Swansea SA4 4AA
☎(01792) 516780
Fax (01792) 516772
e-mail: gorseinon.library@swansea.gov.uk
Library Manager Ms Julie Emmanuel

Morriston Library, Treharne Road, Morriston, Swansea SA6 7AA
☎(01792) 516770
Fax (01792) 516771
e-mail: morriston.library@swansea.gov.uk
Library Manager Ms Pat Perkins

Oystermouth Library, Dunns Lane, Mumbles, Swansea SA3 4AA
☎(01792) 368380
Fax (01792) 369143
e-mail: oystermouth.library@swansea.gov.uk
Library Manager Ms Judy Knight

TORFAEN

Authority: Torfaen County Borough Council
Torfaen Libraries HQ, Ty Blaen Torfaen, Panteg Way, New Inn, Pontypool, Torfaen, Gwent NP4 0LS
☎(01633) 628943
Fax (01495) 766709
url: www.torfaen.gov.uk
Torfaen Library and Information Manager Mrs Christine George BA DipLib MCLIP

Central/largest library
Cwmbran Library, Gwent House, Cwmbran, Torfaen, Gwent NP44 1XQ
☎(01633) 647676
Fax (01633) 647684
e-mail: cwmbranlibrary@torfaen.gov.uk
Senior Librarian Mrs Stephanie Morgan BA (Hons Lib/Hist)
Library Manager Mrs Donna Reardon

Group library
Pontypool Library, Hanbury Road, Pontypool, Torfaen, Gwent NP4 6JL
☎(01495) 762820
e-mail: pontypoollibrary@torfaen.gov.uk
Senior Librarian Mark Tanner BA DipLib MCLIP

VALE OF GLAMORGAN

Authority: Vale of Glamorgan Council
Directorate of Learning and Skills, Provincial House, Kendrick Road, Barry, Vale of Glamorgan CF62 8BF
☎(01446) 709381
url: www.valeofglamorgan.gov.uk/libraries
Chief Librarian Christopher Edwards BA(Hons) DipLib MCLIP (e-mail: cdedwards@valeofglamorgan.gov.uk)

Central/largest library
County Library, King Square, Barry, Vale of Glamorgan CF63 4RW
☎(01446) 422411/422425
Senior Librarian Ms Katherine Owen MCLIP (e-mail: kowen@valeofglamorgan.gov.uk)

Information Librarian Gethin Sheppard BA(Hons) PGDip ACLIP (e-mail: gdsheppard@valeofglamorgan.gov.uk)
Children's Librarian Ms Gillian Southby BA(Hons) PGDip L&IM (e-mail: gsouthby@valeofglamorgan.gov.uk)

Main libraries

Cowbridge Library, Old Hall, Cowbridge, Vale of Glamorgan CF71 7AH
☎(01446) 773941
Community Librarian Ms Melanie Weeks (e-mail: mpweeks@valeofglamorgan.gov.uk)

Dinas Powys Library, The Murch, Dinas Powys, Vale of Glamorgan CF64 4QU
☎029 2051 2556
Community Librarian Paul Templing MSc L&IM (e-mail: ptempling@valeofglamorgan.gov.uk)

Llantwit Major Library, Boverton Road, Llantwit Major, Vale of Glamorgan CF61 1XZ
☎(01446) 792700
Community Librarians Mrs Eironwyn Emlyn-Jones (e-mail: eemlyn-jones@valeofglamorgan.gov.uk), Mrs Christina Scott (e-mail: tscott@valeofglamorgan.gov.uk)

Penarth Library, Stanwell Road, Penarth, Vale of Glamorgan CF64 2YT
☎029 2070 8438
Senior Librarian Marcus Payne BA DipLib MCLIP (e-mail: mmpayne@valeofglamorgan.gov.uk)

WREXHAM

Authority: Wrexham County Borough Council
Library and Information Service, Community Wellbeing and Development Department, Lord Street, Wrexham LL11 1LG
url: www.wrexham.gov.uk
Leisure and Libraries Manager Dylan Hughes BA DipLib MCLIP (01978 298855; e-mail: dylan.hughes@wrexham.gov.uk)

Central/largest library

Wrexham Library, Rhosddu Road, Wrexham LL11 1AU
☎(01978) 292090
e-mail: library@wrexham.gov.uk
Library Services Manager Miss Ann Hughes MA MCLIP (01978 292622; e-mail: ann.hughes@wrexham.gov.uk)
Community Librarian Vacant

Group/branch libraries

Brynteg Library, Quarry Road, Brynteg, Wrexham LL11 6AB
☎(01978) 759523
e-mail: brynteg.library@wrexham.gov.uk
Community Librarian Mrs Marina Thomas MCLIP (01978 292614; e-mail: marina.thomas@wrexham.gov.uk)

Rhos Library, Princes Road, Rhos, Wrexham LL14 1AB
☎(01978) 840328

e-mail: rhos.library@wrexham.gov.uk
Community Librarian Mrs Marina Thomas MCLIP (01978 292614; e-mail:
marina.thomas@wrexham.gov.uk)

CROWN DEPENDENCIES

ALDERNEY

Authority: Alderney
Alderney Library, Church Street, Alderney, Channel Islands GY9 3TE
☎(01481) 824178
e-mail: info@alderneylibrary.org
url: www.alderneylibrary.org
Librarian Ms Kate Russell
Children's Room Ms Joan Banks
(Alderney Library is a voluntary organization)

GUERNSEY

Authority: Guernsey
Guille-Allès Library, Market Street, St Peter Port, Guernsey, Channel Islands GYI IHB
☎(01481) 720392
Fax (01481) 712425
e-mail: ga@library.gg
url: www.library.gg
Chief Librarian Miss Laura Milligan BEd(Hons) MSc(Econ) DipLib MCLIP (e-mail:
lmilligan@library.gg)
Head of Services to Education and Young People Mrs Elizabeth Hutchinson BSc
MCLIP (e-mail: ehutchinson@library.gg)

Priaulx Library, Candie Road, St Peter Port, Guernsey, Channel Islands GYI IUG
☎(01481) 721998
Fax (01481) 713 804
e-mail: priaulx.library@gov.gg
url: www.priaulxlibrary.co.uk
Chief Librarian Ms Amanda Bennett BA(Hons) MA MCLIP
Deputy Chief Librarian Ms Sue Laker DipLib CMS MCLIP
(The Priaulx Library is a reference and lending library specializing in local history and family
history research in the Channel Islands)

ISLE OF MAN

Authority: Isle of Man
**Henry Bloom Noble Library, Douglas Borough Council, 10/12 Victoria Street, Douglas,
Isle of Man IMI 2LH**
☎(01624) 696461
Fax (01624) 696400
e-mail: library.douglas.gov.im
url: www.douglaslibrary.gov.im

Castletown Library, Castletown Commissioners, Farrants Way, Castletown, Isle of Man IM9 INR
☎(01624) 829355
Fax (01624) 829355
e-mail: library@castletown.org.im
Librarian Mrs Angela Teare

Family Library and Mobile Library, Isle of Man Department of Education, Westmoreland Road, Douglas, Isle of Man IMI IRL
☎(01624) 640650
Fax (01624) 671043
url: www.familylibrary.im
Librarian in Charge (Family Library) Ms Mary Cousins BA(Hons) (e-mail: mary.cousins@familylibrary.im)
Librarian in Charge (Mobile Library) Mrs Sandra Henderson MCLIP (e-mail: sandra.henderson@familylibrary.im)

George Herdman Library, Port Erin Commissioners, Bridson Street, Port Erin, Isle of Man IM9 6AL
☎(01624) 832365
Librarian Miss Angela Dryland BSc (e-mail: library@porterin.gov.im)

Onchan Library, Onchan District Commissioners, Willow House, 61-69 Main Road, Onchan, Isle of Man IM3 IAJ
☎(01624) 621228 (tel/fax)
e-mail: onchan.library@onchan.org.im
url: www.library.onchan.org.im
Librarian Mrs Pam Hand

Ramsey Town Library, Ramsey Town Commissioners, Town Hall, Parliament Square, Ramsey, Isle of Man IM8 IRT
☎(01624) 810146
e-mail: ramsey.library@rtc.gov.im
Librarian Paul Boulton BA

Ward Library, Peel Town Commissoners, 38 Castle Street, Peel, Isle of Man IM5 IAL
☎(01624) 843533
e-mail: ward_library@hotmail.com
Librarian Miss Gemma Quilliam

JERSEY

Authority: Jersey
Jersey Library, Halkett Place, St Helier, Jersey, Channel Islands JE2 4WH
☎(01534) 448700 (enquiries), (01534) 448701 (reference), (01534) 448714 (administration)
Fax (01534) 448730
e-mail: je.library@gov.je
url: www.gov.je/library
Chief Librarian Edward Jewell BA MA MSc(Econ) MCLIP

Public Libraries in the Republic of Ireland

CARLOW

Authority: Carlow County Council
Carlow Central Library, Tullow Street, Carlow, Republic of Ireland
☎(00 353 59) 917 0094/912 9705
e-mail: library@carlowcoco.ie
url: www.carlowlibraries.ie
County Librarian Ms Josephine Coyne BSc DLIS
Senior Executive Librarian Ms Deirdre Condron BComm DipLib
Executive Librarian John Shortall BA MSc(Econ)

CAVAN

Authority: Cavan County Council
Johnston Central Library, Farnham Street, Cavan, Republic of Ireland
☎(00 353 49) 437 8505
e-mail: library@cavancoco.ie
url: www.cavanlibrary.ie
County Librarian Ms Josephine Brady BA DLIS
Executive Librarian Tom Sullivan DLIS MSSc
Assistant Librarians Mrs Teresa Treacy BA DLIS, Ms Emma Clancy BA DLIS

CLARE

Authority: Clare County Council
Clare County Library HQ, Mill Road, Ennis, Co Clare, Republic of Ireland
☎(00 353 65) 684 6350/682 1616
Fax (00 353 65) 684 2462
e-mail: mailbox@clarelibrary.ie
url: www.clarelibrary.ie
County Librarian Ms Helen Walsh BSc DLIS LAI

Central/largest library
De Valera Branch Library, Harmony Row, Ennis, Co Clare, Republic of Ireland
☎(00 353 65) 684 6353

Area libraries
Corofin Library, Corofin, Co Clare, Republic of Ireland
☎(00 353 65) 683 7219

Dr Patrick J Hillery Library, Ballard Road, Miltown Malbay, Co Clare, Republic of Ireland
☎(00 353 65) 708 4822

Ennistymon Library, The Square, Ennistymon, Co Clare, Republic of Ireland
☎(00 353 65) 7071245

Kildysart Library, St John Bosco's Community College, Kildysart, Co Clare, Republic of Ireland
☎(00 353 65) 683 2113

Kilfinaghty Library, Church Street, Sixmile Bridge, Co Clare, Republic of Ireland
☎(00 353 61) 369678

Killaloe Library, The Lock House, Killaloe, Co Clare, Republic of Ireland
☎(00 353 61) 376062

Kilmihil Library, St Michael's Community Centre, Church Street, Kilmihil, Co Clare,
Republic of Ireland
☎(00 353 65) 905 0528

Kilrush Library, Kilrush, Co Clare, Republic of Ireland
☎(00 353 65) 905 1504

Lisdoonvarna Library, Kincora Road, Lisdoonvarna, Co Clare, Republic of Ireland
☎(00 353 65) 707 4029

Local Studies Centre, The Manse, Harmony Row, Ennis, Co Clare, Republic of Ireland
☎(00 353 65) 684 6271

Scariff Library, Mountshannon Road, Scariff, Co Clare, Republic of Ireland
☎(00 353 61) 922893

Sean Lemass Library, Town Centre, Shannon, Co Clare, Republic of Ireland
☎(00 353 61) 364266

Library at Culturlann Sweeney, O'Connell Street, Kilkee, Co Clare, Republic of Ireland
☎(00 353 65) 905 6034

Tulla Library, The Market House, Tulla, Co Clare, Republic of Ireland
☎(00 353 65) 683 5919

William Smith O'Brien Library, Kilnasoolagh Park, Newmarket-on-Fergus, Co Clare,
Republic of Ireland
☎(00 353 61) 368411

CORK CITY

Authority: Cork City Council
Cork City Libraries, 57–61 Grand Parade, Cork, Republic of Ireland
☎(00 353 21) 492 4900
Fax (00 353 21) 427 5684
e-mail: libraries@corkcity.ie
url: www.corkcitylibraries.ie
City Librarian Liam Ronayne BCL DipLib ALAI
Executive Librarian (Bibliographic Services) Ms Sinead Feely

Branch libraries

Bishopstown Library, Wilton, Cork, Republic of Ireland
☎(00 353 21) 492 4950
Fax (00 353 21) 434 5428
e-mail: bishopstown_library@corkcity.ie

Blackpool Library, Blackpool, Cork, Republic of Ireland
☎(00 353 21) 492 4933
Fax (00 353 21) 427 5684
e-mail: blackpool_library@corkcity.ie

Children's and Young People's Services, 57 Grand Parade, Cork, Republic of Ireland
☎(00 353 21) 492 4913
Fax (00 353 21) 427 5684
Children's Services Librarian Ms Eibhlín Cassidy (e-mail: childrens_library@corkcity.ie)

Douglas Library, Douglas, Cork, Republic of Ireland
☎(00 353 21) 492 4932
Fax (00 353 21) 427 5684
e-mail: douglas_library@corkcity.ie

Frank O'Connor Library, Old Youghal Road, Mayfield, Cork, Republic of Ireland
☎(00 353 21) 492 4935
Fax (00 353 21) 427 5684
e-mail: mayfield_library@corkcity.ie

Hollyhill Library, Hollyhill, Cork, Republic of Ireland
☎(00 353 21) 492 4928
Fax (00 353 21) 439 3032
e-mail: hollyhill_library@corkcity.ie

Tory Top Road Library, Ballyphehane, Cork, Republic of Ireland
☎(00 353 21) 492 4934
Fax (00 353 21) 427 5684
e-mail: torytop_library@corkcity.ie

CORK COUNTY

Authority: Cork County Council
Cork County Library and Arts Service, Carrigrohane Road, Cork, Republic of Ireland
☎(00 353 21) 454 6499
e-mail: corkcountylibrary@corkcoco.ie
url: www.corkcoco.ie/library
Acting County Librarian Ms Eileen O'Brien

DONEGAL

Authority: Donegal County Council
Donegal County Library Admin. Centre, Rosemount, Letterkenny, Co Donegal, Republic of Ireland
☎(00 353 74) 912 1968 (enquiries and administration)
Fax (00 353 74) 912 1740
e-mail: library@donegalcoco.ie
url: www.donegallibrary.ie
County Librarian and Divisional Manager, Cultural Services Ms Eileen Burgess
Executive Librarian Ms Marianne Lynch (e-mail: marianne.lynch@donegalcoco.ie)

Central/largest library

Central Library, Oliver Plunkett Road, Letterkenny, Co Donegal, Republic of Ireland
☎(00 353 74) 912 4950
Fax (00 353 74) 912 4950
e-mail: central@donegallibrary.ie
Executive Librarian Ms Helen McNutt

DUBLIN

Authority : Dublin City Council
Dublin City Public Libraries, Dublin City Library and Archive, 138–144 Pearse Street, Dublin 2, Republic of Ireland
☎(00 353 1) 674 4800
Fax (00 353 1) 674 4880
e-mail: dublinpubliclibraries@dublincity.ie
url: www.dublincity.ie
City Librarian Ms Margaret Hayes BA DipLib HDipEd ALAI (e-mail: margaret.hayes@dublincity.ie)

Central/largest library

Central Public Library, ILAC Centre, Henry Street, Dublin 1, Republic of Ireland
☎(00 353 1) 873 4333
Fax (00 353 1) 872 1451
e-mail: central.library@dublincity.ie

DÚN LAOGHAIRE–RATHDOWN

Authority: Dún Laoghaire–Rathdown County Council
Public Library Service, Haigh Terrace, Dún Laoghaire, Co Dublin, Republic of Ireland
☎(00 353 1) 214 7970
Fax (00 353 1) 214 7999
e-mail: libraries@dlrcoco.ie
url: www.dlrcoco.ie/library
County Librarian Ms Mairead Owens MA DLIS
Senior Executive Librarian, Finance, IT, Development and Special Projects Ms Geraldine McHugh MA DLIS ALAI
Senior Executive Librarian, Staffing, Health and Safety and Policy Co-ordination Ms Ciara Jones BA DLIS
Senior Executive Librarian, Bibliographic Services, Reader Development and Outreach Ms Marian Keyes BA MA DLIS

Central/largest library

Central Library, Haigh Terrace, Dun Laoghaire, Co Dublin, Republic of Ireland
☎(00 353 1) 280 1147
e-mail: dunlaoghairelib@dlrcoco.ie
Senior Librarian Ms Lisa Murphy BA DLIS

Branch libraries

Blackrock Library, Main Street, Blackrock, Co Dublin, Republic of Ireland
☎(00 353 1) 288 8117
e-mail: blackrocklib@dlrcoco.ie
Senior Librarian Ms Lisa Larkin BA HDipLIS

Cabinteely Library, Old Bray Road, Cabinteely, Dublin 18, Republic of Ireland
☎(00 353 1) 285 5363
e-mail: cabinteelylib@dlrcoco.ie
Senior Librarian Ms Fiona Doherty BA DLIS

Dalkey Library, Castle Street, Dalkey, Co Dublin, Republic of Ireland
☎(00 353 1) 285 5277
e-mail: dalkeylib@dlrcoco.ie
Senior Librarian Ms Carmel Kelly

Deansgrange Library, Clonkeen Drive, Deansgrange, Dublin 18, Republic of Ireland
☎(00 353 1) 285 0860
e-mail: deansgrangelib@dlrcoco.ie
Senior Librarian Ms Oonagh Brennan BA DLIS

Dundrum Library, Upper Churchtown Road, Dublin 14, Republic of Ireland
☎(00 353 1) 298 5000
e-mail: dundrumlib@dlrcoco.ie
Senior Librarian Ms Anne Millane BA DLIS

Shankill Library, Library Road, Shankill, Co Dublin, Republic of Ireland
☎(00 353 1) 282 3081
e-mail: shankilllib@dlrcoco.ie
Librarian Ms Shelley Healy

Stillorgan Library, St Laurence's Park, Stillorgan, Co Dublin, Republic of Ireland
☎(00 353 1) 288 9655
e-mail: stillorganlib@dlrcoco.ie
Senior Librarian Ms Patricia Byrne BA DLIS

FINGAL

Authority: Fingal County Council
Fingal County Libraries, Lower Ground Floor, County Hall, Swords, Co Dublin, Republic of Ireland
☎(00 353 1) 890 5533
Fax (00 353 1) 890 5599
e-mail: libraries@fingal.ie
url: www.fingalcoco.ie/libraries
County Librarian Vacant
Senior Executive Librarian (Admin/Personnel & Finance) Ms Betty Boardman
Senior Librarian (Personnel & Finance) (Bibliographic Services) Ms Carmel Turner
Senior Executive Librarian (Projects Development) Ms Yvonne O'Brien
Librarian (Development & PR) Ms Siobhan Walshe

Largest library
Blanchardstown Library, Civic Centre, Blanchardstown Centre, Dublin 15, Republic of Ireland
☎(00 353 1) 890 5560
Fax (00 353 1) 890 5574
e-mail: blanchlib@fingal.ie
Senior Executive Librarian Ms Yvonne O'Brien
Senior Librarian Ms Ann Byrne

Branch libraries
Balbriggan Library, St George's Square, Balbriggan, Co Dublin, Republic of Ireland

☎(00 353 1) 870 4401
e-mail: balbrigganlibrary@fingal.ie
Senior Librarian Ms Assumpta Hickey

Baldoyle Library, Strand Road, Baldoyle, Dublin 13, Republic of Ireland
☎(00 353 1) 890 6793
e-mail: baldoylelibrary@fingal.ie
Senior Librarian Ms Catherine Keane

County Archives, Clonmel House, Forster Way, Swords, Co Dublin, Republic of Ireland
☎(00 353 1) 870 4496
e-mail: archives@fingal.ie
Archivist Colm McQuinn

Donabate/Portrane Library, Donabate Portrane Community Leisure Centre, Co Dublin, Republic of Ireland
☎(00 353 1) 890 5609
e-mail: donabatelibrary@fingal.ie
Librarian Ms Enid Bebbington

Garristown Library, Main Street, Garristown, Co Dublin, Republic of Ireland
☎(00 353 1) 835 5020
e-mail: garristownlibrary@fingal.ie
Senior Assistant Ms Yvonne Boylan

Housebound Services, Unit 34, Coolmine Industrial Estate, Coolmine, Dublin 15, Republic of Ireland
☎(00 353 1) 822 1564
e-mail: houseboundlibrary@fingal.ie
Librarian Ms Frances Cassidy

Howth Library, Main Street, Howth, Co Dublin, Republic of Ireland
☎(00 353 1) 890 5026
e-mail: howthlibrary@fingal.ie
Librarian Ms Colette Fox

Local Studies, Clonmel House, Forster Way, Swords, Co Dublin, Republic of Ireland
☎(00 353 1) 870 4495
e-mail: local.studies@fingal.ie
Senior Librarian Ms Jacinta Judge

Malahide Library, Main Street, Malahide, Co Dublin, Republic of Ireland
☎(00 353 1) 870 4430
e-mail: malahidelibrary@fingal.ie
Senior Librarian Ms Marjory Sliney

Mobile Library Services, Unit 34, Coolmine Industrial Estate, Coolmine, Dublin 15, Republic of Ireland
☎(00 353 1) 822 1564
e-mail: mobilelibraries@fingal.ie
Senior Librarian Mrs Kathleen Ryan BA MBA FCLIP

Rush Library, Chapel Green, Rush, Co Dublin, Republic of Ireland
☎(00 353 1) 890 8414

e-mail: rushlibrary@fingal.ie
Librarian Charlie Quinn

Skerries Library, Strand Street, Skerries, Co Dublin, Republic of Ireland
☎(00 353 1) 849 1900
e-mail: skerrieslibrary@fingal.ie
Librarian Ms Josephine Knight

Swords Library, Swords Shopping Centre, Rathbeale Road, Swords, Co Dublin, Republic of Ireland
☎(00 353 1) 890 5582
e-mail: swordslibrary@fingal.ie
Senior Librarian Ms Lillian Whelan

GALWAY

Authority: Galway County Council
Galway County Library HQ, Island House, Cathedral Square, Galway, Republic of Ireland
☎(00 353 91) 562471
Fax (00 353 91) 565039
e-mail: info@galwaylibrary.ie
url: www.galwaylibrary.ie
Acting County Librarian Peter Rabbitt BA LLB DipLib
Senior Executive Librarians Mrs Bernadette Kelly BA DipLib, Peter Rabbitt
BA LLB DipLib
Librarian, ICT John Fitzgibbon
Executive Librarian, Schools Mrs Josephine Vahey
Archivist Ms Patricia McWalter BA HDipAS
Librarian, Branch System Ms Catherine Farragher

Central/largest library
Galway City Library, Hynes Building, St Augustine Street, Galway, Republic of Ireland
☎(00 353 91) 561666
Acting Executive Librarian Tom Browne

Branch libraries
Ballinasloe Public Library, Fairgreen, Ballinasloe, Co Galway, Republic of Ireland
☎(00 353 90) 964 3464
Acting Executive Librarian Kieran Shaughnessy

Ballybane Public Library, Castlepark Road, Ballybane, Galway, Republic of Ireland
☎(00 353 91) 380590
Executive Librarian Ms Siobhan Arkins

Carraroe Public Library, Co Galway, Republic of Ireland
☎(00 353 95) 95733
Branch Librarian Ms Triona Mhic Dhonncha

Clifden Public Library, Clifden, Co Galway, Republic of Ireland
☎(00 353 95) 21092
Senior Library Assistant Paul Keogh

Loughrea Public Library, Loughrea, Co Galway, Republic of Ireland
☎(00 353 91) 847220
Assistant Librarian Ms Anne Callanan

Oranmore Public Library, Oranmore, Co Galway, Republic of Ireland
☎(00 353 91) 792117
Staff Officer, Libraries John Lawlor

Portumna Public Library, Portumna, Co Galway, Republic of Ireland
☎(00 353 90) 974 1261
Senior Library Assistant Ms Teresa Tierney

Tuam Public Library, Tuam, Co Galway, Republic of Ireland
☎(00 353 93) 24287
Staff Officer, Libraries Ms Emer Donoghue

Westside Library, Seamus Quirke Road, Galway City, Galway, Republic of Ireland
☎(00 353 91) 520616
Executive Librarian Ms Cora Gunther

KERRY

Authority: Kerry County Council
Kerry Library, Moyderwell, Tralee, Co Kerry, Republic of Ireland
☎(00 353 66) 712 1200
Fax (00 353 66) 712 9202
e-mail: info@kerrylibrary.ie
url: www.kerrylibrary.ie
County Librarian Tommy O'Connor

Area libraries
Ballybunion Library, Sandhill Road, Ballybunion, Co Kerry, Republic of Ireland
☎(00 353 68) 27615
e-mail: ballybunion@kerrylibrary.ie

Caherciveen Library, New Market Street, Caherciveen, Co Kerry, Republic of Ireland
☎(00 353 66) 947 2287
e-mail: caherciveen@kerrylibrary.ie

Castleisland Library, Area Services Centre, Castleisland, Co Kerry, Republic of Ireland
☎(00 353 66) 716 3403
e-mail: castleisland@kerrylibrary.ie

Kenmare Library, Shelbourne Street, Kenmare, Co Kerry, Republic of Ireland
☎(00 353 64) 664 1416
e-mail: kenmare@kerrylibrary.ie

Killarney Library, Rock Road, Killarney, Co Kerry, Republic of Ireland
☎(00 353 64) 663 2655
Fax (00 353 64) 663 6065
e-mail: killarney@kerrylibrary.ie

Killorglin Library, Library Place, Killorglin, Co Kerry, Republic of Ireland
☎(00 353 66) 976 1272
e-mail: killorglin@kerrylibrary.ie

Leabharlann an Daingin, Sráid an Dóirín, An Daingean, Co Kerry, Republic of Ireland
☎(00 353 66) 915 1499
e-mail: dingle@kerrylibrary.ie

Listowel Library, Courthouse Road, Listowel, Co Kerry, Republic of Ireland
☎(00 353 68) 23044
e-mail: listowel@kerrylibrary.ie

Local History and Archives Department, Kerry Library, Moyderwell, Tralee, Co Kerry, Republic of Ireland
☎(00 353 66) 712 1200
e-mail: localhistory@kerrylibrary.ie; archivist@kerrylibrary.ie

Mobile Library Services
Contact details as HQ above

KILDARE

Authority: Kildare County Council
Kildare County Library Service, Riverbank Library and Arts Centre, Main Street, Newbridge, Co Kildare, Republic of Ireland
☎(00 353 45) 431109/431486 (enquiries)
Fax (00 353 45) 432490
e-mail: colibrary@kildarecoco.ie
url: www.kildare.ie/library
Acting County Librarian Ms Marian Higgins

Main branch libraries

Athy Library, Emily Square, Athy, Co Kildare, Republic of Ireland
☎(00 353 59) 863 1144
Fax (00 353 59) 863 1809
e-mail: athylib@kildarecoco.ie
Librarian in Charge Ms Trina Coyne

Celbridge Library, St Patrick's Park, Celbridge, Co Kildare, Republic of Ireland
☎(00 353 1) 627 2207
e-mail: celbridgelib@kildarecoco.ie
Librarian in Charge Ms Aisling Donnelly

Kildare Town Library, Claregate Street, Kildare Town, Co Kildare, Republic of Ireland
☎(00 353 45) 520235
e-mail: kildarelib@kildarecoco.ie
Librarian in Charge Ms Celine Broughal

Leixlip Library, Captain's Hill, Leixlip, Co Kildare, Republic of Ireland
☎(00 353 1) 606 0050
e-mail: leixliplib@kildarecoco.ie
Librarian in Charge Ms Gillian Allen

Maynooth Library, Main Street, Maynooth, Co Kildare, Republic of Ireland
☎(00 353 1) 628 5530
e-mail: maynoothlib@kildarecoco.ie
Librarian in Charge Ms Caroline Farrell

Mobile Library Service, Riverbank Library and Arts Centre, Main Street, Newbridge,
Co Kildare, Republic of Ireland
☎(00 353 45) 448304 (enquiries)
e-mail: mobilelib@kildarecoco.ie
Librarian in Charge Ms Catherine Rafferty (e-mail: crafferty@kildarecoco.ie)

Naas Community Library, Canal Harbour, Naas, Co Kildare, Republic of Ireland
☎(00 353 45) 879111
e-mail: naaslib@kildarecoco.ie
Librarian in Charge Ms Geraldine Whelan

Newbridge Library, Athgarvan Road, Newbridge, Co Kildare, Republic of Ireland
☎(00 353 45) 448353
e-mail: newbridgelib@kildarecoco.ie
Librarian in Charge Ms Suzanne Brosnan

KILKENNY

Authority: Kilkenny County Council
Kilkenny County Library, John's Green House, John's Green, Kilkenny, Republic of Ireland
☎(00 353 56) 779 4160 (enquiries, local studies, mobile, schools, administration)
Fax (00 353 56) 779 4168
e-mail: info@kilkennylibrary.ie
url: www.kilkennylibrary.ie
County Librarian Vacant
Senior Executive Librarian Ms Dorothy O'Reilly DLIS ALAI
Executive Librarian Declan Macauley BSc DLIS
Assistant Librarian Ms Brenda Ward BA HDipLis

Central/largest library
Kilkenny City Library, John's Quay, Kilkenny, Republic of Ireland
☎(00 353 56) 779 4174
e-mail: citylibrary@kilkennylibrary.ie
Senior Library Assistant Ms Aisling Kelly BA HDipLis

Area libraries
Callan Library, Callan, Co Kilkenny, Republic of Ireland
☎(00 353 56) 779 4183
e-mail: callan@kilkennylibrary.ie
Senior Library Assistant Ms Anna Byrne

Castlecomer Library, Kilkenny Street, Castlecomer, Co Kilkenny, Republic of Ireland
☎(00 353 56) 444 0561
e-mail: castlecomer@kilkennylibrary.ie
Library Staff Officer Ms Mary Morrissey

Ferrybank Library, Ferrybank Shopping Centre, Ferrybank, Co Kilkenny, Republic of Ireland
☎(00 353 1) 897200
e-mail: ferrybank@kilkennylibrary.ie
Library Staff Officer Ms Patricia Nolan

Graiguenamanagh Library, Convent Road, Graiguenamanagh, Co Kilkenny, Republic of Ireland
☎(00 353 56) 779 4178
e-mail: graiguenamanagh@kilkennylibrary.ie
Library Staff Officer Ms Alicia Dunphy

Loughboy Library, Loughboy Shopping Centre, Kilkenny, Republic of Ireland
☎(00 353 56) 779 4176
e-mail: loughboy@kilkennylibrary.ie
Senior Library Assistant Ms Catriona Kenneally

Thomastown Library, Marshes Street, Thomastown, Co Kilkenny, Republic of Ireland
☎(00 353 56) 779 4331
e-mail: tomlib@eircom.net
Library Assistant Ms Majella Byrne

Urlingford Library, The Courthouse, Urlingford, Co Kilkenny, Republic of Ireland
☎(00 353 56) 779 4182
e-mail: urlingford@kilkennylibrary.ie
Senior Library Assistant Ms Anna Byrne

LAOIS

Authority: Laois County Council
Laois County Library, Aras An Chontae, JFL Avenue, Portlaoise, Co Laois, Republic of Ireland
☎(00 353 57) 866 4000
Fax (00 353 57) 867 8988
url: www.laois.ie/library
Acting County Librarian Ms Bernie Foran (e-mail: bforan@laoiscoco.ie)

Central/largest library
Portlaoise Branch Library, Dunamase House, Lyster Square, Portlaoise, Co Laois, Republic of Ireland
☎(00 353 57) 862 2333
Librarian Ms Suzanne Carroll

Branch libraries
Abbeyleix Branch Library, Market House, Abbeyleix, Co Laois, Republic of Ireland
☎(00 353 57) 873 0020
Librarian Walter Lawler

Ballylinan Library, Gracefield Shopping Centre, Ballylinan, Co Laois, Republic of Ireland
☎(00 353 59) 862 5007
Librarian Ms Niamh Boyce

Durrow Library, Durrow, Co Laois, Republic of Ireland
☎(00 353 57) 873 6090
Branch Librarian Ms Catherine Hutchinson

Mountmellick Branch Library, Irishtown, Mountmellick, Co Laois, Republic of Ireland
☎(00 353 57) 864 4572
Assistant Librarian Ms Breda Connell

Mountrath Branch Library, Shannon Street, Mountrath, Co Laois, Republic of Ireland
☎(00 353 57) 875 6378
Assistant Librarian Ms Aoife Anton

Portarlington Branch Library, Station Road, Portarlington, Co Laois, Republic of Ireland
☎(00 353 57) 864 3751
Librarian Ms Enda McEvoy

Rathdowney Branch Library, Mill Street, Rathdowney, Co Laois, Republic of Ireland
☎(00 353 505) 46852
Branch Librarian Mrs Catherine Fitzpatrick

Stradbally Branch Library, Court Square, Stradbally, Co Laois, Republic of Ireland
☎(00 353 57) 864 1673
Branch Librarian Ms Julie Ann Stead

LEITRIM (LEABHARLANN CHONTAE LIATROMA)

Authority: Leitrim County Council
Leitrim County Library, Main Street, Ballinamore, Co Leitrim, Republic of Ireland
☎(00 353 71) 964 5582
Fax (00 353 71) 964 5572
e-mail: leitrimlibrary@leitrimcoco.ie
url: www.leitrimlibrary.ie
County Librarian Vacant

LIMERICK CITY AND COUNTY
(the previous authorities of Limerick City and Limerick County have merged to form the
new authority named here)

Authority: Limerick City and County Council
**Limerick City and County Library HQ, Lissanalta House, Dooradoyle Road, Limerick,
Republic of Ireland**
☎(00 353 61) 496526 (enquiries and administration)
Fax (00 353 61) 583135
e-mail: libraryhq@limerickcoco.ie
City and County Librarian Damien Brady BA DLIS
Senior Executive Librarian Damien Dullaghan BA DLIS
Executive Librarian Tony Storan BA DLIS (00 353 61 496529)

Central/largest library
City Library, The Granary, Michael Street, Co Limerick, Republic of Ireland
☎(00 353 61) 407510
Executive Librarian Mike Maguire BA DLIS

Branch libraries
Abbeyfeale Branch Library, Bridge Street, Abbeyfeale, Limerick, Republic of Ireland
☎(00 353 68) 32488
Senior Library Assistant Mike Sweeney

Adare Branch Library, Adare, Co Limerick, Republic of Ireland

☎(00 353 61) 396822
Assistant Librarian Ms Sarah Prendiville BA DLIS

Dooradoyle Branch Library, Crescent Shopping Centre, Dooradoyle Road, Limerick, Republic of Ireland
☎(00 353 61) 301101
Executive Librarian Ms Margaret O'Reilly BA DLIS

Kilmallock Branch Library, Aras Mainchin Seoighe, Millmount, Kilmallock, Co Limerick, Republic of Ireland
☎(00 353 63) 20306
Executive Librarian Ms Noreen O'Neill BA DLIS

Newcastlewest Branch Library, Newcastlewest, Co Limerick, Republic of Ireland
☎(00 353 69) 62273
Executive Librarian Ms Aileen Dillane BA DLIS

Watch House Cross Community Library, Moyross, Limerick, Republic of Ireland
☎(00 353 61) 457726
Executive Librarian Ms Patricia Cusack BA DLIS

LONGFORD

Authority: Longford County Council
Longford County Library, Archives and Heritage Services, Town Centre, Co Longford, Republic of Ireland
☎(00 353 43) 334 1124
Fax (00 353 43) 334 8576
e-mail: library@longfordcoco.ie
url: www.longfordlibrary.ie
County Librarian Ms Mary Carleton-Reynolds DLIS ALAI

Central/largest library
Longford Library, Town Centre, Longford, Co Longford, Republic of Ireland
☎(00 353 43) 334 0727
e-mail: longfordbranchlibrary@longfordcoco.ie
Senior Executive Librarian Willie O'Dowd BComm LLB MLIS

Branch libraries
Ballymahon Library, Main Street, Ballymahon, Co Longford, Republic of Ireland
☎(00 353 90) 643 2546
e-mail: ballymahonlibrary@longfordcoco.ie
Branch Librarian Ms Carmel Kelly

Drumlish Library, Drumlish, Co Longford, Republic of Ireland
☎(00 353 43) 332 4760
e-mail: drumlishlibrary@longfordcoco.ie
Branch Librarian Ms Helen Sheridan

Edgeworthstown Library, Edgeworthstown, Co Longford, Republic of Ireland
☎(00 353 43) 667 1927
e-mail: edgeworthstownlibrary@longfordcoco.ie
Branch Librarian Ms Sheila Walsh

Granard Library, Granard, Co Longford, Republic of Ireland
☎(00 353 43) 668 6164
e-mail: granardlibrary@longfordcoco.ie
Branch Librarian Ms Rosemary Gaynor

Lanesboro Library, Main Street, Lanesboro, Co Longford, Republic of Ireland
☎(00 353 43) 332 1291
e-mail: lanesborolibrary@longfordcoco.ie
Branch Librarian Ms Stella O'Sullivan

LOUTH

Authority: Louth County Council
Louth County Library, Roden Place, Dundalk, Co Louth, Republic of Ireland
☎(00 353 42) 935 3190
e-mail: libraryhelpdesk@louthcoco.ie
url: www.louthcoco.ie/en/Services/Library
County Librarian Ms Bernadette Fennell (e-mail: bernadette.fennell@louthcoco.ie)

MAYO

Authority: Mayo County Council
Mayo County Library, Library HQ, John Moore Road, Castlebar, Co Mayo, Republic of Ireland
☎(00 353 94) 904 7922 (enquiries and administration)
Fax (00 353 94) 902 6491
e-mail: librarymayo@mayococo.ie
url: www.mayolibrary.ie
County Librarian Austin Vaughan BA DLIS (e-mail: avaughan@mayococo.ie)

Central/largest library
Mayo Central Library, The Mall, Castlebar, Co Mayo, Republic of Ireland
☎(00 353 94) 904 7925
Fax (00 353 94) 902 6491
Librarian Ms Paula Leavy McCarthy

MEATH

Authority: Meath County Council
Meath County Library, Railway Street, Navan, Co Meath, Republic of Ireland
☎(00 353 46) 902 1134; 902 1451
e-mail: colibrar@meathcoco.ie
url: www.meath.ie/library
County Librarian Ciaran Mangan BA MLIS
Senior Executive Librarians Ms Geraldine Donnelly DLIS, Ms Frances Tallon MA DLIS
Executive Librarians Ms Dympna Herward BA DLIS, Ms Yvonne Morrison BA DLIS, Tom French BA DLIS (Local Studies Dept), Miss Shauna Henry BA(Hons) DipLib MCLIP

Branch libraries
Ashbourne Library, 1-2 Killegland Court, Ashbourne, Co Meath, Republic of Ireland

☎(00 353 1) 835 8185
Executive Librarian Ms Mary Murphy MSc(LIM) DMS CIM ALAI

Athboy Library, Main Street, Athboy, Co Meath, Republic of Ireland
☎(00 353 46) 943 2539
Senior Library Assistant Mrs Ursula Lynskey

Duleek Library, Main Street, Duleek, Co Meath, Republic of Ireland
☎(00 353 41) 988 0709
Library Assistant David Farnan

Dunboyne Library, Castleview, Dunboyne, Co Meath, Republic of Ireland
☎(00 353 1) 825 1248
Executive Librarian Ms Caroline McLoughlin BA HDipEd DipLIS

Dunshaughlin Library, Main Street, Dunshaughlin, Co Meath, Republic of Ireland
☎(00 353 1) 825 0504
Assistant Librarian Ms Barbara Scally BA DLIS

Kells Library, Maudlin Street, Kells, Co Meath, Republic of Ireland
☎(00 353 46) 924 1592
Branch Librarian Ms Rose Grimes

Navan Library, Railway Street, Navan, Co Meath, Republic of Ireland
☎(00 353 46) 902 1134
Acting Executive Librarian Miss Shauna Henry BA(Hons) DipLib MCLIP

Nobber Library, Nobber, Co Meath, Republic of Ireland
☎(00 353 46) 905 2732
Branch Librarian Ms Imelda Griffin

Oldcastle Library, Millbrook Road, Oldcastle, Co Meath, Republic of Ireland
☎(00 353 49) 854 2084
Senior Library Assistant Ms Anne Price

Rathcairn Library, Rathcairn, Co Meath, Republic of Ireland
☎(00 353 46) 943 0929
Branch Librarian Ms Treasa Uí Mhairtín

Slane Library, Castle Hill, Slane, Co Meath, Republic of Ireland
☎(00 353 41) 982 4955
Branch Librarian Ms Margaret Carolan

Trim Library, High Street, Trim, Co Meath, Republic of Ireland
☎(00 353 46) 943 6014
Executive Librarian Ms Maedhbh Rogan BA DLIS

MONAGHAN

Authority: Monaghan County Council
Monaghan County Library, 98 Avenue, Clones, Co Monaghan, Republic of Ireland
☎(00 353 47) 51143
Fax (00 353 47) 51863
e-mail: moncolib@monaghancoco.ie

url: www.monaghan.ie
Acting County Librarian Ms Catherine Elliott BSocSc

Central/largest library
Monaghan Branch Library, North Road, Monaghan Town, Republic of Ireland
☎(00 353 47) 81830
Fax (00 353 47) 38688
Staff Officer Ms Kay Cassidy (e-mail: kcassidy@monaghancoco.ie)

Branch libraries
Ballybay Library, Main Street, Ballybay, Co Monaghan, Republic of Ireland
☎(00 353 42) 974 1256
Branch Librarian Mrs Rosemary McDonnell

Carrickmacross Branch Library, Market Square, Carrickmacross, Co Monaghan, Republic of Ireland
☎(00 353 42) 966 1148
Assistant Librarian Ms Karen McCague (e-mail: kmccague@monaghancoco.ie)

Castleblayney Branch Library, Iontas Resource Centre, Castleblayney, Co Monaghan, Republic of Ireland
☎(00 353 42) 974 0281
Branch Librarian Ms Pauline Duffy

Clones Branch Library, 98 Avenue, Clones, Co Monaghan, Republic of Ireland
☎(00 353 47) 74712
Fax (00 353 47) 51863
Assistant Librarian Ms Laura Carey (e-mail: lcarey@monaghancoco.ie)

OFFALY

Authority: Offaly County Council
Offaly County Library, O'Connor Square, Tullamore, Co Offaly, Republic of Ireland
☎(00 353 57) 934 6834
e-mail: libraryhq@offalycoco.ie
url: www.offaly.ie/libraries
County Librarian Ms Mary Stuart DLIS
Senior Executive Librarian Diarmuid Bracken BA DLIS

Central/largest library
Tullamore Central Library, O'Connor Square, Tullamore, Co Offaly, Republic of Ireland
☎(00 353 57) 934 6832
e-mail: TullamoreLibrary@offalycoco.ie

ROSCOMMON

Authority: Roscommon County Council
Roscommon County Library, Abbey Street, Roscommon, Republic of Ireland
☎(00 353 90) 663 7272/7274 (enquiries and administration)
Fax (00 353 90) 663 7101
url: www.roscommoncoco.ie

County Librarian Richie Farrell BA DLIS (e-mail: rfarrell@roscommoncoco.ie)
Executive Librarian Ms Mary Butler (e-mail: mbutler@roscommoncoco.ie)

Central/largest library
Roscommon Branch Library, Abbey Street, Roscommon, Republic of Ireland
☎(00 353 90) 663 7277
Fax (00 353 90) 663 7101
e-mail: roslib@roscommoncoco.ie
Assistant Librarian Ms Carolyn Tunney

Branch libraries
Ballaghaderreen Branch Library, Barrack Street, Ballaghaderreen, Co Roscommon, Republic
of Ireland
☎(00 353 94) 987 7044
e-mail: ballaghaderreenlibrary@roscommoncoco.ie
Senior Library Assistant Ms Deirdre Creighton

Boyle Branch Library, The King House, Boyle, Co Roscommon, Republic of Ireland
☎(00 353 71) 966 2800
e-mail: boylelibrary@roscommoncoco.ie
Acting Senior Library Assistant Ms Patricia O'Flaherty

Castlerea Branch Library, Main Street, Castlerea, Co Roscommon, Republic of Ireland
☎(00 353 94) 962 0745
e-mail: castlerealibrary@roscommoncoco.ie
Branch Librarian Ms Maura Carroll

Elphin Branch Library, Main Street, Elphin, Co Roscommon, Republic of Ireland
☎(00 353 71) 963 5775
Branch Librarian Ms Rebecca Thompson

Mobile Library Service, Library HQ, Abbey Street, Roscommon, Republic of Ireland
☎(00 353 90) 663 7279
Senior Library Assistant Ms Meliosa McIntyre

Strokestown Branch Library, Elphin Street, Strokestown, Co Roscommon, Republic of
Ireland
☎(00 353 71) 963 4027
e-mail: strokestownlibrary@roscommoncoco.ie
Branch Librarian Ms Eithne McCaffrey

SLIGO

Authority: Sligo County Council
County Library, Stephen Street, Co Sligo, Republic of Ireland
☎(00 353 71) 911 1850
Fax (00 353 71) 914 6798
e-mail: sligolib@sligococo.ie
url: www.sligolibrary.ie
County Librarian Donal Tinney MA DLIS ALAI (e-mail: dtinney@sligococo.ie)
Senior Executive Librarian Ms Pauline Brennan DLIS (00 353 71 911 1859; e-mail:
pbrenn@sligococo.ie)

Central/largest library

Sligo Central Library, Stephen Street, Co Sligo, Republic of Ireland
☎(00 353 71) 911 1675
e-mail: sligocentrallibrary@sligococo.ie
url: www.sligolibrary.ie
Executive Librarians Ms Patricia Keane (00 353 71 911 1856/1675; e-mail:
pkeane@sligococo.ie), Ultan McNasser MA DLIS (00 353 71 911 1680; e-mail:
umcnasser@sligococo.ie), Ms Caroline Morgan FLAI (00 353 71 911 1849; e-mail:
cmorgan@sligococo.ie)

Branch libraries

Local Studies Library, Stephen Street, Co Sligo, Republic of Ireland
☎(00 353 71) 911 1681
e-mail: sligolib@sligococo.ie
url: www.sligolibrary.ie
Assistant Librarian Patrick Gannon BA DLIS (00 353 71 911 1681; e-mail:
pgannon@sligococo.ie)

Tubbercurry Community Library, Teach Laighne, Humbert Street, Tubbercurry, Co Sligo,
Republic of Ireland
☎(00 353 71) 911 1705
e-mail: tubberlibrary@sligococo.ie
url: www.sligolibrary.ie
Senior Library Assistant Ms Grainne Brett-Mahon (00 353 71 911 1705; e-mail:
gmahon@sligococo.ie)

SOUTH DUBLIN

Authority: South Dublin County Council
Unit I, The Square Industrial Complex, Tallaght, Dublin 24, Republic of Ireland
☎(00 353 1) 459 7834
Fax (00 353 1) 459 7872
e-mail: library@sdublincoco.ie
url: www.southdublinlibraries.ie
Acting County Librarian Kieran Swords (e-mail: kswords@sdublincoco.ie)

Central/largest library

County Library, County Hall, Tallaght, Dublin 24, Republic of Ireland
☎(00 353 1) 462 0073
Fax (00 353 1) 414 9207
e-mail: talib@sdublincoco.ie
Senior Librarians Ms Rosena Hand, Henry Morrin, Ms Margaret Bentley

Branch libraries

Ballyroan Library, Orchardstown Avenue, Rathfarnham, Dublin 14, Republic of Ireland
☎(00 353 1) 494 1900
Fax (00 353 1) 494 7083
e-mail: ballyroan@sdublincoco.ie
Senior Librarian Ms Ann Dunne

Castletymon Library, Castletymon Shopping Centre, Tymon Road North, Tallaght, Dublin 24, Republic of Ireland
☎(00 353 1) 452 4888
Fax (00 353 1) 459 7873
e-mail: castletymon@sdublincoco.ie
Acting Senior Librarian Ms Mary Byron

Clondalkin Library, Monastry Road, Clondalkin, Dublin 22, Republic of Ireland
☎(00 353 1) 459 3315
Fax (00 353 1) 459 5509
e-mail: clondalkin@sdublincoco.ie
Senior Librarian Ms Siobhan Bermingham

John J Jennings Library, Stewarts Hospital, Palmerstown, Dublin 20, Republic of Ireland
☎(00 353 1) 626 4444 (ext 1129)
Fax (00 353 1) 626 1707
e-mail: library@stewartshospital.com
Senior Librarian Ms Siobhan McChrystal

Lucan Library, Superquinn Shopping Centre, Newcastle Road, Lucan, Co Dublin, Republic of Ireland
☎(00 353 1) 621 6422
Fax (00 353 1) 621 6433
e-mail: lucan@sdublincoco.ie
Acting Senior Librarian Ms Catherine Gallagher

Mobile Library Service, Unit 1, The Square Industrial Complex, Tallaght, Dublin 24, Republic of Ireland
☎(00 353 1) 459 7834
Fax (00 353 1) 459 7872
e-mail: mobiles@sdublincoco.ie
Senior Librarian Ms Bernie Meenaghan

Whitechurch Library, Taylor's Lane, Rathfarnham, Dublin 16, Republic of Ireland
☎(00 353 1) 493 0199
e-mail: whitechurch@sdublincoco.ie
Branch Librarian Ms Breda Bollard

Children's and Young People's Library Services
South Dublin Libraries, Unit 1, The Square Industrial Complex, Tallaght, Dublin 24, Republic of Ireland
☎(00 353 1) 459 7834
Fax (00 353 1) 459 7872
e-mail: schools@sdublincoco.ie
Senior Librarians Ms Maria O'Sullivan, Ms Laura Joyce

TIPPERARY (formerly Tipperary Joint Libraries Committee)

Authority: County Tipperary
Tipperary County Library, Castle Avenue, Thurles, Co Tipperary, Republic of Ireland
☎(00 353 504) 21555
Fax (00 353 504) 23442

e-mail: info@tipperarylibraries.ie
url: www.tipperarylibraries.ie
Acting County Librarian Ms Jess Codd

Branch libraries
Borrisokane Library, Main Street, Borrisokane, Co Tipperary, Republic of Ireland
☎(00 353 67) 27199
Branch Librarian Ms Noirin Duggan

Cahir Library, The Square, Cahir, Co Tipperary, Republic of Ireland
☎(00 353 52) 744 2075
Branch Librarian Mrs Ann Tuohy

Carrick-on-Suir Library, Fair Green, Carrick-on-Suir, Co Tipperary, Republic of Ireland
☎(00 353 51) 640591 (tel/fax)
Senior Library Assistant Ms Orla O'Connor

Cashel Library, Friar Street, Cashel, Co Tipperary, Republic of Ireland
☎(00 353 62) 63825
Fax (00 353 62) 63948
e-mail: cashel@tipperarylibraries.ie
Staff Officer (Library) Ms Gemma Larkin

Clonmel Library, Emmet Street, Clonmel, Co Tipperary, Republic of Ireland
☎(00 353 52) 612 4545
Fax (00 353 52) 612 7336
e-mail: clonmel@tipperarylibraries.ie
Executive Librarian Mrs Marie Boland

Cloughjordan Library, Thomas MacDonagh Heritage Centre, Lower Main Street,
Cloughjordan, Co Tipperary, Republic of Ireland
Branch Librarian Mrs Marie Brady

Killenaule Library, Slieveardagh Centre, River Street, Killenaule, Co Tipperary, Republic of
Ireland
☎(00 353 52) 915 7906
Branch Librarian Ms Maure Barrett

Nenagh Library, O'Rahilly Street, Nenagh, Co Tipperary, Republic of Ireland
☎(00 353 67) 34404
Fax (00 353 67) 34405
e-mail: nenagh@tipperarylibraries.ie
Executive Librarian Ms Breffni Hannon

Roscrea Library, Birr Road, Roscrea, Co Tipperary, Republic of Ireland
☎(00 353 505) 22032 (tel/fax)
Assistant Librarian Ms Aine Beausang

Templemore Library, Old Mill Court, Templemore, Co Tipperary, Republic of Ireland
☎(00 353 504) 32555/6
Fax (00 353 504) 32545
e-mail: templemore@tipperarylibraries.ie
Staff Officer (Library) Pat Bracken

Thurles Library, The Source, Cathedral Street, Thurles, Co Tipperary, Republic of Ireland
☎(00 353 504) 29720
Fax (00 353 504) 21344
e-mail: thurles@tipperarylibraries.ie
Executive Librarian Ms Ann Marie Brophy

Tipperary Library, Dan Breen House, Tipperary, Republic of Ireland
☎(00 353 62) 51761 (tel/fax)
Branch Librarians Ms Nollaig Butler, Ms Gerardine Hughes

Tipperary Studies, Thurles Library, The Source, Cathedral Street, Thurles, Co Tipperary,
Republic of Ireland
☎(00 353 504) 29278
e-mail: studies@tipperarylibraries.ie
Staff Officer (Library) Ms Mary Guinan-Darmody

WATERFORD CITY AND COUNTY
(the previous authorities of Waterford City and Waterford County have merged to form
the new authority named here)

Authority: Waterford City and County Council
**Library Headquarters, Waterford City Council Depot, Northern Extension Industrial
Estate, Old Kilmeadan Road, Waterford, Republic of Ireland**
☎(00 353 51) 849839
e-mail: library@waterfordcity.ie
url: www.waterfordcouncil.ie
City and County Librarian Ms Jane Cantwell (e-mail: jcantwell@waterfordcouncil.ie)
Senior Executive Librarians Ms Katherine Collins (e-mail: kcollins@waterfordcouncil.ie),
Ms Melanie Cunningham (e-mail: mcunningham@waterfordcouncil.ie) (Acting)
Executive Librarian Ns Noleen Osborne (e-mail: nosborne@waterfordcouncil.ie)

Central/largest library
Central Library, Lady Lane, Waterford, Republic of Ireland
☎(00 353 51) 849975
e-mail: library@waterfordcouncil.ie
Executive Librarian Ms Sinéad O'Higgins (e-mail: sohiggins@waterfordcouncil.ie)

Area libraries
Dungarvan Branch Library, Davitt's Quay, Dungarvan, Co Waterford, Republic of Ireland
☎(00 353 58) 41231
e-mail: library@waterfordcouncil.ie
Executive Librarian Ger Croughan (e-mail: gcroughan@waterfordcoco.ie)

Ardkeen Library, Ardkeen Shopping Centre, Dunmore Road, Waterford, Republic of Ireland
☎(00 353 51) 849755
e-mail: library@waterfordcouncil.ie
Executive Librarian Ms Sinéad Cummins (e-mail: scummins@waterfordcouncil.ie)

Brown's Road Library, Paddy Brown's Road, Waterford, Republic of Ireland
☎(00 353 51) 849845
e-mail: library@waterfordcouncil.ie
Executive Librarian Ms Sinéad Cummins (e-mail: scummins@waterfordcouncil.ie)

Cappoquin Branch Library, Cappoquin, Waterford, Republic of Ireland
☎(00 353 58) 52263
e-mail: library@waterfordcouncil.ie
Branch Librarian Mrs Bernie Leahy

Dunmore Branch Library, Dunmore East, Waterford, Republic of Ireland
☎(00 353 51) 383211
e-mail: library@waterfordcouncil.ie
Branch Librarian Ms Claire O'Mullain

Kilmacthomas Branch Library, Kilmacthomas, Waterford, Republic of Ireland
☎(00 353 51) 294270
e-mail: library@waterfordcouncil.ie
Branch Librarian Ms Laura Kirwan

Lismore Branch Library, Main Street, Lismore, Waterford, Republic of Ireland
☎(00 353 58) 21377
e-mail: library@waterfordcouncil.ie
Executive Librarian Eddie Byrne (e-mail: ebyrne@waterfordcouncil.ie)

Portlaw Branch Library, The Square, Portlaw, Waterford, Republic of Ireland
☎(00 353 51) 387402
e-mail: library@waterfordcouncil.ie
Librarian Ms Helena Fogarty

Tallow Branch Library, Convent Street, Tallow, Waterford, Republic of Ireland
☎(00 353 58) 56347
e-mail: library@waterfordcouncil.ie
Branch Librarian Ms Evelyn Coady

Tramore Branch Library, Market Square, Tramore, Waterford, Republic of Ireland
☎(00 353 51) 381479
e-mail: library@waterfordcouncil.ie
Executive Librarian Ms Tracy McEneaney (e-mail: tmceneaney@waterfordcouncil.ie)

WESTMEATH

Authority: Westmeath County Council
Westmeath County Library HQ, Dublin Road, Mullingar, Co Westmeath, Republic of Ireland
☎(00 353 44) 933 2162
Fax (00 353 44) 934 2330
url: www.westmeathcoco.ie
Acting County Librarian Mrs Paula O'Dornan BA(Hons) PGDipLIS (e-mail: podornan@westmeathcoco.ie)

Branch libraries
Aidan Heavey Public Library, Athlone Civic Centre, Church Street, Athlone, Co Westmeath, Republic of Ireland
☎(00 353 90) 644 2157/8/9
e-mail: athlib@westmeathcoco.ie
Senior Executive Librarian Gearoid O'Brien DLIS FLAI ALAI (e-mail: gobrien@westmeathcoco.ie)

Ballynacarrigy Library, 2 Kilmurray's Corner, Main Street, Ballynacarrigy, Co Westmeath, Republic of Ireland
☎(00 353 44) 937 3882
e-mail: bnclib@westmeathcoco.ie
Branch Librarian Ms Cecilia Connolly (e-mail: cconnelly@westmeathcoco.ie)

Castlepollard Library, Civic Offices, Mullingar Road, Castlepollard, Co Westmeath, Republic of Ireland
☎(00 353 44) 933 2199
e-mail: cpdlib@westmeathcoco.ie
Staff Officer Ms Nicola Brennan-Gavin (e-mail: ngavin@westmeathcoco.ie)

Kilbeggan Library, Kilbeggan Civic Offices, The Square, Kilbeggan, Co Westmeath, Republic of Ireland
☎(00 353 57) 933 3148
e-mail: killib@westmeathcoco.ie
Senior Library Assistant Ms Margaret Crentsil

Killucan Library, Rathwire Hall, Killucan, Co Westmeath, Republic of Ireland
☎(00 353 44) 937 4260
e-mail: klnlib@westmeathcoco.ie
Branch Librarian Ms Cecilia Connolly (e-mail: cconnelly@westmeathcoco.ie)

Moate Library, Main Street, Moate, Co Westmeath, Republic of Ireland
☎(00 353 90) 648 1888
Fax (00 353 90) 648 1103
e-mail: moatelib@westmeathcoco.ie
Library Assistant Ms Lorna Farrell

Mullingar Library, County Buildings, Mount Street, Mullingar, Co Westmeath, Republic of Ireland
☎(00 353 44) 933 2161
e-mail: mgarlib@westmeathcoco.ie
Executive Librarian Ms Cailin Gallagher DLIS (e-mail: cailin.gallagher@westmeathcoco.ie)

WEXFORD

Authority: Wexford County Council
Library Management Services, County Hall, D-2, Carricklawn, Co Wexford, Republic of Ireland
☎(00 353 53) 919 6571
e-mail: libraryhq@wexfordcoco.ie
url: www.wexford.ie
County Librarian Ms Fionnuala Hanrahan BA DLIS MLIS MCLIP MCLIPI
Senior Executive Librarian Ms Eileen Morrissey BA DLIS

Central/largest library
Wexford County Library, Mallin Street, Wexford, Co Wexford, Republic of Ireland
☎(00 353 53) 919 6760
e-mail: wexfordlib@wexfordcoco.ie
Senior Executive Librarian Ms Sinéad O'Gorman BA DLIS ALAI (e-mail: sinead.ogorman@wexfordcoco.ie)

Area libraries

Bunclody Branch Library, Mill Wood, Carrigduff, Bunclody, Co Wexford, Republic of Ireland
☎(00 353 53) 937 5466
e-mail: bunclodylib@wexfordcoco.ie
Executive Librarian Ms Dearbhla Ní Laighin BA DLIS (e-mail:
dearbhla.nilaighin@wexfordcoco.ie)

Enniscorthy Branch Library, Lymington Road, Enniscorthy, Co Wexford, Republic of Ireland
☎(00 353 53) 923 6055
e-mail: enniscorthylib@wexfordcoco.ie
Executive Librarian Jarlath Glynn BA DipLib (e-mail: jarlath.glynn@wexfordcoco.ie)

New Ross Branch Library, Barrack Lane, New Ross, Co Wexford, Republic of Ireland
☎(00 353 51) 421877
e-mail: newrosslib@wexfordcoco.ie
Executive Librarian Ms Patricia Keenan BA DLIS (e-mail:
patricia.keenan@wexfordcoco.ie)

WICKLOW

Authority: Wicklow County Council
**Wicklow County Library, Library HQ, Boghall Road, Bray, Co Wicklow, Republic of
Ireland**
☎(00 353 1) 286 6566 (enquiries and administration)
Fax (00 353 1) 286 5811
e-mail: wcclhq@eircom.net
url: www.wicklow.ie
County Librarian Brendan Martin BA DLIS
Senior Executive Librarian (Schools and Outreach) Vacant
Senior Executive Librarian (Administration) Ms Carmel Moore DLIS
Executive Librarian (IT) Ms Mary O'Driscoll BSocSc DLIS

Largest library

Bray Public Library, Eglinton Road, Bray, Co Wicklow, Republic of Ireland
☎(00 353 1) 286 2600
Executive Librarian Ms Fiona Scannell

Area libraries

Arklow Public Library, St Mary's Road, Arklow, Co Wicklow, Republic of Ireland
☎(00 353 402) 39977
Assistant Librarian Vacant

Ballywaltrim Public Library, Boghall Road, Bray, Co Wicklow, Republic of Ireland
☎(00 353 1) 272 3205
Assistant Librarian Ms Ciara Brennan

Blessington Public Library, New Town Centre, Blessington, Co Wicklow, Republic of Ireland
☎(00 353 405) 891740
Assistant Librarian Vacant

Greystones Public Library, Church Road, Greystones, Co Wicklow, Republic of Ireland
☎(00 353 1) 287 3548
Assistant Librarian Ms Emer O'Byrne

Wicklow Public Library, Market Square, Co Wicklow, Republic of Ireland
☎(00 353 404) 67025
Assistant Librarian Ms Ann Murdiff

Libraries in Academic Institutions in the United Kingdom

UNIVERSITY OF ABERDEEN

The Sir Duncan Rice Library, University of Aberdeen, Bedford Road, Aberdeen AB24 3AA
☎(01224) 273330 (enquiries/help desk)
Fax (01224) 273382
e-mail: library@abdn.ac.uk
url: www.abdn.ac.uk/library
Head Librarian Ms Diane Bruxvoort
Deputy Librarian and Head of Library Services Laurence W Bebbington (e-mail: laurence.bebbington@abdn.ac.uk)

Site libraries

Medical Library, University of Aberdeen, Polwarth Building, Foresterhill, Aberdeen AB25 2ZD
☎(01224) 437870
Fax (01224) 662454
e-mail: medlib@abdn.ac.uk
Site Services Manager Ms Melanie Bickerton BA

Reid Library, University of Aberdeen, Rowett Institute of Nutrition and Health, Greenburn Road, Bucksburn, Aberdeen AB21 9SB
☎(01224) 438703
e-mail: library@rowett.ac.uk
Librarian Ms Mary Mowat BA MLib MCLIP (e-mail: m.mowat@abdn.ac.uk)

Special Collections Centre, University of Aberdeen, The Sir Duncan Rice Library, Bedford Road, Aberdeen AB24 3AA
☎(01224) 272598 (enquiries)
Fax (01224) 273382
e-mail: speclib@abdn.ac.uk
Head of Special Collections Ms Siobhan Convery

Taylor Library and European Documentation Centre, University of Aberdeen, Taylor Building, Aberdeen AB24 3UB
☎(01224) 272601
Fax (01224) 273893
e-mail: lawlib@abdn.ac.uk
Site Services Manager Ms Nicola Will

ABERTAY UNIVERSITY

Bernard King Library, Abertay University, Bell Street, Dundee DD1 1HG
☎(01382) 308833
Fax (01382) 308877
e-mail: library@abertay.ac.uk
url: http://library.abertay.ac.uk
University Librarian Jim Huntingford

ABERYSTWYTH UNIVERSITY

Hugh Owen Library, Aberystwyth University, Penglais, Aberystwyth, Ceredigion SY23 3DZ
☎(01970) 622400 (enquiries), (01970) 622390 (administration)
Fax (01970) 622404
e-mail: is@aber.ac.uk
url: www.aber.ac.uk
Director of Information Services Tim Davies BSc(Econ) MSc(Econ) MSc MBCS CITP

Thomas Parry Library (Law, Management and Business, Information Sciences), Aberystwyth University, Llanbadarn Fawr, Aberystwyth, Ceredigion SY23 3AS
☎(01970) 622411
e-mail: is@aber.ac.uk
IS Lead for Science Stephen Smith BSc DipLib MCLIP

Site/departmental libraries
Physical Sciences Library (Mathematics, Computer Sciences and Physics), Aberystwyth University, 4th Floor, Physical Sciences Building, Penglais, Aberystwyth, Ceredigion SY23 3BZ
☎(01970) 622400
e-mail: is@aber.ac.uk

ANGLIA RUSKIN UNIVERSITY

University Library, Anglia Ruskin University, East Road, Cambridge CB1 1PT
☎0845 196 2301 or (01223) 363271 ext 2301
Fax 0845 196 2234
url: www.anglia.ac.uk/library
University Librarian Ms Nicky Kershaw BA CertEd MCLIP (0845 196 3763; e-mail: nicky.kershaw@anglia.ac.uk)
Assistant Director of Library Services (Academic Services Division)
Ms Margaret March BA MA MCLIP (0845 196 4644; e-mail: margaret.march@anglia.ac.uk)
Assistant Director of Library Services (Central Services Division) Graham Howorth BA MSc MCLIP (0845 196 3145; e-mail: graham.howorth@anglia.ac.uk)
Assistant Director of Library Services (Customer Services Division)
Roddie Shepherd BA DipLib MCLIP (0845 196 2310; e-mail: roddie.shepherd@anglia.ac.uk)

Chelmsford Library, Anglia Ruskin University, Queens Building, Bishop Hall Lane, Chelmsford, Essex CM1 1SQ
☎(0845) 271 3333

Peterborough Library, Anglia Ruskin University, Education Centre, Peterborough District Hospital, Thorpe Road, Peterborough PE3 6DA
☎(01223) 695570

ARTS UNIVERSITY BOURNEMOUTH
(formerly the Arts University College at Bournemouth)

The Library, Arts University Bournemouth, Wallisdown Road, Poole, Dorset BH12 5HH
☎(01202) 363258

Fax (01202) 537729
e-mail: library@aub.ac.uk
url: www.aub.ac.uk/library
Head of Library and Information Services Ms Julia Waite BSc(Econ) MSc MCLIP FHEA
(e-mail: jwaite@aub.ac.uk)

ASTON UNIVERSITY

**Library & Information Services, Aston University, Aston Triangle, Birmingham B4 7ET
(0121 204 4525 (enquiries)**
Fax 0121 204 4530
e-mail: library@aston.ac.uk
url: www.aston.ac.uk/library/
Director Chris Wanley BA MSc PGCE
Assistant Director (Information Resources) Mrs Heather Whitehouse BSc DipInfSc
Assistant Director (Customer Services) Ms Angela Brady BA DipLIS

BANGOR UNIVERSITY

**Library and Archives Service, Bangor University, College Road, Bangor, Gwynedd
LL57 2DG**
☎(01248) 382981 (enquiries), (01248) 383772 (secretary)
Fax (01248) 382979
e-mail: library@bangor.ac.uk; ill@bangor.ac.uk (interlibrary loans)
url: www.bangor.ac.uk/library
Head of Library and Archives Service Ms Susan Hodges (e-mail:
s.a.hodges@bangor.ac.uk)
Academic Support Librarians Ms Mairwen Owen BA (e-mail:
mairwen.owen@bangor.ac.uk), Ms Jenny Greene (e-mail: j.greene@bangor.ac.uk),
Dr Helen Elizabeth Hall (e-mail: b.hall@bangor.ac.uk), Ms Vashti Zarach (e-mail:
v.zarach@bangor.ac.uk)
Head of Customer Service Tony Heaton (e-mail: t.heaton@bangor.ac.uk)
Collection Management and Library Systems Manager Ms Mieko Yamaguchi BA MA
DipLib (e-mail: m.yamaguchi@bangor.ac.uk)
University Archivist, Welsh and Special Collections Einion Wyn Thomas BA DAA
(e-mail: e.w.thomas@bangor.ac.uk)
Bibliographic Librarian Dr Flora Lewis BSc PhD DipILM (e-mail: f.lewis@bangor.ac.uk)
Digital Services and Development Manager Ms Tracey Randall BA(Hons) MSc (e-mail:
t.randall@bangor.ac.uk)

Site libraries
Education Site Library, Bangor University, Safle'r Normal, Holyhead Road, Bangor,
Gwynedd LL57 2PX
☎(01248) 383048

Healthcare Sciences Library, Bangor University, Archimedes Centre, Technology Park,
Wrexham LL13 7YP
☎(01978) 316370

Main Library, Bangor University, College Road, Bangor, Gwynedd LL57 2DG
☎(01248) 382983

Science Library, Bangor University, Adeilad Deiniol, Deiniol Road, Bangor, Gwynedd
LL57 2UX
☎(01248) 382984

BATH SPA UNIVERSITY

Newton Park Library, Bath Spa University, Newton Park, Newton St Loe, Bath BA2 9BN
☎(01225) 875490
e-mail: library@bathspa.ac.uk/library
url: www.bathspa.ac.uk
Director of Library and Learning Services Ms Alison C. Baud MA DipLib MCLIP
(e-mail: a.baud@bathspa.ac.uk)
Deputy Director Library Services (Academic Services) Ms Ann Siswell BA DipLib
MCLIP (e-mail: a.siswell@bathspa.ac.uk)
Deputy Director Library Services (Electronic Resources) Richard Taylor BA(Hons)
PGDip MCLIP FHEA (01225 875476; e-mail: r.taylor@bathspa.ac.uk)

Campus libraries

Corsham Court Library, Bath Spa University, Corsham Court, Corsham, Wilts SN13 0BZ
☎(01225) 876178
e-mail: library@bathspa.ac.uk
Subject Librarian Ms Rebecca Atkins MSc (e-mail: r.atkins@bathspa.ac.uk)

Sion Hill Library, Bath Spa University, Sion Road, Bath BA1 5SF
☎(01225) 875648
e-mail: library@bathspa.ac.uk
Campus Librarian Ms Helen Rayner BA(Hons) DipInf (e-mail: h.rayner@bathspa.ac.uk)

UNIVERSITY OF BATH

Library, University of Bath, Bath BA2 7AY
☎(01225) 385000 (enquiries), (01225) 386084 (administration)
Fax (01225) 386229
e-mail: library@bath.ac.uk
url: www.bath.ac.uk/library
University Librarian Ms Kate Robinson JP MA FCLIP FRSA

UNIVERSITY OF BEDFORDSHIRE

**Learning Resources Centre, University of Bedfordshire, University Square, Luton, Beds
LU1 3JU**
☎(01582) 743488 (enquiries), (01582) 489398 (administration)
Fax (01582) 489325
e-mail: library.services@beds.ac.uk (administration)
url: www.beds.ac.uk; http://lrweb.beds.ac.uk
Director of Learning Resources Tim Stone MA MCLIP (01582 489310; e-mail:
tim.stone@beds.ac.uk)
University Librarian Marcus Woolley BA MCLIP (01582 489102; e-mail:
marcus.woolley@beds.ac.uk)

Site libraries

Library, University of Bedfordshire, Bedford Campus, Polhill Avenue, Bedford MK41 9EA
☎(01234) 793202

Health Care Learning Resources Centre, Buckinghamshire Campus, University of Bedfordshire, Faculty of Health and Social Sciences, Oxford House, Oxford Road, Aylesbury, Bucks HP21 8SZ
☎(01296) 734301

Butterfield Health Care Learning Resources, University of Bedfordshire, Unit 260–270, Butterfield Park, Hitchin Road, Luton, Beds LU2 8DL
☎(01582) 743803

Putteridge Bury Learning Resources Centre, University of Bedfordshire, Putteridge Bury Campus, Hitchin Road, Luton, Bedfordshire LU2 8LE

BIRMINGHAM CITY UNIVERSITY

Library and Learning Resources, Birmingham City University, Franchise Street, Perry Barr, Birmingham B42 2SU
☎0121 331 5289 (enquiries), 0121 331 6300 (administration)
Fax 0121 356 2875
url: http://library.bcu.ac.uk
Director of Library and Learning Resources Ms Judith Andrews MA DipLib MCLIP (e-mail: judith.andrews@bcu.ac.uk)

UNIVERSITY COLLEGE BIRMINGHAM

Library, University College Birmingham, Summer Row, Birmingham B3 1JB
☎0121 604 1000
url: www.ucb.ac.uk
Head of Library Services Miss Deborah Findlay MSc MCLIP (e-mail: d.findlay@ucb.ac.uk)

UNIVERSITY OF BIRMINGHAM

Library Services, University of Birmingham, Main Library, Edgbaston, Birmingham B15 2TT
☎0121 414 5828 (enquiries)
Fax 0121 471 4691
e-mail: library@bham.ac.uk
url: www.birmingham.ac.uk/libraries
Director of Library Services Ms Diane Job MA DipLIS
Assistant Director: Library Academic Engagement Christopher Cipkin BA MA ARCO MCLIP FHEA
Assistant Director: Library Customer Support Ms Elizabeth Warner-Davies BSc DipLib DipHECouns MBACP
Assistant Director: Collection Management & Development Ms Sarah Price BA

Special Collections, University of Birmingham, Cadbury Research Library, Muirhead Tower, Edgbaston, Birmingham B15 2TT
☎0121 414 5838

e-mail: special-collections@bham.ac.uk
Director of Special Collections Ms Susan Worrall MA(Hons) MArchAd

Site libraries

Barber Fine Art Library, University of Birmingham, Barber Institute of Fine Arts, Edgbaston, Birmingham B15 2TT
☎0121 414 7334
e-mail: fine-arts-library@bham.ac.uk
Manager Ms Jean Scott BA DipLib

Barber Music Library, University of Birmingham, Barber Institute of Fine Arts, Edgbaston, Birmingham B15 2TT
☎0121 414 5852
e-mail: music-library@bham.ac.uk
Manager Ms Jean Scott BA DipLib

Barnes Library, University of Birmingham, Medical School, Vincent Drive, Edgbaston, Birmingham B15 2TT
☎0121 414 3567
e-mail: barneslibrary@contacts.bham.ac.uk
Manager Ms Jean Scott BA DipLib

Education Library, University of Birmingham, Edgbaston, Birmingham B15 2TT
☎0121 414 4869
e-mail: edlib@bham.ac.uk
Manager Ms Dorothy Vuong BSocSc PGDip

Harding Law Library, University of Birmingham, Law School, Edgbaston, Birmingham B15 2TT
☎0121 414 5865
e-mail: law-lib@bham.ac.uk
Manager Ms Dorothy Vuong BSocSc PGDip

Orchard Learning Resource Centre, University of Birmingham, Hamilton Drive, Weoley Park Road, Selly Oak, Birmingham B29 6QW
☎0121 414 8454
e-mail: olrc@bham.ac.uk
Manager Ms Dorothy Vuong BSocSc PGDip

Ronald Cohen Dental Library, Birmingham Dental Hospital, University of Birmingham, St Chad's Queensway, Birmingham B4 6NN
☎0121 466 5502
e-mail: dlib@bham.ac.uk
Manager Ms Jean Scott BA DipLib

Shakespeare Institute Library, University of Birmingham, Shakespeare Institute, Church Street, Stratford upon Avon, Warwicks CV37 6HP
☎0121 414 9525
e-mail: silib@bham.ac.uk
Manager Ms Karin Brown MA PGDip

BISHOP GROSSETESTE UNIVERSITY
(formerly Bishop Grosseteste University College Lincoln)

Library Services, Bishop Grosseteste University, Longdales Road, Lincoln LN1 3DY
☎(01522) 583790
e-mail: library@bishopg.ac.uk
url: www.bishopg.ac.uk/library
Head of Library Services Ms Emma Sansby BA(Hons) MA MCLIP (e-mail:
emma.sansby@bishopg.ac.uk)

UNIVERSITY OF BOLTON

Library, University of Bolton, Deane Road, Bolton, Lancashire BL3 5AB
☎(01204) 903094 (enquiries), (01204) 903160 (administration)
Fax (01204) 903166
url: www.bolton.ac.uk/library
Library Manager Trevor Hodgson BSc(Hons) (01204 903160; e-mail:
t.hodgson@bolton.ac.uk)

BOURNEMOUTH UNIVERSITY

**The Sir Michael Cobham Library, Bournemouth University, Talbot Campus, Fern
Barrow, Poole, Dorset BH12 5BB**
☎(01202) 965959 (enquiries), (01202) 965044 (administration)
Fax (01202) 965475
e-mail: libsupp@bournemouth.ac.uk
url: www.bournemouth.ac.uk/library
Head of Library Services and University Librarian Chris Fowler (e-mail:
cfowler@bournemouth.ac.uk)

Site library

Bournemouth House Library, Bournemouth University, Bournemouth House, 19
Christchurch Road, Bournemouth BH1 3LG
☎(01202) 965959 (enquiries)
Fax (01202) 967298

UNIVERSITY OF BRADFORD

J B Priestley Library, University of Bradford, Bradford BD7 1DP
☎(01274) 233301
Fax (01274) 233398
e-mail: library@bradford.ac.uk
url: www.bradford.ac.uk/library
Director of Information Services Ms Sara Marsh MA MCLIP (01274 233303; e-mail:
s.l.marsh@bradford.ac.uk)
Head of Library Services Ms Grace L Hudson

UNIVERSITY OF BRIGHTON

**Information Services, University of Brighton, Cockcroft Building, Lewes Road, Brighton
BN2 4GJ**
☎(01273) 600900
Fax (01273) 642988
url: www.brighton.ac.uk/libraries

Director of Information Services Terry A Hanson BA DipLib
Assistant Director: Library Services Ms Cath Morgan BEd(Hons) PGDipIS MCLIP
(01273 642760)

Central/largest library
The Aldrich Library, University of Brighton, Cockcroft Building, Lewes Road, Brighton
BN2 4GJ
☎(01273) 642760
Fax (01273) 642988
e-mail: AskAldrich@brighton.ac.uk
Information Services Manager Ms Liz Davey BA

Site libraries
Falmer Library, University of Brighton, Village Way, Falmer, Brighton BN1 9PH
☎(01273) 643569
Fax (01273) 643560
e-mail: AskFalmer@brighton.ac.uk
Information Services Manager Keith Baxter MBA

Hastings Campus Library, University of Brighton, Havelock Road, Hastings, East Sussex
TN34 1BE
☎(01273) 644640
Fax (01273) 644627
e-mail: AskUCH@brighton.ac.uk
Information Services Manager Ms Sarah Friend PGDipIS MCLIP

Queenwood Library, University of Brighton, Darley Road, Eastbourne, East Sussex
BN20 7UN
☎(01273) 643682
Fax (01273) 643825
e-mail: AskQueenwood@brighton.ac.uk
Information Services Manager Ms Margaret Phillips

St Peter's House Library, University of Brighton, 16-18 Richmond Place, Brighton
BN2 8NA
☎(01273) 643221
Fax (01273) 607532
e-mail: AskSPH@brighton.ac.uk
Information Services Manager Ms Lisa Redlinski BA MSc

UNIVERSITY OF BRISTOL

**Arts and Social Sciences Library, University of Bristol, Information Services, Tyndall
Avenue, Bristol BS8 ITJ**
☎0117 928 8000
Fax 0117 925 5334
e-mail: library-enquiries@bristol.ac.uk
url: www.bristol.ac.uk/library
Director of Library Services Dr Jessica Gardner

Biological Sciences Library, University of Bristol, Woodland Road, Bristol BS8 1UG
☎0117 928 7943

Chemistry Library, University of Bristol, School of Chemistry, Cantocks Close, Bristol
BS8 1TS
☎0117 928 8984

Education Library, University of Bristol, 35 Berkeley Square, Bristol BS8 1JA
☎0117 331 4231

Geographical Sciences Library, University of Bristol, University Road, Bristol BS8 1SS
☎0117 928 8116

Medical Library, University of Bristol, Medical School, University Walk, Bristol BS8 1TD
☎0117 331 1501

Physics Library, University of Bristol, H. H. Wills Physics Laboratory, Tyndall Avenue, Bristol
BS8 1TL
☎0117 928 7960

Queen's Library (Engineering, Mathematics, Computer Science), University of Bristol,
Queen's Building, University Walk, Bristol BS8 1TR
☎0117 331 5418

Veterinary Science Library, School of Veterinary Science, University of Bristol, Churchill
Building, Langford, Bristol BS40 5DU
☎0117 928 9205

Wills Memorial Library (Law, Earth Sciences), University of Bristol, Wills Memorial Building,
Queen's Road, Bristol BS8 1RJ
☎0117 954 5398

BRUNEL UNIVERSITY

Library, Brunel University, Middlesex UB8 3PH
☎(01895) 266141 (enquiries), (01895) 266177 (administration)
e-mail: library@brunel.ac.uk
url: www.brunel.ac.uk/services/library
Director of Library Services Mrs Ann Cummings BA MA

UNIVERSITY OF BUCKINGHAM

University Library, University of Buckingham, Hunter Street, Buckingham MK18 1EG
☎(01280) 820218
e-mail: library@buckingham.ac.uk
url: www.buckingham.ac.uk

Site libraries
Franciscan Library, University of Buckingham, Verney Park Campus, Buckingham MK18 1EG
☎(01280) 828207
Fax (01280) 828288
Librarian (Law) Miss Louise Hammond BSc

Hunter Street Library, University of Buckingham, Hunter Street, Buckingham MK18 1EG
☎(01280) 820106
Assistant Librarian (Business and Humanities) Nathan Scrimshaw BA MSc

Assistant Librarian (Science, Education and Foundation) Miss Diana Hilmer DiplBibl MSc

BUCKINGHAMSHIRE NEW UNIVERSITY

Library Services, Buckinghamshire New University, Queen Alexandra Road, High Wycombe, Bucks HPII 2JZ
☎(01494) 522141 ext 5107 (enquiries)
e-mail: library@bucks.ac.uk
url: www.bucks.ac.uk/library
Library Services Manager Ms Ursula Crow (ext 4526; e-mail: ursula.crow@bucks.ac.uk)

UNIVERSITY OF CAMBRIDGE

Cambridge University Library, University of Cambridge, West Road, Cambridge CB3 9DR
☎(01223) 333000
Fax (01223) 333160
e-mail: library@lib.cam.ac.uk
url: www.lib.cam.ac.uk
Librarian Mrs Anne Jarvis MA
Deputy Librarian Ms Sue Mehrer

Dependent libraries

Betty and Gordon Moore Library, University of Cambridge, Wilberforce Road, Cambridge CB3 0WD
☎(01223) 765670
e-mail: moore-library@lib.cam.ac.uk
url: www.lib.cam.ac.uk/BGML
Head of Science Information Services Ms Yvonne Nobis

Central Science Library, University of Cambridge, Benet Street, Cambridge CB2 3PY
☎(01223) 334742
e-mail: lib-csl-inquiries@lib.cam.ac.uk
url: www.lib.cam.ac.uk/CSL
Head of Science Information Services Ms Yvonne Nobis

Medical Library, University of Cambridge, Box 111, Cambridge Biomedical Campus, Cambridge CB2 0SP
☎(01223) 336750
e-mail: library@medschl.cam.ac.uk
url: www.medschl.cam.ac.uk
Librarian Peter B Morgan MA MCLIP

Squire Law Library, University of Cambridge, 10 West Road, Cambridge CB3 9DZ
☎(01223) 330077
Fax (01223) 330048
url: www.squire.law.cam.ac.uk
Librarian David F Wills BA MCLIP (e-mail: dfw1003@cam.ac.uk)

College, Institute and Departmental

Cambridge Union Society

Keynes Library, Cambridge Union Society, 9(A) Bridge Street, Cambridge CB2 1UB
☎(01223) 741289
Fax (01223) 566444
e-mail: librarian@cus.org
url: www.cus.org
Librarian Ms Catherine Wise BA (e-mail: librarian@cus.org)
(Members only)

Christ's College

Christ's College Library, Christ's College, Christ's College, St Andrew's Street, Cambridge CB2 3BU
☎(01223) 334950
e-mail: library@christs.cam.ac.uk
url: www.christs.cam.ac.uk/library
College Librarian Ms Amelie Roper

Churchill College

Library, Churchill College, Storey's Way, Cambridge CB3 0DS
☎(01223) 336138
url: www.chu.cam.ac.uk/library
Librarian Ms Mary Kendall MA MCLIP (e-mail: librarian@chu.cam.ac.uk)
(NB The Library is available to College Members only)

Clare College

Fellows' Library, Clare College, Cambridge CB2 1TL
☎(01223) 333253/333202
Fax (01223) 765560
url: www.clare.cam.ac.uk/The-Fellows-Library
Fellows' Librarian Dr Fiona Edmonds

Forbes Mellon Library, Clare College, Cambridge CB3 9AJ
☎(01223) 333202
e-mail: library@clare.cam.ac.uk
url: www.clare.cam.ac.uk/academic/libraries/index.html
Librarian Mrs Catherine Reid MSc MCLIP

Corpus Christi College

Parker Library, Corpus Christi College, Trumpington Street, Cambridge CB2 1RH
☎(01223) 338025
e-mail: parker-library@corpus.cam.ac.uk
url: www.corpus.cam.ac.uk
Librarian Dr Christopher de Hamel
Sub-Librarians Ms Gill Cannell (e-mail: gc110@cam.ac.uk), Steven Archer (e-mail: sa377@cam.ac.uk)

Taylor Library, Corpus Christi College, Trumpington Street, Cambridge CB2 1RH
☎(01223) 338052
Fax (01223) 338041

e-mail: taylor.library@corpus.cam.ac.uk
url: www.corpus.cam.ac.uk
Taylor Librarian Ms Rebecca Gower (e-mail: rjg58@cam.ac.uk)

Darwin College
Library, Darwin College, Silver Street, Cambridge CB3 9EU
☎(01223) 763547
e-mail: librarian@dar.cam.ac.uk
url: www.dar.cam.ac.uk/library
Librarian Ms Gülay Bozkert

Department of History and Philosophy of Science
Whipple Library, Department of History and Philosophy of Science, Free School Lane,
Cambridge CB2 3RH
☎(01223) 334547
e-mail: hpslib@hermes.cam.ac.uk
url: www.hps.cam.ac.uk/library
Librarian Mrs Anna Jones

Department of Land Economy Library
Mill Lane Library, Department of Land Economy Library, 8 Mill Lane, Cambridge CB2 1RX
☎(01223) 337110
e-mail: landecon-library@lists.cam.ac.uk
url: www.landecon.cam.ac.uk/library/library.htm
(Mill Lane Library also houses the Centre of Latin American Studies and the Centre of
International Studies)

Downing College
The Maitland Robinson Library, Downing College, Regent Street, Cambridge CB2 1DQ
☎(01223) 334829 (enquiries), (01223) 335352 (College Librarian), (01223) 334802
(Library Assistant)
url: www.dow.cam.ac.uk/index.php/about/library
Fellow Librarian Dr Marcus Tomalin PhD
College Librarian Ms Karen Lubarr BA (e-mail: college-librarian@dow.cam.ac.uk)
Archivist Ms Jenny Ulph (e-mail: archivist@dow.cam.ac.uk)

Emmanuel College
Library, Emmanuel College, Cambridge CB2 3AP
☎(01223) 334233
e-mail: library@emma.cam.ac.uk
url: www.emma.cam.ac.uk
Fellow Librarian Dr A S Bendall MCLIP
College Librarian Dr H C Carron BA MA MPhil PhD MCLIP
Assistant Librarian Mrs C E P Bonfield BA

Faculty of Asian and Middle Eastern Studies
Library, Faculty of Asian and Middle Eastern Studies, Sidgwick Avenue, Cambridge CB3 9DA
☎(01223) 335112 (enquiries)
Fax (01223) 335110
e-mail: library@ames.cam.ac.uk

url: www.ames.cam.ac.uk/faclib
Librarian Ms Françoise Simmons MA(Cantab) MA(UCL) (01223 335111)

Faculty of Education
Everton Library and Information Service, Faculty of Education, 184 Hills Road, Cambridge CB2 8PQ
☎(01223) 767700 (enquiries)
e-mail: library@educ.cam.ac.uk
url: www.educ.cam.ac.uk/library
Librarian Ms Angela Cutts BA DipLib MCLIP
Deputy Librarian Ms Emma Jane Batchelor BA DipILS MCLIP

Faculty of Music
Pendlebury Library of Music, Faculty of Music, 11 West Road, Cambridge CB3 9DP
☎(01223) 335182
Fax (01223) 335067
e-mail: pendlebury@mus.ac.ac.uk
url: www.mus.cam.ac.uk/pendlebury
Librarian Ms Anna Pensaert LIC

Fitzwilliam College
Library, Fitzwilliam College, Cambridge CB3 0DG
☎(01223) 332042
Fax (01223) 477976
e-mail: librarian@fitz.cam.ac.uk
url: www.fitz.cam.ac.uk
Librarian Ms Christine E Roberts Lewis BSc(Econ) CertEd

Girton College
Library, Girton College, Cambridge CB3 0JG
☎(01223) 338970
Fax (01223) 339890
e-mail: library@girton.cam.ac.uk
url: www.girton.cam.ac.uk/library
Fellow and Librarian Ms Frances Gandy BA MA MCLIP
Assistant Librarian Mrs Jenny Blackhurst MA MA MCLIP
Archivist Ms Hannah Westall MA(Hons) MA

Gonville and Caius College
Library, Gonville and Caius College, Cambridge CB2 1TA
☎(01223) 332419/339685
e-mail: library@cai.cam.ac.uk
url: www.cai.cam.ac.uk/library
College Librarian M S Statham MA MCLIP
(Upper Library open to members of the College only. Lower Library open to scholars by appointment. All enquiries should be addressed to the College Librarian)

Homerton College
Library, Homerton College, Mary Allan Building, Hills Road, Cambridge CB2 8PH
☎(01223) 747260

e-mail: library@homerton.cam.ac.uk
url: www.homerton.cam.ac.uk
College Librarian Miss Liz Osman MA(Oxon) MA
(Library restricted to use by Homerton College members only. Visits to the library by appointment only)

Institute of Criminology

Radzinowicz Library of Criminology, Institute of Criminology, Sidgwick Avenue, Cambridge CB3 9DA
☎(01223) 335386
Fax (01223) 335356
e-mail: crimlib@hermes.cam.ac.uk
url: www.crim.cam.ac.uk/library
Librarian Stuart Stone BA MPA
Deputy Librarian Ms Alison Chew MA MSc

Jesus College

The Old Library, Jesus College, Jesus Lane, Cambridge CB5 8BL
☎(01223) 339405
Keeper of the Old Library Prof Stephen Heath
Assistant to the Keeper and Archivist Dr Frances Willmoth (e-mail: f.willmoth.jesus.cam.ac.uk)
(Apply in writing)

Quincentenary Library, Jesus College, Jesus Lane, Cambridge CB5 8BL
☎(01223) 339451
e-mail: quincentenary-library@jesus.cam.ac.uk
url: www.jesus.cam.ac.uk/college/infservices/library.html
Quincentenary Librarian Ms Rhona Watson BA(Hons) DipLib MCLIP

King's College Cambridge

Library, King's College Cambridge, Cambridge CB2 1ST
☎(01223) 331232
Fax (01223) 331891
e-mail: library@kings.cam.ac.uk
url: www.kings.cam.ac.uk/library
Librarian James Clements

Lucy Cavendish College

Library, Lucy Cavendish College, Lady Margaret Road, Cambridge CB3 0BU
☎(01223) 332183
e-mail: library@lucy-cav.cam.ac.uk
url: www.lucy-cav.cam.ac.uk
Librarian Ms Celine Carty
(The Library is open only to the members of the College)

Magdalene College

Magdalene College Library, Magdalene College, Magdalene Street, Cambridge CB3 0AG
☎(01223) 332125
e-mail: library@magd.cam.ac.uk

url: www.magd.cam.ac.uk/library
College Librarian Dr Marcus Waithe MA PhD
Deputy Librarian Mrs Annie Gleeson BA MA
(Open 24 hours Monday–Sunday to members of Magdalene College)

Pepys Library, Magdalene College, Magdalene Street, Cambridge CB3 0AG
☎(01223) 332125
e-mail: pepyslibrary@magd.cam.ac.uk
url: www.magd.cam.ac.uk/pepys
Pepys Librarian and Keeper of the Old Library Dr M E J Hughes MA PhD
Deputy Librarian (Pepys and Special Collections) Miss Catherine Sutherland
MA(Cantab) MSc
(Open to visitors 2–4pm Monday to Saturday including Bank Holidays (in summer Saturday
open times are 11.30am–12.30pm and 1.30pm–2.30pm. Closed for Christmas, Easter, and
two weeks in September. Scholars by prior appointment Monday to Friday 10am–5pm)

Old Library, Magdalene College, Magdalene Street, Cambridge CB3 0AG
☎(01223) 332125
e-mail: pepyslibrary@magd.cam.ac.uk
(Open 11.45am–1pm during University Full Term, or scholars by appointment only at other
times)

Murray Edwards College
Rosemary Murray Library, Murray Edwards College, New Hall, Huntingdon Road,
Cambridge CB3 0DF
☎(01223) 762202
Fax (01223) 763110
e-mail: library@murrayedwards.cam.ac.uk
url: www.murrayedwards.cam.ac.uk/exploring/rosemarymurraylibrary
rosemarymurraylibrary/
Librarian Ms Kirstie Preest BA DipILM MA MCLIP
(Admittance to Murray Edwards College members only; reading rights by appointment
with the Librarian during staffed hours)

Newnham College
Library, Newnham College, Sidgwick Avenue, Cambridge CB3 9DF
☎(01223) 335740/335739
url: www.newn.cam.ac.uk/about-newnham/library
Librarian Ms Deborah Hodder MA MCLIP (e-mail: librarian@newn.cam.ac.uk)

Pembroke College
Library, Pembroke College, Cambridge CB2 1RF
☎(01223) 338121
e-mail: library@pem.cam.ac.uk
url: www.pem.cam.ac.uk
Fellow Librarian Nick McBride
Librarian Ms Patricia Aske MA DipLib

Peterhouse
Ward and Perne Libraries, Peterhouse, Cambridge CB2 1RD
☎(01223) 338218 (Ward Library)

e-mail: lib@pet.cam.ac.uk
url: www.pet.cam.ac.uk
Ward Librarian S H Mandelbrote MA
Librarian Ms J K Walker BA MA MCLIP
Library Assistant Mrs E Grayton
Perne Librarian S H Mandelbrote MA
(Perne Library by appointment only)

Queens' College
Library, Queens' College, Silver Street, Cambridge CB3 9ET
☎(01223) 335549/50, Porter's Lodge (01223) 335500
Fax (01223) 335522
e-mail: library@queens.cam.ac.uk
url: www.queens.cam.ac.uk
College Librarian Dr Tim Egginton
Assistant Librarian Mrs Miriam Leonard BSc(Econ)
Fellow Librarian Dr Ian Patterson

Robinson College
Library, Robinson College, Cambridge CB3 9AN
☎(01223) 339124
url: www.robinson.cam.ac.uk
College Librarian Miss Lesley Read MA BA MCLIP

St Catharine's College
Library, St Catharine's College, Cambridge CB2 1RL
☎(01223) 338343
Fax (01223) 338340
e-mail: librarian@caths.cam.ac.uk
url: www.caths.cam.ac.uk/library
Librarian Colin Higgins BA(Med) MSc(Econ) MPhil

St Edmund's College
Library, St Edmund's College, Mount Pleasant, Cambridge CB3 0BN
☎(01223) 336250 (switchboard)
Fax (01223) 762822
url: www.st-edmunds.cam.ac.uk/life/library/index.php
Fellow Librarian Dr Petà Dunstan MA PhD
Assistant Librarian Ms Susanne Jennings (e-mail: librarian@st-edmunds.cam.ac.uk)
(Please write in or e-mail with enquiries)

St John's College
Library, St John's College, Cambridge CB2 1TP
☎(01223) 338661 (administration), (01223) 338662 (enquiries)
Fax (01223) 337035
e-mail: library@joh.cam.ac.uk
url: www.joh.cam.ac.uk/library
Librarian Dr Mark Nicholls MA PhD

Scott Polar Research Institute

Library, Scott Polar Research Institute, Lensfield Road, Cambridge CB2 1ER
☎(01223) 336552
Fax (01223) 336549
e-mail: library@spri.cam.ac.uk
url: www.spri.cam.ac.uk
Librarian Mrs Heather E Lane MA(Oxon) DipLiS MCLIP (e-mail: hel20@cam.ac.uk)

Selwyn College

Library, Selwyn College, Grange Road, Cambridge CB3 9DQ
☎(01223) 335880
e-mail: lib@sel.cam.ac.uk
url: www.sel.cam.ac.uk/library
College Librarian Ms Sonya Adams BA(Oxon) MA(Lond) MA(York)
Assistant Librarian Michael P Wilson BA(Hons) MA

Sidney Sussex College

Richard Powell Library, Sidney Sussex College, Cambridge CB2 3HU
☎(01223) 338852
e-mail: librarian@sid.cam.ac.uk
url: www.sid.cam.ac.uk/life/lib
Librarian Alan Stevens (e-mail: ads63@cam.ac.uk)

Section library

Archive and Muniment Room, Sidney Sussex College, Cambridge CB2 3HU
☎(01223) 338824
Fax (01223) 338884
e-mail: archivist@sid.cam.ac.uk
Archivist Nicholas J Rogers MA MLitt FSA (e-mail: njr1002@cam.ac.uk)

Trinity College

Library, Trinity College, Cambridge CB2 1TQ
☎(01223) 338488
Fax (01223) 338532
e-mail: trin-lib@lists.cam.ac.uk
url: www.trin.cam.ac.uk
Librarian Prof D J McKitterick FBA
(Undergraduate Library open to members of the College only. Wren Library: readers by appointment. Visitors: Mon–Fri 12–2pm; Sat 10.30–12.30, full term only)

Trinity Hall

Library, Trinity Hall, Trinity Lane, Cambridge CB2 1TJ
☎(01223) 332546
Fax (01223) 332537
e-mail: library@trinhall.cam.ac.uk
Director of Library Services Ms Dominique E Ruhlmann MA(Oxon)
Deputy Librarian Tom Sykes

Wolfson College

The Lee Library, Wolfson College, Barton Road, Cambridge CB3 9BB

☎(01223) 335965 (direct), (01223) 335900 (Porters' Lodge)
Fax (01223) 335908
e-mail: library@wolfson.cam.ac.uk
url: www.wolfson.cam.ac.uk/library
Librarian Ms Meg Westbury

CANTERBURY CHRIST CHURCH UNIVERSITY

Library, Canterbury Christ Church University, North Holmes Road, Canterbury, Kent CT1 1QU
☎(01227) 782352 (enquiries)
e-mail: library.enquiries@canterbury.ac.uk
url: www.canterbury.ac.uk/library
Head of Library Services Pete Ryan BA(Hons) MCLIP (e-mail: pete.ryan@canterbury.ac.uk)

Site libraries
Broadstairs Learning Centre, Canterbury Christ Church University, Northwood Road, Broadstairs, Kent CT10 2WA
☎(01843) 609103
Fax (01843) 609130
e-mail: broadstairslc@canterbury.ac.uk
Learning Centre Manager Dennis Corn BSc (e-mail: dennis.corn@canterbury.ac.uk)

Salomons Library, Canterbury Christ Church University, David Salomons Estate, Broomhill Road, Southborough, Tunbridge Wells, Kent TN3 0TG
☎(03330) 117126
e-mail: library.salomans@canterbury.ac.uk
Salomons Librarian Mrs Kathy Chaney MCLIP (e-mail: kathy.chaney@canterbury.ac.uk)

CARDIFF METROPOLITAN UNIVERSITY
(formerly University of Wales Institute, Cardiff)

Library Division, Cardiff Metropolitan University, Llandaff Campus, Western Avenue, Cardiff CF5 2YB
☎029 2041 6240
Fax 029 2041 6908
url: www.cardiffmet.ac.uk
Head of Library Division Ms Emma Adamson BA(Hons) MA (e-mail: eadamson@cardiffmet.ac.uk)

CARDIFF UNIVERSITY

Information Services, Cardiff University, 40–41 Park Place, Cardiff CF10 3BB
☎029 2087 4818
Fax 029 2037 1921
e-mail: library@cardiff.ac.uk
url: www.cardiff.ac.uk/insrv/libraries/index.html
Director of Information Services Martyn Harrow
Director of Libraries and University Librarian Mrs Janet Peters MA MLS MCLIP FHEA FRSA (029 2087 9362)

Site libraries

Aberconway Library, Cardiff University, PO Box 430, Cardiff CF24 0DE
☎029 2087 4770
e-mail: abcyliby@cardiff.ac.uk
Library Manager Miss Sally Earney

Archie Cochrane Library, Education Centre, Cardiff University, University Hospital
Llandough, Penarth, Cardiff CF64 2XX
☎029 2071 5497
Fax 029 2071 6497
e-mail: cochraneliby@cardiff.ac.uk
Hospitals Librarian Ms Rosemary Soper

Architecture Library, Cardiff University, King Edward VII Avenue, Cardiff CF10 3NB
☎029 2087 5974
e-mail: archliby@cardiff.ac.uk
Site Librarian Bute, Architecture, Senghennydd. Subject Librarian – Mathematics
Mrs Helen Staffer (e-mail: helen.staffer@wales.gsi.gov.uk)
Subject Librarian – Architecture Ms Sarah Nicholas

Arts and Social Studies Library, Cardiff University, PO Box 430, Cardiff CF24 0DE
☎029 2087 4818
Fax 029 2037 1921
e-mail: asslliby@cardiff.ac.uk
**Site Librarian ASSL. Law Service and Subject Librarian – History and
Archaeology** Duncan Montgomery

Biomedical Sciences Library, Cardiff University, PO Box 430, Cardiff CF24 0DE
☎029 2087 4090
e-mail: biomedliby@cardiff.ac.uk
Biomedical Scences and Science Librarian Mrs Linda Davies
Subject Librarian – Biosciences Nigel Morgan

Brian Cooke Dental Library, Cardiff University, 4th Floor, Dental School, Heath Park,
Cardiff CF14 4XY
☎029 2074 2525
e-mail: dentliby@cardiff.ac.uk
Dental Librarian Ms Delyth Morris

Bute Library, Cardiff University, PO Box 430, Cardiff CF24 0DE
☎029 2087 4611
e-mail: buteliby@cardiff.ac.uk
Site Librarian Bute, Architecture, Senghennydd. Subject Librarian – Mathematics
Mrs Helen Staffer (e-mail: helen.staffer@wales.gsi.gov.uk)

Cancer Research Wales Library, Cardiff University, Ground Floor, Cancer Research Wales
Building, Velindre Hospital, Velindre Road, Whitchurch, Cardiff CF14 2TL
☎029 2031 6291
e-mail: crwlibrary@wales.nhs.uk
Library Manager Mrs Bernadette Coles

Health Library, Cardiff University, The Cochrane Building, University Hospital of Wales,
Heath Park, Cardiff CF14 4XN
☎029 2068 8137

Fax 029 2068 8138
e-mail: healthlibrary@cardiff.ac.uk
Medical Librarian Mrs Lindsay Roberts

Law Library, Cardiff University, PO Box 430, Cardiff CF24 0DE
☎029 2087 4971
Fax 029 2037 1921
e-mail: lawliby@cardiff.ac.uk
Subject Librarians – Law Matthew Davies, Ms Lynn Goodhew

Music Library, Cardiff University, PO Box 430, Cardiff CF24 0DE
☎029 2087 4387
e-mail: musicliby@cardiff.ac.uk
Subject Librarian – Music Ms Charity Dove

Science Library, Cardiff University, PO Box 430, Cardiff CF24 0DE
☎029 2087 4085
Fax 029 2087 4995
e-mail: sciliby@cardiff.ac.uk
Biomedical Sciences and Science Librarian Mrs Linda Davies

Senghennydd Library, Cardiff University, PO Box 430, Cardiff CF24 0DE
☎029 2087 4158
e-mail: sengliby@cardiff.ac.uk
Site Librarian Bute, Architecture, Senghennydd. Subject Librarian – Mathematics
Mrs Helen Staffer (e-mail: helen.staffer@wales.gsi.gov.uk)

Trevithick Library, Cardiff University, PO Box 430, Cardiff CF24 0DE
☎029 2087 4286
e-mail: trevliby@cardiff.ac.uk
Trevithick Librarian and Subject Librarian – Computer Sciences and Engineering
Mrs Ruth Thornton

UNIVERSITY OF CENTRAL LANCASHIRE

Learning Information Service, University of Central Lancashire, Preston, Lancs PR1 2HE
☎(01772) 895355 (LIS Customer Support)
Fax (01772) 892991
e-mail: liscustomersupport@uclan.ac.uk
url: www.uclan.ac.uk
Acting Director of Learning and Information Services Ms Lisa Banks (01772 892674;
e-mail: lbanks2@uclan.ac.uk)
Head of Library and IT Services Jeremy Andrew BSc (01772 892264; e-mail:
jsandrew@uclan.ac.uk)
Acting Head of Customer Services Ms Nicola Rostron (01772 895051; e-mail:
nrostron@uclan.ac.uk)
Head of Technical Services James Crooks (01772 893802; e-mail: jdcrooks@uclan.ac.uk)

Site library
Burnley HE Library, University of Central Lancashire, Burnley Campus, Princess Way,
Burnley, Lancs BB12 0EQ
☎(01772) 895355
Librarian Michael Hargreaves (01772 892127; e-mail: mhargreaves@uclan.ac.uk)

CENTRAL SCHOOL OF SPEECH AND DRAMA
see ROYAL CENTRAL SCHOOL OF SPEECH AND DRAMA

UNIVERSITY OF CHESTER

Learning and Information Services, Seaborne Library, University of Chester, Parkgate Road, Chester CH1 4BJ
☎(01244) 511234 (enquiries); (01244) 511000 (switchboard)
e-mail: lis.helpdesk@chester.ac.uk
url: www.chester.ac.uk
Director of Learning and Information Services Brian Fitzpatrick BSc MBA (01244 512025; e-mail: b.fitzpatrick@chester.ac.uk)
Deputy Director and Head of Learning Technology Henry Blackman BSc MBCS CITP MHEA (01244 513374; e-mail: h.blackman@chester.ac.uk)
Deputy Director (Health Libraries, Print and Desktop Services) Mrs Wendy Fiander BSc MA MCLIP FHEA (01244 511193; e-mail: w.fiander@chester.ac.uk)
Deputy Director (Academic and User Services) Mrs Angela Walsh BLib MA MCLIP (01244 513308; e-mail: a.walsh@chester.ac.uk)
Deputy Director (Warrington and Network Services) Nigel Williams MSc (01925 534211; e-mail: nigel.williams@chester.ac.uk)

Broomhead Library, University of Chester, Warrington Campus, Crab Lane, Warrington, Cheshire WA2 0DB
☎(01925) 534284
Fax (01925) 530001
Librarian Mrs Emma Walsh BA MCLIP (e-mail: e.walsh@chester.ac.uk)

Learning and Information Services, University of Chester, Riverside Building, Castle Drive, Chester CH1 1SL
☎(01244) 512345
e-mail: riverside.library@chester.ac.uk
Senior Librarian Mrs Claire Norton
Site Librarian Mrs Karen Spencer

Sutton Library, University of Chester, Thornton Science Park, Pool Lane, Ince, Chester CH2 4NU
☎(01244) 513456
Librarian Paul Verlander (e-mail: p.verlander@chester.ac.uk)

Faculty of Health and Social Care Education Centre Libraries
Clatterbridge Library, University of Chester, Wirral Campus, Clatterbridge Hospital, Bebington, Wirral, Cheshire CH63 4JY
☎(01925) 534056
Librarian Ms Jacqui Maung MA (e-mail: j.maung@chester.ac.uk)

JET (Joint Education and Training) Library, University of Chester, Leighton Hospital, Middlewich Road, Crewe, Cheshire CW1 4QJ
☎(01270) 612538
Fax (01270) 252611
Librarian Ms Susan Smith (e-mail: susan.smith@chester.ac.uk)

UNIVERSITY OF CHICHESTER

Learning Resources Centre, University of Chichester, Bishop Otter Campus, College Lane, Chichester, West Sussex PO19 6PE
☎(01243) 816222
e-mail: help@chi.ac.uk
url: www.chi.ac.uk/student-life/life-campus/library-services
Director of Learning and Information Services Ms Anna O'Neill (01243 816090; e-mail: a.oneill@chi.ac.uk)

Campus library
Library, University of Chichester, Bognor Regis Campus, Upper Bognor Road, Bognor Regis, West Sussex PO21 1HR
☎(01243) 816222
Deputy Librarian Steve Bowman (01243 812082; e-mail: s.bowman@chi.ac.uk)

CITY UNIVERSITY LONDON

University Library, City University London, Northampton Square, London EC1V 0HB
☎020 7040 4061 (enquiries)
Fax 020 7040 8969 (switchboard)
e-mail: library@city.ac.uk
url: www.city.ac.uk/library
Director of Library Services Ms Louise Doolan BA(Hons) MA (e-mail: louise.doolan@city.ac.uk)

Site libraries
Learning Resource Centre, City University London, Cass Business School, 106 Bunhill Row, London EC1Y 8TZ
☎020 7040 8787 (enquiries)
e-mail: cklib@city.ac.uk
url: www.cass.city.ac.uk/library
Head of LRC Ms Jacqui Gaul MA MCLIP

Library Services, City University London, City Law School Library, 4 Gray's Inn Place, Gray's Inn, London WC1R 5DX
☎020 7400 3605 (enquiries)
e-mail: lawlibrary@city.ac.uk
url: www.city.ac.uk/law

Library Services, City University London, City Law School Library, Innovation Centre, Whiskin Street, London EC1R 0JT
e-mail: lawlibrary@city.ac.uk
url: www.city.ac.uk/law

COVENTRY UNIVERSITY

Lanchester Library, Coventry University, Frederick Lanchester Building, Gosford Street, Coventry CV1 5DD
☎024 7765 7575 (enquiries); 024 7765 7515 (administration)

url: www.coventry.ac.uk
University Librarian Phil Brabban (e-mail: aa2950@coventry.ac.uk)

CRANFIELD UNIVERSITY

Kings Norton Library, Cranfield University, Cranfield, Beds MK43 0AL
☎(01234) 754444 (general enquiries)
e-mail: library@cranfield.ac.uk
url: www.cranfield.ac.uk
Director of Library Services and University Librarian Simon Bevan BSc(Econ) MA

Other libraries

Barrington Library, Defence Academy of Management and Technology, Cranfield University,
Shrivenham, Swindon SN6 8LA
☎(01793) 785743 (general enquiries)
Fax (01793) 785555
e-mail: library.barrington@cranfield.ac.uk
url: http://diglib.shrivenham.cranfield.ac.uk
Head of Barrington Library Ms Sally Wilkinson BA(Hons) DipLib DipComp MCLIP

Management Information Resource Centre, Cranfield University, Cranfield, Beds MK43 0AL
☎(01234) 754440
Fax (01234) 751806
Head of Research and Learning Support John Harrington BA(Hons) MA DipLib MCLIP
(e-mail: j.harrington@cranfield.ac.uk)

UNIVERSITY FOR THE CREATIVE ARTS

**Library and Student Services, University for the Creative Arts, Falkner Road, Farnham,
Surrey GU9 7DS**
☎(01252) 892709
e-mail: library@ucreative.ac.uk
url: www.ucreative.ac.uk/lss
Director of Library & Student Services Ms Janice Conway (e-mail:
JConway3@ucreative.ac.uk)
Discovery Systems Manager Ms Jill Gravestock (e-mail: jgravestock@ucreative.ac.uk)

Elaine Thomas Library, University for the Creative Arts, Falkner Road, Farnham, Surrey
GU9 7DS
☎(01252) 892709
e-mail: LibraryFARN@ucreative.ac.uk
url: www.ucreative.ac.uk/lss
Gateway Services Manager Simon Harper (e-mail: sharper2@ucreative.ac.uk)

Campus libraries

University Library Canterbury, University for the Creative Arts, New Dover Road,
Canterbury, Kent CT1 3AN
☎(01227) 817302
e-mail: LibraryCANT@ucreative.ac.uk
url: www.ucreative.ac.uk/lss
Gateway Services Manager Nicholas Ross MSc MCLIP (e-mail: nross@ucreative.ac.uk)

University Library Epsom, University for the Creative Arts, Ashley Road, Epsom, Surrey
KT18 5BE
☎(01372) 202461
e-mail: LibraryEPSM@ucreative.ac.uk
url: www.ucreative.ac.uk/lss
Gateway Services Manager Ms Hilary Wicks (e-mail: hwicks@ucreative.ac.uk)

University Library Rochester, University for the Creative Arts, Fort Pitt, Rochester, Kent
ME1 1DZ
☎(01634) 888734
e-mail: LibraryROCH@ucreative.ac.uk
url: www.ucreative.ac.uk/lss
Gateway Services Manager Ms Louise Jennings (e-mail: ljennings@ucreative.ac.uk)

UNIVERSITY OF CUMBRIA

Harold Bridges Library, University of Cumbria, Bowerham Road, Lancaster LA1 3JD
☎(01524) 590871
e-mail: liss@cumbria.ac.uk
url: www.cumbria.ac.uk/liss
Head of Library and Student Services Ms Margaret Weaver BA MSc MCLIP FHEA
(e-mail: margaret.weaver@cumbria.ac.uk)
Customer Services Manager Ms Lisa Toner BA DipLib MCLIP (01524 384682; e-mail:
lisa.toner@cumbria.ac.uk)

Campus libraries
Brampton Road Library, University of Cumbria, Carlisle, Cumbria CA3 9AY
☎(01228) 400341
e-mail: liss@cumbria.ac.uk
Customer Services Manager Ms Lisa Toner BA DipLib MCLIP (01524 384682; e-mail:
lisa.toner@cumbria.ac.uk)

Fusehill Street Library, University of Cumbria, Skiddaw Building, Fusehill Street, Carlisle
CA1 2HH
☎(01228) 616218
e-mail: liss@cumbria.ac.uk
Customer Services Manager Ms Lisa Toner BA DipLib MCLIP (01524 384682; e-mail:
lisa.toner@cumbria.ac.uk)

London Library, University of Cumbria, 58 East India Dock Road, London E14 6JE
☎020 7517 4805
e-mail: liss@cumbria.ac.uk
Customer Services Manager Ms Lisa Toner BA DipLib MCLIP (01524 384682; e-mail:
lisa.toner@cumbria.ac.uk)

The Barn, University of Cumbria, Rydal Road, Ambleside, Cumbria LA22 9BB
☎(01539) 430274
e-mail: ambleside@cumbria.ac.uk
Customer Services Manager Ms Lisa Toner BA DipLib MCLIP (01524 384682; e-mail:
lisa.toner@cumbria.ac.uk)

DE MONTFORT UNIVERSITY

Kimberlin Library, De Montfort University, The Gateway, Leicester LEI 9BH
☎0116 257 7165
Fax 0116 257 7046
url: www.library.dmu.ac.uk
Director of Library and Learning Services Ms Jo Webb MA MLib MBA FCLIP FRSA
FHEA (e-mail: jwebb@dmu.ac.uk)
Head of User Experience Richard Partridge BA(Hons) PGDipLIS (e-mail:
rpartridge@dmu.ac.uk)
Head of Archives and Resource Management Dr Alan Brine BA MSc PhD MCLIP (e-
mail: abrine@dmu.ac.uk)
Head of Academic Liaison and Administration Ms Jane Mortimer BA(Hons) PGDipLib
DMS PGDipHRM MCLIP AHEA

UNIVERSITY OF DERBY

Learning Enhancement, University of Derby, Kedleston Road, Derby DE22 IGB
☎(01332) 591215
e-mail: library@derby.ac.uk
url: www.derby.ac.uk/library
Dean of Learning Enhancement Dr Ruth Ayres BSc(Hons) PhD DIC CBiol MIBiol
PGCTLHE FHEA
University Librarian Ms Pat Johnson MCLIP (e-mail: p.a.johnson@derby.ac.uk)
Deputy University Librarian Ms Maria Carnegie BA(Hons) (e-mail:
m.a.carnegie@derby.ac.uk)

UNIVERSITY OF DUNDEE

Library and Learning Centre, University of Dundee, Small's Wynd, Dundee DDI 4HN
☎(01382) 384087 (enquiries), (01382) 384084 (administration)
Fax (01382) 386228
e-mail: library@dundee.ac.uk
url: www.dundee.ac.uk/library
Chief Information Officer & Director of LLC & University Librarian Dr Richard
Parsons MSc PhD

Site libraries

Duncan of Jordanstone College Library, University of Dundee, Matthew Building, 13 Perth
Road, Dundee DDI 4HT
☎(01382) 385255 (enquiries)
Fax (01382) 384094
e-mail: doj-library@dundee.ac.uk
Librarian Ms Yvonne McKenzie BA MCLIP

Robertson Trust Medical Library, University of Dundee, Ninewells Hospital and Medical
School, Dundee DDI 9SY
☎(01382) 383031
Fax (01382) 383032
e-mail: ninewells-library@dundee.ac.uk
Librarian Andrew Jackson BA(Hons) MCLIP

School of Nursing and Midwifery Library – Kirkcaldy, University of Dundee, Fife School of Nursing and Midwifery, Forth Avenue, Kirkcaldy, Fife KY2 5YS
☎(01382) 385930
Fax (01382) 385931
e-mail: fife-library@dundee.ac.uk
Librarian Andrew Jackson BA(Hons) MCLIP

DURHAM UNIVERSITY

Bill Bryson Library, Durham University, Stockton Road, Durham DH1 3LY
☎0191 334 2968
Fax 0191 334 2971
e-mail: main.library@durham.ac.uk
url: www.dur.ac.uk/library
Librarian and Director of Heritage Collections Jon Purcell BA MBA DMS DipLib MCLIP
Deputy Librarian Pete Maggs BA MA MBA DipLib
Deputy Director (Heritage Collections/Cultural Engagement) Dr Keith Bartlett BA PhD

Departmental libraries
Durham Business School Library, Durham University, Mill Hill Lane, Durham DH1 3LB
☎0191 334 5213
Fax 0191 334 5201
Academic Liaison Librarian Colin Theakston BA MPhil

Education Library, Durham University, Leazes Road, Durham DH1 1TA
☎0191 334 8137
Fax 0191 334 8311
Library Supervisor Dr Richard Lawrie BA PhD

Palace Green Library, Durham University, Palace Green, Durham DH1 3RN
☎0191 334 2932
Fax 0191 334 2942
Head of Heritage Collections Dr Sheila M Hingley BA MA PhD MCLIP FSA
Head of Learning and Access Dr Sarah Price BA PhD
Head of University Museums Dr Craig Barclay MA MLitt PhD AMA FSA MIFA

Queen's Campus Library, Durham University, University Boulevard, Stockton-on-Tees, Co Durham TS17 6BH
☎0191 334 0270
Fax 0191 334 0271
e-mail: stockton.library@durham.ac.uk
Queen's Campus Library Manager Ms Jane A Hodgson BA DipLib

UNIVERSITY OF EAST ANGLIA

Library, University of East Anglia, Norwich NR4 7TJ
☎(01603) 592421 (enquiries), (01603) 592407 (administration)
Fax (01603) 591010
e-mail: library@uea.ac.uk
url: www.lib.uea.ac.uk

Director of Information Services Jonathan Colam-French BSc MSc MBA (01603 593858; e-mail: j.colam@uea.ac.uk)
Library Director Nicholas Lewis BA PGCE MA (e-mail: nicholas.lewis@uea.ac.uk)
Head of Resources Ed Chamberlain BA(Hons) MA (01603 592429; e-mail: edmund.chamberlain@uea.ac.uk)
Head of User Services Mrs Heather Wells BSc MSc MCLIP (01603 593440; e-mail: heather.wells@uea.ac.uk)
Faculty Librarian (Social Science Faculty) Ms Carly Sharples BA MSc (01603 591712; e-mail: c.sharples@uea.ac.uk)
Faculty Librarian (Sciences) Dr Elizabeth Clarke BSc PhD (01603 591249; e-mail: e.clarke@uea.ac.uk)
Faculty Librarian (Arts and Humanities) Ms Sarah Elsegood BSc MCLIP ILTM
Faculty Librarian (Sciences) Ms Rachel Henderson (01603 592428; e-mail: rachel.henderson@uea.ac.uk)
Faculty Librarian (Health) William Jones BSc DipLib MCLIP (01603 592412; e-mail: w.jones@uea.ac.uk)
Information Compliance Officer David Palmer BA LLB MLS (01603 593523; e-mail: david.palmer@uea.ac.uk)
Systems Librarian Alan Exelby BA DipLib (01603 592432; e-mail: a.exelby@uea.ac.uk)
User Services Library Manager Ms Catherine Breame BA (01603 593507; e-mail: catherine.breame@uea.ac.uk)
Head of Academic Liaison Ms Jane Helgesen BA MA MCLIP (01603 592221; e-mail: j.helgesen@uea.ac.uk)
Information Policy & Compliance Manager Ms Ellen Paterson BA MSc (01603 592431; e-mail: e.paterson@uea.ac.uk)

UNIVERSITY OF EAST LONDON

Library and Learning Services, University of East London, Water Lane, London E15 4LZ
☎020 8223 4646
url: www.uel.ac.uk/lls
Director of Library and Learning Services Ms Cathy Walsh MA PGDipLib (e-mail: c.walsh@uel.ac.uk)
Associate Director, Client Services Ms Libby Homer (e-mail: l.homer@uel.ac.uk)
Academic Services Manager Paul Chopra MA PGDipLib MCLIP (e-mail: p.chopra@uel.ac.uk)
Learning Services Manager Ms Simone Okolo (e-mail: s.n.okolo@uel.ac.uk)

Campus library and learning centres

Docklands Library and Learning Centre, University of East London, 4–6 University Way, London E16 2RD
☎020 8223 3434 (enquiries)
Campus Library and Learning Centre Manager Ms Cath Johnson (e-mail: c.johnson@uel.ac.uk)

Stratford Library and Learning Centre, University of East London, Water Lane, Stratford, London E15 4LZ
☎020 8223 4646 (enquiries)
Campus Library and Learning Centre Manager Ms Florence Achen-Owor (e-mail: florence@uel.ac.uk

EDGE HILL UNIVERSITY

Learning Services, Edge Hill University, St Helens Road, Ormskirk, Lancs L39 4QP
☎(01695) 650800 (enquiries), (01695) 584284 (administration)
e-mail: lshelpdesk@edgehill.ac.uk
url: http://library.edgehill.ac.uk
Dean of Learning Services Ms Alison Mackenzie (01695 584284; e-mail:
alison.mackenzie@edgehill.ac.uk)
Assistant Head of Learning Services Ms Maria Mirza (01695 584334; e-mail:
maria.mirza@edgehill.ac.uk)

Site libraries
Aintree Library and Information Resource Centre, Edge Hill University, Clinical Sciences
Centre, University Hospital Aintree, Longmoor Lane, Liverpool L9 7AL
☎0151 529 5851

Armstrong House Library, Edge Hill University, Faculty of Health and Social Care,
Armstrong House, Manchester Technology Centre, Brancaster Road, Manchester
M1 7ED
☎(01695) 650797

Learning Services, Edge Hill University, Woodlands Campus, Southport Road, Chorley,
Lancs PR7 1QR
☎(01257) 517136

EDINBURGH COLLEGE OF ART AT THE UNIVERSITY OF EDINBURGH

**Library, Edinburgh College of Art at the University of Edinburgh, Evolution House, 78
West Port, Edinburgh EH1 2LE**
☎0131 651 5700
Fax 0131 651 5919
e-mail: eca@ed.ac.uk
url: www.ed.ac.uk/schools-departments/information-services/library-museum-gallery/
using-library/lib-locate/eca-library
Academic Support Librarian Ms Jane Furness
Site & Service Supervisor Andrew Baxter MA(Hons) MSc

EDINBURGH NAPIER UNIVERSITY

**Craiglockhart Campus Library, Edinburgh Napier University, Craiglockhart Campus,
Edinburgh EH14 1DJ**
☎0131 455 4260
url: www.napier.ac.uk/
Director of Information Services Chris Pinder BA MLib DipLib FCLIP (0131 455 4270)
Assistant Director (Customer Services) Ms Margaret Lobban MA MSc DipLib
DipEdTech MCLIP (0131 455 4272)
Head of Learning and Research Services Malcolm Jones BA DipLib MCLIP
(0131 455 2693)

Campus libraries
Merchiston Campus Library, Edinburgh Napier University, Merchiston Campus, Edinburgh EH10 5DT
☎0131 455 2582

Sighthill Campus Learning Resource Centre, Edinburgh Napier University, Sighthill Campus, Edinburgh EH11 4BN
☎0131 455 5616

UNIVERSITY OF EDINBURGH
Main Library, University of Edinburgh, George Square, Edinburgh EH8 9LJ
☎0131 650 3409 (Access and Lending Services); 0131 650 8379 (Special Collections)
Fax 0131 651 5041
e-mail: IS.Helpdesk@ed.ac.uk
url: www.ed.ac.uk/schools-departments/information-services/library-museum-gallery
Director of Library and University Collections Dr John Scally BA(Hons) PhD DipILS
(e-mail: john.scally@ed.ac.uk)

Site libraries
Law and Europa Library, University of Edinburgh, Old College, South Bridge, Edinburgh EH8 9YL
☎0131 650 2044
e-mail: IS.Helpline@ed.ac.uk
Site and Services Supervisor Ms Frances Fullarton (e-mail: f.fullarton@ed.ac.uk)

Moray House Library, University of Edinburgh, Dalhousie Land, St John Street, Edinburgh EH8 8JR
☎0131 651 6193
e-mail: IS.Helpline@ed.ac.uk
Site and Services Supervisor David Fairgrieve MA DipLib MCLIP (e-mail: david.fairgrieve@ed.ac.uk)

New College Library (Divinity), University of Edinburgh, Mound Place, Edinburgh EH1 2LU
☎0131 650 8957
e-mail: IS.Helpline.ed.ac.uk
Site and Services Supervisor Ms Sheila Dunn BA (e-mail: s.dunn@ed.ac.uk)

Noreen and Kenneth Murray Library, University of Edinburgh, King's Buildings, West Mains Road, Edinburgh EH9 3JF
☎0131 650 5784
e-mail: IS.Helpline@ed.ac.uk
Site and Services Supervisor Ms Judy Melville BA(Hons) (e-mail: judith.melville@ed.ac.uk)

Royal Infirmary Library, University of Edinburgh, Chancellor's Building, Little France Crescent, Edinburgh EH6 4SB
☎0131 242 6341
e-mail: IS.Helpline@ed.ac.uk
Site and Services Supervisor Ms Claire Leach BSc(Hons) PGDipLib (e-mail: claire.leach@ed.ac.uk)

The Lady Smith of Kelvin Veterinary Library, University of Edinburgh, Royal (Dick) School of Veterinary Studies, Easter Bush, Roslin, Midlothian EH25 9RG
☎0131 650 6405
e-mail: IS.Helpline@ed.ac.uk
Site and Services Supervisor Ms Claire Leach BSc(Hons) PGDipLib (e-mail: claire.leach@ed.ac.uk)

Western General Library, University of Edinburgh, Crewe Road South, Edinburgh EH4 2XU
☎0131 537 2299
e-mail: IS.Helpline@ed.ac.uk
Site and Services Supervisor Ms Claire Leach BSc(Hons) PGDipLib (e-mail: claire.leach@ed.ac.uk)

UNIVERSITY OF ESSEX

The Albert Sloman Library, University of Essex, Wivenhoe Park, Colchester, Essex CO4 3SQ
☎(01206) 873188
Fax (01206) 872289
url: www.essex.ac.uk
Librarian Robert Butler MSc

UNIVERSITY OF EXETER

University Forum Library, University of Exeter, Stocker Road, Exeter, Devon EX4 4PT
☎(01392) 263867 (enquiries)
Fax (01392) 263871
e-mail: library@exeter.ac.uk
url: www.exeter.ac.uk/library/
Head of Library & Culture Services Ms Clare Powne BMus MA MCLIP

Campus libraries

Research Commons, University of Exeter, Old Library Building, Prince of Wales Road, Exeter, Devon EX4 4SB
☎(01392) 264052
e-mail: library@exeter.ac.uk

St Luke's Campus Library, University of Exeter, Heavitree Road, Exeter, Devon EX1 2LU
☎(01392) 264785

Tremough Learning Resources Centre, University of Exeter, Penryn Campus, Treliever Road, Penryn, Cornwall TR10 9FE
☎(01326) 370441
Fax (01326) 370437
url: http://library.fxplus.ac.uk

Woodlane Library, University of Exeter, Falmouth Campus, Woodlane, Falmouth, Cornwall TR11 4RH
☎(01326) 213815
Fax (01326) 213827

FALMOUTH UNIVERSITY (formerly University College Falmouth)

Tremough Library, Falmouth University, Penryn Campus, Treliever Road, Penryn, Cornwall TRIO 9FE
☎(01326) 370441
e-mail: library@falmouth.ac.uk
url: www.falmouth.ac.uk
Head of Library and Information Services Ms Doreen Pinfold BA(Hons) PGDipLib MCLIP (e-mail: doreen.pinfold@fxplus.ac.uk)
User Services Librarian Ms Christina Carson (e-mail: christina.carson@fxplus.ac.uk)
Systems Librarian Steve Pellow BA(Hons) PGCE (e-mail: stevep@fxplus.ac.uk)
Technical Services Librarian Stephen Atkinson BSc DipLib MCLIP (e-mail: stephena@fxplus.ac.uk)
(Tremough LRC also serves University of Exeter)

Woodlane Library, Falmouth University, Woodlane Library, Falmouth Campus, Falmouth, Cornwall TRI1 4RH
☎(01326) 213815
e-mail: library@falmouth.ac.uk
url: www.library.fxplus.ac.uk
Art and Design Librarian Ms Dawn Lawrence (e-mail: dawn.lawrence@fxplus.ac.uk)
Campus Librarian Ms Rosalind Tyley MA (e-mail: rosalind.tyley@fxplus.ac.uk), Alan Doherty (e-mail: alan.doherty@fxplus.ac.uk) (job share)
(Woodlane Library also serves University of Exeter)

UNIVERSITY OF GLAMORGAN *see* UNIVERSITY OF SOUTH WALES

GLASGOW CALEDONIAN UNIVERSITY

University Library Services, Saltire Centre, Glasgow Caledonian University, Cowcaddens Road, Glasgow G4 0BA
☎0141 273 1000
Fax 0141 273 1183
e-mail: library@gcu.ac.uk
url: www.gcu.ac.uk/library
Director, Library Services Robert Ruthven MA DipLIS MCLIP

GLASGOW SCHOOL OF ART

Library, Glasgow School of Art, 167 Renfrew Street, Glasgow G3 6RQ
☎0141 353 4551
url: www.gsa.ac.uk/library
Head of Learning Resources Ms Alison Stevenson (e-mail: a.stevenson@gsa.ac.uk)

UNIVERSITY OF GLASGOW

Library, University of Glasgow, Hillhead Street, Glasgow GI2 8QE
☎0141 330 6704/5 (enquiries), 0141 330 5634 (administration)

Fax 0141 330 4952
e-mail: library@lib.gla.ac.uk
url: www.lib.gla.ac.uk
University Librarian Ms Helen Durndell MA PGDipLib

UNIVERSITY OF GLOUCESTERSHIRE

Learning and Information Services, University of Gloucestershire, The Park Campus, Cheltenham, Glos GL50 2RH
☎(01242) 714333 (enquiries), (01242) 715442 (administration)
e-mail: lcinfopark@glos.ac.uk
url: www.glos.ac.uk/library
Head of Library and Information Services Mrs Lesley Castens LLB(Hons)

Site libraries

Francis Close Hall Learning Centre, University of Gloucestershire, Swindon Road, Cheltenham, Glos GL50 4AZ
☎(01242) 714600
e-mail: libraryfch@glos.ac.uk
Faculty Librarian, BEPS Ms Sue Turner (e-mail: sturner@glos.ac.uk)

Oxstalls Learning Centre, University of Gloucestershire, Oxstalls Lane, Longlevens, Gloucester GL2 9HW
☎(01242) 175100
e-mail: libraryoxstalls@glos.ac.uk
Faculty Librarian Matt Durant (e-mail: mdurant@glos.ac.uk)

Park Learning Centre, University of Gloucestershire, Reynolds Building, The Park, Cheltenham, Glos GL50 2RH
☎(01242) 714333
e-mail: librarypark@glos.ac.uk
Customer Services Manager Scott Jordan BA (e-mail: sjordan@glos.ac.uk)

GLYNDŴR UNIVERSITY

Library, Glyndŵr University, Plas Coch, Mold Road, Wrexham LL11 2AW
☎(01978) 293250
url: www.glyndwr.ac.uk
Head of Library and Student Services Paul Jeorrett BA MCLIP PGDip (e-mail: p.jeorrett@glyndwr.ac.uk)
Academic Liaison Co-ordinator Nicola Watkinson BSc MCLIP FHEA (e-mail: nicolaw@glyndwr.co.uk)

UNIVERSITY OF GREENWICH

Greenwich Campus Library, University of Greenwich, The Library, Park Row, Greenwich, London SE10 9LS
☎020 8331 8000
url: www.gre.ac.uk/lib
Director of Information and Library Services Paul Butler (020 8331 8521; e-mail: p.butler@gre.ac.uk)

Head of Library Services Ms Virginia Malone (020 8331 9660; e-mail: v.g.malone@gre.ac.uk)
Senior Academic Services Librarian Ms Sarah Crofts (020 8331 9078; e-mail: s.j.crofts@gre.ac.uk)

Campus libraries
Avery Hill Campus Library, University of Greenwich, Bexley Road, London SE9 2PQ
☎020 8331 8484
Senior Academic Services Librarian Ms Barbara Gallagher (e-mail: b.r.gallagher@gre.ac.uk)

Drill Hall Library, University of Greenwich, Universities at Medway, North Road, Chatham Maritime, Kent ME4 4TB
☎(01634) 883278
Drill Hall Library Manager Dave Puplett (e-mail: d.r.puplett@gre.ac.uk)
(shared library with Canterbury Christ Church University and University of Kent)

GUILDHALL SCHOOL OF MUSIC AND DRAMA

Library, Guildhall School of Music and Drama, Silk Street, Barbican, London EC2Y 8DT
☎020 7382 7178 (direct)
e-mail: library@gsmd.ac.uk
url: www.gsmd.ac.uk
Senior Librarian Mrs Kate Eaton BA(Hons) MA MCLIP (e-mail: kate.eaton@gsmd.ac.uk)

HARPER ADAMS UNIVERSITY

Library, Harper Adams University, Edgmond, Newport, Shropshire TF10 8NB
☎(01952) 820280
e-mail: libhelp@harper-adams.ac.uk
url: www.harper-adams.ac.uk
Librarian Ms Kathryn Greaves BLib(Hons) MCLIP (e-mail: kgreaves@harper-adams.ac.uk)

HERIOT-WATT UNIVERSITY

University Library, Heriot-Watt University, Edinburgh EH14 4AS
☎0131 451 3582
e-mail: libhelp@hw.ac.uk
url: www.hw.ac.uk/library
Director of Information Services Mike Roch

UNIVERSITY OF HERTFORDSHIRE

Information Hertfordshire, University of Hertfordshire, College Lane, Hatfield, Herts AL10 9AB
☎(01707) 284678
Fax (01707) 284701
e-mail: helpdesk@herts.ac.uk
url: www.herts.ac.uk
Chief Information Officer Dr David Ford (e-mail: d.m.ford@herts.ac.uk)

Learning resources centres

Hatfield College Lane Campus Learning Resources Centre, University of Hertfordshire, College Lane, Hatfield, Herts AL10 9AB
☎(01707) 284678

Hatfield de Havilland Campus Learning Resources Centre, University of Hertfordshire, Hatfield, Herts AL10 9AY
☎(01707) 284678
(post c/o College Lane address above)

UNIVERSITY OF THE HIGHLANDS AND ISLANDS

(formerly UHI Millennium Institute)

UHI Library Services, University of the Highlands and Islands, Executive Office, Ness Walk, Inverness IV3 5SQ
☎(01463) 279000
Fax (01463) 279001
url: www.uhi.ac.uk
Acting Director of Library and Information Systems John Maher (e-mail: john.maher@uhi.ac.uk)

Academic Partner libraries

Argyll College UHI, University of the Highlands and Islands, Stewart Road, Campbeltown, Argyll PA28 6AT
☎(01631) 559673
Learning Resources Contact Ms Liz Richardson (e-mail: liz.richardson@argyllcollege.ac.uk)

Highland Theological College, University of the Highlands and Islands, High Street, Dingwall, Ross-shire IV15 9HA
☎(01349) 780215
Fax (01349) 780001
Librarian Martin Cameron BA DipLib MCLIP (e-mail: martin.cameron@uhi.ac.uk)

Inverness College UHI, University of the Highlands and Islands, 3 Longman Road, Inverness IV1 1SA
☎(01463) 273248
Fax (01463) 711977
Learning Resources Contact Ms Carol Hart DipLIS MCLIP

Lews Castle College UHI, University of the Highlands and Islands, Stornoway, Western Isles, Isle of Lewis, Hebrides HS2 0XR
☎(01851) 770408
Fax (01851) 770001
e-mail: lelibrary@uhi.ac.uk
Library Contact Ms Caroline Brick

Moray College UHI, University of the Highlands and Islands, Moray Street, Elgin, Moray IV30 1JJ
☎(01343) 576206
Fax (01343) 576001
Library Officer Mrs Linda K Mutch BSC(Econ) (e-mail: linda.mutch.moray@uhi.ac.uk)

NAFC Marine Centre UHI, North Atlantic Fisheries College, University of the Highlands and Islands, Port Arthur, Scalloway, Shetland ZE1 0UN
☎(01595) 772000
Fax (01595) 772001
e-mail: library@nafc.uhi.ac.uk
url: www.nafc.ac.uk
Learning Resources Contact Ms Ruth Priest BA DipLib MCLIP (e-mail: ruth.priest@shetland.uhi.ac.uk)

North Highland College UHI, University of the Highlands and Islands, Ormlie Road, Thurso, Caithness KW14 7EE
☎(01847) 889293/4
e-mail: nhc.library@uhl.ac.uk
Learning Resource Assistant Ms Janet Parker (e-mail: janet.parker@uhi.ac.uk)

Orkney College UHI, University of the Highlands and Islands, East Road, Kirkwall, Orkney KW15 1LX
☎(01856) 569272
Fax (01856) 569001
e-mail: oclibrary@uhi.ac.uk
Librarian Ms Anette Andersen (01856 569272)

Perth College UHI, University of the Highlands and Islands, Crieff Road, Perth PH1 2NX
☎(01738) 877721
e-mail: library@perth.uhi.ac.uk
url: www.perth/support/library/Pages/default.aspx
College Librarian Donald MacLean MA(Hons) PGDipILS ACLIB (e-mail: donald.maclean@perth.uhi.ac.uk)

Sabhal Mòr Ostaig, University of the Highlands and Islands, Colaiste Ghàidhlig na h-Alba, An Teanga, Slèite, An t-Eilean Sgitheanach IV44 8RQ
☎(01471) 888447/888431
e-mail: sm00ll@uhi.ac.uk
url: www.smo.uhi.ac.uk/
College Librarian Ms Cairistìona Cain MA(Hons) MSc DipPsych

SAMS UHI, Scottish Association for Marine Science, University of the Highlands and Islands, Dunstaffnage Marine Laboratory, Dunbeg, Oban, Argyll PA37 1QA
☎(01631) 559000
Fax (01631) 559001
Learning Resources Contact Ms Olga Kimmins BA(Hons) (e-mail: olga.kimmins@sams.uhi.ac.uk)

Shetland College UHI, University of the Highlands and Islands, Gremista, Lerwick, Shetland ZE1 0PX
☎(01595) 771258
e-mail: library@shetland.uhi.ac.uk
Learning Resources Contact Ms Ruth Priest BA DipLib MCLIP (e-mail: ruth.priest@shetland.uhi.ac.uk)

West Highland College UHI, University of the Highlands and Islands, Carmichael Way, Fort William, Lochaber, Inverness-shire PH33 6FF
☎(01397) 874277

Learning Resources Contact Ms Louise Penny
(previously Lochaber College)

UNIVERSITY OF HUDDERSFIELD

Library and Computing Centre, University of Huddersfield, Queensgate, Huddersfield, Yorkshire HD1 3DH
☎(01484) 473888 (enquiries)
e-mail: library@hud.ac.uk
url: www.hud.ac.uk
Director of Computing and Library Services Ms Sue White BA(Hons) DipLib MCLIP FHEA

UNIVERSITY OF HULL

The Brynmor Jones Library, University of Hull, Cottingham Road Campus, Cottingham Road, Kingston upon Hull HU6 7RX
☎(01482) 466581
e-mail: libhelp@hull.ac.uk
url: http://library.hull.ac.uk
Director of Library and Learning Innovation and University Librarian Dr Richard Heseltine BA DPhil DipLib

Campus library

Keith Donaldson Library, University of Hull, Scarborough Campus, Filey Road, Scarborough, North Yorks YO11 3AZ
☎(01723) 357277
Fax (01723) 357328
e-mail: libhelp-scar@hull.ac.uk

IMPERIAL COLLEGE LONDON

Central Library, Imperial College London, South Kensington, London SW7 2AZ
☎020 7594 8810 (enquiries), 020 7594 8816 (administration)
Fax 020 7594 8876
e-mail: library@imperial.ac.uk
url: www.imperial.ac.uk/library
Director of Library Services Ms Chris Banks FRSA (e-mail: chris.banks@imperial.ac.uk)
Assistant Director, Library Academic Services Ms Frances Boyle (e-mail: f.boyle@imperial.ac.uk)
Assistant Director, Library Resource and Innovation Services Ms Susan Howard BA MSc DipLib MCLIP (020 7594 8622; e-mail: s.howard@imperial.ac.uk)

Medical libraries

Charing Cross Campus Library, Imperial College London, Charing Cross Campus, St Dunstan's Road, London W6 8RP
☎020 7594 0755
e-mail: cxissuedesk@imperial.ac.uk

Chelsea and Westminster Campus Library, Imperial College London, Chelsea and Westminster Hospital, 369 Fulham Road, London SW10 9NH

☎020 8746 8107
e-mail: librarycw@imperial.ac.uk

Hammersmith Campus Library, Imperial College London, Hammersmith Campus, Du Cane Road, London W12 0NN
☎020 8383 3246
e-mail: libhamm@imperial.ac.uk

Royal Brompton Campus Library, Imperial College London, Guy Scadding Building, Dovehouse Street, London SW3 6LY
☎020 7594 7917
e-mail: br.library@imperial.ac.uk

St Mary's Fleming Library, Imperial College London, St Mary's Campus, Norfolk Place, London W2 1PG
☎020 7594 3692
e-mail: sm-lib@imperial.ac.uk

Silwood Park Campus Library, Imperial College London, Silwood Park Campus, Buckhurst Road, Ascot, Berks SL5 7TA
☎020 7594 2461
e-mail: silwood.library@imperial.ac.uk

INSTITUTE OF DEVELOPMENT STUDIES

British Library for Development Studies, Institute of Development Studies, University of Sussex, Falmer, Brighton BNI 9RE
☎(01273) 915660
url: blds.ids.ac.uk
Acting Head of Library Ms Helen Rehin (e-mail: h.rehin@ids.ac.uk)

ISLE OF MAN COLLEGE OF FURTHER AND HIGHER EDUCATION

Library, Isle of Man College of Further and Higher Education, Homefield Road, Douglas, Isle of Man IM2 6RB
☎(01624) 648207
e-mail: libiomc@manx.net
Senior Librarian Miss Carole Graham BA MSc MCLIP (e-mail: Carole.Graham@iomcollege.ac.im)
College Librarian Tim Kenyon BA MA MCLIP (e-mail: Tim.Kenyon@iomcollege.ac.im)

KEELE UNIVERSITY

Library Services, Keele University, Keele, Staffs ST5 5BG
☎(01782) 733535 (enquiries), (01782) 733232 office
Fax (01782) 734502
e-mail: library.help@keele.ac.uk
url: www.keele.ac.uk/library
University Librarian Paul Reynolds MA MCLIP (e-mail: p.r.reynolds@keele.ac.uk)

Departmental library
Health Library, Keele University, Clinical Education Centre, University Hospital of North Staffordshire, Newcastle Road, Stoke-on-Trent ST4 6QG
☎(01782) 679500
Fax (01782) 679582
Health Library Manager J V P Hutchins MA DipLib (e-mail: j.v.p.hutchins@keele.ac.uk)

UNIVERSITY OF KENT

Templeman Library, University of Kent, Canterbury, Kent CT2 7NU
☎(01227) 823124
Fax (01227) 823984
e-mail: library-enquiry@kent.ac.uk
url: www.kent.ac.uk/library
Director of Information Services John Sotillo BSc
Assistant Director (Library Collections) Ms Trudy Turner
Assistant Director (Customer Support) Sam Thornton

Site libraries
Drill Hall Library, Universities at Medway, University of Kent, North Road, Chatham Maritime, Chatham, Kent ME4 4TB
☎(01634) 883278
Fax (01634) 883567
url: http://campus.medway.ac.uk/library
Library Manager Dave Puplett (e-mail: d.r.puplett@gre.ac.uk)
(Shared library with Canterbury Christ Church University and University of Greenwich)

KINGSTON UNIVERSITY

Library and Learning Services, Kingston University, Penrhyn Road, Kingston upon Thames, Surrey KT1 2EE
☎020 8417 2101 (enquiries), 020 8417 2099 (administration)
e-mail: library@kingston.ac.uk
url: www.kingston.ac.uk/library
Co-Director of Library and Learning Services/Head of Content Development
Mrs Elizabeth Malone BA(Hons) DipLib MCLIP (020 8417 2100; e-mail: e.malone@kingston.ac.uk)
Co-Director of Library and Learning Services/Head of Learning and Research Support Ms Sandy Leitch BA(Hons) DipLib (020 8417 7785; e-mail: s.leitch@kingston.ac.uk)

Campus libraries
Library and Learning Services, Kingston University, Nightingale Centre, Kingston Hill, Kingston upon Thames, Surrey KT2 7LB
☎020 8417 5380

Library and Learning Services, Kingston University, Dame Elizabeth Esteve-Coll Centre, Knights Park, Kingston upon Thames, Surrey KT1 2QJ
☎020 8417 4214

Library and Learning Services, Kingston University, Sir Sydney Camm Centre, Roehampton Vale, Friars Avenue, London SW15 3DW
☎020 8417 4760

LANCASTER UNIVERSITY

University Library, Lancaster University, Bailrigg, Lancaster LA1 4YH
☎(01524) 592516 (enquiries), 01524 592535 (administration)
Fax (01524) 65719
e-mail: library@lancaster.ac.uk (Library user services)
url: www.libweb.lancs.ac.uk
Director of Computing & Library Services Paul Harness

LEEDS BECKETT UNIVERSITY

(formerly Leeds Metropolitan University)

Sheila Silver Library, Leeds Beckett University, Leslie Silver Building, Woodhouse Lane, Leeds LS1 3ES
☎0113 812 1000
e-mail: library@leedsbeckett.ac.uk
url: www.library.leedsbeckett.ac.uk
Director of Libraries and Learning Innovation Ms Jo Norry BA(Hons) MA DipLib PGDip FCLIP FHEA (0113 812 5966; e-mail: j.norry@leedsbeckett.ac.uk)

Campus libraries
Headingley Library, Leeds Beckett University, James Graham Building, Headingley Campus, Church Wood Avenue, Leeds LS6 3HF
☎0113 812 1000
e-mail: library@leedsbeckett.ac.uk

LEEDS COLLEGE OF MUSIC

Library, Leeds College of Music, 3 Quarry Hill, Leeds LS2 7PD
☎0113 222 3458 (enquiries)
e-mail: lcmlibrary@lcm.ac.uk
url: www.lcm.ac.uk
Head of Library eLearning and Technical Services Ms Jay Glasby BA MCLIP (e-mail: j.glasby@lcm.ac.uk)
Jazz Archivist Ms Claire Marsh BMus MSc MCLIP (e-mail: c.marsh@lcm.ac.uk)

LEEDS TRINITY UNIVERSITY
(formerly Leeds Trinity & All Saints College)

Library, Leeds Trinity University, Brownberrie Lane, Horsforth, Leeds LS18 5HD
☎0113 283 7244
Fax 0113 283 7200
url: www.leedstrinity.ac.uk/services/library
Director of Library and Learning Resources Nick Goodfellow BA MA MCLIP
(e-mail: n.goodfellow@leedstrinity.ac.uk)

Liaison Librarians Ms Rebecca Coombes BA(Hons) MSc (e-mail:
r.coombes@leedstrinity.ac.uk), Ms Rachel Davies (e-mail: r.davies@leedstrinity.ac.uk),
Ms Sarah Munks (e-mail: s.munks@leedstrinity.ac.uk)

UNIVERSITY OF LEEDS

University Library, University of Leeds, Leeds LS2 9JT
☎0113 343 5663
e-mail: library@leeds.ac.uk
url: www.leeds.ac.uk/library
University Librarian/Keeper of the Brotherton Collection Dr Stella Butler BSc PhD
AMA (e-mail: s.butler@leeds.ac.uk)
Deputy Librarian Brian Clifford BA MA HonFCLIP (e-mail: b.e.clifford@leeds.ac.uk)

UNIVERSITY OF LEICESTER

**David Wilson Library, University of Leicester, PO Box 248, University Road, Leicester
LEI 9QD**
☎0116 252 2043 (general enquiries), 0116 252 2031 (Librarian's secretary)
Fax 0116 252 2066
e-mail: library@leicester.ac.uk
url: www.le.ac.uk/library
University Librarian Mrs Caroline Taylor (0116 252 2034)
Deputy University Librarian Ben Wynne (0116 252 5048)

UNIVERSITY OF LINCOLN

University Library, University of Lincoln, Brayford Pool, Lincoln LN6 7TS
☎(01522) 886222 (general enquiries), (01522) 886427 (administration)
Fax (01522) 886311
url: www.library.lincoln.ac.uk
University Librarian Ian Snowley BA MBA FCLIP
Deputy Librarian Ms Lys Ann Reiners (e-mail: lreiners@lincoln.ac.uk)
Head of Electronic Library Services Dave Masterson (e-mail:
dmasterson@lincoln.ac.uk)
Customer Services Team Manager Mrs Lesley Thompson (01522 886222; e-mail:
lthompson@lincoln.ac.uk)

Campus libraries

Holbeach Campus Library, University of Lincoln, Minerva House, Holbeach Technology
Park, Park Road, Holbeach, Spalding, Lincs PE12 7PT
☎(01406) 493007
Fax (01406) 493030
Library Officer Ms Julie Smith

LIVERPOOL HOPE UNIVERSITY

The Sheppard-Worlock Library, Liverpool Hope University, Hope Park, Liverpool LI6 9JD
☎0151 291 2000 (Help Point), 0151 291 2001 (administration), 0151 291 2007/2079
(enquiries)

Fax 0151 291 2037
e-mail: askalibrarian@hope.ac.uk
url: www.hope.ac.uk//gateway/library
Head of Library Services Ms Susan Murray BSc MA MCLIP ILTM (0151 291 2002;
e-mail: murrays@hope.ac.uk)

LIVERPOOL INSTITUTE FOR PERFORMING ARTS

**Learning Services, Liverpool Institute for Performing Arts, Mount Street, Liverpool
LI 9HF**
☎0151 330 3111
url: www.lipa.ac.uk/lrc
Learning Services Manager Ms C Holmes BA(Hons) PGDipLib (0151 332 3111; e-mail:
c.holmes@lipa.ac.uk)

LIVERPOOL JOHN MOORES UNIVERSITY

**Library and Student Support, Liverpool John Moores University, Aldham Robarts
Learning Resource Centre, Maryland Street, Liverpool LI 9DE**
☎0151 231 3179
url: www.ljmu.ac.uk
Director of Library and Student Support Ms Maxine Melling BA PGDipLib MLib
MCLIP (0151 231 3682; e-mail: m.melling@ljmu.ac.uk)

Site libraries
Aldham Robarts Learning Resource Centre, Liverpool John Moores University, 29 Maryland
Street, Liverpool LI 9DE
☎0151 231 3179

Avril Robarts Learning Resource Centre, Liverpool John Moores University, 79 Tithebarn
Street, Liverpool L2 2ER
☎0151 231 3179

I M Marsh Learning Resource Centre, Liverpool John Moores University, Barkhill Road,
Liverpool L17 6BD
☎0151 231 3179

UNIVERSITY OF LIVERPOOL

University Library, University of Liverpool, Liverpool L69 3DA
☎0151 794 2679 (enquiries), 0151 794 2674 (administration)
Fax 0151 794 2681/5417
url: www.liv.ac.uk/library
University Librarian Phil Sykes BA MCLIP

Site libraries
Harold Cohen Library (Science, Medicine, Engineering, Veterinary and Dental Science),
University of Liverpool, Ashton Street, Liverpool L69 3DA
☎0151 794 5411
Fax 0151 794 5417
User Services Manager Ms Lesley Butler BA MCLIP (e-mail: l.m.butler@liv.ac.uk)

Sydney Jones Library (Humanities, Social Sciences, Special Collections and Archives),
University of Liverpool, Chatham Street, Liverpool L69 3DA
☎0151 794 2679
Fax 0151 794 2681
User Services Manager Ms Laura Dunn BA DipLib MCLIP (e-mail: l.dunn@liv.ac.uk)

LONDON CONTEMPORARY DANCE SCHOOL

**Library, London Contemporary Dance School, The Place, 16 Flaxman Terrace, London
WCIH 9AT**
☎020 7121 1110
e-mail: library@theplace.org.uk
url: www.lcds.ac.uk/library
Learning Resources Manager Ms Tiffany Hore MA(Cantab) MA (e-mail:
tiffanyhore@theplace.org.uk)

LONDON METROPOLITAN UNIVERSITY

**Calcutta House Library, London Metropolitan University, Calcutta House, Old Castle
Street, London EI 7NT**
☎020 7133 4444
e-mail: library@londonmet.ac.uk
url: www.londonmet.ac.uk
Interim Head of Library Resources Julian Roland BA DipLib MCLIP (e-mail:
j.roland@londonmet.ac.uk)
Head of Library Customer Services Development Ms Laura Simmons BSc(Hons)
MAEd (e-mail: l.simmons@londonmet.ac.uk)
Reader Services Manager, City Campus Libraries Ms Federica Arisco BA(Hons) LLM
PGDipInfManag (020 7320 1181; e-mail: f.arisco@londonmet.ac.uk)
Reader Services Manager, Holloway Road Mrs Gulten Tufekci BSc MAInfManag
(020 7133 2089; e-mail: g.tufekci@londonmet.ac.uk)
Senior Academic Liaison Librarian Ms Anne Foley (e-mail: a.foley@londonmet.ac.uk)

Other libraries
Commercial Road Library, London Metropolitan University, 41 Commercial Road, London
EI ILA

Holloway Road Library, London Metropolitan University, 236–250 Holloway Road, London
N7 6PP

Special collections
TUC Library Collections, London Metropolitan University, Holloway Road Library,
236–250 Holloway Road, London N7 6PP
☎020 7133 3726
Fax 020 7133 2529
e-mail: tuclib@londonmet.ac.uk
Academic Liaison Librarian Jeff Howarth (e-mail: j.howarth@london.met.ac.uk)
(The Women's Library previously housed at London Metropolitan is now at the London
School of Economics – *see under* University of London)

LONDON SOUTH BANK UNIVERSITY

Perry Library, London South Bank University, 250 Southwark Bridge Road, London SE1 6NJ
☎020 7815 6647
Fax 020 7815 6629
url: www.my.lsbu.ac.uk/general/library.aspx
Director of Library and Learning Resources Ms Margaret Kitching (020 7815 6695; e-mail: kitchinm@lsbu.ac.uk)
Assistant Director and Head of Academic Liaison Ms Alison Chojna (020 7815 6608; e-mail: chojnaa@lsbu.ac.uk)
Site Manager (Perry Library) Alan Doherty (020 7815 6626; e-mail: dohertaa@lsbu.ac.uk)

Site library

Havering Campus, London South Bank University, Goldcrest Way, Romford, Essex RM3 0BE
☎020 7815 5982
Fax 020 7815 4786
e-mail: lisex@lsbu.ac.uk

UNIVERSITY OF LONDON

Senate House Library, University of London, Senate House, Malet Street, London WC1E 7HU
☎020 7862 8500 (enquiries), 020 7862 8411 (administration)
Fax 020 7862 5562
e-mail: senatehouselibrary@london.ac.uk
url: www.senatehouselibrary.ac.uk
Senate House Librarian Ms Jackie Marfleet (e-mail: jackie.marfleet@london.ac.uk)
Associate Director, Historic Collections Mrs Christine Wise (e-mail: christine.wise@london.ac.uk)
Associate Director, Modern Collections David Clover DipLib MA (e-mail: david.clover@london.ac.uk)
Associate Director, Information Systems and Services Vacant
(Includes libraries of the Australian and Canadian High Commissions)

Depository Library, University of London, Spring Rise, Egham, Surrey TW20 9PP
☎(01784) 434560 (enquiries), 020 7862 8425 (administration)
e-mail: shl.depository@london.ac.uk

Any enquiries relating to the Depository Library should be directed to James Cook (020 7862 8425)

College, Institute and Departmental

Each College listed below is an independent self-governing institution funded, where applicable, by HEFCE, and awarding degrees of the University of London, of which each is a member.

Australian and Canadian High Commission Libraries *see* University of London, Senate House

Birkbeck

Library, Birkbeck, Malet Street, London WC1E 7HX
☎020 7631 6064 (administration), 020 7631 6063/6239 (enquiries)
Fax 020 7631 6066
e-mail: libhelp@bbk.ac.uk
url: www.bbk.ac.uk/lib/
Director of Library and Media Studies Robert Atkinson MA DipLib MCLIP (020 7631 6250; e-mail: r.atkinson@bbk.ac.uk)

Courtauld Institute of Art

Library, Courtauld Institute of Art, Somerset House, Strand, London WC2R 0RN
☎020 7848 2701 (enquiries)
url: www.courtauld.ac.uk
Kilfinan Librarian, Head of Book, Witt and Conway Libraries Antony Hopkins
(e-mail: antony.hopkins@courtauld.ac.uk)

Goldsmiths

Library, Goldsmiths, New Cross, London SE14 6NW
☎020 7919 7150 (enquiries), 020 7919 7161 (administration)
Fax 020 7919 7165
e-mail: library@gold.ac.uk
url: www.gold.ac.uk/library
Acting Librarian Ms Veronica Lawrence (e-mail: v.lawrence.gold.ac.uk)

Heythrop College

Library, Heythrop College, Kensington Square, London W8 5HN
☎020 7795 4250 (Philosophy Library), 020 7795 4254 (Theology Library)
e-mail: library@heythrop.ac.uk
url: www.heythrop.ac.uk
Acting Librarian Michael Morgan (e-mail: m.morgan@heythrop.ac.uk)

Institute of Advanced Legal Studies

Library, Institute of Advanced Legal Studies, School of Advanced Study, 17 Russell Square, London WC1B 5DR
☎020 7862 5790
Fax 020 7862 5770
e-mail: ials@sas.ac.uk
url: www.ials.sas.ac.uk/library
Librarian Jules R Winterton BA LLB MCLIP
Deputy Librarian David R Gee BA MA MCLIP

Institute of Cancer Research

Library, Institute of Cancer Research, Brookes Lawley Building, 15 Cotswold Road, Belmont, Sutton, Surrey SM2 5NG
☎020 8722 4230
Fax 020 8722 4323
e-mail: library@icr.ac.uk
url: www.icr.ac.uk

Librarian Barry Jenkins BA DipLib (e-mail: barry.jenkins@icr.ac.uk)
Library Information Officer Miss Sue Rogers (e-mail: sue.rogers@icr.ac.uk)

Site library
Library, Institute of Cancer Research, Chester Beatty Labs, 237 Fulham Road, London
SW3 6JB
☎020 7153 5542
e-mail: library@icr.ac.uk
url: www.icr.ac.uk
Librarian Barry Jenkins BA DipLib (e-mail: barry.jenkins@icr.ac.uk)
Library Assistant Ms June Greenwood

Institute of Classical Studies
Institute of Classical Studies Library and Joint Library of the Hellenic and Roman Societies,
Institute of Classical Studies, Senate House, Malet Street, London WC1E 7HU
☎020 7862 8709
e-mail: iclass.enquiries@london.ac.uk
url: http://library.icls.sas.ac.uk
Librarian Colin H Annis MA MCLIP (e-mail: colin.annis@sas.ac.uk)

Institute of Education
Newsam Library and Archives, Institute of Education, 20 Bedford Way, London
WC1H 0AL
☎020 7612 6080 (enquiries)
Fax 020 7612 6093
e-mail: lib.enquiries@ioe.ac.uk
url: www.ioe.ac.uk/is
Director of Library and Archive Services Andrew McDonald FCLIP FRSA

Institute of Historical Research
Library, Institute of Historical Research, School of Advanced Study, Senate House, Malet
Street, London WC1E 7HU
☎020 7862 8760
e-mail: ihr.Library@sas.ac.uk
url: www.history.ac.uk/library
Acting Librarian Ms Kate Wilcox BA MSc (e-mail: kate.wilcox@sas.ac.uk)

King's College London

Denmark Hill Campus
Weston Education Centre Library, King's College London, Weston Education Centre,
Cutcombe Road, London SE5 9RJ
☎020 7848 5541
Fax 020 7848 5550
Customer Services Manager, Space and Environment Ms Susan Isaac
Operational Managers Ms Vanessa Farrier, Ms Lucy Royle

Guy's Campus
Information Services Centre, King's College London, New Hunt's House, Guy's Campus,
London SE1 1UL

☎020 7848 6600
Fax 020 7848 6743
Information Services Centre Manager Ms Sally Brock BA DipLib MA MCLIP

Institute of Psychiatry
Institute of Psychiatry Library, King's College London, 16 De Crespigny Park, London
SE5 8AF
☎020 7848 0204
Customer Services Manager, Space and Environment Ms Susan Isaac
Operational Managers Ms Vanessa Farrier, Ms Lucy Royle

St Thomas' Campus
Information Services Centre, King's College London, St Thomas' House, St Thomas'
Hospital, Lambeth Palace Road, London SE1 7EH
☎020 7188 3740
Fax 020 7188 8358
Information Services Centre Manager Ms Helen Butler

Strand Campus
Maughan Library, King's College London, Chancery Lane, London WC2A 1LR
☎020 7848 2424
Fax 020 7848 2277
e-mail: libraryservices@kcl.ac.uk
url: www.kcl.ac.uk/library
Director of Library Services Robert Hall BA MA (e-mail: robert.hall@kcl.ac.uk)
Deputy Director of Library Services Ms Erin Caseley BA MA (e-mail:
erin.caseley@kcl.ac.uk)
Library Operations Managers Ms Alison Charlesworth BA(Hons) MA (e-mail:
alison.charlesworth@kcl.ac.uk), Ms Anna-Lena Kleinert (e-mail:
anna-lena.kleinert@kcl.ac.uk)

Waterloo Campus
Information Services Centre, King's College London, Franklin-Wilkins Building, 150
Stamford Street, London SE1 9NH
☎020 7848 4378
Operational Managers Ms Samantha Appleyard, Ms Holly Wicks

London Business School
Library, London Business School, Regent's Park, London NW1 4SA
☎020 7000 7620
e-mail: library@london.edu
url: www.london.edu/library
Head of Library Planning Paul Banks BA(Hons) DipLib MCLIP (e-mail:
pbanks@london.ac.uk)
Director, IT and Library Ian Capp

London School of Economics and Political Science
LSE Library (British Library of Political and Economic Science), London School of
Economics and Political Science, 10 Portugal Street, London WC2A 2HD
☎020 7955 7229 (enquiries), 020 7955 7219 (administration)

Fax 020 7955 7454
e-mail: library.enquiries@lse.ac.uk
url: www.library.lse.ac.uk
Director of Library Services Ms Elizabeth Chapman BA MA DipLib FECert FCLIP
(020 7955 7224; e-mail: e.chapman@lse.ac.uk)
Deputy Director of Library Services Ms Nicola Wright (020 7955 7217; e-mail:
n.c.wright@lse.ac.uk)
Technical Services Manager Glyn Price BA DipLib MCLIP (020 7955 6755; e-mail:
g.price@lse.ac.uk)

The Women's Library, LSE Library, 10 Portugal Street, London WC2A 2HD
☎020 7955 7229
e-mail: library.enquiries@lse.ac.uk
url: www.library.lse.ac.uk
Academic Services Manager Martin Reid

London School of Hygiene & Tropical Medicine
Library & Archives Service, London School of Hygiene & Tropical Medicine, Keppel Street,
London WC1E 7HT
☎020 7927 2276 (enquiries), 020 7927 2283 (administration)
Fax 020 7927 2273
e-mail: library@lshtm.ac.uk
url: www.lshtm.ac.uk/library
Head of Library & Archives Service Ms Caroline Lloyd BA MA MCLIP (e-mail:
caroline.lloyd@lshtm.ac.uk)

London School of Jewish Studies
Library, London School of Jewish Studies, Schaller House, 44A Albert Road, London
NW4 2SJ
☎020 8203 6427
Fax 020 8203 6420
url: www.lsjs.ac.uk
Librarian Mrs Erla Zimmels DipLib (e-mail: erla.zimmels@lsjs.ac.uk)

Queen Mary
Library, Queen Mary, 327 Mile End Road, London E1 4NS
☎020 7882 8800
Fax 020 8981 0028
e-mail: library@qmul.ac.uk
url: www.library.qmul.ac.uk
Director of Student Services Ms Emma Bull BA(Hons) DipInf MCLIP (020 7882 7385;
e-mail: e.j.bull@qmul.ac.uk)
Assistant Directors Ms June Hayles BA MCLIP (020 7882 7290; e-mail:
j.m.hayles@qmul.ac.uk), Ms Pat Simons (020 7882 3877; e-mail: p.simons@qmul.ac.uk)

Site libraries
Medical and Dental Library (Whitechapel), Queen Mary, Barts and the London School of
Medicine and Dentistry, Church of St Augustine with St Philip, Newark Street, London
E1 2AD
☎020 7882 8800
e-mail: library@qmul.ac.uk

Medical School Library (West Smithfield), Queen Mary, St Bartholomew's Hospital, West Smithfield, London EC1A 7BE
☎020 7882 8818
Fax 020 7601 7853
e-mail: library@qmul.ac.uk

Victoria Park Library, Queen Mary, Education Centre, London Chest Hospital, Bonner Road, London E2 9JX
☎020 7882 8800
e-mail: library@qmul.ac.uk
(Reference only except on Thursday afternoons)

Royal Holloway
Library, Royal Holloway, University of London, Egham, Surrey TW20 0EX
☎(01784) 443823 (enquiries), (01784) 443334 (administration)
e-mail: library@royalholloway.ac.uk
url: www.royalholloway.ac.uk/library
Director of Library Services John Tuck
Associate Director (Academic and User Services) Matthew Brooke BA(Hons) MA (e-mail: m.brooke@royalholloway.ac.uk)
Associate Director (E-Strategy and Technical Services) Ms Amy Warner (e-mail: amy.warner@royalholloway.ac.uk)

Royal Veterinary College
Library, Camden Campus, Royal Veterinary College, Royal College Street, London NW1 0TU
☎020 7468 5162
e-mail: library@rvc.ac.uk
url: www.rvc.ac.uk
Customer Services Manager Gwyn Jervis (e-mail: gjervis@rvc.ac.uk)

Library, Hawkshead Campus, Royal Veterinary College, Eclipse Building, Hawkshead Lane, North Mimms, Hatfield, Herts AL9 7TA
☎(01707) 666214
e-mail: library@rvc.ac.uk
url: www.rvc.ac.uk
Director of Library and Information Services Simon Jackson MA MCLIP (e-mail: sjackson@rvc.ac.uk)
Customer Services Manager Ms Sally Burton (e-mail: sburton@rvc.ac.uk)

St George's, University of London
St George's Library, St George's, University of London, Hunter Wing, Cranmer Terrace, London SW17 0RE
☎020 8725 5466 (direct line)
e-mail: library@sgul.ac.uk
url: www.sgul.ac.uk/services/library
Learning and Research Support Manager Mrs Sue David (e-mail: sdavid@sgul.ac.uk)

School of Oriental and African Studies
Library, School of Oriental and African Studies, Thornhaugh Street, Russell Square, London WC1H 0XG

☎020 7898 4163 (enquiries), 020 7898 4160 (library office)
e-mail: libenquiry@soas.ac.uk
url: www.soas.ac.uk/library
Director of Library and Information Services John Robinson BA MA (e-mail:
j.robinson@soas.ac.uk)

School of Pharmacy
Library, School of Pharmacy, 29–39 Brunswick Square, London WC1N 1AX
☎020 7753 5833
e-mail: sop.library@ucl.ac.uk
url: www.pharmacy.ac.uk
Head of Library and Information Services Ms Michelle Wake BA MA MCLIP (e-mail:
m.wake@ucl.ac.uk)

UCL (University College London)
UCL Library Services, UCL (University College London), Gower Street, London WC1E 6BT
☎020 7679 7793
e-mail: library@ucl.ac.uk
url: www.ucl.ac.uk/library
**Director and Acting Group Manager, Planning & Resources and Academic
Support Group** Dr Paul Ayris MA PhD (e-mail: p.ayris@ucl.ac.uk)
Group Manager, Reader Services Dr Vincent Matthews BSc(Econ) MA MA PhD
(020 7679 2607; e-mail: v.matthews@ucl.ac.uk)
Acting Group Manager, IT Services and Bibliographic Services Martin Moyle (e-mail:
m.moyle@ucl.ac.uk)

Site libraries
Library and Information Services, UCL School of Slavonic and East European Studies, UCL
(University College London), 16 Taviton Street, London WC1H 0BW
☎020 7679 8701
Fax 020 7679 8710
e-mail: ssees-library@ssees.ucl.ac.uk
url: www.ssees.ucl.ac.uk/library
Librarian and Director of Information Services Ms Lesley Pitman BA DipLib (e-mail:
l.pitman@ucl.ac.uk)

Queen Square Library, Archive and Museum Library, UCL Institute of Neurology and The
National Hospital for Neurology and Neurosurgery, UCL (University College London),
Queen Square, London WC1N 3BG
☎020 3448 4709
e-mail: neurolibrary@ucl.ac.uk
Librarian Ms Sarah Lawson (e-mail: sarah.lawson@ucl.ac.uk)
Deputy Librarian Ms Kate Brunskill (e-mail: k.brunskill@ucl.ac.uk)

Royal Free Medical Library, UCL Library Services, UCL (University College London), Royal
Free Hospital, Rowland Hill Street, London NW3 2PF
☎020 7794 0500 ext 33202
Fax 020 7794 3534
e-mail: rlibrary@ucl.ac.uk
url: www.ucl.ac.uk/medicalschool/rfhmedlib

Librarian Ms Betsy Anagnostelis BSc(Hons) MSc DipLib (e-mail:
b.anagnostelis@medsch.ucl.ac.uk)

UCL Bartlett Library, UCL (University College London), Ground Floor, Central House, 14
Upper Woburn Place, London WC1H 0NN
☎020 7679 4900
Fax 020 7679 7373
e-mail: library@ucl.ac.uk
Site Librarians Ms Suzanne Tonkin BA(Hons) MSc (e-mail: suzanne.tonkin@ucl.ac.uk),
Ms Caroline Fletcher (e-mail: caroline.fletcher@ucl.ac.uk) (job share)

UCL Cruciform Library, UCL (University College London), The Cruciform Hub, 90 Gower
Street, London WC1E 6BT
☎020 7679 6079
e-mail: lib-crucienq@ucl.ac.uk
url: www.ucl.ac.uk/Library/crucilib.shtml
Site Librarian Ms Kate Cheney BA MSc MCLIP (e-mail: k.cheney@ucl.ac.uk)

UCL Ear Institute and Action on Hearing Loss Libraries, UCL (University College London),
Royal National Throat, Nose and Ear Hospital, 330–336 Gray's Inn Road, London
WC1X 8EE
☎020 3456 5145
Fax 020 3456 5143
e-mail: rnidlib@ucl.ac.uk
url: www.ucl.ac.uk/Library/rnidlib.shtml
Librarian Alex Stagg MA (e-mail: a.stagg@ucl.ac.uk)

UCL Eastman Dental Institute Library, UCL (University College London), 256 Gray's Inn
Road, London WC1X 8LD
☎020 3456 1045/2331
e-mail: edi-library@ucl.ac.uk
url: www.ucl.ac.uk/eastman
Librarian Ms Anna Di Iorio MA (e-mail: a.diiorio@ucl.ac.uk) (On maternity leave until
April 2015)
Acting Librarian Robbie Lumsden (e-mail: r.lumsden@ucl.ac.uk) (up to April 2015)

UCL Institute of Archaeology Library, UCL (University College London), 31–34 Gordon
Square, London WC1H 0PY
☎020 7679 4788
Fax 020 7679 7393
e-mail: lib-archaeology@ucl.ac.uk
url: www.ucl.ac.uk/archaeology/about/library
Librarian Robert Kirby MA (e-mail: r.kirby@ucl.ac.uk)

UCL Institute of Child Health Library, UCL (University College London), 30 Guilford
Street, London WC1N 1EH
☎020 7905 2847
Fax 020 7831 0488
e-mail: ich.library@ucl.ac.uk
url: www.ucl.ac.uk/ich/services/library
Librarian John Clarke MA DipLib (e-mail: j.clarke@ucl.ac.uk)
Deputy Librarian Ms Grazia Manzotti (e-mail: g.manzotti@ucl.ac.uk)

UCL Institute of Ophthalmology Library, UCL (University College London), 11–43 Bath Street, London EC1V 9EL
☎020 7608 6814
e-mail: ophthlib@ucl.ac.uk
url: www.ucl.ac.uk/ioo/The_Joint_Library.php
Librarian Ms Debbie Heatlie BA (020 7608 6815; e-mail: d.heatlie@ucl.ac.uk)
(Joint library with Moorfields Eye Hospital)

UCL Institute of Orthopaedics Library, UCL (University College London), Sir Herbert Seddon Teaching Centre, Royal National Orthopaedic Hospital, Brockley Hill, Stanmore, Middlesex HA7 4LP
☎020 8909 5351
Fax 020 8909 5390
e-mail: orthlib@ucl.ac.uk
url: www.ucl.ac.uk/Library/iorthlib.shtml
Librarian Ms Julie Noren MLS (e-mail: j.noren@ucl.ac.uk)

UCL Language and Speech Science Library, UCL (University College London), Chandler House, 2 Wakefield Street, London WC1N 1PF
☎020 7679 4207
Fax 020 7679 4238
e-mail: lib-lass@.ucl.ac.uk
url: www.ucl.ac.uk/library/lasslib.shtml
Librarian Ms Breege Whiten MA (e-mail: b.whiten@ucl.ac.uk)

UCL Library Special Collections, UCL (University College London), Gower Street, London WC1E 6BT
☎020 7679 7827
e-mail: spec.coll@ucl.ac.uk
url: www.ucl.ac.uk/Library/special-coll/; http://archives.ucl.ac.uk
Head of Special Collections and Archivist Ms Gillian Furlong BA DipArchMan RMSA (020 7679 2619; e-mail: g.furlong@ucl.ac.uk)

Warburg Institute
Library, Warburg Institute, School of Advanced Study, Woburn Square, London WC1H 0AB
☎020 7862 8935/6 (Reading Room)
Fax 020 7862 8939
e-mail: warburg.library@sas.ac.uk
url: http://warburg.sas.ac.uk/library
Librarian Dr Raphaële Mouren (e-mail: raphaele.mouren@sas.ac.uk)

LOUGHBOROUGH UNIVERSITY

Pilkington Library, Loughborough University, Loughborough, Leics LE11 3TU
☎(01509) 222360
Fax (01509) 223993
e-mail: library@lboro.ac.uk
url: www.lboro.ac.uk/services/library
Acting University Librarian Jeff Brown BA MA DipLib (01509 222400; e-mail: j.j.brown@lboro.ac.uk)

MANCHESTER METROPOLITAN UNIVERSITY

Sir Kenneth Green Library, Manchester Metropolitan University, All Saints, Manchester MI5 6BH
☎0161 247 3096
Fax 0161 247 6349
url: www.library.mmu.ac.uk
Head of Library Services Ms Ruth Jenkins BSc MA (0161 247 6101; e-mail: r.jenkins@mmu.ac.uk)

Site libraries
Crewe Library, Manchester Metropolitan University, Crewe Green Road, Crewe, Cheshire CWI IDU
☎0161 247 5002
Library Service Manager Vacant

THE UNIVERSITY OF MANCHESTER

The John Rylands University Library, The University of Manchester, Main Library, Oxford Road, Manchester MI3 9PP
☎0161 275 3751
Fax 0161 273 7488
url: www.manchester.ac.uk/library
University Librarian and Director of The John Rylands Library Ms Jan Wilkinson BA(Hons) DipLib DMS FCLIP FRSA (e-mail: jan.wilkinson@manchester.ac.uk)
Head of Research Services and Deputy Librarian Simon Bains MA (e-mail: simon.bains@manchester.ac.uk)

Site libraries
Alan Gilbert Learning Commons, The University of Manchester, Oxford Road, Manchester MI3 9PP
☎0161 306 4923
Learning Commons Development Manager Ms Rosie Jones BA(Hons) PGDip PGCert FHEA (e-mail: rosemary.jones@manchester.ac.uk)

The John Rylands Library, The University of Manchester, 150 Deansgate, Manchester M3 3EH
☎0161 306 0555
e-mail: uml.special-collections@manchester.ac.uk
Head of Special Collections and Associate Director of The John Rylands Library Ms Rachel Beckett MA MCLIP (e-mail: rachel.beckett@manchester.ac.uk)

The Joule Library, The University of Manchester, Sackville Street Building, Manchester MI3 9PL
☎0161 306 4923
Customer Services Manager – Sites and Customer Relations Mrs Debbie Allan BA DipLib MSc (e-mail: debbie.allan@manchester.ac.uk)

MIDDLESEX UNIVERSITY

Library and Student Support, Middlesex University, Sheppard Library, The Burroughs, Hendon, London NW4 4BT

☎020 8411 6060
url: http://unihub.mdx.ac.uk/study/library/services/visitors/index.aspx
Director of Library and Student Support Nick Bevan BSc MSc(Econ) DipLib
MSc(InfSc) (020 8411 5234; e-mail: n.bevan@mdx.ac.uk)
Deputy Director Ms Ruth Moore BA (020 8411 6947; e-mail: r.moore@mdx.ac.uk)
Assistant Director, Library and Learner Development Matthew Lawson BA MA
MCLIP (020 8411 4126; e-mail: m.lawson@mdx.ac.uk)

NEWCASTLE UNIVERSITY

**Robinson Library, Newcastle University, Jesmond Road West, Newcastle upon Tyne
NE2 4HQ**
☎0191 222 7662 (enquiries), 0191 222 7674 (administration)
Fax 0191 208 6235
e-mail: libraryhelp@ncl.ac.uk
url: www.ncl.ac.uk/library/
Director of Academic Services and University Librarian Wayne Connolly BA DipLib
(e-mail: wayne.connolly@ncl.ac.uk)

Divisional libraries

Law Library, Newcastle University, Newcastle Law School, 21–24 Windsor Terrace,
Newcastle upon Tyne NE1 7RU
☎0191 222 7944
e-mail: libraryhelp@ncl.ac.uk
Senior Library Assistant Ms Catherine Dale

The Walton Library (Medical and Dental), Newcastle University, The Medical School,
Framlington Place, Newcastle upon Tyne NE2 4HH
☎0191 222 7550
Medical Librarian Ms Erika Gavillet BA(Hons) MA DipLib (e-mail:
erika.gavillet@ncl.ac.uk)

NEWMAN UNIVERSITY (formerly Newman University College)

Library, Newman University, Genners Lane, Bartley Green, Birmingham B32 3NT
☎0121 476 1181 ext 1208
e-mail: library@newman.ac.uk
url: www.newman.ac.uk/library
Director of Library and Learning Services Ms Christine Porter BA MLib MCLIP (ext
1327; e-mail: c.porter@newman.ac.uk)
Library Liaison Manager David Crozier BA MSc(Econ) DipMan MCLIP (ext 1339; e-mail:
d.crozier@newman.ac.uk)
Systems Librarian Ms Janet Smith BA(Hons) (ext 1526; e-mail: janet.smith@newman.ac.uk)

UNIVERSITY OF NORTHAMPTON

**Park Campus Library, University of Northampton, Boughton Green Road, Northampton
NN2 7AL**
☎(01604) 735500 ext 2477 (enquiries), ext 2041 (administration)
Fax (01604) 718819

e-mail: libraryhelp@northampton.ac.uk
url: www.northampton.ac.uk
Head of Library and Learning Services Chris Powis BA MA MLib PGDipTHE MCLIP FHEA FRSA (ext 2229; e-mail: chris.powis@northampton.ac.uk)

Avenue Campus Library, University of Northampton, Maidwell Building, St George's Avenue, Northampton NN2 6JD
☎(01604) 735500 ext 3900
Fax (01604) 719618
(other details as above)

NORTHERN SCHOOL OF CONTEMPORARY DANCE

Library, Northern School of Contemporary Dance, 98 Chapeltown Road, Leeds LS7 4BH
☎0113 219 3020
Fax 0113 219 3030
url: http://nscdlibrary.wordpress.co.uk
Librarian/CDD Library Advisor and OpenAthens Administrator Miss Samantha King BA(Hons) MCLIP (e-mail: samantha.king@nscd.ac.uk)

NORTHUMBRIA UNIVERSITY

University Library, Northumbria University, Sandyford Road, Newcastle upon Tyne NE1 8ST
☎0191 227 4125
e-mail: ask4help@northumbria.ac.uk
url: http://library.northumbria.ac.uk
Director of Academic Services and University Librarian Professor Jane Core BA Mlib

Site library
Coach Lane Campus Library, Northumbria University, East Block, Coach Lane, Newcastle upon Tyne NE7 7XA
☎0191 215 6540

NORWICH UNIVERSITY OF THE ARTS

(formerly Norwich University College of the Arts)

Learning Resource Centre, Norwich University of the Arts, Francis House, 3–7 Redwell Street, Norwich NR2 4SN
☎(01603) 610561
Fax (01603) 615728
e-mail: library@nua.ac.uk
url: www.nua.ac.uk
Librarian Tim Giles BA (e-mail: t.giles@nua.ac.uk)
Assistant Librarians Ms Jan McLachlan BA(Hons) DipLIS (e-mail: j.mclachlan@nua.ac.uk), Gordon Burnett MA MCLIP (e-mail: g.burnett@nua.ac.uk)

NOTTINGHAM TRENT UNIVERSITY

Libraries and Learning Resources, Nottingham Trent University, Goldsmith Street, Nottingham NG1 5LS
☎0115 848 6446
Fax 0115 848 2286
url: www.ntu.ac.uk
Head of Libraries and Learning Resources Mark Toole MA(Cantab) (e-mail: mark.toole@ntu.ac.uk)
Deputy University Librarian (Customer Services) Mike Berrington BA(Hons) MA DipLib (0115 848 6059; e-mail: mike.berrington@ntu.ac.uk)
Deputy University Librarian (Information Resources and Planning) Ms Ruth Stubbings BA(Hons) MA DipLib MCLIP (e-mail: ruth.stubbings@ntu.ac.uk)

Site libraries
The Boots Library, Nottingham Trent University, Goldsmith Street, Nottingham NG1 5LS
☎0115 848 2175 (enquiries)
Fax 0115 848 4425

Brackenhurst Campus Library, Nottingham Trent University, Southwell Road, Southwell, Notts NG25 0QF
☎(01636) 817049 (enquiries)
Fax (01636) 817077

Clifton Campus Library, Nottingham Trent University, Clifton Lane, Nottingham NG11 8NS
☎0115 848 3570/6612
Fax 0115 848 6304

UNIVERSITY OF NOTTINGHAM

Libraries and Research and Learning Resources, University of Nottingham, University Park, Nottingham NG7 2RD
☎0115 951 6393 (library helpline)
url: www.nottingham.ac.uk/library
Director, Libraries and Research and Learning Resources Ms Caroline Williams MA

Library sites
Business Library, University of Nottingham, Business School, Jubilee Campus, Wollaton Road, Nottingham NG8 1BB
☎0115 846 8069
Fax 0115 846 8064

Denis Arnold Music Library, University of Nottingham, University Park, Nottingham NG7 2RD
☎0115 951 4596
Fax 0115 951 4558

Djanogly LRC (Education, Computer Science), University of Nottingham, Jubilee Campus, Wollaton Road, Nottingham NG8 1BB
☎0115 846 6700
Fax 0115 846 6705

George Green Library of Science and Engineering, University of Nottingham, University Park, Nottingham NG7 2RD
☎0115 951 4570
Fax 0115 951 4578

Greenfield Medical Library, University of Nottingham, Queen's Medical Centre, Nottingham NG7 2UH
☎0115 823 0555
Fax 0115 823 0549

Hallward Library (Arts and Humanities, Law, Social Sciences), University of Nottingham, University Park, Nottingham NG7 2RD
☎0115 951 4555
Fax 0115 951 4558

James Cameron-Gifford Library (Applied Biosciences, Veterinary Medicine and Science), University of Nottingham, Sutton Bonington Campus, Sutton Bonington, nr Loughborough, Leics LE12 5RD
☎0115 951 6390
Fax 0115 951 6389

Manuscripts and Special Collections, University of Nottingham, King's Meadow Campus, Lenton Lane, Nottingham NG7 2NR
☎0115 951 4565
Fax 0115 846 8651
Keeper Mark Dorrington

OPEN UNIVERSITY

Library Services, Open University, Walton Hall, Milton Keynes MK7 6AA
☎(01908) 653138
Fax (01908) 653571
e-mail: lib-help@open.ac.uk
url: www.open.ac.uk; http://library.open.ac.uk
Director of Library Services Mrs Nicky Whitsed MSc FCLIP (01908 653254; e-mail: nicky.whitsed@open.ac.uk)
Associate Director – Business Performance and Management Ms Ann Davies BSc(Hons) MSc (01908 652057; e-mail: ann.davies@open.ac.uk)
Associate Director – Academic and Student Services Ms Patricia Heffernan BA(Hons) DipLib (01908 654850; e-mail: tricia.heffernan@open.ac.uk)
Associate Director – Information Management and Innovation Ms Gill Needham BA(Hons) DipLib CertMan MSc(Econ) (01908 858369; e-mail: gill.needham@open.ac.uk)

OXFORD BROOKES UNIVERSITY

Headington Library, Oxford Brookes University, Headington Campus, Gipsy Lane, Headington, Oxford OX3 0BP
☎(01865) 483156 (enquiries), (01865) 483130 (administration)
e-mail: library@brookes.ac.uk
url: www.brookes.ac.uk/library
Director of Learning Resources Dr Helen M Workman PhD MCLIP (e-mail: h.workman@brookes.ac.uk)

Head of Service Development and Delivery Ms Jan Haines BLib MA DipM MCLIP
(e-mail: jan.haines@brookes.ac.uk)

Site libraries
Harcourt Hill Library, Oxford Brookes University, Harcourt Hill Campus, Oxford OX2 9AT
☎(01865) 488222
Fax (01865) 488224
Customer Services Team Leader Ms Madeleine Bentley BA(Hons) (e-mail:
mbentley@brookes.ac.uk)

Wheatley Library, Oxford Brookes University, Wheatley Campus, Wheatley, Oxford
OX33 1HX
☎(01865) 485869
Fax (01865) 485750
Customer Services Team Leader Ms Ruth Wilkinson BA(Hons) (e-mail:
rwilkinson@brookes.ac.uk)

UNIVERSITY OF OXFORD

The Bodleian Libraries
The Bodleian Library, The Bodleian Libraries, Broad Street, Oxford OX1 3BG
☎(01865) 277162
Fax (01865) 277182
e-mail: reader.services@bodleian.ox.ac.uk
url: www.bodleian.ox.ac.uk
Bodley's Librarian Richard Ovenden MA FRSA FSA (e-mail:
richard.ovenden@bodleian.ox.ac.uk)
Director of Administration and Finance Ms Laura How (e-mail:
laura.how@bodleian.ox.ac.uk)
Associate Director, Collections and Resource Description Ms Catriona Cannon
(e-mail: catriona.cannon@bodleian.ox.ac.uk)
Associate Director, Digital Libraries Vacant

Accessible Resources Acquisition and Creation Unit, The Bodleian Libraries, University of
Oxford, Osney Mead, Oxford OX2 0EW
☎(01865) 283862
e-mail: aracu@bodleian.ox.ac.uk
url: www.bodleian.ox.ac.uk/using/disability
Director/Manager Ms Teresa Pedroso BA(Hons) (01865 283861; e-mail:
teresa.pedroso@bodleian.ox.ac.uk)

Alexander Library of Ornithology, Edward Grey Institute of Field Ornithology, University of
Oxford, Department of Zoology, Tinbergen Building, South Parks Road, Oxford
OX1 3PS
☎(01865) 271143
e-mail: enquiries.rsl@bodleian.ox.ac.uk
url: www.libguides.bodleian.ox.ac.uk/alexanderlibrary
Alexander Librarian Ms Sophie Wilcox (e-mail: sophie.wilcox@bodleian.ox.ac.uk)

Bodleian Japanese Library, University of Oxford, 27 Winchester Road, Oxford OX2 6NA
☎(01865) 284506

Fax (01865) 284500
e-mail: japanese@bodleian.ox.ac.uk
url: www.bodleian.ox.ac.uk/bjl
Librarian Mrs Izumi Tytler MA

Bodleian KB Chen China Centre Library, University of Oxford, Dickson Poon Building,
Canterbury Road, Oxford OX2 6LU
☎(01865) 280430
Fax (01865) 280431
e-mail: chinese.studies.library@bodleian.ox.ac.uk
url: www.bodleian.ox.ac.uk/dept/oriental/csl.htm
Librarian Minh Chung MA

Bodleian Law Library, University of Oxford, St Cross Building, Manor Road, Oxford
OX1 3UR
☎(01865) 271462
Fax (01865) 271475
e-mail: law.library@bodleian.ox.ac.uk
url: www.bodleian.ox.ac.uk/law
Law Librarian Ms Ruth Bird BA TSTC GradDipLib (e-mail: ruth.bird@bodleian.ox.ac.uk)
Academic Services Librarian Ms Margaret Watson MA DipLib MCLIP (e-mail:
margaret.watson@bodleian.ox.ac.uk)
Information Resources Librarian Ms Helen Garner BA(Hons) DipILM MCLIP (e-mail:
helen.garner@bodleian.ox.ac.uk)

Bodleian Music Faculty Library, University of Oxford, Faculty of Music, St Aldate's, Oxford
OX1 1DB
☎(01865) 276148 (enquiries)
e-mail: music.library@bodleian.ox.ac.uk
url: www.bodleian.ox.ac.uk/music
Librarian and Alfred Brendel Curator of Music Martin Holmes

Bodleian Social Science Library, University of Oxford, Manor Road Building, Manor Road,
Oxford OX1 3UQ
☎(01865) 278721 (Librarian), (01865) 271093 (Library)
Fax (01865) 271072
e-mail: ssl@bodleian.ox.ac.uk
url: www.bodleian.ox.ac.uk/ssl
Librarian Mrs Jo Gardner (e-mail: jo.gardner@bodleian.ox.ac.uk)

Department of Education Library, University of Oxford, 15 Norham Gardens, Oxford
OX2 6PY
☎(01865) 274028
e-mail: education.library@bodleian.ox.ac.uk
url: www.bodleian.ox.ac.uk/education
Education Librarian Ms Catherine Scutt (e-mail: catherine.scutt@bodleian.ox.ac.uk)

Department of Experimental Psychology, Library, University of Oxford, Tinbergen Building,
9 South Parks Road, Oxford OX1 3UD
☎(01865) 271312
Fax (01865) 310447
e-mail: library@psy.ox.ac.uk
url: www.psy.ox.ac.uk/library; www.bodleian.ox.ac.uk/libraries

Librarian Ms Karine Barker (e-mail: karine.barker@bodleian.ox.ac.uk)

English Faculty Library, University of Oxford, St Cross Building, Manor Road, Oxford
OX1 3UQ
☎(01865) 271050
Fax (01865) 271054
e-mail: efl-enquiries@bodleian.ox.ac.uk
url: www.bodleian.ox.ac.uk/english
English Librarian Ms Sue Usher BA(Hons) DipLib MCLIP

Foreign Cataloguing, University of Oxford, Bodleian Libraries, Osney 1 Building, Osney
Mead, Oxford OX2 0EW
☎(01865) 277027
Principal Library Assistant Mrs Nathalie Chaddock-Thomas (e-mail:
nathalie.thomas@bodleian.ox.ac.uk)

History Faculty Library, University of Oxford, Radcliffe Camera, Bodleian Library, Oxford
OX1 3BG
☎(01865) 277262
e-mail: library@history.ox.ac.uk
url: www.bodleian.ox.ac.uk/history
History Librarian Ms Isabel Holowaty BA(Hons) MSc (e-mail:
isabel.holowaty@bodleian.ox.ac.uk) (based at Upper Reading Room, Bodleian Library,
Oxford OX1 3BG)
Librarian in charge Mrs Rachel D'Arcy Brown MA(Hons) MSc (e-mail:
rachel.darcy-brown@bodleian.ox.ac.uk)

Latin American Centre, St Antony's College, University of Oxford, 1 Church Walk, Oxford
OX2 6JF
☎(01865) 274486
Fax (01865) 274489
e-mail: laclib@bodleian.ox.ac.uk
url: www.bodleian.ox.ac.uk/lac
Bodleian Latin American Centre Librarian Frank Egerton (e-mail:
frank.egerton@ouls.ox.ac.uk)

Oriental Institute Library, University of Oxford, Pusey Lane, Oxford OX1 2LE
☎(01865) 278202
Fax (01865) 278204
e-mail: oriental.institute@bodleian.ox.ac.uk
url: www.bodleian.ox.ac.uk/oil
Librarian i/c Dr Dinah Manisty (e-mail: dinah.manisty@bodleian.ox.ac.uk)

Philosophy and Theology Faculties Library, University of Oxford, Radcliffe Humanities,
Radcliffe Observatory Quarter, Woodstock Road, Oxford OX2 6GG
☎(01865) 276927
e-mail: ptfl@bodleian.ox.ac.uk
url: www.bodleian.ac.uk/ptfl
Librarian Dr Hilla A Wait MA DPhil

Radcliffe Science Library, University of Oxford, Parks Road, Oxford OX1 3QP
☎(01865) 272800
Fax (01865) 272821

e-mail: enquiries.rsl@bodleian.ox.ac.uk
url: www.bodleian.ox.ac.uk/science
Keeper of Scientific Books Ms Alena Ptak-Danchak (e-mail:
alena.ptak-danchak@bodleian.ox.ac.uk)

Rewley House Continuing Education Library, University of Oxford, Rewley House,
I Wellington Square, Oxford OXI 2JA
☎(01865) 270454
Fax (01865) 270309
e-mail: library@conted.ox.ac.uk
url: http://library.conted.ox.ac.uk
Librarian Ms S Pemberton BA DipLib MCLIP

Sackler Library, University of Oxford, I St John Street, Oxford OXI 2LG
☎(01865) 278092
Fax (01865) 278098
e-mail: sac-enquiries@bodleian.ox.ac.uk
url: www.bodleian.ox.ac.uk/sackler
Librarian Dr Graham Piddock PhD (e-mail: graham.piddock@bodleian.ox.ac.uk)
(Access to the Library is limited to members of Oxford University and holders of Bodleian
Library reader's tickets)

Sainsbury Library, University of Oxford, Saïd Business School, Park End Street, Oxford
OXI IHP
☎(01865) 288880
e-mail: library@sbs.ox.ac.uk
url: www.sbs.ox.ac.uk
Bodleian Business Librarian Ms Chris Flegg (e-mail: chris.flegg@sbs.ox.ac.uk)

Taylor Institution Library, University of Oxford, St Giles, Oxford OXI 3NA
☎(01865) 278154 (office), 278158/278161 (main desk)
Fax (01865) 278165
e-mail: tay-loans@bodleian.ox.ac.uk
url: www.bodleian.ox.ac.uk/taylor
Taylor Librarian James Legg MA MA(Lond) (01865 278160; e-mail:
james.legg@bodleian.ox.ac.uk)
(The Taylor Institution Modern Languages Faculty Library can also be found at this location;
the Taylor Bodleian, Slavonic and Greek Library can be found at 47 Wellington Square,
Oxford OXI 2JF; tel: 01865 270464)

Vere Harmsworth Library (Rothermere American Institute), University of Oxford, Bodleian
Libraries, IA South Parks Road, Oxford OXI 3UB
☎(01865) 282700
e-mail: vhl@bodleian.ox.ac.uk
url: www.bodleian.ox.ac.uk/vhl
Librarian i/c Ms Jane Rawson MA MA (e-mail: jane.rawson@ouls.ox.ac.uk)

Bodleian Health Care Libraries

Cairns Library, University of Oxford, Oxford Radcliffe Hospitals NHS Trust, The John
Radcliffe Hospital, Headley Way, Headington, Oxford OX3 9DU
☎(01865) 221936
Fax (01865) 221941

e-mail: hcl-enquiries@bodleian.ox.ac.uk
url: www.bodleian.ox.ac.uk/medicine
Head of Health Care Libraries Donald M Mackay MA(Hons) MA MCLIP

College, Institute and Departmental

All Souls College
Codrington Library, All Souls College, Oxford OX1 4AL
☎(01865) 279318
Fax (01865) 279299
e-mail: codrington.library@all-souls.ox.ac.uk
url: www.asc.ox.ac.uk
Fellow Librarian Prof I W F Maclean FBA (e-mail: ian.maclean@all-souls.ox.ac.uk)
Librarian Ms Gaye Morgan MA PGDip

Balliol College
Library, Balliol College, Oxford OX1 3BJ
☎(01865) 277709
Fax (01865) 277803
e-mail: library@balliol.ox.ac.uk
url: www.balliol.ox.ac.uk
Fellow Librarian Seamus Perry
Librarian Ms Naomi Tiley

Brasenose College
Library, Brasenose College, Radcliffe Square, Oxford OX1 4AJ
☎(01865) 277827
e-mail: library@bnc.ox.ac.uk
url: www.bnc.ox.ac.uk
Fellow Librarian Professor Simon Palfrey
College Librarian Ms Liz Kay (e-mail: liz.kay@bnc.ox.ac.uk)

Campion Hall
Library, Campion Hall, Brewer Street, Oxford OX1 1QS
☎(01865) 286100
url: www.campion.ox.ac.uk
Librarian Revd Dr Joseph A Munitiz DèsLettres MA
Assistant Librarian Laurence Weeks MA

Christ Church
Library, Christ Church, Oxford OX1 1DP
☎(01865) 276169
e-mail: library@chch.ox.ac.uk
url: www.chch.ox.ac.uk/library
Senior Assistant Librarians Mrs J E McMullin MA MCLIP (e-mail: janet.mcmullin@chch.ox.ac.uk), Dr C M Neagu DPhil MCLIP (e-mail: cristina.neagu@chch.ox.ac.uk)

Corpus Christi College
Library, Corpus Christi College, Merton Street, Oxford OX1 4JF

☎(01865) 276744
Fax (01865) 276767
e-mail: library.staff@ccc.ox.ac.uk
url: www.ccc.ox.ac.uk/Library-and-Archives/
Librarian Miss Joanna Snelling MA MCLIP (e-mail: joanna.snelling@ccc.ox.ac.uk)

Exeter College
Library, Exeter College, Turl Street, Oxford OX1 3DP
☎(01865) 279657
e-mail: library@exeter.ox.ac.uk
url: www.exeter.ox.ac.uk
Fellow Librarian Professor Faramerz Dabhoiwala (e-mail:
faramerz.dabhoiwala@exeter.ox.ac.uk)
College Librarian Ms Joanna Bowring (e-mail: joanna.bowring@exeter.ox.ac.uk)

Green Templeton College
Library, Green Templeton College, 43 Woodstock Road, Oxford OX2 6HG
☎(01865) 274788
e-mail: library@gtc.ox.ac.uk
url: www.gtc.ox.ac.uk
Head of Library and Information Services Ms Kirsty Taylor
Librarian Ms Gill Edwards BSc (e-mail: gill.edwards@gtc.ox.ac.uk)

Harris Manchester College
Library, Harris Manchester College, Mansfield Road, Oxford OX1 3TD
☎(01865) 271016 (library), (01865) 281472 (office)
Fax (01865) 271012
e-mail: librarian@hmc.ox.ac.uk
url: www.hmc.ox.ac.uk
Fellow Librarian Ms Sue Killoran BA MA(Oxon) PGDipLib MCLIP (e-mail:
susan.killoran@hmc.ox.ac.uk)
Assistant Librarian Ms Katrina Malone BA MSc MCLIP (e-mail:
katrina.malone@hmc.ox.ac.uk)

Hertford College
Library, Hertford College, Catte Street, Oxford OX1 3BW
☎(01865) 279409
e-mail: library@hertford.ox.ac.uk
url: www.hertford.ox.ac.uk
Fellow Librarian and Archivist Dr Oliver Noble Wood BA MSt DPhil (e-mail:
oliver.noblewood@mod-langs.ox.ac.uk)
Librarian Mrs Alice Roques MSc InfLibMan (e-mail: alice.roques@hertford.ox.ac.uk)

Jesus College
Celtic Library, Jesus College, Turl Street, Oxford OX1 3DW
☎(01865) 279704
url: http://libguides.bodleian.ox.ac.uk/jesus-celtic
Librarian Owen McKnight MMath MA

College Archives, Jesus College, Turl Street, Oxford OX1 3DW

☎(01865) 279761
Archivist Christopher Jeens BA DipArchAdmin (01865 279761; e-mail: archivist@jesus.ox.ac.uk)

Fellows' Library, Jesus College, Turl Street, Oxford OX1 3DW
☎(01865) 279704
e-mail: librarian@jesus.ox.ac.uk
url: http://libguides.bodleian.ox.ac.uk/jesus-specialcollections
Fellow Librarian Professor T M O Charles-Edwards

Meyricke Library, Jesus College, Turl Street, Oxford OX1 3DW
☎(01865) 279704
e-mail: library@jesus.ox.ac.uk
url: www.jesus.ox.ac.uk/library
Fellow Librarian Dr Marion Turner
College Librarian Owen McKnight MMath MA
(Visits by bona fide scholars are available only by prior appointment with the College Librarian or Archivist as appropriate)

Keble College
Library, Keble College, Oxford OX1 3PG
☎(01865) 272797
e-mail: library@keble.ox.ac.uk
url: www.keble.ox.ac.uk/about/library
Librarian Ms Yvonne D Murphy BA(Hons) MSSc (e-mail: librarian@keble.ox.ac.uk)
Deputy Librarian Dr Gillian A Beattie
Archivist and Records Manager Miss Eleanor L Fleetham (e-mail: archives@keble.ox.ac.uk)

Lady Margaret Hall
Library, Lady Margaret Hall, Norham Gardens, Oxford OX2 6QA
☎(01865) 274361
Fax (01865) 511069
e-mail: library.admin@lmh.ox.ac.uk
url: www.lmh.ox.ac.uk
Fellow Librarian Dr Grant Tapsell
Librarian Miss Roberta Staples BA (e-mail: roberta.staples@lmh.ox.ac.uk)
Archivist Oliver Mahony (e-mail: oliver.mahony@mansfield.ox.ac.uk)
(The library is for the use of members of college only, though bona fide researchers may be allowed access to books by arrangement with the Librarian)

Linacre College
Library, Linacre College, St Cross Road, Oxford OX1 3JA
☎(01865) 271661
e-mail: library@linacre.ox.ac.uk
url: www.linacre.ox.ac.uk
Fellow Librarian Ms Louise Clarke (e-mail: louise.clarke@bodleian.ox.ac.uk)
Librarian Ms Fiona Richardson (e-mail: fiona.richardson@linacre.ox.ac.uk)

Lincoln College
Library, Lincoln College, Turl Street, Oxford OX1 3DR

☎(01865) 279831
e-mail: library@lincoln.ox.ac.uk
url: www.lincoln.ox.ac.uk
Librarian Mrs Fiona Piddock BA DipLib

Magdalen College

Library, Magdalen College, Oxford OX1 4AU
☎(01865) 276045 (direct)
e-mail: library@magd.ox.ac.uk
url: www.magd.ox.ac.uk
Fellow Librarian Dr C Y Ferdinand BA MA MA MA DPhil (e-mail:
christine.ferdinand@magd.ox.ac.uk)
Reader Services Librarian James Fishwick BA MA(LIS) (e-mail:
james.fishwick@magd.ox.ac.uk)

Mansfield College

Library, Mansfield College, Mansfield Road, Oxford OX1 3TF
☎(01865) 270975
Fax (01865) 270970
url: www.mansfield.ox.ac.uk
Fellow Librarian Dr David Leopold
Librarian Ms Sally Jones (e-mail: librarian@mansfield.ox.ac.uk)

Merton College

Library, Merton College, Oxford OX1 4JD
☎(01865) 276380
Fax (01865) 276361
e-mail: library@merton.ox.ac.uk
url: www.merton.ox.ac.uk
Fellow and Librarian Dr Julia Walworth BA MA PhD (01865 276308; e-mail:
julia.walworth@merton.ox.ac.uk)
Assistant Librarian Dr Petra Hofmann BA MA PhD
Archivist Julian Reid (e-mail: julian.reid@merton.ox.ac.uk)

New College

Library, New College, Oxford OX1 3BN
☎(01865) 279580 (enquiries and administration)
url: www.new.ox.ac.uk/library-and-archives
Librarian Mrs Naomi van Loo MA BA MCLIP (e-mail: naomi.vanloo@new.ox.ac.uk)

Nuffield College

Library, Nuffield College, New Road, Oxford OX1 1NF
☎(01865) 278550
Fax (01865) 278621
e-mail: library-enquiries@nuffield.ox.ac.uk
url: www.nuffield.ox.ac.uk/library
Librarian Ms Elizabeth Martin DipLib MA MCLIP (e-mail: librarian@nuffield.ox.ac.uk)

Oriel College

Library, Oriel College, Oxford OX1 4EW
☎(01865) 276558 (direct)

e-mail: library@oriel.ox.ac.uk
url: www.oriel.ox.ac.uk
Librarian Mrs Marjory Szurko BA MRes DipLib MCLIP

Pembroke College
McGowin Library, Pembroke College, St Aldate's, Oxford OXI IDW
☎(01865) 276409 (direct)
Fax (01865) 276418
e-mail: library@pmb.ox.ac.uk
url: www.pmb.ox.ac.uk
Librarian Ms Laura Cracknell (e-mail: laura.cracknell@pmb.ox.ac.uk)
Archivist Ms Amanda Ingram (e-mail: archivist@pmb.ox.ac.uk)
(Visitors wishing to consult the archives are admitted by prior appointment only)

The Queen's College
Library, Queen's College, The, Oxford OXI 4AW
☎(01865) 279130
e-mail: library@queens.ox.ac.uk
url: www.queens.ox.ac.uk/library
Librarian Ms Amanda Saville MA MCLIP (01865 279213)
Reader Services Librarian Ms Tessa Shaw BA DipLib
Technical Services Librarian Ms Lynette Dobson MA MCLIP

Regent's Park College
Library, Regent's Park College, Pusey Street, Oxford OXI 2LB
☎(01865) 288120 (College); (01865) 288142 (Library direct line)
Fax (01865) 288121
e-mail: library@regents.ox.ac.uk
url: www.rpc.ox.ac.uk
College Librarian Revd Emma Walsh (e-mail: emma.walsh@regents.ox.ac.uk)
(General College Library open to members of College only. The Angus Library, a research
library for Baptist history, which also incorporates the former libraries of the Baptist Union
of Great Britain and the Baptist Historical Society, and the archives of the Baptist
Missionary Society on deposit, available by appointment)

St Anne's College
Library, St Anne's College, Woodstock Road, Oxford OX2 6HS
☎(01865) 274810
Fax (01865) 274899
e-mail: library@st-annes.ox.ac.uk
url: www.st-annes.ox.ac.uk/about/library
Librarian Dr David Smith MA DPhil MCLIP (e-mail: david.smith@st-annes.ox.ac.uk)
Deputy Librarian Ms Sally Speirs BA MStud MLIS

St Antony's College
Russian and Eurasian Studies Centre Library, St Antony's College, 62 Woodstock Road,
Oxford OX2 6JF
☎(01865) 284728
url: www.sant.ox.ac.uk
Librarian Richard Ramage (e-mail: richard.ramage@sant.ox.ac.uk)

St Benet's Hall

Library, St Benet's Hall, 38 St Giles, Oxford OX1 3LN
☎(01865) 280598
Fax (01865) 280792
e-mail: librarian@stb.ox.ac.uk
url: www.st-benets.ox.ac.uk
Librarian Father Michael Phillips OSB (e-mail: michael.phillips@stv.ox.ac.uk)

St Catherine's College

Library, St Catherine's College, Manor Road, Oxford OX1 3UJ
☎(01865) 271707
e-mail: library@stcatz.ox.ac.uk
url: www.stcatz.ox.ac.uk
Fellow Librarian Dr Gervase Rosser MA PhD
Assistant Librarians Ms Renée Prud'Homme, Ms Ludmila Gromova

St Cross College

Library, St Cross College, St Giles, Oxford OX1 3LZ
☎(01865) 278481
Fax (01865) 279484
e-mail: librarian@stx.ox.ac.uk
url: www.stx.ox.ac.uk/about-st-cross/library
Librarian Mrs Sheila Allcock BSc

St Edmund Hall

Library, St Edmund Hall, Queen's Lane, Oxford OX1 4AR
☎(01865) 279062
url: www.seh.ox.ac.uk
Librarian Ms Blanca Martin BA Dip (e-mail: blanca.martin@seh.ox.ac.uk)
(The Library is for the use of members of St Edmund Hall only)

St Hilda's College

Kathleen Major Library, St Hilda's College, Cowley Place, Oxford OX4 1DY
☎(01865) 276849 (general enquiries)
Fax (01865) 276816
e-mail: library@st-hildas.ox.ac.uk
url: www.st-hildas.ox.ac.uk
Librarian Miss Maria Croghan MA (e-mail: maria.croghan@st-hildas.ox.ac.uk)

St Hugh's College

Library, St Hugh's College, St Margaret's Road, Oxford OX2 6LE
☎(01865) 274938
Fax (01865) 274912
e-mail: library@st-hughs.ox.ac.uk
url: www.st-hughs.ox.ac.uk/library
Librarian Ms Nora Khayi (e-mail: nora.khayi@st-hughs.ox.ac.uk)

St John's College

Library, St John's College, St Giles, Oxford OX1 3JP
☎(01865) 277300 (main lodge), (01865) 277330/1 (direct to library)

Fax (01865) 277435 (College office)
e-mail: library@sjc.ox.ac.uk
url: www.sjc.ox.ac.uk
Fellow Librarian Dr Alastair Wright
Librarian Stewart Tiley BA(Hons) MA DipILM MCLIP
Deputy Librarian Mrs Ruth Ogden BA DipLib (e-mail: ruth.ogden@sjc.ox.ac.uk)

St Peter's College
Library, St Peter's College, New Inn Hall Street, Oxford OX1 2DL
☎(01865) 278882
Fax (01865) 278855
e-mail: library@spc.ox.ac.uk
url: www.spc.ox.ac.uk
Librarian Dr David Johnson MA(Lond) DPhil(Oxon) (e-mail: david.johnson@spc.ox.ac.uk)
Assistant Librarian Mrs Janet Foot (e-mail: janet.foot@spc.ox.ac.uk)

Somerville College
Library, Somerville College, Woodstock Road, Oxford OX2 6HD
☎(01865) 270694
e-mail: library@some.ox.ac.uk
url: www.some.ox.ac.uk
Librarian Dr Anne Manuel MA MSc MEd PhD
Assistant Librarian Miss Susan Purver MA DipLIS (01865 270694)

Trinity College
Library, Trinity College, Broad Street, Oxford OX1 3BH
☎(01865) 279863 (enquiries and administration)
Fax (01865) 279902
url: www.trinity.ox.ac.uk/college/library
Librarian Ms Sharon Cure (e-mail: sharon.cure@trinity.ox.ac.uk)

University College
Library, University College, High Street, Oxford OX1 4BH
☎(01865) 276621
Fax (01865) 276987
e-mail: library@univ.ox.ac.uk
url: www.univ.ox.ac.uk
Fellow Librarian Professor Tiffany Stern MA PhD(Cantab)
College Librarian Ms Elizabeth J Adams BAppSci(Curtin)

Wadham College
Library, Wadham College, Parks Road, Oxford OX1 3PN
☎(01865) 277900 (College); (01865) 277914 (direct)
Fax (01865) 277937
e-mail: library@wadh.ox.ac.uk
url: www.wadham.ox.ac.uk
Librarian Tim Kirtley
Fellow Librarian Professor Robin Fiddian

Wolfson College
The Library, Wolfson College, Oxford OX2 6UD
☎(01865) 274076
e-mail: library@wolfson.ox.ac.uk
url: www.wolfson.ox.ac.uk/library
Librarian Ms Fiona E Wilkes BA MA DipLib MCLIP
(Open to members of College and Common Room only)

Worcester College
Library, Worcester College, Walton Street, Oxford OX1 2HB
☎(01865) 278354/278370 (library); (01865) 278300 (porter's lodge)
Fax (01865) 278387
e-mail: library@worc.ox.ac.uk
url: www.worc.ox.ac.uk
Librarian Dr Joanna Parker MA DPhil (e-mail: joanna.parker@worc.ox.ac.uk)

UNIVERSITY OF PLYMOUTH

Charles Seale-Hayne Library, University of Plymouth, Drake Circus, Plymouth PL4 8AA
☎(01752) 232323/588588 (enquiries); (01752) 587100 (administration)
Fax (01752) 587101
url: www.plymouth.ac.uk/library
Head of Library and Digital Support Ms Jane Gosling BSc DipLib MCLIP (e-mail:
jane.gosling@plymouth.ac.uk)

UNIVERSITY OF PORTSMOUTH

University Library, University of Portsmouth, Cambridge Road, Portsmouth PO1 2ST
☎023 9284 3228/9 (enquiries), 023 9284 3222 (administration)
e-mail: elibrary@port.ac.uk
url: www.port.ac.uk/library
University Librarian Ms Roisin Gwyer (e-mail: roisin.gwyer@port.ac.uk)

QUEEN MARGARET UNIVERSITY, EDINBURGH

**Learning Resource Centre, Queen Margaret University, Edinburgh, Queen Margaret
University Drive, Musselburgh, East Lothian EH21 6UU**
☎0131 474 0000
Fax 0131 474 0001
e-mail: lrchelp@qmu.ac.uk
url: www.qmu.ac.uk/lb
Head of Learning Services Mrs Jo Rowley BA(Hons) MSc

QUEEN'S UNIVERSITY OF BELFAST

**Information Services Directorate, Queen's University of Belfast, McClay Library,
10 College Park, Belfast BT7 1LP**
☎028 9097 6346
url: www.qub.ac.uk/lib
Director of Information Services John Gormley (e-mail: j.gormley@qub.ac.uk)

Assistant Director (Library Services and Research Support) Ms Elizabeth Traynor BA MA MCLIP (e-mail: e.traynor@qub.ac.uk)

RAVENSBOURNE

Library Services, Ravensbourne, 6 Penrose Way, Peninsula Square, London SEIO OEW
☎020 3040 3500
Fax 020 8325 8320
url: www.ravensbourne.ac.uk
Learning Resources Manager Ms Sarah Maule BA(Hons) MA (e-mail: s.maule@rave.ac.uk)
Library Services Co-ordinator Ms Jill Dye MA Mphil (e-mail: j.dye@rave.ac.uk)

UNIVERSITY OF READING

University Library and Collections Services, University of Reading, Whiteknights, PO Box 223, Reading RG6 6AE
☎0118 378 8770 (enquiries), 0118 378 8773 (administration)
e-mail: library@reading.ac.uk
url: www.reading.ac.uk/library
Head of University Library and Collections Services and University Librarian
Mrs Julia Munro BSc MSc MBA MCLIP (0118 378 8774; e-mail: j.h.munro@reading.ac.uk)
Head of Academic Liaison and Support Ms Helen Hathaway (0118 378 4642; e-mail: h.m.hathaway@reading.ac.uk)
Head of Collections and Space Paul Johnson (0118 378 6784; e-mail: p.b.johnson@reading.ac.uk)
Head of Services and Systems Miss Celia A Ayres BSc DipInfSc MCLIP (0118 378 8781; e-mail: c.a.ayres@reading.ac.uk)
Facilities Manager/Head of Administration Robin Hunter (0118 378 8775; e-mail: r.d.hunter@reading.ac.uk)

THE ROBERT GORDON UNIVERSITY

University Library, The Robert Gordon University, Riverside East, Garthdee Road, Aberdeen ABIO 7GJ
☎(01224) 263450
Fax (01224) 263455
e-mail: library@rgu.ac.uk
url: www.rgu.ac.uk/library
Director of Knowledge and Information Services Ms Michelle Anderson BA(Hons) MA PGDip
Associate Director, Operational Services Ms Judith Moynagh MA MCLIP (e-mail: j.moynagh@rgu.ac.uk)
Associate Director, Client Services Miss Margaret Buchan MA MCLIP (e-mail: m.buchan@rgu.ac.uk)

UNIVERSITY OF ROEHAMPTON

Library Services, University of Roehampton, The University Library, Roehampton Lane, London SWI5 5SZ

☎020 8392 3770 (general enquiries)
Fax 020 8392 3026
e-mail: enquiry.desk@roehampton.ac.uk
url: www.roehampton.ac.uk/library
University Librarian Ms Susan Scorey BA(Hons) PGCE MCLIP (020 8392 3058; e-mail: susan.scorey@roehampton.ac.uk)
Head of Library Academic Liaison Ms Anne Pietsch BA(Hons) MSc (020 8392 3774; e-mail: a.pietsch@roehampton.ac.uk)
Head of Library Central Services Ms Collette Xavier BA MA DipEdTech DipInf MCLIP (020 8392 3211; e-mail: collette.xavier@roehampton.ac.uk)
Head of Library User Services Ms Faye Jackson (020 8392 3351; e-mail: f.jackson@roehampton.ac.uk)
Collections Development Manager Chris Foreman (020 8392 3352; e-mail: c.foreman@roehampton.ac.uk)
Archivist Ms Kornelia Cepok MA (020 8392 3323; e-mail: k.cepok@roehampton.ac.uk)

ROSE BRUFORD COLLEGE OF THEATRE AND PERFORMANCE

Learning Resources Centre, Rose Bruford College of Theatre and Performance, Lamorbey Park, Burnt Oak Lane, Sidcup, Kent DA15 9DF
☎020 8308 2626
Fax 020 8308 0542
url: www.bruford.ac.uk
College Librarian Frank Trew BA(Hons) PGDipInf (e-mail: frank.trew@bruford.ac.uk)
Assistant Librarian Terence Connolly BA(Hons) PGDipILS (e-mail: terry.connolly@bruford.ac.uk)

ROYAL ACADEMY OF DRAMATIC ART

RADA Library, Royal Academy of Dramatic Art, 18 Chenies Street, London WC1E 7PA
☎020 7636 7076 (ask for Library)
e-mail: library@rada.ac.uk
url: www.rada.ac.uk
Library Manager James Thornton
Senior Library Assistant Ms Jean Madden
Researcher/Assistant Ms Roe Lane

ROYAL ACADEMY OF MUSIC

Library, Royal Academy of Music, Marylebone Road, London NW1 5HT
☎020 7873 7323 (enquiries and administration)
Fax 020 7873 7322
e-mail: library@ram.ac.uk
url: www.ram.ac.uk
Librarian Ms Kathryn Adamson BA MA DipLib HonFRAM

ROYAL AGRICULTURAL UNIVERSITY

(formerly Royal Agricultural College)

Library, Royal Agricultural University, Stroud Road, Cirencester, Glos GL7 6JS
☎(01285) 652531
Fax (01285) 889844
e-mail: library@rau.ac.uk
url: www.rau.ac.uk/library
Head of Library Services Peter Brooks BA MA PGCE MCLIP (01285 652531 ext 2276)

ROYAL CENTRAL SCHOOL OF SPEECH AND DRAMA (formerly Central School of Speech and Drama)

Library Services, Royal Central School of Speech and Drama, Embassy Theatre, 64 Eton Avenue, London NW3 3HY
☎020 7559 3942 (enquiries)
Fax 020 7722 4132
e-mail: library@cssd.ac.uk
url: www.cssd.ac.uk
Head of Library Services Ms Helen Davies BA PGCE MSc MCLIP (e-mail: helen.davies@cssd.ac.uk)
Collections and Services Manager Ms Diana Watt (e-mail: diana.watt@cssd.ac.uk)

ROYAL COLLEGE OF ART

College Library, Royal College of Art, Kensington Gore, London SW7 2EU
☎020 7590 4224 (enquiries)
e-mail: library@rca.ac.uk
url: www.rca.ac.uk
Head of Library Services Ms Darlene Maxwell (e-mail: darlene.maxwell@rca.ac.uk)
Archives & Collections Manager Neil Parkinson (e-mail: neil.parkinson@rca.ac.uk)

ROYAL COLLEGE OF MUSIC

Library, Royal College of Music, Prince Consort Road, London SW7 2BS
☎020 7591 4325
Fax 020 7591 4326
e-mail: library@rcm.ac.uk
url: www.rcm.ac.uk
Librarian Peter Linnitt BMus DipLib (020 75914323; e-mail: peter.linnitt@rcm.ac.uk)
Reference Librarian Dr Peter Horton MA DPhil DipLib MCLIP (020 7591 4324; e-mail: phorton@rcm.ac.uk)

ROYAL COLLEGE OF NURSING OF THE UNITED KINGDOM

Royal College of Nursing Library and Heritage Services, Royal College of Nursing of the United Kingdom, 20 Cavendish Square, London WIG ORN
☎020 7647 3668

Fax 020 7647 3420
e-mail: rcn.library@rcn.org.uk
url: www.rcn.org.uk/development/library
Acting Library and Information Services Manager Ms Sarah Cull
Archives and Information Services Manager Ms Teresa Doherty
(Access for non-members is by appointment)

ROYAL CONSERVATOIRE OF SCOTLAND

(formerly Royal Scottish Academy of Music and Drama)

Whittaker Library, Royal Conservatoire of Scotland, 100 Renfrew Street, Glasgow G2 3DB
☎0141 270 8268
Fax 0141 270 8353
e-mail: library@rcs.ac.uk
url: www.rcs.ac.uk/library
Head of Information Services Ms Caroline Cochrane (0141 270 8269; e-mail: c.cochrane@rcs.ac.uk)

ROYAL NORTHERN COLLEGE OF MUSIC

Library, Royal Northern College of Music, 124 Oxford Road, Manchester M13 9RD
☎0161 907 5243
Fax 0161 273 7611
e-mail: library@rncm.ac.uk
url: www.rncm.ac.uk
Librarian Mrs Anna Wright BA MA MCLIP HonRNCM (e-mail: anna.wright@rncm.ac.uk)
Deputy Librarian Geoffrey Thomason MusB MusM ARCM LTCL DipLib (e-mail: geoff.thomason@rncm.ac.uk)

ROYAL SCOTTISH ACADEMY OF MUSIC AND DRAMA see ROYAL CONSERVATOIRE OF SCOTLAND

ROYAL WELSH COLLEGE OF MUSIC AND DRAMA

Library, Royal Welsh College of Music and Drama, Castle Grounds, Cathays Park, Cardiff CF10 3ER
☎029 2034 2854
Fax 029 2039 1304
url: library.rwcmd.ac.uk
Librarian Mrs Judith Agus BA BMus MCLIP (029 2039 1330; e-mail: judith.agus@rwcmd.ac.uk)

RUSKIN COLLEGE

Library, Ruskin College, Dunstan Road, Oxford OX3 9BZ
☎(01865) 759607

Fax (01865) 554372
e-mail: library@ruskin.ac.uk
url: www.ruskin.ac.uk
Director of Library and Learning Resources Ms Valerie Moyses BA(Hons) MCLIP DipLib
(Admission by appointment only)

UNIVERSITY OF ST ANDREWS

Library, University of St Andrews, University Library, North Street, St Andrews, Fife KY16 9TR
☎(01334 462281 (enquiries and administration), 01334 462301 (Director's Office)
Fax (01334) 462282
e-mail: library@st-andrews.ac.uk
url: www.st-andrews.ac.uk/library
University Librarian & Director of Library Services John MacColl FRSE (e-mail: jam31@st-andrews.ac.uk)
Deputy Director Library Services Jeremy Upton MA DipLib BMus(Hons)

UNIVERSITY OF ST MARK & ST JOHN

(formerly University College Plymouth St Mark & St John)

Library, University of St Mark & St John, Derriford Road, Plymouth PL6 8BH
☎(01752) 636845 (enquiries), (01752) 636700 ext 4206 (administration)
e-mail: libraryenquiries@marjon.ac.uk
url: www.marjon.ac.uk
Head of Library Mrs Wendy Evans BA(Hons) AHEA MCLIP (01752 636700 ext 4206; e-mail: wevans@marjon.ac.uk)

ST MARY'S UNIVERSITY COLLEGE TWICKENHAM

Learning Resources Centre, St Mary's University College Twickenham, Waldegrave Road, Strawberry Hill, Twickenham, Middlesex TW1 4SX
☎020 8240 4097
e-mail: enquiry@smuc.ac.uk
url: www.smuc.ac.uk/it-and-library-services
Director of Library and Learning Technology Martin Scarrott BA DipLib MCLIP FHEA
(e-mail: martin.scarrott@smuc.ac.uk)

UNIVERSITY OF SALFORD

The Library, University of Salford, Clifford Whitworth Building, Salford M5 4WT
☎0161 295 5535
e-mail: library@salford.ac.uk
url: www.library.salford.ac.uk
University Librarian Ms Julie Berry
Associate University Librarian (Learning and Research Support) David Clay
Associate University Librarian (Library Services) James Anthony-Edwards
Head of Library Business, Planning and Quality Lynne Leader

Campus libraries

Adelphi Library, University of Salford, Adelphi Building, Peru Street, Salford M3 6EQ
☎0161 295 5535

Clifford Whitworth Library, University of Salford, Salford M5 4WT
☎0161 295 2444
Fax 0161 295 6624

MediaCityUK, University of Salford, Salford Quays, Salford M50 2HE
☎0161 295 5535

SCOTTISH AGRICULTURAL COLLEGE see SRUC – SCOTLAND'S RURAL COLLEGE

SHEFFIELD HALLAM UNIVERSITY

Student and Learning Services, Sheffield Hallam University, City Campus, Sheffield S1 1WB
☎0114 225 3333
Fax 0114 225 3859
e-mail: learning.centre@shu.ac.uk
url: www.shu.ac.uk/services/sls/learning/library.html
Director, Learning and Academic Services Ms Nuala Devlin BA(Hons) MA MCLIP
Academic Services Manager Ms Alison Ward BA MA MCLIP (e-mail: a.ward@shu.ac.uk)
Information Resources Manager Ms Ann Betterton (e-mail: a.betterton@shu.ac.uk)
Advisory and Operations Maurice Teasdale (e-mail: m.teasdale@shu.ac.uk)

Campus Learning Centres

Adsetts Centre, Sheffield Hallam University, Student and Learning Services, City Campus,
Sheffield S1 1WB
☎0114 225 3333
Fax 0114 225 3859

Collegiate Learning Centre, Sheffield Hallam University, Student and Learning Services,
Collegiate Crescent Campus, Sheffield S10 2BP
☎0114 225 3333
Fax 0114 225 2476

THE UNIVERSITY OF SHEFFIELD

Western Bank Library, The University of Sheffield, Western Bank, Sheffield S10 2TN
☎0114 222 7200 (general enquiries); 0114 222 7224 library (administration)
e-mail: library@sheffield.ac.uk
url: www.shef.ac.uk/library
Director of Library Services and University Librarian Martin J Lewis MA DipLib MCLIP

Major libraries

Health Sciences Library, The University of Sheffield, Beech Hill Road, Sheffield S10 2RX
☎0114 222 7200
Fax 0114 278 0923
e-mail: library@sheffield.ac.uk

Information Commons, The University of Sheffield, 44 Leavygreave Road, Sheffield S3 7RD
☎0114 222 9999
e-mail: infocommons@sheffield.ac.uk

St George's Library, The University of Sheffield, Mappin Street, Sheffield S1 4DT
☎0114 222 7200
e-mail: library@sheffield.ac.uk

UNIVERSITY OF SOUTH WALES

(formerly University of Glamorgan and University of Wales Newport)

**Library and Student Centre, University of South Wales, Llantwit Road, Treforest,
Pontypridd, Rhondda Cynon Taf CF37 1DL**
☎(01443) 483400 (enquiries)
e-mail: lrsupport@southwales.ac.uk
url: www.studentlibrary@southwales.ac.uk
Director of Student Support and Library Services Dr Gillian Jack BA(Hons) MBA PhD
(e-mail: gillian.jack@southwales.ac.uk)
Library Services Manager Dr Andrew Dalgleish MA PhD MCLIP (e-mail: andrew.dalgleish@southwales.ac.uk), Ms Ann Cross Blib(Hons) PGCE FHEA MCLIP
(e-mail: ann.cross@southwales.ac.uk)

SOUTHAMPTON SOLENT UNIVERSITY

Mountbatten Library, Southampton Solent University, Southampton SO14 0RJ
☎023 8201 3681 (enquiries), 023 8031 3248 (administration)
Fax 023 8031 3672
url: www.solent.ac.uk/library/
Head of Library and Learning Services Steve Rose BA(Hons) DipLib MSc (023 8031
3342; e-mail: steve.rose@solent.ac.uk)
Deputy University Librarian (Customer Services and Operations) Graeme Barber
MSc BA(Hons) DipLib MCLIP (023 8031 3867; e-mail: graeme.barber@solent.ac.uk)
Deputy University Librarian (Information Services and Systems) Ms Margaret
Feetham MA MCLIP (023 8201 3220; e-mail: margaret.feetham@solent.ac.uk)
Dean, Learning and Information Service Ms Elizabeth Selby BA DMS MCLIP (023
8031 3679; e-mail: elizabeth.selby@solent.ac.uk)

Site library

Warsash Library, Southampton Solent University, Newtown Road, Warsash, Southampton
SO31 9ZL
☎023 8201 4269

UNIVERSITY OF SOUTHAMPTON

Hartley Library, University of Southampton, Highfield, Southampton SO17 1BJ
☎023 8059 2180 (enquiries), 023 8059 3450 (administration)
Fax 023 8059 5451
e-mail: library@soton.ac.uk
url: www.soton.ac.uk/library
University Librarian Ms Jane Savidge MA MA MCLIP (e-mail: j.c.savidge@soton.ac.uk)

Deputy Librarian Richard Wake MA MA CertMgmt MCLIP (023 8059 2371; e-mail: rlw1@soton.ac.uk)
Senior Archivist Ms Karen Robson (023 8059 2721; e-mail: k.robson@soton.ac.uk)

Site libraries
Health Services Library MP 883, University of Southampton, Level A, South Academic Block, Southampton General Hospital, Tremona Road, Southampton SO16 6YD
☎023 8079 6547
Fax 023 8079 8939
e-mail: hslib@soton.ac.uk
url: www.soton.ac.uk/library/about/hsl
Head of MHLS Library Services Ric Paul (e-mail: r.m.paul@soton.ac.uk)

Library, University of Southampton, Winchester School of Art, Park Avenue, Winchester, Hants SO23 8DL
☎023 8059 6986
e-mail: wsaenqs@soton.ac.uk
url: www.soton.ac.uk/library/about/wsal
Head of Library and Information Services Ms Linda Newington BA(Hons) PGDip MCLIP (e-mail: lan1@soton.ac.uk)

National Oceanographic Library, University of Southampton, Southampton Oceanography Centre, Waterfront Campus, European Way, Southampton SO14 3ZH
☎023 8059 6666
e-mail: mias@noc.soton.ac.uk (marine inf/adv serv); nol@noc.soton.ac.uk (general)
url: www.soton.ac.uk/library/about/nol
Head of Library Information Services and Head of Library Services for the Faculties of Engineering and the Environment, Natural and Environmental Sciences, and Physical Sciences and Engineering Mrs Jane Stephenson BLib MCLIP (023 8059 6111; e-mail: j.stephenson@soton.ac.uk)

SPURGEON'S COLLEGE

Library, Spurgeon's College, 189 South Norwood Hill, London SE25 6DJ
☎020 8653 0850
Fax 020 8771 0959
e-mail: library@spurgeons.ac.uk
url: www.spurgeons.ac.uk
Librarian Ms Annabel Haycraft BA MA DASP (e-mail: a.haycraft@spurgeons.ac.uk)

SRUC – SCOTLAND'S RURAL COLLEGE
(formerly Scottish Agricultural College)

SRUC Ayr Riverside Campus Library, SRUC – Scotland's Rural College, University Avenue, Ayr KA8 0SX
☎(01292) 886414/886413
Fax (01292) 886199
e-mail: libraryau@sruc.ac.uk
url: www.sruc.ac.uk/library
Head of Library Services Ms Elaine P Muir MA PGDipLib MCLIP (e-mail: elaine.muir@sac.ac.uk)

Campus libraries

SRUC Aberdeen Campus Library, SRUC – Scotland's Rural College, Ferguson Building, Craibstone Estate, Bucksburn, Aberdeen AB21 9YA
☎(01224) 711057
Fax (01224) 711291
e-mail: libraryab@sruc.ac.uk
url: www.sac.ac.uk
Site Librarian Ms Gillian Holmes BSc PGDip (e-mail: gillian.holmes@sruc.ac.uk)
Site Librarian Olubunmi Adebajo BA(Hons) MSc MCLIP (e-mail: olubunmi.adebajo@sruc.ac.uk)

SRUC Barony Campus Library, SRUC – Scotland's Rural College, Barony College, Parkgate, Dumfries DG1 3NE
☎(01387) 860251 ext 224
e-mail: baronylibrary@sruc.ac.uk
Site Librarian Ms J K Garnett BSc MA MBA MCLIP (e-mail: karen.garnett@sruc.ac.uk)

SRUC Edinburgh Campus Library, SRUC – Scotland's Rural College, Peter Wilson Building, King's Buildings, West Mains Road, Edinburgh EH9 3JG
☎0131 535 4117
e-mail: librarykb@sruc.ac.uk
url: www.sruc.ac.uk
Site Librarian Ms Rachel Atkinson MA(Hons) MSc (e-mail: rachel.atkinson@sruc.ac.uk)

SRUC Elmwood Campus Library, SRUC – Scotland's Rural College, Carslogie Road, Cupar, Fife KY15 4JB
☎(01334) 658810
e-mail: elmwoodlibrary@sruc.ac.uk
Site Librarian Ms Marjory Bruce McKean MA MSc (e-mail: marjory.mckean@sruc.ac.uk)

SRUC Oatridge Campus Library, SRUC – Scotland's Rural College, Ecclesmachan, Broxburn, West Lothian EH52 6NH
☎(01506) 864800
e-mail: OatridgeResourceCentreTeam@sruc.ac.uk
Site Librarian Ms Lesley Reade (e-mail: lesley.reade@sruc.ac.uk)

STAFFORDSHIRE UNIVERSITY

Information Services, Staffordshire University, College Road, Stoke-on-Trent ST4 2DE
☎(01782) 295770 (enquiries); (01782) 294443 (administration)
Fax (01782) 295799
e-mail: library@staffs.ac.uk
url: www.staffs.ac.uk
Director of Information Services Bernard Shaw (e-mail: b.shaw@staffs.ac.uk)
Associate Director of Learning, Technology and Information Services David Parkes BA(Hons) MSc MA MCLIP (01782 294369; e-mail: d.parkes@staffs.ac.uk)

Site libraries

Law Library, Staffordshire University, Leek Road, Stoke-on-Trent, Staffs ST4 2DF
☎(01782) 294307
e-mail: libraryhelpdesk@staffs.ac.uk
Law and Business Librarian Ms Alison Pope

Nelson Library, Staffordshire University, PO Box 368, Beaconside, Stafford ST18 0DP
☎(01785) 353236
e-mail: libraryhelpdesk@staffs.ac.uk
Customer Services and Operations Manager Mrs Rebecca Hodgetts

Shrewsbury Health Library, Staffordshire University, School of Health, Royal Shrewsbury
Hospital, Mytton Oak Road, Shrewsbury SY3 8XQ
☎(01743) 261440
Fax (01743) 261061
Subject and Learning Support Librarian Mrs Shirley Kennedy

Thompson Library, Staffordshire University, PO Box 664, College Road, Stoke-on-Trent
ST4 2DE
☎(01782) 295750 (helpdesk); (01782) 294443 (administration)
Fax (01782) 295799
e-mail: libraryhelpdesk@staffs.ac.uk
Customer Services and Site Liaison Manager Mrs Janice Broad

UNIVERSITY OF STIRLING

University Library, University of Stirling, Stirling FK9 4LA
☎(01786) 467250 (Information Centre), (01786) 467235 (Library), (01786) 467235
(administration)
e-mail: library@stir.ac.uk/infocentre@stir.ac.uk
url: www.stir.ac.uk/is
Acting Director of Information Services Ms Kathy McCabe

Campus library
Highland Health Sciences Library, University of Stirling, Centre for Health Science, Old
Perth Road, Inverness IV2 3JH
☎(01463) 255600 (ext 7600)
Fax (01463) 255605
e-mail: hhsl-inverness@stir.ac.uk
Librarian Mrs Anne Gillespie BA DipLibStud MCLIP (e-mail: ag5@stir.ac.uk)

UNIVERSITY OF STRATHCLYDE

**Andersonian Library, University of Strathclyde, Curran Building, 101 St James' Road,
Glasgow G4 0NS**
☎0141 548 4444 (enquiries)
Fax 0141 552 3304
e-mail: library@strath.ac.uk
url: www.strath.ac.uk/library
University Librarian Ms Dilys Young BA DMS MSc(Econ) MLIS FHEA (0141 548 4618;
e-mail: dilys.young@strath.ac.uk)

UNIVERSITY OF SUNDERLAND

**Student and Learning Support, University of Sunderland, Unit 2 Technical Park, Chester
Road, Sunderland SR1 3SD**
☎0191 515 2230

url: www.sunderland.ac.uk/sls
Director of Student and Learning Support Ms Kirsten Black BA DipISTech
(0191 515 3904)
Assistant Directors Oliver Pritchard BA MA MA MCLIP (0191 515 2903; e-mail:
oliver.pritchard@sunderland.ac.uk), Ivan Whitfield BA MBA (0191 515 2978; e-mail:
ivan.whitfield@sunderland.ac.uk)

Campus libraries
London Campus Library, University of Sunderland, London Campus, 197 Marsh Wall,
Docklands, London E14 9SG
☎020 7531 7333
Campus Librarian Ms Mehves Kayani-Hogan BA MA MA MCLIP (020 7531 7333; e-mail:
mehves.kayani-hogan@sunderland.ac.uk)

The Murray Library, University of Sunderland, Chester Road, Sunderland SR1 3SD
☎0191 515 3149
Campus Manager Ms Sandra Marsh BA(Hons) FHEA (0191 515 3570; e-mail:
sandra.marsh@sunderland.ac.uk)

St Peter's Library, University of Sunderland, Prospect Building, St Peter's Riverside
Campus, St Peter's Way, Sunderland SR6 0DD
☎0191 515 3318
Campus Manager Ms Rachel Dolan BA(Hons) MA FHEA (0191 515 3391; e-mail:
rachel.dolan@sunderland.ac.uk)

UNIVERSITY OF SURREY

University Library, University of Surrey, Guildford, Surrey GU2 7XH
☎(01483) 683325 (enquiries), 01483 689232 (administration)
Fax (01483) 689500
e-mail: library-enquiries@surrey.ac.uk
url: www.surrey.ac.uk/library
Director of Library and Learning Support Services Ms Caroline Rock BA(Hons) MA
MCLIP

UNIVERSITY OF SUSSEX

University Library, University of Sussex, Falmer, Brighton BN1 9QL
☎(01273) 678163 (enquiries), (01273) 877097 (administration)
Fax (01273) 678441
e-mail: library@sussex.ac.uk
url: www.sussex.ac.uk/library
University Librarian Ms Kitty Inglis
Head of Library Academic Services & Special Collections Ms Jane Harvell
Head of Library Operations Adrian Hale
Head of Library Planning & Administration Ms Sally Faith

SWANSEA METROPOLITAN UNIVERSITY see
UNIVERSITY OF WALES TRINITY ST DAVID

SWANSEA UNIVERSITY

Library and Information Centre, Swansea University, Singleton Park, Swansea SA2 8PP
☎(01792) 295697 (enquiries), (01792) 295175 (administration)
Fax (01792) 295851
e-mail: library@swansea.ac.uk
url: www.swansea.ac.uk/iss/libraries
Deputy Director, Information Services and Systems Steve Williams BA PGDip FBCS
(01792 295167; e-mail: s.r.williams@swansea.ac.uk)

Site library
South Wales Miners' Library, Swansea University, Hendrefoelan Campus, Gower Road,
Swansea SA2 7NB
☎(01792) 518603
e-mail: miners@swansea.ac.uk
Librarian Ms Siân F Williams BSc MCLIP

TEESSIDE UNIVERSITY

Library and Information Services, Teesside University, Middlesbrough TS1 3BA
☎(01642) 342100 (enquiries), (01642) 342103 (administration)
Fax (01642) 342190
e-mail: libraryhelp@tees.ac.uk
url: www.lis.tees.ac.uk
Director, Library & Information Services Ms Liz Jolly BA(Hons) DipILS FCLIP FRSA
(e-mail: liz.jolly@tees.ac.uk)

THAMES VALLEY UNIVERSITY see UNIVERSITY OF WEST LONDON

TRINITY LABAN

**Jerwood Library of the Performing Arts, Trinity Laban, King Charles Court, Old Royal
Naval College, Greenwich, London SE10 9JF**
☎020 8305 3950 (enquiries)
e-mail: jlpa@trinitylaban.ac.uk
url: www.trinitylaban.ac.uk/jerwoodlibrary
Head Librarian Miss Claire Kidwell BA(Hons) MA (e-mail: ckidwell@tcm.ac.uk)

Library, Laban, Trinity Laban, Creekside, London SE8 3DZ
☎020 8305 9400 (switchboard)
e-mail: librarians-dance@trinitylaban.ac.uk
url: www.trinitylaban.ac.uk
Head of Library and Archive Ralph Cox

UNIVERSITY OF THE ARTS LONDON

**Information Services, University of the Arts London, 272 High Holborn, London
WC1V 7EY**
☎020 7514 6000 (switchboard)

url: www.arts.ac.uk/library
Director of Libraries and Academic Support Services Ms Pat Christie BA MCLIP (020
7514 8072; e-mail: p.christie@arts.ac.uk)

College/site libraries

Camberwell College of Arts
Library Services, Camberwell College of Arts, 43–45 Peckham Road, London SE5 8UF
☎020 7514 6349
Fax 020 7514 6324
Learning Resources Manager Peter Jennett MA MCLIP (e-mail:
p.jennett@wimbledon.arts.ac.uk)
Assistant Learning Resources Manager Ms Mandy Cumbridge
Librarians Ms Catherine Lauriol, Ms Jan Morgan, Ms Jane Mann, Gustavo Grandal
Montero MA MCLIP

Central St Martins College of Art and Design
Library and Learning Resources, Central St Martins College of Art and Design, Granary
Building, I Granary Square, Kings Cross, London NIC 4AA
☎020 7514 7037
url: www.arts.ac.uk/csm
Learning Resources Manager Ms Rowan Williamson (e-mail:
r.williamson@arts.csm.ac.uk)
Assistant Learning Resources Manager Ms Jayne Batch (e-mail:
j.batch@csm.arts.ac.uk)

Library and Learning Resources, Central St Martins College of Art and Design, 107 Charing
Cross Road, London WC2H 0DU
☎020 7310/7311
Assistant Learning Resources Manager Ms Jayne Batch (e-mail:
j.batch@csm.arts.ac.uk)

Chelsea College of Arts
Library and Learning Resources, Chelsea College of Arts, 16 John Islip Street, London
SWIP 4JU
☎020 7514 7773/4
Fax 020 7514 7785
url: www.arts.ac.uk/study-at-ual/library-services
Learning Resources Manager Peter Jennett MA MCLIP (e-mail:
p.jennett@wimbledon.arts.ac.uk)
Assistant Learning Resources Manager Kevin Canning
Librarians Gustavo Grandal Montero MA MCLIP, Ms Sarah Turk MA, Ms Cassy Sachar MA,
Ms Alessia Borri MA

London College of Communication
Library and Learning Resources, London College of Communication, Elephant and Castle,
London SE1 6SB
☎020 7514 6527 or 8026
e-mail: library@lcc.arts.ac.uk
url: www.arts.ac.uk/library; arts.ac.libanswers.com (enquiries)

Learning Resources Manager Ms Tania Olsson MA MCLIP (e-mail: t.olsson@lcc.arts.ac.uk)

London College of Fashion
Library Services, London College of Fashion, 20 John Princes Street, Oxford Circus, London WIG 0BJ
☎020 7514 7455
Learning Resources Manager Ms Karen Ellis-Rees MA (e-mail: k.ellis-rees@fashion.arts.ac.uk)

Wimbledon College of Arts
Library Services, Wimbledon College of Arts, Merton Hall Road, London SW19 3QA
☎020 7514 9690 (enquiries)
Fax 020 7514 9642
url: www.wimbledon.arts.ac.uk; www.arts.ac.uk/study-at-ual/library-services
Learning Resources Manager Peter Jennett MA MCLIP (e-mail: p.jennett@wimbledon.arts.ac.uk)
Librarians Peter Crollie BA(Hons) (e-mail: p.crollie@wimbledon.arts.ac.uk), Ms Lorna Scott BA MCLIP (e-mail: l.a.scott@wimbledon.arts.ac.uk), Ms Alice Bloom BA (e-mail: a.bloom@wimbledon.arts.ac.uk)

UNIVERSITY OF ULSTER

Library, University of Ulster, Coleraine Campus, Cromore Road, Coleraine, Co Londonderry BT52 ISA
☎028 7032 3128
Fax 028 7032 4928
url: www.library.ulster.ac.uk
University Librarian Mrs Janet Peden BLS BA MSc PGCHEP FHEA MCLIP (028 7032 4743; e-mail: je.peden@ulster.ac.uk)

Campus libraries
Library, Belfast Campus, University of Ulster, York Street, Belfast BT15 1ED
☎028 9026 7268
Fax 028 9026 7278
Campus Library Manager Mrs Marion Khorshidian BA DipLIS MCLIP (e-mail: m.khorshidian@ulster.ac.uk)

Library, Coleraine Campus, University of Ulster, Cromore Road, Coleraine, Co Londonderry BT52 ISA
☎028 7032 4345
Fax 028 7032 4928
Campus Library Manager Mrs Stephanie McLaughlin BA LibStud (e-mail: sa.mclaughlin@ulster.ac.uk)

Library, Jordanstown Campus, University of Ulster, Shore Road, Newtownabbey, Co Antrim BT37 0QB
☎028 9036 6399
Fax 028 9036 6849
Campus Library Manager Ms Laura Mills BA PGDipLIS (e-mail: lj.mills@ulster.ac.uk)

Library, Magee Campus, University of Ulster, Northland Road, Londonderry BT48 7JL
☎028 7137 5264
Fax 028 7137 5626
Campus Library Manager Vacant

UNIVERSITY OF WALES INSTITUTE, CARDIFF see CARDIFF METROPOLITAN UNIVERSITY

UNIVERSITY OF WALES, NEWPORT see UNIVERSITY OF SOUTH WALES

UNIVERSITY OF WALES TRINITY ST DAVID
(Now includes the libraries of the former Swansea Metropolitan University)

Library, University of Wales Trinity St David, Learning Resources Centre, Lampeter Campus, College Street, Lampeter, Ceredigion SA48 7ED
☎(01570 424798 (enquiries/Librarian)
e-mail: lampeterlibrary@tsd.uwtsd.ac.uk
url: www.uwtsd.ac.uk/library
Head of Library and Learning Resources: Carmarthen & Lampeter
Ms Alison Harding MA MSc MCLIP (e-mail: a.harding@tsd.ac.uk)
Deputy Head of Library and Learning Resources: Carmarthen & Lampeter
Ms Sarah Jones (e-mail: s.b.jones@tsd.ac.uk)

Library, University of Wales Trinity St David, Learning Resources Centre, Carmarthen
Campus, College Road, Carmarthen SA31 3EP
☎(01267) 676780
e-mail: carmarthenlibrary@tsd.uwtsd.ac.uk
url: www.uwtsd.ac.uk/carmarthen-library

Griffith Library, University of Wales Trinity St David, Learning Resources Centre, Dynevor
Centre for Art, Design & Media, De La Beche Street, Swansea SA1 3EU
☎(01792) 481030
url: www.uwtsd.ac.uk/swansea-libraries/griffith-library
Deputy Head of Library and Learning Resources: Swansea Ms Helen Beale (e-mail:
helen.beale@sm.uwtsd.ac.uk)

Owen Library, University of Wales Trinity St David, Mount Pleasant, Swansea SA1 6ED
☎(01792) 481141
url: www.uwtsd.ac.uk/swansea-libraries/owen-library
Head of Library and Learning Resources: Swansea Ms Anne Harvey LLB DipLib
(e-mail: anne.harvey@sm.uwtsd.ac.uk)

Roderic Bowen Library & Archives, University of Wales Trinity St David, Lampeter,
Ceredigion SA48 7ED
☎(01570) 424716
e-mail: rodericbowenlibrary@tsd.ac.uk
url: www.uwtsd.ac.uk/rbla

Swansea Business Library, University of Wales Trinity St David, Powell Street, Swansea
SA1 1NE

☎(01792) 481023
url: www.uwtsd.ac.uk/swansea-libraries/swansea-business-library
Head of Library and Learning Resources: Swansea Ms Anne Harvey LLB DipLib
(e-mail: anne.harvey@sm.uwtsd.ac.uk)

Townhill Library, University of Wales Trinity St David, Townhill Road, Swansea SA2 0UT
☎(01792) 482113
url: www.uwtsd.ac.uk/swansea-libraries/townhill-library
Deputy Head of Library and Learning Resources: Swansea Ms Mari Thomas BA
DipLib MCLIP (e-mail: mari.thomas@sm.uwtsd.ac.uk)

UNIVERSITY OF WARWICK

Library, University of Warwick, Gibbet Hill Road, Coventry CV4 7AL
☎024 7652 2026
Fax 024 7652 4211
e-mail: library@warwick.ac.uk
url: www2.warwick.ac.uk/services/library
Librarian Robin Green BA MA DipLib

THE UNIVERSITY OF WEST LONDON

(formerly Thames Valley University)

Library Services, West London University, St Mary's Road, Ealing, London W5 5RF
☎020 8231 2248
e-mail: library@uwl.ac.uk
url: www.uwl.ac.uk/library
Director of Library Services Tim Wales BA(Hons) MSc MCLIP FHEA (e-mail:
tim.wales@uwl.ac.uk)

Libraries

Berkshire Institute for Health Library, West London University, Ninth Floor, Fountain
House, 2 Queens Walk, Reading RG1 7QF
☎020 8209 4470
Customer Experience Librarian Michael Sharrocks (020 8231 4470; e-mail:
mike.sharrocks@uwl.ac.uk)

Paragon House Library, West London University, 2nd Floor, Paragon House, Boston Manor
Road, Brentford, Middlesex TW8 9GA
☎020 8209 4043
Customer Experience Librarian Imran Hussain (020 8209 2109; e-mail:
imran.hussain@uwl.ac.uk)
(Note: this library will be closing Summer 2015)

St Mary's Road Library, West London University, Ealing, London W5 5RF
☎020 8231 2248
Customer Experience Librarian Imran Hussain (020 8209 2109; e-mail:
imran.hussain@uwl.ac.uk)

UNIVERSITY OF THE WEST OF ENGLAND, BRISTOL

Library Services, University of the West of England, Bristol, Frenchay Campus, Coldharbour Lane, Bristol BS16 IQY
☎0117 328 2277 (enquiries), 0117 328 2404 (administration)
Fax 0117 328 2407
url: www.uwe.ac.uk/library
Director of Library Services Jason Briddon BSc MA PGCE PGCHE MCLIP

UNIVERSITY OF THE WEST OF SCOTLAND

Library, University of the West of Scotland, High Street, Paisley, Renfrewshire PAI 2BE
☎0141 848 3758 (enquiries)
Fax 0141 848 3761
e-mail: library@uws.ac.uk
url: www.uws.ac.uk/library
University Librarian Ms Jan Howden (e-mail: jan.howden@uws.ac.uk)
Campus Librarian (Paisley) Ms Philomena Millar (e-mail: philomena.millar@uws.ac.uk)

Site Libraries

Ayr Campus Library, University of the West of Scotland, Beech Grove, Ayr KA8 0SR
☎(01292) 886345
Fax (01292) 886288
e-mail: libraryayr@uws.ac.uk
Campus Librarian (Ayr) Neal Buchanan (e-mail: neal.buchanan@uws.ac.uk)

Dumfries Campus Crichton Library, University of the West of Scotland, Dumfries Campus, Dumfries DGI 4UQ
☎(01387) 734323
Campus Librarian (Dumfries) Ms Avril Goodwin (e-mail: avril.goodwin@uws.ac.uk)

Hamilton Campus Library, University of the West of Scotland, Almada Street, Hamilton, Lanarkshire ML3 0JB
☎(01698) 894424
Fax (01698) 286856
Campus Librarian (Hamilton) John Burke (e-mail: john.burke@uws.ac.uk)

UNIVERSITY OF WESTMINSTER

Information Services, University of Westminster, Cavendish House, 101 New Cavendish Street, London WIW 6XH
☎020 7911 5095
url: www.westminster.ac.uk
Director of Information Services Ms Suzanne Enright BA DipLib MCLIP (e-mail: s.enright@westminster.ac.uk)
Associate Director Library and Archive Services Ms Carole Satchwell BA MCLIP (e-mail: c.satchwell@westminster.ac.uk)
Library Services Manager Ms Elaine Salter BA MLib FCLIP (e-mail: e.salter@westminster.ac.uk)

Academic Liaison Manager Ms Fiona O'Brien MA MCLIP FRSA (e-mail: f.obrien@westminster.ac.uk)

Libraries

Archive Services, University of Westminster, Regent Campus, 4–12 Little Titchfield Street, London W1W 7UW
☎020 3506 9602
University Archivist Ms Elaine Penn MA RMSA (e-mail: e.s.penn@westminster.ac.uk)

Cavendish Library, University of Westminster, 115 New Cavendish Street, London W1W 6UW
☎020 3506 4050/4051
Assistant Library Manager Ms Clare Dowsett (e-mail: c.dowsett@westminster.ac.uk)

Harrow LRC, University of Westminster, Watford Road, Northwick Park, Harrow, Middlesex HA1 3TP
☎020 3506 7920
Library Services Site Manager Ms Sally Bannard BA PGCDipHistArt (e-mail: s.bannard@westminster.ac.uk)

Marylebone Library, University of Westminster, 35 Marylebone Road, London NW1 5LS
☎020 3506 7063
Library Services Site Manager Ms Nikki Trigg (e-mail: n.trigg@westminster.ac.uk)

Regent Library, University of Westminster, 4–12 Little Titchfield Street, London W1W 7UW
☎020 3506 9614
Library Services Site Manager Ms Katherine Marshall MA

UNIVERSITY OF WINCHESTER

Library, University of Winchester, Sparkford Road, Winchester, Hants SO22 4NR
☎(01962) 827306
Fax (01962) 827443
url: www.winchester.ac.uk/library
Librarian David Farley BA(Hons) CertMan(OU) MCLIP (01962 827306; e-mail: david.farley@winchester.ac.uk)
Deputy Librarian (Technical Services) Ms Sarah Bulger BA(Hons) MA (01962 827306; e-mail: sarah.bulger@winchester.ac.uk)
Deputy Librarian (Reader Services) Mrs Susan Renshaw BA(Hons) PGDip MCLIP (01962 827306; e-mail: susan.renshaw@winchester.ac.uk)

UNIVERSITY OF WOLVERHAMPTON

Harrison Learning Centre, University of Wolverhampton, Wulfruna Street, Wolverhampton WV1 1RH
☎(01902) 321333 (enquiries)
e-mail: www.wlv.ac.uk/lib/contacts/ask_a_librarian.aspx
url: www.wlv.ac.uk/lib
Director of Learning and Information Services Ms Fiona Parsons BA MLib PGCE (01902 321673)
Assistant Director of Learning and Information Services Mrs Trish Fouracres BA(Hons) MA MCLIP, John Dowd BA(Hons)

Site libraries

Telford Learning Centre, University of Wolverhampton, Old Shifnal Road, Priorslee, Telford, Shropshire TF2 9NT
☎(01902) 321333 (enquiries)

Walsall Learning Centre, University of Wolverhampton, Gorway, Walsall, West Midlands WS1 3BD
☎(01902) 321333 (enquiries)

School of Health site library
Burton Learning Centre, University of Wolverhampton, Burton Nurse Education Centre, Belvedere Road, Burton upon Trent, Staffs DE13 0RB
☎(01902) 321333 (enquiries)

UNIVERSITY OF WORCESTER

Information and Learning Services, University of Worcester, Peirson Library, Henwick Grove, Worcester WR2 6AJ
☎(01905) 666222
e-mail: askalibrarian@worc.ac.uk
url: www.worcester.ac.uk/ils
Director of Information and Learning Services Ms Anne Hannaford BA(Hons) DipLib (e-mail: a.hannaford@worc.ac.uk)

The Hive, University of Worcester, Sawmill Walk, The Butts, Worcester WR1 3PB
☎(01905) 822866
url: www.thehiveworcester.org
(Note: Joint academic/public library of the University of Worcester and Worcestershire County Council)

WRITTLE COLLEGE

Library, Writtle College, Chelmsford, Essex CM1 3RR
☎(01245) 424245
Fax (01245) 420456
e-mail: thelibrary@writtle.ac.uk
url: www.writtle.ac.uk
Head of Learning Information Services Mrs R M Hewings BSc(Econ) DMS DipLib FCLIP FHEA (ext 26009; e-mail: rachel.hewings@writtle.ac.uk)
Academic Liaison Librarian Ms Mary Davidson MSc (e-mail: mary.davidson@writtle.ac.uk)

YORK ST JOHN UNIVERSITY

Information Learning Services, York St John University, Fountains Learning Centre, Lord Mayor's Walk, York YO31 7EX
☎(01904) 876696
Fax (01904) 876324
e-mail: ils@yorksj.ac.uk
url: www.yorksj.ac.uk/library/index.aspx
Director of Information Learning Services Ms Debbi Boden-Angell

Deputy Director of Information Learning Services Steven Patterson
University Librarian Ms Helen Westmancoat BA MCLIP
Academic Liaison Librarians Ms Jane Munks BA MCLIP (e-mail: j.munks@yorksj.ac.uk),
Ms Victoria Watt MA (e-mail: v.watt@yorksj.ac.uk), Ms Lottie Alexander BA (e-mail:
l.alexander@yorksj.ac.uk), Ms Clare McCluskey BA MCLIP (e-mail: c.mccluskey@yorksj.ac.uk)
Resource Acquisitions Librarian Bryan Jones BA (e-mail: b.jones@yorksj.ac.uk)
Database Librarian Ms Ruth Mardall BA MA (e-mail: r.mardall2@yorksj.ac.uk)

UNIVERSITY OF YORK

The University Library, University of York, Heslington, York YO10 5DD
☎(01904) 323873 (enquiries)
Fax (01904) 323806
e-mail: lib-enquiry@york.ac.uk
url: www.york.ac.uk/library
Director of Information Stephen Town MA DipLib FCLIP MCIM

Branch/department library

King's Manor Library, University of York, Exhibition Square, York YO1 7EP
☎(01904) 323969

York Minster Library, University of York, The Old Palace, Dean's Park, York YO1 7JQ
☎(0844) 9390021

Selected government, national and special libraries in the UK

ACTION ON HEARING LOSS LIBRARY

(formerly RNID Library)

Action on Hearing Loss Library, UCL Ear Institute and RNID Libraries at the Royal National Throat, Nose and Ear Hospital, 330–332 Gray's Inn Road, London WC1X 8EE
☎020 3456 5253 (also for Minicom)
Fax 020 3456 5143
e-mail: rnidlib@ucl.ac.uk
url: www.ucl.ac.uk/library/rnidlib.shtml
Librarian Alex Stagg MA (e-mail: a.stagg@ucl.ac.uk)

Specialism(s): Audiology; Deaf studies

ADVOCATES LIBRARY

Advocates Library, Parliament House, Edinburgh EH1 1RF
☎0131 260 5683 (enquiries), 0131 260 5637 (Librarian)
Fax 0131 260 5663 (9am–5pm weekdays)
e-mail: inqdesk@advocates.org.uk
url: www.advocates.org.uk
Senior Librarian Ms Andrea Longson BSc DipLib MBA (e-mail: andrea.longson@advocates.org.uk)
(Open to members only. Non-members may access stock at the National Library of Scotland.)

Specialism(s): Law

ALDERSHOT MILITARY MUSEUM

Military Museum and Archive, Aldershot Military Museum, Evelyn Woods Road, Queens Avenue, Aldershot, Hants GU11 2LG
☎(01252) 314598
url: www.hants.gov.uk/aldershot-museum
Curator Ms Jenny Stevens (e-mail: jenny.stevens@hants.gov.uk)
(Accessible to enquirers by appointment)

Specialism(s): Military and local history relating to Aldershot and Farnborough

AMBLESS SOCIETY LIBRARY

Ambless Society Library, Shalom House, Lower Celtic Park, Enniskillen, Co Fermanagh BT74 6HP
☎028 6632 0320; Ambless Accident Supportline: 028 6632 0321 (tel/fax/smstext/voicemail/RBS)
Fax 028 6632 0320
e-mail: ambless.hq@btinternet.com
Librarian John Wood

Specialism(s): Private research library working closely with the charity Ambless, which offers care and support to accident sufferers and their families

AMERICAN MUSEUM IN BRITAIN

Library, American Museum in Britain, Claverton Manor, Bath BA2 7BD
☎(01225) 823016
Fax (01225) 469160
e-mail: info@americanmuseum.org; library@americanmuseum.org (by appointment only)
url: www.americanmuseum.org
Librarian Dr Cathryn Spence (e-mail: cathryn.spence@americanmuseum.org)

Specialism(s): American history and decorative arts; Religions, e.g. Shakers; North American Indians

AMGUEDDFA CYMRU – NATIONAL MUSEUM WALES

Library, Amgueddfa Cymru – National Museum Wales, Cathays Park, Cardiff CFI0 3NP
☎029 2057 3202
e-mail: library@museumwales.ac.uk
url: www.museumwales.ac.uk
Principal Librarian Ms Kristine Chapman
Assistant Librarian Ms Jennifer Evans (02920 573202; e-mail: jennifer.evans@museumwales.ac.uk)

Specialism(s): Archaeology; Fine and decorative arts; Botany; Geology; Zoology; Architecture; Welsh history and topography

ANIMAL HEALTH AND VETERINARY LABORATORIES AGENCY

(formerly Veterinary Laboratories Agency)

Library, Animal Health and Veterinary Laboratories Agency, New Haw, Addlestone, Surrey KTI5 3NB
☎(01932) 357314 (enquiries)
Fax (01932) 357608
e-mail: library@ahvla.defra.gsi.gov.uk
url: www.defra.gov.uk/ahvla-en
Librarian and Records Officer Mrs Heather Hulse BA(Hons)
Library Services Manager Mrs Sonja van Montfort BA(Hons) (e-mail: sonja.vanmontfort@ahvla.gsi.gov.uk)

Specialism(s): Veterinary science and medicine; Animal husbandry; Diseases of commercial farm animals

THE ARMITT MUSEUM AND LIBRARY

Library, The Armitt Museum and Library, Rydal Road, Ambleside, Cumbria LA22 9BL
☎(01539) 431212
e-mail: info@armitt.com
url: www.armitt.com
Curator Ms Deborah Walsh

Specialism(s): Specialist Lake District collection (literature, topography, natural history); Cumbria; Mountaineering; Kurt Schwitters; Beatrix Potter; Brunskill and Abraham Brothers (Photographic glass plates), Herbert Bell (Photography), Harriet Martineau, William Green

ASSOCIATION OF COMMONWEALTH UNIVERSITIES

Reference Library, Association of Commonwealth Universities, Woburn House, 20–24 Tavistock Square, London WC1H 9HF
☎020 7380 6700
Fax 020 7387 2655
e-mail: info@acu.ac.uk
url: www.acu.ac.uk
Librarian Nicholas Mulhern MA MA DipLIS MCLIP

Specialism(s): Higher Education in the Commonwealth

BANK OF ENGLAND

Information Centre, Bank of England, Threadneedle Street, London EC2R 8AH
☎020 7601 4715 (enquiries), 020 7601 4668 (administration)
e-mail: informationcentre@bankofengland.co.uk
url: www.bankofengland.co.uk
Information Centre Manager Mark Faulkner BA(Hons)

Specialism(s): Economics; Central banking

BG GROUP PLC

Information Centre, BG Group plc, Faraday Building 2, 100 Thames Valley Park Drive, Reading RG6 1PT
☎(0118) 929 2496 (enquiries and administration)
Fax (0118) 929 2414
url: www.bg-group.com
Information Analyst David Freemantle (0118 929 2497; e-mail: david.freemantle@bg-group.com)

Specialism(s): Reference collection, mainly energy industry

BIRMINGHAM AND MIDLAND INSTITUTE

The Birmingham Library, Birmingham and Midland Institute, 9 Margaret Street, Birmingham B3 3BS
☎0121 236 3591
Fax 0121 212 4577
e-mail: admin@bmi.org.uk
url: www.bmi.org.uk
Librarian Vacant
(Private members' library)

Specialism(s): History; Literature; Natural history; Science; Travel; Fiction; Biography; Music

BISHOPSGATE INSTITUTE

Bishopsgate Library, Bishopsgate Institute, 230 Bishopsgate, London EC2M 4QH
☎020 7392 9270
Fax 020 7392 9275
e-mail: library@bishopsgate.org.uk
url: www.bishopsgate.org.uk
Library and Archives Manager Stefan Dickers (e-mail:
stefan.dickers@bishopsgate.org.uk)

Specialism(s): London history and topography; Labour history; 19thC trades union history;
Co-operative movement; Freethought movement; Humanism

BRITANNIA ROYAL NAVAL COLLEGE

College Library, Britannia Royal Naval College, Dartmouth, Devon TQ6 0HJ
☎(01803) 677278
url: www.brnc.ac.uk
College Librarian Peter Barr BA(Hons) MA MCLIP (e-mail: peter.barr@brnc.ac.uk)
Training Facilitator Ms Gill Smith (e-mail: gillian.smith@brnc.ac.uk)
(Prior appointment necessary)*Specialism(s)*: Strategic studies; Naval history;
Marine environment; Leadership

BRITISH ANTARCTIC SURVEY

Library, British Antarctic Survey, High Cross, Madingley Road, Cambridge CB3 0ET
☎(01223) 221312
e-mail: baslib@bas.ac.uk
url: www.antarctica.ac.uk
Library Services Manager Andrew Gray

Specialism(s): Geology; Geophysics; Glaciology; Climatology; Upper atmosphere physics;
Marine and terrestrial biology (all with accent on Antarctic region)

BRITISH BROADCASTING CORPORATION

**BBC Information and Archives, British Broadcasting Corporation, BC3 D6 Broadcast
Centre, 201 Wood Lane, London W12 7TP**
☎020 8008 2250
url: www.bbc.co.uk
Controller, BBC Archives Ms Sarah Hayes (e-mail: sarah.hayes.01@bbc.co.uk)

BRITISH COUNCIL

**Customer Services, British Council, Bridgewater House, 58 Whitworth Street,
Manchester M1 6BB**
☎0161 957 7755
e-mail: general.enquiries@britishcouncil.org
url: www.britishcouncil.org

(For details of British Council information services in 110 countries and territories see
website: www.britishcouncil.org.)

BRITISH DENTAL ASSOCIATION

Library, British Dental Association, 64 Wimpole Street, London WIG 8YS
☎020 7563 4545
Fax 020 7935 6492
e-mail: library@bda.org
url: www.bda.org.uk
Head of Library and Knowledge Services Roger Farbey MBE BA DipLib FCLIP (e-mail: r.farbey@bda.org)

BRITISH FILM INSTITUTE

BFI Reuben Library, British Film Institute, BFI Southbank, Belvedere Road, South Bank, London SEI 8XT
☎020 7255 1444
e-mail: library@bfi.org.uk
url: www.bfi.org.uk/education-research/bfi-reuben-library
Library Manager Ms Emma Smart (e-mail: emma.smart@bfi.org.uk)
(Incorporates Independent Television Commission Library collections)

Specialism(s): The moving image (national film and television collection and archives)

BRITISH GEOLOGICAL SURVEY

Research Knowledge Services, British Geological Survey, Kingsley Dunham Centre, Keyworth, Nottingham NGI2 5GG
☎0115 936 3205
Fax 0115 936 3200
e-mail: libuser@bgs.ac.uk
url: www.bgs.ac.uk
Head of Research Knowledge Services Ken Hollywood BA MSc DipLib MCLIP (e-mail: ken.hollywood@nerc.ac.uk)

Branch libraries

Library, British Geological Survey, Scottish Regional Office, Murchison House, West Mains Road, Edinburgh EH9 3LA
☎0131 650 0322
Fax 0131 668 2683
e-mail: mhlib@bgs.ac.uk
Site Librarian Ms Gail Gray BSc PGDipLIS

London Information Office, British Geological Survey, Natural History Museum Earth Galleries, Cromwell Road, South Kensington, London SW7 5BD
☎020 7589 4090
Fax 020 7589 4090
e-mail: bgslondon@bgs.ac.uk
Officer-in-Charge Ms Clare Tombleson (e-mail: cto@bgs.ac.uk)

BRITISH HOROLOGICAL INSTITUTE

Library, British Horological Institute, Upton Hall, Upton, Newark, Notts NG23 5TE

☎(01636) 813795 (switchboard); 817602 (Library)
Fax (01636) 812258
e-mail: clocks@bhi.co.uk
url: www.bhi.co.uk
Librarian and Curator Viscount Alan Midleton FBHI
(Library open to members only; research available to non-members on request)

BRITISH LIBRARY

British Library, 96 Euston Road, London NW1 2DB
☎01937 546 060 (general and visitor enquiries), 0330 333 1144 (switchboard)
url: www.bl.uk
Chair Baroness Blackstone
Chief Executive Roly Keating
Chief Financial Officer Steve Morris
Director of Collections Caroline Brazier
Director of Audiences Ms Frances Brindle
Chief Digital Officer Richard Boulderstone
Chief Operating Officer Phil Spence

Enquiry points
The following are based at 96 Euston Road, London NW1 2DB. Admission to the Library's
London reading rooms is by pass only. Most of the Library's catalogues are available on its
website, www.bl.uk. For general enquiries about the collection, reader services and
advance reservations, tel: 020 7412 7676, e-mail: reader-services-enquiries@bl.uk.

St Pancras Reading Rooms
Asian and African Studies enquiries
☎020 7412 7873; Fax: 020 7412 7641
Business and Intellectual Property enquiries
☎020 7412 7454
Humanities Reference Service and Sound & Vision Reference Service
☎020 7412 7831
Librarianship and Information Science Service
☎020 7412 7831
Manuscripts and Maps Reference Team
☎020 7412 7513/7702
Music Collections
☎020 7412 7772
News Reference Service
☎020 7412 7377
Rare Books Reference Team
☎020 7412 7564
Science, Technology and Medicine
☎020 7412 7288
Social Sciences Reference Service
☎020 7412 7894
Sound & Vision Reference Service
☎020 7412 7831

Other useful numbers/e-mail addresses

Reader Registration (advice on who may use the Library and how to apply for a reader's pass)
020 7412 7676, e-mail: Reader-Registration@bl.uk

Visitor Services (for general enquiries and details of exhibitions, events)
01937 546 060, e-mail: customer-services@bl.uk

Northern Site, British Library, Boston Spa, Wetherby, West Yorks LS23 7BQ
☎01937 546060
e-mail: customer-services@bl.uk

BRITISH MEDICAL ASSOCIATION

BMA Library, British Medical Association, BMA House, Tavistock Square, London
WC1H 9JP
☎020 7383 6625
Fax 020 7388 2544
e-mail: bma-library@bma.org.uk
url: www.bma.org.uk/library
Librarian Ms Jacky Berry BA(Hons) MBA MCLIP

BRITISH MUSEUM

Anthropology Library, Centre for Anthropology, Department of AOA, British Museum,
Great Russell Street, London WC1B 3DG
☎020 7323 8031
e-mail: anthropologylibrary@thebritishmuseum.ac.uk
Senior Librarian Mrs Jan Ayres (020 7323 8069; e-mail: jayres@thebritishmuseum.ac.uk)
(The Anthropology Library in the British Museum is a major anthropological collection. It
incorporates the stock of the former library of the Royal Anthropological Institute. It
covers every aspect of anthropology – cultural anthropology (with emphasis on material
culture), archaeology, biological anthropology, linguistics and such related fields as history,
sociology, description and travel. It also houses a Pictorial Collection. The Library is open
to researchers and the general public (proof of identity will be required).

BRITISH PSYCHOLOGICAL SOCIETY

Psychology Library, British Psychological Society, Senate House Library, University of
London, Malet Street, London WC1E 7HU
☎020 7862 8461
e-mail: enquiries@shl.lon.ac.uk
url: www.shl.lon.ac.uk
Psychology Librarian, Senate House Library, University of London Mrs Mura Ghosh
MLS MBA (020 7862 8449; e-mail: mura.ghosh@london.ac.uk)
(The BPS collection of periodicals is held at the Psychology Library and amalgamated with
the University of London Library collection of psychology periodicals.)

BRITISH STANDARDS INSTITUTION

Knowledge Centre, British Standards Institution, 389 Chiswick High Road, London
W4 4AL

☎020 8996 7004
Fax 020 8996 7005
e-mail: knowledgecentre@bsigroup.com
url: www.bsigroup.com
Knowledge Centre Manager Ms Lucy Ahmed BA(Hons) PGDipILM
(The Library may be used for reference free of charge by members and students. For non-members there is a charge. Please contact us in advance to arrange a visit.)

Specialism(s): Standards

BRITISH UNIVERSITIES FILM & VIDEO COUNCIL

Information Service, British Universities Film & Video Council, 77 Wells Street, London WIT 3QJ
☎020 7393 1500 (switchboard); 020 7393 1506 (direct)
Fax 020 7393 1555
e-mail: ask@bufvc.ac.uk
url: www.bufvc.ac.uk
Head of Membership Services and Information Sergio Angelini

Specialism(s): Film; Television; Radio

THE BRITTEN-PEARS FOUNDATION

Library, The Britten-Pears Foundation, The Red House, Golf Lane, Aldeburgh, Suffolk IP15 5PZ
☎(01728) 451700
Fax (01728) 453076
e-mail: library@brittenpears.org; enquiries@brittenpears.org
url: www.brittenpears.org
Director of Collections and Heritage Dr Christopher Grogan BMus PhD DipLIS (01728 451707)
Librarian Dr Nicholas Clark PhD DipILS (01728 451702)

BROMLEY HOUSE LIBRARY

Bromley House Library, Bromley House, Angel Row, Nottingham NGI 6HL
☎0115 947 3134
e-mail: enquiries@bromleyhouse.org
Librarian Mrs Carol Barstow BSc DipLib MA MCLIP
(Subscription library also available to the public for reference purposes only, by prior appointment)

CANCER RESEARCH UK

Library and Information Services, Cancer Research UK, London Research Institute, 44 Lincoln's Inn Fields, London WC2A 3LY
☎020 7269 3206
Fax 020 7269 3084
e-mail: lib.info@cancer.org.uk
url: www.cancerresearchuk.org

Library Administrator Ms Michelle Trowsdale (e-mail:
michelle.trowsdale@cancer.org.uk)
(Note: this is a workplace/research library not open to the public)

CANTERBURY CATHEDRAL

Cathedral Library and Archives, Canterbury Cathedral, The Precincts, Canterbury, Kent CTI 2EH
☎(01227) 865287
e-mail: library@canterbury-cathedral.org
url: www.canterbury-cathedral.org/library.html
Librarian Ms Karen Brayshaw BA(Hons) MA (e-mail:
brayshawk@canterbury-cathedral.org)

Specialism(s): Theology; Liturgy; Church history; Local (Kentish) history; Anti-slavery movement; Natural history

CENTRE FOR ECOLOGY & HYDROLOGY

Library & Archive Service, Centre for Ecology & Hydrology Edinburgh, Bush Estate, Penicuik, Midlothian EH26 0QB
☎0131 445 4343
Fax 0131 445 3943
e-mail: cehlib@ceh.ac.uk
url: www.ceh.ac.uk
(This library is unstaffed. Please contact for information)

Research station libraries
Library, Centre for Ecology & Hydrology Bangor, Environment Centre for Wales,
University of Wales, Deiniol Road, Bangor, Gwynedd
LL57 2UW
☎(01248) 370045
Fax (01248) 362133
(This library is unstaffed. Please contact for information)

Library, Centre for Ecology & Hydrology Lancaster, Lancaster Environment Centre, Library
Avenue, Bailrigg, Lancaster LA1 4AP
☎(01524) 595800
Head of CEH Library & Archive Service Steve Prince BSc DipLib MCLIP (e-mail:
sjpr@ceh.ac.uk)
CEH Library Manager Ms Pam Moorhouse (e-mail: pmo@ceh.ac.uk)
Librarian Ms Jeanette Coward (e-mail: jcowa@ceh.ac.uk)

Library, Centre for Ecology & Hydrology Wallingford, Maclean Building, Crowmarsh
Gifford, Wallingford, Oxon OX10 8BB
☎(01491) 838800
e-mail: wllibrary@ceh.ac.uk
Librarians Adrian Smith BSc AIMgt MCLIP, Ms Dee Galliford

Specialism(s): Environment (esp. terrestrial and freshwater sciences), Hydrology

CENTRE FOR POLICY ON AGEING

Reference Library, Centre for Policy on Ageing, 28 Great Tower Street, London EC3R 5AT
☎020 7553 6500
Fax 020 7553 6501
e-mail: informationservices@cpa.org.uk
url: www.cpa.org.uk
Director Ms Gillian Crosby (e-mail: gcrosby@cpa.org.uk)

CHARTERED INSTITUTE OF LIBRARY AND INFORMATION PROFESSIONALS (CILIP)

Member Services Team, Chartered Institute of Library and Information Professionals (CILIP), 7 Ridgmount Street, London WC1E 7AE
☎020 7255 0500
e-mail: memberservices@cilip.org.uk
url: www.cilip.org.uk
Development Officer (Member Support) Matthew Wheeler (e-mail: matthew.wheeler@cilip.org.uk)

THE CHARTERED INSTITUTE OF LOGISTICS AND TRANSPORT

Knowledge Centre, The Chartered Institute of Logistics and Transport, Earlstrees Court, Earlstrees Road, Corby, Northants NN17 4AX
☎(01536) 740113 (library), (01536) 740100 (reception)
Fax (01536) 740102 (FAO Knowledge Centre Manager)
url: www.ciltuk.org.uk
Knowledge Centre Manager Peter Huggins MA (e-mail: peter.huggins@ciltuk.org.uk)
Knowledge Centre and Webshop Senior Executive Ms Fiona Palmer (e-mail: fiona.palmer@ciltuk.org.uk)
(Access: free to Institute members and full-time students; a charge is made for non-member use.)

Specialism(s): Logistics; Supply-chain; Passenger transport

CHARTERED INSURANCE INSTITUTE

CII Knowledge Services, Chartered Insurance Institute, 20 Aldermanbury, London EC2V 7HY
☎020 7417 4415/4416
e-mail: knowledge@cii.co.uk
url: www.cii.co.uk/knowledge
Knowledge Services Team Leader Mrs Hannah Nilsumran BA(Hons) MA MSc

Specialism(s): Insurance, risk and related financial services

CHETHAM'S LIBRARY

Chetham's Library, Long Millgate, Manchester M3 1SB
☎0161 834 7961

Fax 0161 839 5797
e-mail: librarian@chethams.org.uk
url: www.chethams.org.uk
Chetham's Librarian Michael Powell BD PhD

Specialism(s): Rare books; Local history

CIVIL AVIATION AUTHORITY

Information Management Department, Civil Aviation Authority, Aviation House, Gatwick Airport South, West Sussex RH6 0YR
☎(01293) 573781
Fax (01293) 573181
e-mail: infoservices@caa.co.uk
url: www.caa.co.uk
Information Resources Manager Vagn Pedersen MA MCLIP (01293 573966)

Specialism(s): UK aviation and aviation safety

CMI, CHARTERED MANAGEMENT INSTITUTE

KnowledgeDirect, CMI, Chartered Management Institute, Management House, Cottingham Road, Corby, Northants NN17 1TT
☎(01536) 207434
Fax (01536) 401013
e-mail: enquiries@managers.org.uk
url: www.managers.org.uk
Information and Content Developer Ms Catherine Baker
(Information services, principally to Institute members)

Specialism(s): Management theory, practice and techniques

COLLEGE OF OCCUPATIONAL THERAPISTS

Library, College of Occupational Therapists, 106–114 Borough High Street, Southwark, London SE1 1LB
☎020 7450 2303/2320/2316
Fax 020 7450 2364
e-mail: library@cot.co.uk
url: www.cot.org.uk
Librarian Ms Anne Jenkins
Deputy Librarian Ms Lorna Rutherford BA(Hons) PGDip
Assistant Librarian Andy Hughes BA(Hons) MA

COMMONWEALTH SECRETARIAT

Library and Archives, Commonwealth Secretariat, Marlborough House, Pall Mall, London SW1Y 5HX
☎020 7747 6164
Fax 020 7747 6168
e-mail: library@commonwealth.int
url: www.thecommonwealth.org

Librarian Mrs Nsekanji Pelekamoyo BA BA(Hons) MBA (e-mail: n.pelekamoyo@commonwealth.int))

Specialism(s): The Commonwealth (Democracy; Economic Development; Governance; Small States; Social Development; Youth)

COMPETITION AND MARKETS AUTHORITY
(formerly Competition Commission)

Information Centre, Competition and Markets Authority, Victoria House, Southampton Row, London WCIB 4AD
☎020 3738 6261
e-mail: info@cma.gsi.gov.uk
url: www.gov.uk/cma
Information Centre Manager Miss L J Fisher MA MCLIP
Chief Media Relations Officer Rory Taylor
(Open to government libraries by appointment. Not open to the public)

CONSERVATIVE PARTY ARCHIVE

Conservative Party Archive, c/o Bodleian Library, Broad Street, Oxford OXI 3BG
☎(01865) 277181; (01865) 277046
e-mail: conservative.archives@bodleian.ox.ac.uk; modern.papers@bodleian.ox.ac.uk
url: www.bodleian.ox.ac.uk/cpa; www.cparchive.org.uk;
www.bodley.ox.ac.uk/dept/scwmss/cpa
Archivist Jeremy McIlwaine MArAd (01865 277181; e-mail:
jeremy.mcilwaine@bodleian.ox.ac.uk)
(Open to the public – subject to Bodleian access conditions)

COUNTRYSIDE COUNCIL FOR WALES (CYNGOR CEFN GWLAD CYMRU) see NATURAL RESOURCES WALES (CYFOETH NATURIOL CYMRU)

CPRE (CAMPAIGN TO PROTECT RURAL ENGLAND)

Library and Information Unit, CPRE (Campaign to Protect Rural England), 5–11 Lavington Street, London SEI 0NZ
☎020 7981 2800 (switchboard); 020 7981 2809 (direct)
Fax 020 7981 2899
url: www.cpre.org.uk
Library and Information Services Officer Oliver Hilliam BA (e-mail:
oliverh@cpre.org.uk)

Specialism(s): Planning; Environment; Transport

CROWN PROSECUTION SERVICE

Library Information Services, Crown Prosecution Service, Rose Court, 2 Southwark Bridge Road, London SE1 9HS
☎020 3357 0915 (direct)
e-mail: cps.libraryinformationservices@cps.gsi.gov.uk
url: www.cps.gov.uk
CPS Librarian Robert Brall BA DipLib MCLIP

CROWTHER CENTRE FOR MISSION EDUCATION

Library, Crowther Centre for Mission Education, Church Mission Society, Watlington Road, Cowley, Oxford OX4 6BZ
☎(01865) 787552
Fax (01865) 776375
url: www.cms-uk.org/heritage
Librarian Ken Osborne (e-mail: ken.osborne@cms-uk.org)

Specialism(s): History and theology of mission of the Anglican Church

DEPARTMENT FOR COMMUNITIES AND LOCAL GOVERNMENT (DCLG)

Knowledge and Information Access Team, Department for Communities and Local Government (DCLG), 2nd Floor NW, Fry Building, 2 Marsham Street, London SW1P 4DF
☎0303 444 2361
e-mail: contactus@communities.gov.uk
url: www.communities.gov.uk
Knowledge Management Policy, Library and Information Services Branch Head
Ms Maewyn Cumming

Specialism(s): Housing; Local Government; Planning

DEPARTMENT FOR CULTURE, MEDIA AND SPORT (DCMS)

Libraries Team, Department for Culture, Media and Sport (DCMS), 4th Floor, 100 Parliament Street, London SW1A 2BQ
☎020 7211 6000 (enquiries)
e-mail: enquiries@culture.gsi.gov.uk
url: www.culture.gov.uk
Head of Libraries Ms Keira Shaw (020 7211 6391; e-mail: keira.shaw@culture.gsi.gov.uk)
(There is no longer a library at DCMS, but the Library Policy Team deals with national library policy issues)

DEPARTMENT FOR EDUCATION (DFE)

Ministerial and Public Communications Division, Department for Education (DFE), Piccadilly Gate, Store Street, Manchester M1 2WD
☎0370 000 2288

e-mail: https://www.education.gov.uk/help/contactus
url: www.gov.uk/dfe

Specialism(s): Education theory and policy

DEPARTMENT FOR ENVIRONMENT, FOOD AND RURAL AFFAIRS (DEFRA)

Intelligence Hub, Department for Environment, Food and Rural Affairs (Defra), Area 4D, Nobel House, 17 Smith Square, London SW1P 3JR
☎020 7238 1523
e-mail: intelligencehub@defra.gsi.gov.uk
url: www.gov.uk/defra
Head of Knowledge and Intelligence Services Ms Katherine Woolf

Specialism(s): Environment; Farming; Food; Rural issues; Agriculture; Climate change and sustainable development

DEPARTMENT FOR INTERNATIONAL DEVELOPMENT (DFID)

eLibrary, Knowledge and Information Management Unit, Department for International Development (DFID), 22 Whitehall, London SW1A 2EG
☎020 7023 0000
Fax 020 7023 0012
url: https://www.gov.uk/government/organisations/department-for-international-development
Senior Knowledge and Information Manager Ms Sharon Skelton BA(Hons)
(Note: eLibrary services only; no visiting)

DEPARTMENT FOR REGIONAL DEVELOPMENT

Library, Department for Regional Development, Room G-40, Clarence Court, 10–18 Adelaide Street, Belfast BT2 8GB
☎028 9054 1045/6
Fax 028 9054 1081
e-mail: library@drdni.gov.uk
url: www.drdni.gov.uk
Librarian Ms Fiona Sawey BA(Hons)
Assistant Librarian Ms Gillian Potter MA(Hons) MA

DEPARTMENT FOR WORK AND PENSIONS (DWP)

Caxton House Library, Department for Work and Pensions (DWP), Ground Floor, Tothill Street, London SW1H 9NA
☎020 7449 5897
Fax 020 7449 7997
e-mail: library.services@dwp.gsi.gov.uk
url: www.dwp.gov.uk
Head of Library Profession Graham Monk BA(Hons) MCLIP
Deputy Head of Library Ms Melanie Harris BA(Hons) DipLib MCLIP

Library Manager Mrs Anoja Fernando BSc(Hons) MCLIP
Information Management and New Technologies Senior Librarian
Ms Helen Skelton BA(Hons)Lib MSc
Information Managers Ms Naomi Lees BA(Hons) MSc, Ms Helen Nolan BA(Hons) MSc MSc
Librarian Archivist Ms Angela Tailby BA(Hons)
Knowledge, Information and Records Management Librarian Ms Karen Gommersall
BA FCLIP
Central Analysis Division (CAD) Librarian Knowledge Management
Ms Andria Lannon BA(Hons) MA DipLib MCLIP

DEPARTMENT OF HEALTH (DH)

**Knowledge Centre, Department of Health (DH), Quarry House, Quarry Hill, Leeds
LS2 7UE**
☎0113 254 5080
Fax 0113 254 5084
e-mail: knowledgecentre-qh@dh.gsi.gov.uk
url: https://www.gov.uk/government/organisations/department-of-health
Senior Librarian (Customer Services) Mrs Natalie Gudgeon BSc(Hons)
Senior Librarian (Resource Development) Ms Sarah Long

Specialism(s): Public health, health services, health services policy and management,
medicine, hospitals, social care

DEPARTMENT OF JUSTICE NI

**Records and Information Management Branch, Department of Justice NI, Knockview
Buildings, Block 2, Stormont Estate, Belfast BT4 3SU**
☎(0)28 90 588617
Records and Information Management Team (e-mail: DOJFOI@dojni.x.gsi.gov.uk)

ENERGY INSTITUTE

**Energy Institute Knowledge Service (EIKS), Energy Institute, 61 New Cavendish Street,
London WIG 7AR**
☎020 7467 7114/5 (enquiries), 020 7467 7111 (administration)
Fax 020 7255 1472
e-mail: info@energyinst.org
url: www.energyinst.org
Knowledge and Information Manager Mrs Catherine M Cosgrove BSc(Hons) BA
MCLIP FEI
Librarian Chris L Baker BA(Hons) MEI

ENGLISH FOLK DANCE AND SONG SOCIETY

**Vaughan Williams Memorial Library, English Folk Dance and Song Society, Cecil Sharp
House, 2 Regent's Park Road, London NWI 7AY**
☎020 7485 2206 exts 229/233
e-mail: library@efdss.org
url: www.vwml.org

Library Director Malcolm Taylor BA(Lib) MCLIP OBE
Librarian Ms Laura Smyth BA(Hons) PGDip
Assistant Librarian Nicholas Wall MA
Archivist Ms Claire Norman BA(Hons) PGDip
Cataloguer Ms Elaine Bradtke PhD

Specialism(s): Traditional music and folk culture

ENGLISH HERITAGE

Library, English Heritage, The Engine House, Fire Fly Avenue, Swindon SN2 2EH
☎(01793) 414632
e-mail: library@english-heritage.org.uk
url: www.english-heritage.org.uk
Librarians Ms Nicola Cryer BA(Hons) MA (e-mail: nicola.cryer@english-heritage.org.uk),
Ms Diana Sims BSc(Hons) PGCE DipInfSc

Specialism(s): English archaeology and architecture

EQUALITY AND HUMAN RIGHTS COMMISSION (EHRC)

**Library and Information Services, Equality and Human Rights Commission (EHRC), 2nd
Floor, Arndale House, Arndale Centre, Manchester M4 3AQ**
☎0161 829 8308
Fax 0161 829 8110
url: www.equalityhumanrights.com
Library and Information Services Manager David Sparrow BA(Hons) MA MCLIP
(e-mail: david.sparrow@equalityhumanrights.com)

Specialism(s): Information relating to all equality strands: age, disability, gender, human rights, race, religion and belief, and sexual orientation. EHRC's mission is to reduce inequality, eliminate discrimination, strengthen good relations between people, and protect human rights.

FOOD STANDARDS AGENCY

**Information Management Services, Food Standards Agency, Aviation House, 125
Kingsway, London WC2B 6NH**
☎020 7276 8181
Fax 020 7276 8289
e-mail: infocentre@foodstandards.gsi.gov.uk
url: www.food.gov.uk
Chief Information Officer Ken Anderson (e-mail: ken.anderson@foodstandards.gsi.gov.uk)
(Public access by appointment only)

Specialism(s): Food safety; Food science and nutrition.

FORESTRY COMMISSION

**Library, Forestry Commission, Forest Research Station, Alice Holt Lodge, Wrecclesham,
Farnham, Surrey GU10 4LH**

☎(01420) 22255, (01420) 526216 (direct line)
Fax (01420) 23653
e-mail: library@forestry.gsi.gov.uk
url: www.forestry.gov.uk; www.forestry.gov.uk/forestresearch
Librarian Mrs Kirsten Hutchison MA DipEd MSc(Lib&InfStud) (e-mail: kirsten.hutchison@forestry.gsi.gov.uk)

Specialism(s): Forestry; Arboriculture; Plant sciences; Ecology

FRANCIS SKARYNA BELARUSIAN LIBRARY AND MUSEUM

Francis Skaryna Belarusian Library and Museum, 37 Holden Road, London NI2 8HS
☎020 8445 5358
Fax 020 8445 5358
e-mail: library@skaryna.org.uk
url: www.skaryna.org.uk
Librarian Mgr Alexander Nadson

Specialism(s): Books, periodicals and archives relating to Belarus

FRESHWATER BIOLOGICAL ASSOCIATION

Library, Freshwater Biological Association, The Ferry Landing, Far Sawrey, Ambleside, Cumbria LA22 0LP
☎(01539) 442468
Fax (01539) 446914
e-mail: lis@fba.org.uk
url: www.fba.org.uk
Collections Manager Ms Tamsin Vicary MA (e-mail: tvicary@fba.org.uk)

Specialism(s): Freshwater biology; Water chemistry; Algology; Ichthyology

GEOLOGICAL SOCIETY OF LONDON

Library, Geological Society of London, Burlington House, Piccadilly, London WIJ 0BG
☎020 7432 0999
Fax 020 7439 3470
e-mail: library@geolsoc.org.uk
url: www.geolsoc.org.uk/library
Library and Information Services Manager Ms Fabienne Michaud (e-mail: fabienne.michaud@geolsoc.org.uk)

GERMAN HISTORICAL INSTITUTE LONDON

Library, German Historical Institute London, 17 Bloomsbury Square, London WCIA 2NJ
☎020 7309 2050 (enquiries)
e-mail: library@ghil.ac.uk
url: www.ghil.ac.uk
Head Librarian Dr Christiane Swinbank
Librarians Ms J Gambus, Ms A-M Klauk, Ms J Schumann

GLADSTONE'S LIBRARY (formerly St Deiniol's Residential Library)

Gladstone's Library, Church Lane, Hawarden, Flintshire CH5 3DF
☎(01244) 532350
Fax (01244) 520643
e-mail: enquiries@gladlib.org.uk
url: www.gladstoneslibrary.org
Director of Research and Collections Dr Louisa Yates (e-mail: louisa.yates@gladlib.org)
Library Assistant Gary Butler (e-mail: library@gladlib.org)
(Modern residential accommodation is available at modest charges. Day readers welcome.
Testimonial required.)

Specialism(s): This is a residential library specializing in theology, history and Victorian
studies. The collection of over 250,000 volumes includes W E Gladstone's personal library.

GOETHE-INSTITUT LONDON

Library, Goethe-Institut London, 50 Princes Gate, Exhibition Road, London SW7 2PH
☎020 7596 4020
e-mail: library@london.goethe.org
url: www.goethe.de/london
Head of Information Services and Translation Programme Jens Boyer (e-mail:
boyer@london.goethe.org)

Specialism(s): Contemporary German culture, literature and language

GREATER LONDON AUTHORITY

**Information Services, Greater London Authority, City Hall, The Queen's Walk, London
SE1 2AA**
☎020 7983 4000 (GLA switchboard)
Fax 020 7983 4674
e-mail: glaenquiries@idoxgroup.com
Information Services Manager Ms Alexia Pipe

GUILDFORD INSTITUTE

Library, Guildford Institute, Ward Street, Guildford, Surrey GU1 4LH
☎(01483) 562142
Fax (01483) 451034
e-mail: library@guildford-institute.org.uk
url: www.guildford-institute.org.uk
Librarian Ms Pamela Keen
(Lending service to members. Research enquiries welcomed)

Specialism(s): General collection of literature, humanities and science work dating from late
Victorian period to present; Local history collections of Surrey and Guildford.

HEALTH AND SAFETY EXECUTIVE

**Information Management Unit, Health and Safety Executive, I.G. Redgrave Court,
Merton Road, Bootle, Merseyside L20 7HS**

☎0151 951 4382
Fax 0151 951 3674
url: www.hse.gov.uk
Head of Information Management Unit and Security Mrs June Rafferty
Head of Information Services Ms Sue King BA(Hons) MCLIP FRSA (e-mail:
sue.king@hse.gsi.gov.uk)

Knowledge Centre
Health and Safety Executive, Knowledge Centre, 1.G. Redgrave Court, Merton Road,
Bootle, Merseyside L20 7HS
☎0151 951 4382
Fax 0151 951 3674
Site Manager Ms Sue Cornmell BA(Hons) PGDipLib LLB(Hons) MCLIP

(General requests for information on health and safety at work to the HSE Infoline Tel:
0845 345 0055; Minicom: 0845 408 9577. Written enquiries to HSE Infoline, Caerphilly
Business Park, Caerphilly CF83 3GG; e-mail: hse.infoline@connaught.plc.uk; Fax: 0845 408
9566)

HEALTH MANAGEMENT LIBRARY AND INFORMATION SERVICE

**Health Management Library and Information Service, NHS Scotland, Scottish Health
Service Centre, Crewe Road South, Edinburgh EH4 2LF**
☎0131 275 7760
e-mail: nss.hmilibrary@nhs.net
url: www.healthmanagementonline.co.uk
Library Services Manager Mrs Gill Earl BA(Hons) MCLIP
Librarian Mrs Alison Bogle MA DipLib MCLIP

Specialism(s): Health care management

HEALTH PROTECTION AGENCY see PUBLIC HEALTH ENGLAND

HEREFORD CATHEDRAL

Library & Archives, The Cathedral, Hereford HR1 2NG
☎(01432) 374225/6
Fax (01432) 374220
e-mail: library@herefordcathedral.org
url: www.herefordcathedral.org
Canon Chancellor Revd Canon Chris Pullin
Librarian Dr Rosemary Firman PhD MA BMus (e-mail:
rosemary.firman@herefordcathedral.org)
Archivist Mrs Rosalind Caird
(Open to the public)

HIGH COMMISSION OF INDIA

Library, High Commission of India, India House, Aldwych, London WC2B 4NA
☎020 7632 3142
Fax 020 7632 3172
e-mail: att.pni@hcilondon.in
url: www.hcilondon.in
Librarian Lakshmana Sudhakar Nivas
Hon Librarian Miss M S Travis
(Staff library only. Collection is for reference only; no interlibrary lending; visiting at the discretion of Head of Press and Information Department)

HIGHGATE LITERARY AND SCIENTIFIC INSTITUTION

Library, Highgate Literary and Scientific Institution, II South Grove, Highgate, London N6 6BS
☎020 8340 3343
e-mail: librarian@hlsi.net
url: www.hlsi.net
Librarian Ms Margaret Mackay DipLib BEd(Hons) MCLIP
(Public access allowed for reference)

Specialism(s): Biography; Fiction; London/local history; Samuel Taylor Coleridge; John Betjeman

HM TREASURY AND CABINET OFFICE

Research Library Service, HM Treasury and Cabinet Office, I Horse Guards Road, London SWIA 2HQ
☎020 7270 5290 (enquiries)
e-mail: research.library@hm-treasury.gsi.gov.uk
url: https://www.gov.uk/government/organisations/hm-treasury
Research Advisor Ms Emma Wallis (e-mail: emma.wallis@hmtreasury.gsi.gov.uk)
(Note: not open to the public. For all general enquiries contact the Correspondence and Enquiries Unit on: public.enquiries@hm-treasury.gov.uk)

Specialism(s): Economics and finance; Public administration; Parliamentary material

HMS SULTAN

Library, HMS Sultan, Military Road, Gosport, Hants POI2 3BY
☎023 9254 2678
e-mail: Sultan-librarian@fleetfost.mod.uk
url: www.royalnavy.mod.uk
Sultan Librarian Nigel Sturt BA(Hons) MCLIP
(Visits by arrangement)

Specialism(s): Mechanical, electrical, marine and aeronautical engineering; Naval science, technology and history

HOME OFFICE

Information Services Centre, Home Office, Lower Ground Floor, Seacole Building, 2 Marsham Street, London SWIP 4DF
☎020 7035 6699
Fax 0870 336 9266
e-mail: informationservicescentre@homeoffice.gsi.gov.uk
url: www.homeoffice.gov.uk
Information Team Manager Mrs Susan Payne
Information and Library Manager (Provision) Andrew Glancy
Information and Library Manager (Resources) Ms Karen Richardson BA(Hons)

HOUSE OF COMMONS

Department of Information Services, House of Commons, Information Office, London SWIA 0AA
☎020 7219 4272
e-mail: hcinfo@parliament.uk
url: www.parliament.uk
Librarian of the House of Commons Vacant
Head of the Information Office Matthew Ringer (e-mail: ringerm@parliament.uk)
(There are specialist sections which deal with enquiries from Members of Parliament only. Outside enquirers should approach the Department's public interface, the House of Commons Information Office (contact details as above)

HOUSE OF LORDS

Library, House of Lords, London SWIA 0PW
☎020 7219 5242 (enquiries), 020 7219 3240 (administration)
e-mail: hllibrary@parliament.uk
url: www.parliament.uk/lords
Director of Information Services and Librarian Dr Elizabeth Hallam Smith PhD FSA FRSA FRHistS
Director of Library Services Alex Brocklehurst

HULTON/ARCHIVE – GETTY IMAGES

Hulton/Archive – Getty Images, Unique House, 21–31 Woodfield Road, London W9 2BA
☎0020 7579 5700 (Reception)
e-mail: archiveresearch@gettyimages.com
url: www.gettyimages.co.uk
Archive Research Manager Ms Caroline Theakstone (020 7604 8607)

Specialism(s): Social history; Personalities; Entertainment; Sport; War; Royalty; Events up to 1980s

IMPERIAL WAR MUSEUM

Department of Collections Access, Imperial War Museum, Lambeth Road, London SEI 6HZ
☎020 7416 5342
e-mail: collections@iwm.org.uk

url: http://collections.iwm.org.uk
Head of Collections Access Fergus Read MA PGCE AMA (e-mail: fread@iwm.org.uk)
(Services: Research Room (appointment required) Mon–Fri 10–5; telephone enquiry service Mon–Fri. Please note: In addition to our Research Room, we now also offer gallery visitors the Explore History Centre where, without an appointment, visitors can make reference enquiries, ask about family history research and browse digitized sound, image and archival collections. Explore History is open seven days a week)

Specialism(s): Conflicts since 1914 involving Great Britain and Commonwealth countries – military, civilian and social historical aspects. NB Research Room access now includes IWM Sound Archive listening facilities

INSTITUT FRANÇAIS D'ÉCOSSE (FRENCH INSTITUTE)

Library, Institut français d'Écosse (French Institute), 13 Randolph Crescent, Edinburgh EH3 7TT
☎0131 225 5366
Fax 0131 220 0648
e-mail: library@ifecosse.org.uk
url: www.ifecosse.org.uk
Librarian Mrs Catherine Guiat

Specialism(s): French language and culture

INSTITUT FRANÇAIS DU ROYAUME-UNI

La Médiathèque, Institut français du Royaume-Uni, 17 Queensberry Place, London SW7 2DT
☎020 7871 3545
Fax 020 7871 3519
e-mail: library@institutfrancais.org.uk
url: www.institut-francais.org.uk
Director Ms Ophélie Ramonatxo
Deputy Director and Head of Adult Library Christopher Bonilla de la Plata

Children's Library, Institut français du Royaume-Uni, 32 Harrington Road, London SW7 2DT
☎020 7871 3550
Head of Children's Library Ms Aude Larribau

Specialism(s): Multimedia library on contemporary France (books, audio-books, press-cuttings, DVD, magazines). Free French Archives; CampusFrance: information desk for Studies in France. Children's section. Interlibrary loans. Contributes to joint catalogue COPAC. Culturethèque: digital platform: e-books and documentaries online.

INSTITUTE AND FACULTY OF ACTUARIES

(formerly Institute of Actuaries)

Library, Institute and Faculty of Actuaries, Level 2, Exchange Crescent, 7 Conference Square, Edinburgh EH3 8RA
☎0131 240 1311

Fax 0131 240 1313
e-mail: libraries@actuaries.org.uk
url: www.actuaries.org.uk
Librarian David Hood BA MSc MCLIP

Library, Institute and Faculty of Actuaries, 7th Floor, Holborn Gate, London WC1V 7PP
☎020 7632 2114
Fax 020 7632 2121
e-mail: libraries@actuaries.org.uk
url: www.actuaries.org.uk
Librarian David Raymont BA DipLIS DipRSA

Specialism(s): Actuarial science; Pensions; Insurance; Finance and investment; Demography; Risk management; Resource and environment

INSTITUTE FOR ANIMAL HEALTH see THE PIRBRIGHT INSTITUTE

INSTITUTE OF CHARTERED ACCOUNTANTS IN ENGLAND AND WALES

Library and Information Service, Institute of Chartered Accountants in England and Wales, Chartered Accountants' Hall, Moorgate Place, London EC2R 6EA
☎020 7920 8620
Fax 020 7920 8621
e-mail: library@icaew.com
url: www.icaew.com/library
Head of Advisory and Information Services Mrs Anna Burmajster MA MCLIP (e-mail: anna.burmajster@icaew.com)
Manager, Outreach and Engagement Ms Rowena Mann (e-mail: rowena.mann@icaew.com)
(The Library is located in the Business Centre within Chartered Accountants' Hall and is for members of the ICAEW and ICAEW-registered students; ACT and IFA members and non-members by arrangement and paying a daily or weekly fee for access. E-mail: businesscentre.reception@icaew.com)

Specialism(s): Accountancy; Auditing; Taxation; Law; Company information; Finance; Management; IT

INSTITUTE OF CHARTERED SECRETARIES AND ADMINISTRATORS

Information Centre, Institute of Chartered Secretaries and Administrators, Saffron House, 6–10 Kirby Street, London EC1N 8TS
☎020 7580 4741*
e-mail: info@icsa.co.uk
url: www.icsa.org.uk
Policy Manager Ms Sheila Doyle
(*Technical enquiries should be sent by e-mail)

Specialism(s): Company law; Corporate governance; Company secretarial practice; Charity law

INSTITUTE OF CLINICAL RESEARCH

Resource Centre, Institute of Clinical Research, 10 Cedar Court, Grove Park, White Waltham Road, Maidenhead, Berks SL6 3LW
☎(01628) 501700
Fax (01628) 501709
e-mail: info@icr-global.org
url: www.icr-global.org
Head of Media Andrew Smith (01628 536975; e-mail: asmith@icr-global.org)
(Note: Members only professional library; not open to the public)

Specialism(s): Specialist subjects relate to nature of clinical research; Regulations; Ethical issues, the clinical trial process and the personal development of professionals involved in clinical research; Course materials, job descriptions and resource lists

INSTITUTE OF DIRECTORS

Business Library, Institute of Directors, 116 Pall Mall, London SW1Y 5ED
☎020 7451 3100
Fax 020 7321 0145
e-mail: businessinfo@iod.com
url: www.iod.com/ias
Head of Information and Advisory Services Miss S Watts MSc

Specialism(s): Corporate governance; Directorship; Boardroom practice

INSTITUTE OF MATERIALS, MINERALS AND MINING

David West Library, Institute of Materials, Minerals and Mining, 1 Carlton House Terrace, London SW1Y 5DB
☎020 7451 7300 (switchboard)
Fax 020 7451 7405
url: www.iom3.org
Information and Library Co-ordinator Ms Hilda Kaune BA(Hons) DipLib (020 7451 7360 (direct); e-mail: hilda.kaune@iom3.org)
Information Officer Mrs Frances Perry BA (020 7451 7324 (direct); e-mail: frances.perry@iom3.org)

Specialism(s): Materials; Metals; Polymers; Ceramics; Composites; Packaging; Clay; Minerals and Mining; Materials Science; Wood

INSTITUTE OF OCCUPATIONAL MEDICINE

Library, Institute of Occupational Medicine, Research Avenue North, Riccarton, Edinburgh EH14 4AP
☎0131 449 8000
Fax 0131 449 8084

e-mail: info@iom-world.org
url: www.iom-world.org
Information Scientist Ken Dixon MA(Hons) MA MCLIP (0131 449 8017; e-mail: ken.dixon@iom-world.org)

Specialism(s): Occupational medicine and environmental issues

INSTITUTE OF PSYCHOANALYSIS

Library, Institute of Psychoanalysis, II2A Shirland Road, Maida Vale, London W9 2BT
☎020 7563 5008
Fax 020 7563 5001
e-mail: library@iopa.org.uk
url: www.psychoanalysis.org.uk
Head Librarian (Mr) Saven Morris

INSTITUTION OF CIVIL ENGINEERS

Library, Institution of Civil Engineers, One Great George Street, Westminster, London SWIP 3AA
☎020 7665 2251
Fax 020 7976 7610
e-mail: library@ice.org.uk
url: www.ice.org.uk
Library Manager Ms Rose Marney MCLIP (e-mail: rose.marney@ice.org.uk)

THE INSTITUTION OF ENGINEERING AND TECHNOLOGY

Library, The Institution of Engineering and Technology, I Birdcage Walk, London SWIH 9JJ
☎020 7344 5461 (general library enquiries)
e-mail: libdesk@theiet.org
url: www.theiet.org
Library and Archives Manager Ms Anne Locker (e-mail: alocker@theiet.org)
(Temporary address. IET will move back to 2 Savoy Place, London WC2R 0BL in late 2015)

Archives Centre, The Institution of Engineering and Technology, Savoy Hill House, 7–10 Savoy Hill, London WC2R 0BU
☎020 7344 8407
e-mail: archives@theiet.org

Specialism(s): Electrical, electronic, control and manufacturing engineering; Telecommunications, computing and information technology

INSTITUTION OF MECHANICAL ENGINEERS

Information and Library Service, Institution of Mechanical Engineers, I Birdcage Walk, London SWIH 9JJ
☎020 7973 1274
Fax 020 7222 8762

e-mail: library@imeche.org
url: www.imeche.org.uk/library
Head of Library Service Ms Sarah Rogers MA MCLIP
Information Officers Adrian Clement MA MCLIP, Ms Laura Beduz MA
Archivists Ms Karyn Stuckey MA, Ms Sarah Broadhust MA

INSTITUTION OF OCCUPATIONAL SAFETY AND HEALTH

Technical Enquiry and Information Service, The Institution of Occupational Safety and Health, The Grange, Highfield Drive, Wigston, Leicester LE18 1NN
☎0116 257 3100
Fax 0116 257 3101
e-mail: reception@iosh.co.uk
url: www.iosh.co.uk
Technical Information Service Co-ordinator Miss Anne Wells (e-mail: anne.wells@iosh.co.uk)

INSTITUTO CERVANTES

Library, Instituto Cervantes, 102 Eaton Square, London SW1W 9AN
☎020 7235 0353
e-mail: biblon1@cervantes.es
url: www.cervantes.es; http://londres.cervantes.es
Head Librarian Ms Mayte Azorin

Site library

Jorge Edwards Library, Instituto Cervantes, 326–330 Deansgate, Campfield Avenue Arcade, Manchester M3 4FN
☎0161 661 4201 (direct)
Fax 0161 661 4203
e-mail: bibman@cervantes.es
url: http://manchester.cervantes.es
Librarian Francisco Duch Martínez
A further site library (located in Dublin) can be found in the Academic, National and Special Libraries in the Republic of Ireland section.

Specialism(s): Spanish culture, history, literature, language and teaching.

THE INTERNATIONAL INSTITUTE FOR STRATEGIC STUDIES (IISS)

Library and Information Department, The International Institute for Strategic Studies (IISS), Arundel House, 13–15 Arundel Street, London WC2R 3DX
☎020 7395 9122 (library enquiries), 020 7379 7676 (main switchboard)
Fax 020 7836 3108
e-mail: library@iiss.org
url: www.iiss.org/en/library
Chief Librarian Mrs Ellena Jamie MA(Oxon) MSc

Deputy Librarian Ms Catherine Micklethwaite BSc(Econ) MA
Assistant Librarian Mrs Hilary Morris BA MCLIP

Specialism(s): International relations; War studies

INTERNATIONAL MARITIME ORGANIZATION

Maritime Knowledge Centre, International Maritime Organization, 4 Albert Embankment, London SE1 7SR
☎020 7587 3164
e-mail: maritimeknowledgecentre@imo.org
url: www.imo.org
Head, Maritime Knowledge Centre Ms Sharon Lynn Grant

Specialism(s): Official IMO documentation, IMO conventions and instruments, maritime safety, maritime security, maritime law, marine environment, human element & seafarers rights, prevention of marine pollution by ships, liability and compensation for damage caused by ships

ISLE OF MAN FAMILY HISTORY SOCIETY

Library, Isle of Man Family History Society, Derby Lodge, Derby Road, Peel, Isle of Man IM5 1HH
☎(01624) 843105
e-mail: iomfhs@manx.net
url: www.isle-of-man.com/community/geneaology/iomfhs
Librarian Mrs Doreen Quayle
(Open Wednesdays and Saturdays, 2–5pm)

ISLE OF MAN PARLIAMENT/LEGISLATURE OF THE ISLE OF MAN

Tynwald Library, Isle of Man Parliament/Legislature of the Isle of Man, Legislative Buildings, Douglas, Isle of Man IM1 3PW
☎(01624) 685520
Fax (01624) 685522
e-mail: library@tynwald.org.im
url: www.tynwald.org.im
Head of Service Ms Joann Corkish

Specialism(s): Manx Parliamentary and Isle of Man Government publications and Isle of Man laws

ITALIAN CULTURAL INSTITUTE (ISTITUTO ITALIANO DI CULTURA)

Eugenio Montale Library, Italian Cultural Institute (Istituto Italiano di Cultura), 39 Belgrave Square, London SW1X 8NX
☎020 7235 1461 (switchboard), 020 7235 1461 ext 203, 020 7396 4425 (library direct line)
Fax 020 7235 4618

e-mail: library.icilondon@esteri.it
url: www.icilondon.esteri.it
Librarian in charge Ms Maria Riccobono Reidy
(The Library is open for reference to the general public: Monday to Thursday 12.30pm to
7.30pm (excluding public holidays). Friday, Saturday and Sunday the Library is closed.)
Please check website for updated information about changes in opening times during
Summer term, Easter and Christmas period and for a list of public holidays)

Specialism(s): Italian culture and language; Literature and visual arts; Collection of DVDs on
Italian cinema

JOINT SERVICES COMMAND AND STAFF COLLEGE

**Library, Joint Services Command and Staff College, Faringdon Road, Watchfield,
Swindon SN6 8LA**
☎(01793) 788236
Fax (01793) 788281
e-mail: library.jscsc@defenceacademy.mod.uk
Head of Library Services C M Hobson MCLIP MBE

Specialism(s): Defence studies; International affairs; Military history

THE KENNEL CLUB

Library & Art Gallery, The Kennel Club, 1–5 Clarges Street, London W1J 8AB
☎020 7518 1009
Fax 020 7518 1045
e-mail: library@thekennelclub.org.uk
url: www.thekennelclub.org.uk/library
Library and Collections Manager Ms Ciara Farrell BA HDipLIS
(Open Mondays to Fridays, 9.30 am–4.30 pm by appointment)

Specialism(s): Canine literature, registrations and show catalogues, canine art

THE KING'S FUND

**Information and Knowledge Services, The King's Fund, 11–13 Cavendish Square, London
W1G 0AN**
☎020 7307 2568
e-mail: library@kingsfund.org.uk
url: www.kingsfund.org.uk/library
Head of Information Services Ms Deena Maggs (e-mail: d.maggs@kingsfund.org.uk)

Specialism(s): Health and social care policy/management

LABOUR PARTY

Communications Unit, Labour Party, One Brewer's Green, London SW1H 0RH
☎0845 092 2299
url: www.labour.org.uk/contact

Communications Unit Manager London Jim Harvey

Specialism(s): Labour Party and Government policy

LAMBETH PALACE LIBRARY

Lambeth Palace Library, Lambeth Palace Road, London SEI 7JU
☎020 7898 1400
e-mail: archives@churchofengland.org
url: www.lambethpalacelibrary.org
Director of Libraries and Archives Declan Kelly MSc MCLIP (e-mail:
declan.kelly@churchofengland.org)
Librarian and Archivist Giles Mandelbrote MA FSA (e-mail:
giles.mandelbrote@churchofengland.org)

Related libraries

Church of England Record Centre, Lambeth Palace Library, 15 Galleywall Road,
Bermondsey, London SE16 3PB
☎020 7898 1030
e-mail: archives@churchofengland.org
(Reading room access via Lambeth Palace Library.)*Specialism(s)*: Archives of the central
organization of the Church of England, in particular the Church Commissioners; The
Archbishops' Council; the General Synod.

Church Care Library, Lambeth Palace Library, Church House, Great Smith Street, London
SWIP 3AZ
☎020 7898 1884
e-mail: churchcare@churchofengland.org

Specialism(s): Ecclesiastical architecture and archaeology; Church fittings and furnishings;
Stained glass, organs, bells, monuments

THE LAW SOCIETY

Library, The Law Society, II3 Chancery Lane, London WC2A IPL
☎020 7320 5946
Fax 020 7831 1687
e-mail: library@lawsociety.org.uk; document delivery service: lawdocs@lawsociety.org.uk
url: www.lawsociety.org.uk/library
Online catalogue: www.lawsociety.org.uk/libraryonline
Librarian and Head of Information Services Chris Holland BA MCLIP

Specialism(s): Law; Parliamentary material; Historical legal material

THE LIBRARY AND MUSEUM OF FREEMASONRY

**The Library and Museum of Freemasonry, Freemasons' Hall, Great Queen Street,
London WC2B 5AZ**
☎020 7395 9257
Fax 020 7404 7418
e-mail: libmus@freemasonry.london.museum
url: www.freemasonry.london.museum

Director Ms Diane Clements
Librarian Martin Cherry
Curator Mark Dennis
Archivist Ms Susan Snell

LIBRARY FOR IRANIAN STUDIES

Library for Iranian Studies, The Woodlands Hall, Crown Street, London W3 8SA
☎020 8993 6384
Fax 020 8752 1300
e-mail: info@iranianlibrary.org.uk
url: www.iranianlibrary.org.uk
Head of Library Dr Mashaallah Ajoudani

LINCOLN CATHEDRAL

Library, Lincoln Cathedral, Minster Yard, Lincoln LN2 1PX
☎(01522) 561640
Fax (01522) 561641
e-mail: librarian@lincolncathedral.com
url: www.lincolncathedral.com
Librarian Mrs Julie Taylor (e-mail: librarian@lincolncathedral.com)

LINEN HALL LIBRARY

The Linen Hall Library, 17 Donegall Square North, Belfast BT1 5GB
☎028 9032 1707
Fax 028 9043 8586
e-mail: info@linenhall.com
url: www.linenhall.com
Librarian John Killen MA MLS

Specialism(s): Irish history and culture

LINNEAN SOCIETY OF LONDON

Library, Linnean Society of London, Burlington House, Piccadilly, London W1J 0BF
☎020 7434 4479
Fax 020 7287 9364
e-mail: library@linnean.org
url: www.linnean.org
Librarian and Linnaeus Link Co-ordinator Mrs Lynda Brooks BA DipLib MCLIP FLS
(e-mail: lynda@linnean.org)
Deputy Librarian Ms Elaine Charwat MA MSc (e-mail: elainec@linnean.org)

Specialism(s): Natural history; Taxonomy; Evolutionary ecology; History of natural history; Conservation and environment

LITERARY AND PHILOSOPHICAL SOCIETY OF NEWCASTLE UPON TYNE

The Lit and Phil Library, Literary and Philosophical Society of Newcastle upon Tyne, 23 Westgate Road, Newcastle upon Tyne NEI ISE
☎0191 232 0192
Fax 0191 261 4494
e-mail: library@litandphil.org.uk
url: www.litandphil.org.uk
Librarian Ms Kay Easson MA DipLib MCLIP

Specialism(s): Humanities

LONDON CHAMBER OF COMMERCE AND INDUSTRY

Information Centre, London Chamber of Commerce and Industry, 33 Queen Street, London EC4R IAP
☎020 7203 1866 (direct)
Fax 020 7203 1812
url: www.londonchamber.co.uk
Business Information Executive Ms Alexa Michael MA (e-mail: amichael@londonchamber.co.uk)
(Note: this is a member only service)

Specialism(s): General business information

LONDON LIBRARY

London Library, 14 St James's Square, London SWIY 4LG
☎020 7930 7705
Fax 020 7766 4766
e-mail: membership@londonlibrary.co.uk
url: www.londonlibrary.co.uk
Librarian Miss Inez T P A Lynn BA MLitt MCLIP
Deputy Librarian Ms Mary Gillies BA MA PGDip

Specialism(s): History; Literature; The arts; Related subjects in major European languages

LONDON METROPOLITAN ARCHIVES

Library, London Metropolitan Archives, 40 Northampton Road, London ECIR OHB
☎020 7332 3820
Fax 020 7833 9136
e-mail: ask.lma@cityoflondon.gov.uk
url: www.cityoflondon.gov.uk
Principal Archivist – Public Services Ms Elizabeth Scudder

Specialism(s): London (local government history; social history)

LONDON TRANSPORT MUSEUM

Information Desk and Library, London Transport Museum, 39 Wellington Street, Covent Garden, London WC2E 7BB
☎020 7565 7280
Fax 020 7565 7252
e-mail: enquiry@ltmuseum.co.uk
url: www.ltmuseum.co.uk
Information Services Manager Ms Caroline Warhurst BA MCLIP
Ms Helen Grove MA
(Visitors by appointment. Opening hours: Wed and Thurs 10am–5pm; Fri 11am–5pm)

Specialism(s): History and development of London's transport past, present and future; information about Transport for London, London Transport and predecessor companies; special emphasis on the development of art, architecture and design in London Transport

MACMILLAN CANCER SUPPORT

Corporate Library, Macmillan Cancer Support, Intelligence and Research, 89 Albert Embankment, London SE1 7UQ
☎020 7840 7830
e-mail: library@macmillan.org.uk
url: www.macmillan.org.uk
Library and Information Specialist (Corporate Library) Chris Wilson (e-mail: cwilson@macmillan.orguk)

MANX NATIONAL HERITAGE

National Library and Archives, Manx National Heritage, Manx Museum, Douglas, Isle of Man IM1 3LY
☎(01624) 648000; (01624) 648040
e-mail: library@mnh.gov.im
url: www.manxnationalheritage.im/what-we-do/our-collections/library-archives/
Library and Archive Services Officer Paul Weatherall BSc MA PGCE MCLIP (e-mail: paul.weatherall.gov.im)
Librarian Alan G Franklin MA MCLIP (e-mail: alan.franklin@mnh.gov.im)
Archivist Ms Wendy Thirkettle BA DipAS (e-mail: wendy.thirkettle@mnh.gov.im)

Specialism(s): History and development of the Isle of Man; Combined local studies, Archive and diocesan record office and place of deposit for public records

MARINE BIOLOGICAL ASSOCIATION

National Marine Biological Library, Marine Biological Association, Citadel Hill, Plymouth PL1 2PB
☎(01752) 633266
Fax (01752) 633102
e-mail: nmbl@mba.ac.uk
url: www.mba.ac.uk/nmbl/
Head of Library and Information Services Miss Linda Noble BSc MCLIP (01752 633270; e-mail: lno@mba.ac.uk)

Specialism(s): Marine sciences including marine biology, pollution, oceanography and chemistry, fisheries; dating back to 19th century

MARX MEMORIAL LIBRARY

Marx Memorial Library, 37A Clerkenwell Green, London ECIR 0DU
☎020 7253 1485
e-mail: info@marxlibrary.org.uk
url: www.marx-memorial-library.org
Administrator Dr Laura Miller

MARYLEBONE CRICKET CLUB

MCC Library, Marylebone Cricket Club, Lord's Ground, St John's Wood, London NW8 8QN
☎020 7616 8657
Fax 020 7616 8659
e-mail: mcclibrary@mcc.org.uk
url: www.lords.org/history/mcc-library
Curator Adam Chadwick (020 7616 8655)
Research Officer Neil Robinson (020 7616 8559)

MATERIALS PROCESSING INSTITUTE

(formerly part of Tata Steel)

Knowledge and Library Services, Teesside Technology Centre, PO Box II, Eston Road, Grangetown, Middlesbrough, Cleveland TS6 6US
☎(01642) 382000
Fax (01642) 460321
Manager, Customised Information Services Ms Carol Patton

Specialism(s): Steel engineering and manufacturing

MEDICAL RESEARCH COUNCIL (MRC)

Medical Research Council (MRC), Head Office Swindon, Polaris House, North Star Avenue, Swindon SN2 IFL
☎(01793) 416200
url: www.mrc.ac.uk

Medical Research Council (MRC), Head Office London, 14th Floor, One Kemble Street, London WC2B 4AN
☎01793 416200
url: www.mrc.ac.uk
Knowledge & Information Management Team Contact Ms Claire Barnes
Chief Press Officer Ms Carmel Turner (020 7395 2273; e-mail: carmel.turner@headoffice.mrc.ac.uk)

MET OFFICE

National Meterological Library, Met Office, FitzRoy Road, Exeter, Devon EXI 3PB

☎(01392) 884841 (enquiries)
e-mail: metlib@metoffice.gov.uk
url: www.metoffice.gov.uk
Library and Archive Manager Ms Sarah Pankiewicz
(Open to the public)

National Meteorological Archive, Met Office, Great Moor House, Bittern Road, Sowton, Exeter, Devon EX2 7NL
☎(01392) 360987
e-mail: metlib@metoffice.gov.uk
url: www.metoffice.gov.uk
Archivist Dr Catherine Ross
(Open to the public by appointment)

MINISTRY OF DEFENCE

DBS Knowledge and Information, Whitehall Library, Ministry of Defence, Ground Floor, Zone D, Main Building, Whitehall, London SW1A 2HB
☎020 7218 4445 (general enquiries)
e-mail: dbski-libraryoffice@mod.uk
url: www.mod.uk
DBS KI-Library Resources Manager Ms Bozena Adamiec (020 7218 0139; e-mail: DBSKI-LibraryResMgr@mod.uk)

MINISTRY OF JUSTICE

Library, Ministry of Justice, 102 Petty France, London SW1H 9AJ
☎020 3334 3000
Fax 020 3334 4198
e-mail: moj.library@justice.gsi.gov.uk
url: www.justice.gov.uk
Librarian Miss Kathy Turner BSc MSc MCLIP

MORRAB LIBRARY

Morrab Library, Morrab Gardens, Penzance, Cornwall TR18 4DA
☎(01736) 364474
e-mail: morrablibrary@hotmail.co.uk
url: www.morrablibrary.org.uk
Librarian Mrs Annabelle Read
(Available on payment of an annual subscription or a daily fee)

Specialism(s): Cornish literature and history; Napoleonic collection

MUSEUM OF LONDON

Library, Museum of London, London Wall, London EC2Y 5HN
☎020 7001 9844
Fax 020 7600 1058
e-mail: library@museumoflondon.org.uk
url: www.museumoflondon.org.uk

Librarian Ms Sally Brooks MA MCLIP
(Readers by appointment only)

NATIONAL AEROSPACE LIBRARY

National Aerospace Library, The Hub, Fowler Avenue, Farnborough Business Park, Farnborough, Hants GU14 7JP
☎(01252) 701060
e-mail: hublibrary@aerosociety.com
url: www.aerosociety.com/nal
Chief Librarian Brian Riddle (01252 701060; e-mail: brian.riddle@aerosociety.com)
(Incorporating the Royal Aeronautical Society Library formerly located in London)

Specialism(s): Extensive collection of material relating to the development and recent technical advances in aeronautics, aviation and aerospace technology. Includes collections of the Royal Aeronautical Society. A guide to some of the key collections held at the National Aerospace Library is available as a series of pdfs that are available via the following website: www.aerosociety.com/About-Us/nal/speccollections. The National Aerospace Library is a free-to-access public reference library which is open Tuesday-Friday 10am-4pm.

THE NATIONAL ARCHIVES

Library, The National Archives, Kew, Richmond, Surrey TW9 4DU
☎020 8876 3444
e-mail: library@nationalarchives.gov.uk
url: www.nationalarchives.gov.uk
Chief Executive Jeff James
Director of Public Services and HR Ms Caroline Ottaway-Searle
Interim Head of Advice and Records Knowledge Lee Oliver
Head of Library and Deployment Services Ms Helen Pye-Smith MA (020 8392 5278; e-mail: helen.pye-smith@nationalarchives.gsi.gov.uk)

NATIONAL ARMY MUSEUM

(Closed for redevelopment until late 2016. For access to library and archive collections, please e-mail tsc@nam.ac.uk)

Templer Study Centre, National Army Museum, Royal Hospital Road, London SW3 4HT
☎020 7730 0717
Fax 020 7823 6573
e-mail: tsc@nam.ac.uk
url: www.nam.ac.uk
Collections Access and Outreach Manager Michael Ball MA AMA
Templer Study Centre Manager Ms Kate Swann MA

Specialism(s): Military history; British army; Indian and Commonwealth armies

NATIONAL ART LIBRARY

Word and Image Department, National Art Library, Victoria and Albert Museum, Cromwell Road, South Kensington, London SW7 2RL

☎020 7942 2400 (enquiries)
e-mail: nal.enquiries@vam.ac.uk
url: www.vam.ac.uk/nal
Head of Information Services Martin Flynn

Site library
Archive of Art and Design, National Art Library, Blythe House, 23 Blythe Road, West
Kensington, London W14 0QF
☎020 7603 1514
e-mail: archive@vam.ac.uk
Archivist Christopher Marsden

NATIONAL ASSEMBLY FOR WALES

Library, National Assembly for Wales, Cardiff Bay, Cardiff CF99 INA
☎029 2089 8629
url: www.assemblywales.org
Head of Library Mrs Stephanie Wilson (e-mail: stephanie.wilson@wales.gov.uk)

Specialism(s): Information resources to support the work of Assembly Members, also the
Research Service, which provides expert and impartial research to support Assembly
Members and Committees in fulfilling the scrutiny, legislative and representative functions
of the National Assembly for Wales

NATIONAL CHILDREN'S BUREAU

Information Centre, National Children's Bureau, 8 Wakley Street, London EC1V 7QE
☎020 7843 6000
e-mail: library@ncb.org.uk
url: www.ncb.org.uk
Information Centre Manager Ms Anna Kassman-McKerrell (020 7843 6303; e-mail:
akassman-mckerrell@ncb.org.uk)
(Ring for appointment to visit)

NATIONAL COAL MINING MUSEUM FOR ENGLAND

**Library, National Coal Mining Museum for England, Caphouse Colliery, New Road,
Overton, West Yorks WF4 4RH**
☎(01924) 848806
Fax (01924) 840694
e-mail: info@ncm.org.uk
url: www.ncm.org.uk
Librarians Mrs Anisha Christison BSc(Hons) MSc MCLIP (e-mail:
curatorial.librarian@ncm.org.uk), Mrs Jill Clapham BA(Hons) PGDipLib (e-mail:
curatorial.librarian@ncm.org.uk) (job share)

NATIONAL GALLERY

Research Centre, The National Gallery, Trafalgar Square, London WC2N 5DN

☎020 7747 2542
Fax 020 7747 2892
e-mail: research.centre@ng-london.org.uk
url: www.nationalgallery.org.uk
Research Centre Manager Alan Crookham (020 7747 2831;
e-mail: alan.crookham@ng-london.org.uk)
(Readers by appointment only)

Specialism(s): Western European painting 1200–1900

NATIONAL INSTITUTE FOR HEALTH AND CLINICAL EXCELLENCE (NICE)

Information Services, National Institute for Health and Clinical Excellence (NICE), Clinical, Public Health and Social Care, 10 Spring Gardens, London SW1A 2BU
☎0300 003 7780
Fax 0300 003 7785
e-mail: nice@nice.org.uk
url: www.nice.org.uk
Associate Director for Information Services Dr Sarah Cumbers (e-mail:
sarah.cumbers@nice.org.uk)

Specialism(s): Evidence-based healthcare; Health technology evaluation; Clinical guidelines;
Evidence-based public health

NATIONAL INSTITUTE OF ECONOMIC AND SOCIAL RESEARCH

Library, National Institute of Economic and Social Research, 2 Dean Trench Street, Smith Square, London SW1P 3HE
☎020 7222 7665
Fax 020 7654 1900
e-mail: library@niesr.ac.uk
url: www.niesr.ac.uk
Librarian Ms Sarah Stevens (020 7654 1907; e-mail: s.stevens@niesr.ac.uk)

NATIONAL LIBRARY OF SCOTLAND

National Library of Scotland, George IV Bridge, Edinburgh EH1 1EW
☎0131 623 3700
Fax 0131 623 3701
e-mail: enquiries@nls.uk
url: www.nls.uk
Chief Executive Officer and National Librarian Dr John Scally BA(Hons) PhD DipILS
(e-mail: john.scally@ed.ac.uk)

Branch/regional libraries
Map Collections Reading Room, National Library of Scotland, 33 Salisbury Place, Edinburgh
EH9 1SL
☎0131 623 3970

Fax 0131 623 3971
e-mail: maps@nls.uk

Reading Rooms and Reference Services, Exhibitions and Events, National Library of Scotland, George IV Bridge, Edinburgh EH1 1EW
☎0131 623 3907/3908
Fax 0131 623 3830
e-mail: enquiries@nls.uk

Scottish Screen Archive, National Library of Scotland, 39–41 Montrose Avenue, Hillington Park, Glasgow G52 4LA
☎(0845) 366 4600
Fax (0845) 366 4601
e-mail: ssaenquiries@nls.uk

Specialism(s): Scottish history and culture

NATIONAL LIBRARY OF WALES: LLYFRGELL GENEDLAETHOL CYMRU

National Library of Wales: Llyfrgell Genedlaethol Cymru, Aberystwyth, Ceredigion SY23 3BU
☎(01970) 632800
Fax (01970) 615709
e-mail: holi@llgc.org.uk
url: www.llgc.org.uk
Chief Executive and Librarian Dr Aled Gruffydd Jones MA PhD FRHistS FLSW

Specialism(s): Legal deposit library housing books, MSS, maps, photographs, paintings, audiovisual and electronic materials; important digitization and exhibitions programmes

NATIONAL MARITIME MUSEUM see ROYAL MUSEUMS GREENWICH

NATIONAL MEDIA MUSEUM

Royal Photographic Society Collection, National Media Museum, Pictureville, Bradford BD1 1NQ
☎0844 856 3797
e-mail: research@nationalmediamuseum.org.uk
url: www.nationalmediamuseum.org.uk
Curator of Photographs Greg Hobson (01274 203324; e-mail: greg.hobson@nationalmediamuseum.org.uk)
Associate Curator Brian Liddy (01274 203376; e-mail: brian.liddy@nationalmediamuseum.org.uk)
(Prior appointment essential for members and non-members)

Science and Society Picture Library, SCMG Enterprises Ltd, Science Museum Group, Exhibition Road, South Kensington, London SW7 2DD
☎020 7942 4400

Fax 020 7942 4401
e-mail: piclib@nmsi.ac.uk
url: www.scienceandsociety.co.uk
(Holds the National Collections of Photography (including the Royal Photographic Society Collection), as well as Cinematography and Television)

Specialism(s): The science, technology and art of the still and moving image and its impact on our lives

NATIONAL MUSEUM OF SCOTLAND

(formerly known as National Museums Scotland)

Library, National Museum of Scotland, Chambers Street, Edinburgh EHI IJF
☎0131 247 4137 (enquiries)
Fax 0131 220 4819
e-mail: library@nms.ac.uk
url: www.nms.ac.uk
Head of Information Services Ms Evelyn Simpson (e-mail: e.simpson@nms.ac.uk)

Branch library

Library, National War Museum of Scotland, The Castle, Edinburgh EH1 2NG
☎0131 247 4137

Specialism(s): Decorative arts; Archaeology; Ethnography; History of science and technology; Natural sciences; Museology; Military history

NATIONAL PHYSICAL LABORATORY

Library, National Physical Laboratory, Hampton Road, Teddington, Middlesex TWII 0LW
☎020 8943 6417
Fax 020 8614 0424
e-mail: library@npl.co.uk
url: www.npl.co.uk
Information Service Manager Ian O'Leary MA DLIS (020 8943 6809; e-mail: ian.o-leary@npl.co.uk)

Specialism(s): Physics; Material science; Mathematics; Metrology

NATIONAL POLICE LIBRARY

(formerly National Policing Improvement Agency)

National Police Library, College of Policing, Bramshill, Hook, Hants RG27 0JW
☎(01256) 602650 (enquiries), (01256) 602100 (main switchboard)
Fax (01256) 602285
e-mail: library@college.pnn.police.uk
url: www.college.police.uk/library
Librarian Ms Patricia Hughes BA(Hons) MCLIP (e-mail: patricia.hughes@college.pnn.police.uk)

NATIONAL PORTRAIT GALLERY

Heinz Archive and Library, National Portrait Gallery, 39–40 Orange Street, London WC2H 7HS
☎020 7321 6617
Fax 020 7306 0056 (FAO Heinz Archive & Library)
e-mail: archive@npg.org.uk
url: www.npg.org.uk/research/archive
Head of Archive and Library Robin K Francis BSc(Hons) MA MCLIP
Librarian Joseph Ripp BA MSLS
(Readers by appointment only)

Specialism(s): British portraiture

NATIONAL RAILWAY MUSEUM

Search Engine, National Railway Museum, Leeman Road, York YO26 4XJ
☎(08448) 153139 (all enquiries)
e-mail: search.engine@nrm.org.uk
url: www.nrm.org.uk
Librarian Ms Karen Baker BA MA MCLIP (01904 685745; e-mail: karen.baker@nrm.org.uk)
(National Railway Museum is part of the Science Museum Group)

NATIONAL STEM CENTRE

National STEM Centre, University of York, Heslington, York, North Yorks YO10 5DD
☎(01904) 328314
Fax (01904) 328328
url: www.nationalstemcentre.org.uk
Resources Co-ordinator Andrew Jones (e-mail: a.jones@nationalstemcentre.org)

Specialism(s): A national collection and archive of Science, Maths, Technology and Engineering (STEM) education resources, including full-text digital resources

NATURAL ENGLAND

Information and Library Services, Natural England, Suite D, Unex House, Bourges Boulevard, Peterborough PE1 1NG
☎0845 600 3078 (switchboard)
e-mail: library@naturalengland.org.uk
url: www.naturalengland.org.uk
Senior Adviser Ms Anne Beach (e-mail: anne.beach@naturalengland.org.uk)

Specialism(s): Sustainable use and management of the natural environment: biodiversity; wildlife; landscapes; access and recreation; conservation of marine and coastal environments

NATURAL HISTORY MUSEUM

Library, Natural History Museum, Cromwell Road, London SW7 5BD
☎020 7942 5460 (enquiries)

Fax 020 7942 5559
e-mail: library@nhm.ac.uk
url: www.nhm.ac.uk/library
Head of Library and Archives Ms Jane Smith (e-mail: jane.smith@nhm.ac.uk)
(The Library holds one of the world's leading collections of literature and art on natural
history, including comprehensive holdings in taxonomy and systematics. International in
coverage, the physical and digital collections provide a unique resource for scientific, arts
humanities and social science researchers.)

Site library

Ornithology and Rothschild Library, Natural History Museum, Natural History Museum
Tring, Akeman Street, Tring, Herts HP23 6AP
☎020 7942 5460
Fax 020 7942 6150
e-mail: ornlib@nhm.ac.uk
url: www.nhm.ac.uk/tring

NATURAL RESOURCES WALES (CYFOETH NATURIOL CYMRU)

(formerly Countryside Council for Wales (Cyngor Cefn Gwlad Cymru)

**Llyfrgell Library, Natural Resources Wales (Cyfoeth Naturiol Cymru), Maes y Ffynnon,
Penrhosgarnedd, Bangor, Gwynedd LL57 2DW**
☎(01248) 385522
Fax (01248) 385510
e-mail: library@cyfoethnaturiolcymru.gov.uk
url: www.nrw.gov.uk
Records and Information Services Team Leader Ms Dwynwen Lloyd BA MCLIP

NETWORK RAIL INFRASTRUCTURE LTD

**Knowledge Centre, Network Rail Infrastructure Ltd, The Quadrant:MK, Elder Gate,
Milton Keynes MK9 IEN**
☎(01908) 782777
url: www.networkrail.co.uk
Librarian Neil Dixon (e-mail: neil.dixon@networkrail.co.uk)
(Not open to the public but queries welcomed from professional organizations and
researchers.)

Specialism(s): UK railway history, legislation, engineering, health and safety

NHS HEALTH SCOTLAND

**Knowledge Services, NHS Health Scotland, Gyle Square, I South Gyle Crescent,
Edinburgh EHI2 9EB**
☎0141 414 2762
e-mail: nhs.healthscotland-knowledge@nhs.net
url: www.healthscotland.com/knowledge
Knowledge Services Manager Ms Julia Green BA DipLib MSc

Librarian Ms Julie Arnot

Specialism(s): Public health; Health inequalities; Health improvement

NHS NATIONAL SERVICES SCOTLAND

Information Services Division, NHS National Services Scotland, Area l43e, Gyle Square, I South Gyle Crescent, Edinburgh EHI2 9EB
☎0131 275 6423
e-mail: NSS.isdlibrary@nhs.net
url: www.isdscotland.org
Manager, ISD Library Services Alan Jamieson MA DipLib (e-mail: alan.jamieson@nhs.net)

Specialism(s): Health statistics; Official circulars; Media monitoring

NORTHERN IRELAND ASSEMBLY

Library, Northern Ireland Assembly, Parliament Buildings, Balymiscaw, Stormont, Belfast BT4 3XX
☎028 9052 1250
Fax 028 9052 1922
e-mail: library@niassembly.gov.uk
url: www.niassembly.gov.uk
Enquiry Services Librarian Seán McGeown (e-mail: sean.mcgeown@niassembly.gov.uk)

Specialism(s): Legislation and official publications relating especially to N Ireland, government, politics and Irish history

NORTHERN IRELAND OFFICE

Library, Northern Ireland Office, I Horse Guards Road, London SWIA 2HQ
☎020 7210 0253
Fax 020 7210 0212
url: www.nio.gov.uk
Records Officer Ms Claire O'Neill (e-mail: claire.o'neill@nio.x.gsi.gov.uk)

OFFICE FOR NATIONAL STATISTICS

Library and Information Service, Office for National Statistics, Room I.063, Government Buildings, Cardiff Road, Newport, Gwent NPI0 8XG
☎(01633) 456582
e-mail: kim.team@ons.gsi.gov.uk
url: www.ons.gov.uk
Knowledge and Information Manager Ms Catty Bennett BA MA (01633 456582; e-mail: catty.bennett@ons.gsi.gov.uk)
(The library is open to the public by appointment only)

OFFICE OF RAIL REGULATION

Information Centre, Office of Rail Regulation, I Kemble Street, London WC2B 4AN
☎020 7282 2001

Fax 020 7282 2040
e-mail: info.centre@orr.gsi.gov.uk
url: http://orr.gov.uk
Information Manager Ms Sue MacSwan BA MSc

OFFICE OF THE PARLIAMENTARY AND HEALTH SERVICE OMBUDSMAN (OFFICE OF THE PARLIAMENTARY COMMISSIONER FOR ADMINISTRATION AND HEALTH SERVICE COMMISSIONER FOR ENGLAND)

Learning and Resource Centre, Office of the Parliamentary and Health Service Ombudsman (Office of the Parliamentary Commissioner for Administration and Health Service Commissioner for England), 15th Floor, Millbank Tower, Millbank, London SW1P 4QP
☎0300 061 4104
e-mail: lrc@ombudsman.org.uk
url: www.ombudsman.org.uk
Librarian Ms Deanne Mitchell BA DipLib MCLIP

Specialism(s): Ombudsman issues; Maladministration

OFGEM (OFFICE OF GAS AND ELECTRICITY MARKETS)

Research and Information Centre, OFGEM (Office of Gas and Electricity Markets), 9 Millbank, London SW1P 3GE
☎020 7901 7003
Fax 020 7901 7378
e-mail: library@ofgem.gov.uk
url: www.ofgem.gov.uk
Librarian Keith Smith
Assistant Librarian Ms Victoria Leadbetter

OMNIBUS SOCIETY

The John F Parke Memorial Library, The Omnibus Society, 100 Sandwell Street, Walsall, West Midlands WS1 3EB
☎(01922) 629358
e-mail: libadmin@omnibus-society.org
url: www.omnibus-society.org
Librarian Alan Mills (01922 631867; e-mail: alanavrilmills@hotmail.com)
(Manned by volunteers, the Library is currently open to casual callers on Wednesdays (09.15–16.00), although other appointments can be made by prior arrangement.)

Specialism(s): Road passenger transport; Unique collection of timetables, book stock and photographs

PIRA INTERNATIONAL see SMITHERS PIRA

THE PIRBRIGHT INSTITUTE

(formerly Institute for Animal Health)

Library, The Pirbright Institute, Ash Road, Woking, Surrey GU24 0NF
☎(01483) 232441
e-mail: pirbright.library@pirbright.ac.uk
url: www.pirbright.ac.uk
Librarian Mrs Liz Pritchard (e-mail: elizabeth.pritchard@pirbright.ac.uk)

PLUNKETT FOUNDATION

Library, Plunkett Foundation, The Quadrangle, Woodstock, Oxon OX20 ILH
☎(01993) 810730
e-mail: info@plunkett.co.uk
url: www.plunkett.co.uk
Head of Information and Communications Mike Perry

Specialism(s): Focus on history and practice of co-operatives and rural enterprise; Agriculture

PLYMOUTH PROPRIETARY LIBRARY

Plymouth Proprietary Library, Alton Terrace, III North Hill, Plymouth PL4 8JY
☎(01752) 660515
Librarians Ms Chloe Adams, John Horton

Specialism(s): 19th- and early 20th-century classical fiction (available to members only)

POETRY LIBRARY

Saison Poetry Library, Level 5, Royal Festival Hall, South Bank Centre, London SE1 8XX
☎020 7921 0943/0664
e-mail: info@poetrylibrary.org.uk
url: www.poetrylibrary.org.uk; www.poetrymagazines.org.uk
Poetry Librarian Chris McCabe BA(Hons) PGDip MA

POLISH LIBRARY

Polish Library, 238–246 King Street, London W6 0RF
☎020 8741 0474
e-mail: library@polishlibrary.co.uk; ccl@polishlibrary.co.uk
url: www.posk.org
Library Director Mrs Dobroslawa Platt

PORTICO LIBRARY

The Portico Library, 57 Mosley Street, Manchester M2 3HY
☎0161 236 6785
url: www.theportico.org.uk
Librarian Miss Emma Marigliano BA(Hons) (e-mail: librarian@theportico.org.uk)

(Tours by arrangement. Nineteenth-century stock available for scholarly research and for members. Exhibitions and events, reflective of a late Georgian polite society, open to the public.)

PUBLIC HEALTH ENGLAND

(formerly the Health Protection Agency)

Knowledge and Library Services, Public Health England, 5th Floor, Wellington House, 133–155 Waterloo Road, London SE1 8UG
☎020 3682 0086
e-mail: libraries@phe.gov.uk
url: www.phe.gov.uk
Head of Knowledge and Library Services Ms Anne Brice (e-mail: anne.brice@phe.gov.uk)
Knowledge and Library Services Manager Ms Sarah Brittan (e-mail: sarah.brittan@phe.gov.uk)
Senior Knowledge and Evidence Manager Ms Heather Lodge (e-mail: heather.lodge@phe.gov.uk)

Library, Public Health England, Colindale Library, 61 Colindale Avenue, London NW9 5EQ
☎020 8327 7616 (enquiries)
e-mail: libraries@phe.org.uk
url: www.phe.org.uk

Library, Public Health England, Porton Down, Salisbury, Wilts SP4 0JG
☎(01980) 612450
e-mail: libraries@phe.org.uk
url: www.phe.org.uk

Library, Public Health England, Chilton, Didcot, Oxon OX11 0RQ
☎(01235) 825404
e-mail: libraries@phe.org.uk
url: www.phe.org.uk

RELIGIOUS SOCIETY OF FRIENDS IN BRITAIN (QUAKERS)

Library, Religious Society of Friends in Britain (Quakers), Friends House, 173–177 Euston Road, London NW1 2BJ
☎020 7663 1135
e-mail: library@quaker.org.uk
url: www.quaker.org.uk/library
Head of Library and Archives David Blake

Specialism(s): Quakerism (17th century to the present); Peace and pacifism; Anti-slavery; Prison reform and penal affairs; Humanitarian assistance; Temperance

RESEARCH COUNCILS UK

Strategy Unit, Research Councils UK, Polaris House, North Star Avenue, Swindon, Wilts SN2 1ET

☎(01793) 444000
url: www.rcuk.ac.uk

Arts and Humanities Research Council (AHRC), Research Councils UK, Polaris House, North Star Avenue, Swindon, Wilts SN2 1FL
☎(01793) 444000
e-mail: enquiries@ahrc.ac.uk
Head of Information Service Patrick Ffinch (01793 416017; e-mail: p.ffinch@ahrc.ac.uk)

Biotechnology and Biological Sciences Research Council (BBSRC), Research Councils UK, Polaris House, North Star Avenue, Swindon, Wilts SN2 1UH
☎(01793) 413200
url: www.bbsrc.ac.uk

Economic and Social Research Council (ESRC), Research Councils UK, Polaris House, North Star Avenue, Swindon, Wilts SN2 1UJ
☎(01793) 413000
url: www.esrc.ac.uk

Engineering and Physical Sciences Research Council (EPSRC), Research Councils UK, Polaris House, North Star Avenue, Swindon, Wilts SN2 1ET
☎(01793) 444000
url: www.epsrc.ac.uk

Natural Environment Research Council (NERC), Research Councils UK, Polaris House, North Star Avenue, Swindon, Wilts SN2 1EU
☎(01793) 411500
url: www.nerc.ac.uk

RNIB NATIONAL LIBRARY SERVICE

RNIB National Library Service, Bakewell Road, Orton Southgate, Peterborough PE2 6WS
☎0303 123 9999
e-mail: helpline@rnib.org.uk
url: www.rnib.org.uk/reading
Reading Services Senior Manager James Moscicki
Manager Vacant
(RNIB National Library Service offers a comprehensive range of books and accessible information for adults and children with sight loss. Books are posted free of charge using the Articles for the Blind service.)

Specialism(s): Talking Books: the UK's largest collection (20,000) titles of unabridged audio books, both fiction and non-fiction; Braille and Moon books: books in giant print (24pt type); Braille Music Library: 14,000 Braille music scores (the largest collection outside the USA) plus books about music and music theory and audio tutorials on CD; Online catalogues, e-mail discussion group and web message boards for book lovers; reader magazines and help with choosing books; RNIB Research Library: the most comprehensive UK collection of print material relating to sight loss (tel: 020 7391 2052)

RNID see ACTION ON HEARING LOSS LIBRARY

ROTHAMSTED RESEARCH

Rothamsted Library, Rothamsted Research, Harpenden, Herts AL5 2JQ
☎(01582) 763133
Fax (01582) 760981
e-mail: res.library@rothamsted.ac.uk
url: www.rothamsted.ac.uk/library-and-information-services
Librarian Mrs S E Allsopp BA DipLib (e-mail: liz.allsopp@rothamsted.ac.uk)

Specialism(s): Arable crops research; Sustainable land development

ROYAL ACADEMY OF ARTS

Library, Royal Academy of Arts, Burlington House, Piccadilly, London W1J 0BD
☎020 7300 5737 (enquiries), 020 7300 5740 (administration)
Fax 020 7300 5765
e-mail: library@royalacademy.org.uk
url: www.royalacademy.org.uk
Head of Library Services Adam Waterton (e-mail:
adam.waterton@royalacademy.org.uk)
Assistant Librarians Ms Miranda Stead BA(Hons) LipLIS, Ms Linda Macpherson

Specialism(s): British art and artists from 18th century to present; History of the Academy since 1768

ROYAL AIR FORCE COLLEGE

College Library, Royal Air Force College, Cranwell, Sleaford, Lincs NG34 8HB
☎(01400) 266219
Fax (01400) 262532
e-mail: chom.library@btconnect.com
College Librarian Miss Andrea Sevier BA(Hons) MCLIP (01400 266602; e-mail:
rn-spt-collegelibrarian@mod.uk)

ROYAL AIR FORCE MUSEUM

Royal Air Force Museum, Grahame Park Way, Hendon, London NW9 5LL
☎020 8205 2266 ext 4873, 020 8358 4873
Fax 020 8200 1751
e-mail: research@rafmuseum.org
url: www.rafmuseum.org
Head of Archives P J V Elliott MA BSc MCLIP RMARA
(Prior appointment necessary)

Specialism(s): Military aviation

ROYAL ASTRONOMICAL SOCIETY

Library, Royal Astronomical Society, Burlington House, Piccadilly, London W1J 0BQ
☎020 7734 3307/4582
Fax 020 7494 0166
e-mail: librarian@ras.org.uk

url: www.ras.org.uk; www.sciencephotolibrary.com
Librarian Ms Siân Prosser (e-mail: sp@ras.org.uk)
(Enquiries in writing or by e-mail preferred, access by appointment)

Specialism(s): Extensive archive and rare book collection covering astronomy and geophysics

ROYAL AUTOMOBILE CLUB

Library, Royal Automobile Club, 89 Pall Mall, London SW1Y 5HS
☎020 7747 3398
Fax 0870 460 6285
e-mail: library@royalautomobileclub.co.uk
url: www.royalautomobileclub.co.uk
Club Librarian Trevor G Dunmore BA(Hons) DipLib

Specialism(s): History of motoring and motor sport

ROYAL BOTANIC GARDEN EDINBURGH

Library & Archives, Royal Botanic Garden Edinburgh, 20a Inverleith Row, Edinburgh EH3 5LR
☎0131 248 2853 (enquiries), 0131 248 2850 (administration)
Fax 0131 248 2901
e-mail: library@rbge.ac.uk
url: www.rbge.org.uk/science/library-and-archives
Head of Library Ms Lorna Mitchell BSc DipLib MCLIP (e-mail: l.mitchell@rbge.ac.uk)

Specialism(s): Botany; Horticulture; Garden history and botanical art

ROYAL BOTANIC GARDENS, KEW

Library, Art & Archives, Royal Botanic Gardens, Kew, Richmond, Surrey TW9 3AE
☎020 8332 5414
Fax 020 8332 5430
e-mail: library@kew.org
url: www.kew.org
Head of Library, Art and Archives Christopher Mills BA MA DipLib MCLIP FLS
(020 8332 5412; e-mail: c.mills@kew.org.uk)

ROYAL COLLEGE OF PHYSICIANS AND SURGEONS OF GLASGOW

Library, Royal College of Physicians and Surgeons of Glasgow, 232–242 St Vincent Street, Glasgow G2 5RJ
☎0141 227 3241 (enquiries), 0141 221 6072 (administration)
Fax 0141 221 1804
e-mail: library@rcpsg.ac.uk
url: www.rcpsg.ac.uk
Library and Heritage Manager Mrs Carol Parry BA(Hons) MA DAA (e-mail: carol.parry@rcpsg.ac.uk)

Modern Resources Officer Ms Clare Harrison BA MSc (e-mail:
claire.harrison@rcpsg.ac.uk)
Information Officer Andrew McAinsh BA(Hons) MSc (e-mail:
andrew.mcainsh@rcpsg.ac.uk)

Specialism(s): History of medicine, modern library resources

ROYAL COLLEGE OF PHYSICIANS OF EDINBURGH

Sibbald Library, Royal College of Physicians of Edinburgh, 9 Queen Street, Edinburgh EH2 IJQ
☎0131 225 7324
Fax 0131 220 3939
e-mail: library@rcpe.ac.uk
url: www.rcpe.ac.uk
Sibbald Librarian Iain A Milne MLib MCLIP

ROYAL COLLEGE OF PHYSICIANS OF LONDON

Library, Royal College of Physicians of London, II St Andrews Place, Regent's Park, London NWI 4LE
☎020 3075 1539
Fax 020 7486 3729
e-mail: enquiries@rcplondon.ac.uk
url: www.rcplondon.ac.uk
Minicom 020 7486 5687
Head of Library, Archive and Museum Services Mrs Julie Beckwith BA MSc MCLIP
(e-mail: julie.beckwith@rcplondon.ac.uk)
Library Manager Ms Karen Reid BSc MSc (e-mail: karen.reid@rcplondon.ac.uk)

Jerwood Medical Education Resource Centre, Royal College of Physicians of London, Peto Place, Rear of St Andrews Place, London NWI 4LE
☎020 3075 1490
e-mail: merc@rcplondon.ac.uk

Specialism(s): UK health policy; Public health; History of medicine; Medical biography; separately managed Jerwood Medical Education Resource Centre

ROYAL COLLEGE OF PSYCHIATRISTS

Library and Information Service, Royal College of Psychiatrists, 21 Prescot Street, London EI 8BB
☎020 7235 2351 ext 2520
Fax 020 3701 2661
e-mail: infoservices@rcpsych.ac.uk
url: www.rcpsych.ac.uk
Library and Information Manager Ms Beverley Berry

Specialism(s): Antiquarian psychiatry textbooks dating from 15th century

ROYAL COLLEGE OF SURGEONS OF ENGLAND

Library and Lumley Study Centre, Royal College of Surgeons of England, 35–43 Lincoln's Inn Fields, London WC2A 3PE
☎020 7869 6555/6556 (enquiries), 020 7405 3474 (College switchboard)
e-mail: library@rcseng.ac.uk; archives@rcseng.ac.uk
url: www.rcseng.ac.uk
Director of Library and Surgical Information Services Mrs Thalia Knight MA MA MCLIP (e-mail: tknight@rcseng.ac.uk)
Head of Library and Surgical Information Services Tom Bishop BA(Hons) MA (e-mail: tbishop@rcseng.ac.uk)

ROYAL COLLEGE OF VETERINARY SURGEONS

RCVS Knowledge Library, Royal College of Veterinary Surgeons, Belgravia House, 62–64 Horseferry Road, London SWIP 2AF
☎020 7202 0752
Fax 020 7202 0751
e-mail: library@rcvsknowledge.org
url: www.rcvsknowledge.org
Head of Library and Information Service Ms Clare Boulton

ROYAL COMMISSION ON THE ANCIENT AND HISTORICAL MONUMENTS OF WALES

Library and Enquiries Service, Royal Commission on the Ancient and Historical Monuments of Wales, Crown Building, Plas Crug, Aberystwyth, Ceredigion SY23 INJ
☎(01970) 621200
Fax (01970) 627701
e-mail: nmr.wales@rcahmw.gov.uk
url: www.rcahmw.gov.uk
Secretary Ms Hilary Malaws
Information Services Manager Ms Penny Icke

Specialism(s): Archaeology; Architectural history and heritage of Wales

ROYAL COURTS OF JUSTICE

Library, Royal Courts of Justice, Ministry of Justice, Strand, London WC2A 2LL
☎020 7947 7671
Fax 020 7947 6661
e-mail: rcj.library@justice.gsi.gov.uk
url: www.justice.gov.uk
Librarian Ms Stephanie Curran BA GradDipLibStudies MIT (e-mail: stephanie.curran@justice.gsi.gov.uk)
(Note: not open to the public)

ROYAL ENGINEERS MUSEUM, ARCHIVES AND LIBRARY

Royal Engineers Museum, Archives and Library, Brompton Barracks, Chatham, Kent ME4 4UG
☎(01634) 822221
url: www.re-museum.co.uk
Deputy Curator (Collections Management) Ms Danielle Sellers (e-mail: DocsOfficer@rhqre.co.uk)

ROYAL ENTOMOLOGICAL SOCIETY

Library, Royal Entomological Society, The Mansion House, Chiswell Green Lane, St Albans, Herts AL2 3NS
☎(01727) 899387
Fax (01727) 894797
e-mail: lib@royensoc.co.uk
url: www.royensoc.co.uk
Librarian Mrs Val McAtear BA(Hons)Lib
(The library is open by appointment only)

ROYAL GEOGRAPHICAL SOCIETY (with the INSTITUTE OF BRITISH GEOGRAPHERS)

Foyle Reading Room, Royal Geographical Society (with the Institute of British Geographers), 1 Kensington Gore, London SW7 2AR
☎020 7591 3044
Fax 020 7591 3001
e-mail: enquiries@rgs.org
url: www.rgs.org
Principal Librarian Eugene Rae MA DipLIS
Deputy Librarian Miss Janet Turner BA(Hons)
Map Librarian David McNeill BA

Specialism(s): Geography; Travel; Exploration

ROYAL HORTICULTURAL SOCIETY

Lindley Library London, Royal Horticultural Society, 80 Vincent Square, London SWIP 2PE
☎020 7821 3083
e-mail: library.london@rhs.org.uk
url: www.rhs.org.uk/education-learning/libraries-at-rhs
Head of Libraries and Exhibitions Ms Fiona Davison

ROYAL INSTITUTE OF BRITISH ARCHITECTS

British Architectural Library, Royal Institute of British Architects, 66 Portland Place, London WIB IAD
☎020 7580 5533 (switchboard); Public information line: 020 7307 3882

e-mail: info@riba.org
url: www.architecture.com
Director Ms Wendy Fish BA DipLib

Branch library
British Architectural Library Drawings and Archives Collection, Royal Institute of British Architects, Henry Cole Wing, Victoria and Albert Museum, Exhibition Road, London SW7 2RL
☎020 7307 3708 (Study Room)
e-mail: drawings&archives@riba.org
Chief Curator and H J Heinz Curator of Drawings Charles Hind
(Study room by appointment only)

ROYAL INSTITUTE OF INTERNATIONAL AFFAIRS

Library, Royal Institute of International Affairs, Chatham House, 10 St James's Square, London SW1Y 4LE
☎020 7957 5723 (enquiries)
Fax 020 7957 5710
e-mail: library@chathamhouse.org
url: www.chathamhouse.org
Librarian David Bates (020 7314 3610; e-mail: dbates@chathamhouse.org)

Specialism(s): International affairs; Politics; Economics; Security; Environment

ROYAL INSTITUTE OF NAVIGATION

The Cundall Library, Royal Institute of Navigation, 1 Kensington Gore, London SW7 2AT
☎020 7591 3134
Fax 020 7591 3131
url: www.rin.org.uk
Librarian Tony Fyler (020 7591 3133)
(The library is free to members and open to the public on an appointment-only basis.)

Specialism(s): Land, sea and air navigation

ROYAL INSTITUTION OF CHARTERED SURVEYORS

Library and Information Services, Royal Institution of Chartered Surveyors, Parliament Square, London SW1P 3AD
☎0870 333 1600 ext 3714; 020 7334 3714
e-mail: library@rics.org
url: www.rics.org
Head of Reference Services Ms Cathy Linacre BA DipLib MCLIP (020 7334 3748; e-mail: clinacre@rics.org)

ROYAL INSTITUTION OF GREAT BRITAIN

Library, Royal Institution of Great Britain, 21 Albemarle Street, London W1S 4BS

☎020 7670 2939
Fax 020 7670 2920
e-mail: ril@ri.ac.uk
url: www.rigb.org
Head of Collections and Heritage Prof Frank James (020 7670 2924; e-mail: fjames@ri.ac.uk)

ROYAL INSTITUTION OF NAVAL ARCHITECTS

Library, Royal Institution of Naval Architects, 8–9 Northumberland Street, London WC2N 5DA
☎020 7235 4622
Fax 020 7259 5912
e-mail: hq@rina.org.uk
url: www.rina.org.uk
Information Manager Graeme Mitchell (e-mail: gmitchell@rina.org.uk)

ROYAL MILITARY ACADEMY SANDHURST

Central Library, Royal Military Academy Sandhurst, Camberley, Surrey GU15 4PQ
☎(01276) 412367
Fax (01276) 412538
url: www.sandhurst.mod.uk
Senior Librarian Andrew Orgill MA DipLib (e-mail: rmas-library-snrlibrarian@mod.uk)

Specialism(s): Military history and international affairs

ROYAL MUSEUMS GREENWICH
(formerly National Maritime Museum)

Caird Library, Royal Museums Greenwich, National Maritime Museum, Greenwich, London SE10 9NF
☎020 8312 6516
Fax 020 8312 6599
e-mail: library@rmg.co.uk; manuscripts@rmg.co.uk
url: www.rmg.co.uk/cairdlibrary
Head of Archive and Library Stuart Bligh BSc(Hons)
Library Manager Gareth Bellis MA
Librarian (Systems and Serials) Ms Penny Allen MSc LITDip

Specialism(s): Maritime history; Horology; Astronomy; Shipbuilding; Navigation

ROYAL PHARMACEUTICAL SOCIETY

Library, Royal Pharmaceutical Society, 1 Lambeth High Street, London SE1 7JN
☎020 7735 9141 (switchboard); 020 7572 2300 (direct)
Fax 020 7735 7629
e-mail: library@rpharms.com
url: www.rpharms.com/home/home.asp
Librarian Ms Jane Trodd MA (e-mail: jane.trodd@rpharms.com)

Specialism(s): Pharmacy; Medicines; Therapeutics; Pharmaceutical science

ROYAL SOCIETY

Library, Royal Society, 6–9 Carlton House Terrace, London SWIY 5AG
☎020 7451 2606
Fax 020 7930 2170
e-mail: library@royalsociety.org
url: http://royalsociety.org
Head of Library and Information Services Keith Moore MA
Library Manager Rupert Baker

ROYAL SOCIETY FOR THE PREVENTION OF ACCIDENTS

Information Centre, Royal Society for the Prevention of Accidents, RoSPA House, 28 Calthorpe Road, Edgbaston, Birmingham BI5 IRP
☎0121 248 2063
e-mail: infocentre@rospa.com
url: www.rospa.com
Information Services Manager Ms Helen Shaw (e-mail: hshaw@rospa.com)

ROYAL SOCIETY OF CHEMISTRY

Library and Information Centre, Royal Society of Chemistry, Burlington House, Piccadilly, London WIJ OBA
☎020 7440 3373 (direct)
Fax 020 7437 8883
e-mail: library@rsc.org
url: www.rsc.org/library
Library Operations Specialist Ms Kate Bennett

ROYAL SOCIETY OF MEDICINE

Library, Royal Society of Medicine, I Wimpole Street, London WIG OAE
☎020 7290 2940/2941 (enquiries), 020 7290 2931 (administration)
Fax 020 7290 2939
e-mail: library@rsm.ac.uk
url: www.rsm.ac.uk
Director of Library Services Wayne Sime BSc(Econ) FCLIP

ROYAL STATISTICAL SOCIETY

Library, Royal Statistical Society, 12 Errol Street, London ECIY 8LX
☎020 7638 8998
url: www.rss.org.uk
Archives and Records Management Consultant Ms Janet Foster (e-mail: j.foster@rss.org.uk)
(Historical book collection and Society archives. Viewing by appointment only.)

Albert Sloman Library, Royal Statistical Society, University of Essex, Wivenhoe Park, Colchester, Essex CO4 3SQ

☎(01206) 873181/873172 (enquiries)
Deputy Librarian Nigel Cochrane (e-mail: nigelc@essex.ac.uk)
Assistant Librarian Ms Sandy Macmillen (e-mail: amacmi@essex.ac.uk)
(Houses the Library of the RSS.)

Specialism(s): Statistics; Social history

RSA

Library, RSA, 8 John Adam Street, London WC2N 6EZ
☎020 7451 6847
e-mail: library@rsa.org.uk
url: www.thersa.org/fellowship/fellows-facilities/library
Head of Library Vacant

Archive, RSA, 8 John Adam Street, London WC2N 6EZ
☎020 7451 6847
e-mail: archive@rsa.org.uk
url: www.thersa.org/about-us/history-and-archive
Head of Archive Ms Eve Watson
(Access by appointment)

ST FAGANS: NATIONAL HISTORY MUSEUM

Library, St Fagans: National History Museum, St Fagans, Cardiff CF5 6XB
☎029 2057 3446
Fax 029 2057 3490
url: www.museumwales.ac.uk/St Fagans
Library Assistant Richard Edwards (e-mail: richard.edwards@museumwales.ac.uk)

Specialism(s): Material, social and cultural history of Wales

SCIENCE AND TECHNOLOGY FACILITIES COUNCIL

Chadwick Library, Science and Technology Facilities Council, Daresbury Laboratory, SciTech Daresbury, Warrington, Cheshire WA4 4AD
☎(01925) 603397
Fax (01925) 603779
e-mail: librarydl@stfc.ac.uk
url: www.facebook.com/STFCChadwickLibrary
Library Services Development Manager Mrs Debbie Franks BSc MCLIP (01925 603189; e-mail: debbie.franks@stfc.ac.uk)

Library, Science and Technology Facilities Council, Rutherford Appleton Laboratory, Harwell, Didcot, Oxon OX11 0QX
☎(01235) 445384 (general enquiries)
Fax (01235) 446403
e-mail: library@stfc.ac.uk
url: www.stfc.ac.uk/SCD/support/43929.aspx
Site Librarian Mrs Linda Gilbert BSc(Econ) MCLIP (01235 446151)

SCIENCE FICTION FOUNDATION COLLECTION

Science Fiction Foundation Collection, University of Liverpool Library, PO Box 123, Liverpool L69 3DA
☎0151 794 2696 (library)
Fax 0151 794 2681
url: www.sfhub.ac.uk
Librarian/Administrator Andy Sawyer MPhil MCLIP (0151 794 3142; e-mail: asawyer@liverpool.ac.uk)

SCIENCE MUSEUM LIBRARY

Science Museum Library, Exhibition Road, London SW7 2DD
The London library is now closed to the public. A new Research Centre with library facilities will open at the Science Museum in late 2015.

Site library

Science Museum Library & Archives, Science Museum Library, Science Museum at Wroughton, Hackpen Lane, Wroughton, Swindon SN4 9NS
☎(01793) 846222
Fax (01793) 815413
e-mail: smlwroughton@sciencemuseum.ac.uk
url: www.sciencemuseum.org.uk/library
Library Collections Manager John Underwood (01793 846248; fax: 01793 798021; e-mail: john.underwood@sciencemuseum.org.uk)
(Open free to the public for reference on Fridays 10am-5pm; by advance appointment at Swindon.)

Specialism(s): A national library for the history and public understanding of science and technology

SCOTTISH ENTERPRISE

Economic Research, Scottish Enterprise, Atrium Court, 50 Waterloo Street, Glasgow G2 6HQ
☎0141 248 2700 (main), 0141 228 2268 (direct line)
Fax 0141 248 1600
url: www.scottish-enterprise.com
Manager of Economic Research Mrs Gail Rogers MA DipLib (e-mail: gail.rogers@scotent.co.uk)

Specialism(s): Business information

SCOTTISH GOVERNMENT

ISIS Information Management and Assurance, Scottish Government Library, GD Bridge, Victoria Quay, Commercial Street, Edinburgh EH6 6QQ
☎0131 244 4556
Fax 0131 244 4545
e-mail: SGLibrary@scotland.gsi.gov.uk
Head Librarian Vacant

Librarian Ms Jenny Foreman

Specialism(s): Scottish Government and official publications

SCOTTISH NATURAL HERITAGE

Library Services, Scottish Natural Heritage, Great Glen House, Leachkin Road, Inverness IV3 8NW
☎(01463) 725290 (enquiries); (01463) 725291 (library management)
Fax (01463) 725067
e-mail: library@snh.gov.uk
url: www.snh.org.uk
Library Team Leader Paul R Longbottom MCLIP (e-mail: paul.longbottom@snh.gov.uk)

SCOTTISH PARLIAMENT

Scottish Parliament Information Centre (SPICe), Scottish Parliament, Edinburgh EH99 ISP
☎0131 348 5300
Fax 0131 348 5050
e-mail: spice@scottish.parliament.uk
url: www.scottish.parliament.uk
Head of Collections Ms Kathryn Appleby (e-mail: kathryn.appleby@scottish.parliament.uk)
Head of Enquiries Ms Shona Shackle

SIGNET LIBRARY

Signet Library, Parliament Square, Edinburgh EHI IRF
☎0131 220 3249
Fax 0131 220 4016
e-mail: library@wssociety.co.uk
url: www.wssociety.co.uk
Research Principal James Hamilton

Specialism(s): Scottish history, Scots law

SMITHERS PIRA (formerly PIRA International)

Smithers PIRA, Shawbury, Shrewsbury, Shropshire SY4 4NR
☎(01939) 250383 (enquiries)
e-mail: pirabase@smithers.com
url: www.pirabase.com
Database Operations Manager Ms Rosie Kirkwood (e-mail: rkirkwood@smithers.com)
(The library is no longer open to the public.)

Specialism(s): Abstracts database and document delivery – Papermaking; Printing; Packaging; Publishing

SOCIÉTÉ JERSIAISE

Lord Coutanche Library, Société Jersiaise, 7 Pier Road, St Helier, Jersey, Channel Islands JE2 4XW
☎(01534) 730538 (enquiries), (01534) 633392 (administration)
Fax (01534) 888262
e-mail: library@societe-jersiaise.org
url: www.societe-jersiaise.org
Librarian Ms Bronwyn Matthews (e-mail: bronwyn.matthews@societe-jersiaise.org)
Library Assistant Ms Anna Baghiani (e-mail: anna.baghiani@societe-jersiaise.org)

Specialism(s): Local studies; Local and family history; Maps, prints, newspapers and ephemera

SOCIETY FOR COOPERATION IN RUSSIAN AND SOVIET STUDIES

Library, Society for Cooperation in Russian and Soviet Studies, 320 Brixton Road, London SW9 6AB
☎020 7274 2282
Fax 020 7274 3230
e-mail: ruslibrary@scrss.org.uk
url: www.scrss.org.uk
Hon Librarian John Cunningham

Specialism(s): Literature, arts and history of Russia/Soviet Union in the 20th century

SOCIETY OF ANTIQUARIES OF LONDON

Library, Society of Antiquaries of London, Burlington House, Piccadilly, London W1J 0BE
☎020 7479 7084
Fax 020 7287 6967
e-mail: library@sal.org.uk
url: www.sal.org.uk
Head of Library and Collections Ms Heather Rowland BA MCLIP

Specialism(s): Archaeology; Antiquities and historic monuments in Britain and Europe

SOCIETY OF GENEALOGISTS

Library, Society of Genealogists, 14 Charterhouse Buildings, Goswell Road, London EC1M 7BA
☎020 7251 8799
Fax 020 7250 1800
e-mail: librarian@sog.org.uk
url: www.sog.org.uk; online catalogue at www.sog.org.uk/the-library
Head of Library Services Tim Lawrence (020 7702 5484; e-mail: librarian@sog.org.uk)

Specialism(s): Family, local and national history; Topography; Biography; Heraldry; Demography; Material on most countries worldwide

TATA STEEL, RESEARCH, DEVELOPMENT AND TECHNOLOGY

Knowledge and Library Services, Tata Steel, Research, Development and Technology, Swinden Technology Centre, Moorgate, Rotherham, South Yorks S60 3AR
☎(01709) 820166
Fax (01709) 825337
url: www.Tatasteel.com
(Library has no on-site personnel. Enquiries will be dealt with by colleagues in Ijmuiden, Netherlands)

Specialism(s): Steel engineering and manufacturing

TATE LIBRARY AND ARCHIVE

Hyman Kreitman Reading Rooms, Tate Library and Archive, Tate Britain, Millbank, London SW1P 4RG
☎020 7887 8838
e-mail: reading.rooms@tate.org.uk
url: www.tate.org.uk/research/researchservices/readingrooms
Head of Library, Archive and Collection Access Ms Jane Bramwell
Library Collections Manager Ms Maxine Miller BA(Hons) DipLib MCLIP
Archivist Adrian Glew
Gallery Records Manager Miss Jane Kennedy
Reader Services and Systems Manager Andrew Gent
Opening hours: 11am–5pm Monday–Friday (appointments required)

Specialism(s): Library: British art and international modern art – over 150,000 exhibition catalogues and 50,000 monographs; artists books. Archive: Archive of British Art since 1900: unpublished and semi-published documentation about fine artists in all media including commercial galleries and dealers, critics, societies and institutions. Gallery Records: Tate's official records

TAVISTOCK AND PORTMAN NHS FOUNDATION TRUST

Library, Tavistock and Portman NHS Foundation Trust, 120 Belsize Lane, London NW3 5BA
☎020 7435 7111 (switchboard); 020 8938 2520 (direct line)
e-mail: library@tavi-port.ac.uk
url: www.library.tavistockandportman.ac.uk
Head of Library and Information Services Ms Angela Douglas MCLIP BSc MA (e-mail: angeladouglas@tavi-port.ac.uk)

Specialism(s): Psychoanalysis; Psychotherapy; Educational psychology

TPS CONSULT LTD

The Information Centre, TPS Consult Ltd, Centre Tower, Whitgift Centre, Croydon CR9 0AU
☎020 8256 4110
Fax 0844 244 0591

e-mail: info@tpsconsult.co.uk
url: www.tpsconsult.co.uk
Marketing and Information Services Manager Gursel Ziynettin (e-mail:
ziynettin.gursel@tpsconsult.co.uk)

Specialism(s): Construction and design

TRADES UNION CONGRESS LIBRARY COLLECTIONS

Trades Union Congress Library Collections, Holloway Road Learning Centre, London Metropolitan University, 236–250 Holloway Road, London N7 6PP
☎020 7133 3726
Fax 020 7133 2529
e-mail: tuclib@londonmet.ac.uk
url: www.londonmet.ac.uk/libraries/tuc; www.unionhistory.info
Librarian Jeff Howarth (e-mail: j.howarth@london.met.ac.uk)

Specialism(s): Trade unions; Industrial relations; Politics; Economic history; International affairs

UNITED STATES EMBASSY

Information Resource Center, United States Embassy, 24 Grosvenor Square, London WIA IAE
☎020 7894 0925 (10am–12 noon (public enquiries)), 020 7499 9000 ext 2643
(administration)
Fax 020 7629 8288
e-mail: reflond@state.gov
url: http://london.usembassy.gov
Director Ms Anna Girvan

Specialism(s): US government and foreign policy; Current affairs

V&A THEATRE AND PERFORMANCE DEPARTMENT

Research Collections, V&A Theatre and Performance Department, Blythe House, 23 Blythe Road, London WI4 0QX
☎020 7942 2697 (enquiries); 020 7942 2698 (reading room)
e-mail: tmenquiries@vam.ac.uk
url: www.vam.ac.uk/theatre/page/t/theatre-and-performance
Head of Collections Management Ms Claire Hudson BA MCLIP
Librarian Ms Beverley Hart (e-mail: b.hart@vam.ac.uk)

Specialism(s): Performing arts; Stage design

VETERINARY LABORATORIES AGENCY see ANIMAL HEALTH AND VETERINARY LABORATORIES AGENCY

WATER SERVICES REGULATION AUTHORITY (OFWAT)

Enquiries and Information Rights, Water Services Regulation Authority (OFWAT), Centre City Tower, 7 Hill Street, Birmingham B5 4UA
☎0121 644 7644 (general enquiries); 0121 644 7500 (switchboard)
Fax 0121 625 1400
e-mail: mailbox@ofwat.gsi.gov.uk
url: www.ofwat.gov.uk
Head of Public Affairs Simon Markall

THE WELDING INSTITUTE (TWI)

Information Services, The Welding Institute (TWI), TWI Ltd, Granta Park, Great Abington, Cambridge CB21 6AL
☎(01223) 899000
Fax (01223) 891264
e-mail: library@twi.co.uk
url: www.twi-global.com
Manager, Information Services Ms Linda Dumper (e-mail: linda.dumper@twi.co.uk)
Librarian Mrs Joanne Cooper BA(Hons) DipInfStud MCLIP (e-mail: joanne.cooper@twi.co.uk)

WELLCOME LIBRARY

Wellcome Library, 183 Euston Road, London NW1 2BE
☎020 7611 8628
e-mail: library@wellcome.ac.uk
url: http://wellcomelibrary.org
Head of Library Dr Simon Chaplin
Library Administrator Ms Tracy Tillotson

Wellcome Images
☎020 7611 8348
Fax 020 7611 8577
e-mail: images@wellcome.ac.uk

Moving Image and Sound Collections
☎020 7611 8766
Fax 020 7611 8765
e-mail: misc@wellcome.ac.uk

Specialism(s): History of medicine and allied science subjects

WELSH GOVERNMENT (formerly Welsh Assembly Government)

Library and Archive Service, Welsh Government, Department for Finance & Corporate Services, Cathays Park, Cardiff CF10 3NQ
☎029 2082 5449
e-mail: welshgovernmentlibrary@wales.gsi.gov.uk
url: www.wales.gov.uk

Head of the Library and Archive Service Ms Marlize Palmer (e-mail: marlize.palmer@wales.gsi.gov.uk)

Specialism(s): Welsh government publications

WESTMINSTER ABBEY

Muniment Room and Library, Westminster Abbey, London SWIP 3PA
☎020 7654 4830
e-mail: library@westminster-abbey.org
url: www.westminster-abbey.org
Librarian Dr Tony Trowles MA DPhil (e-mail: tony.trowles@westminster-abbey.org)

Specialism(s): History of Westminster Abbey; Coronations; Early printed books (pre-1800)

WIENER LIBRARY FOR THE STUDY OF THE HOLOCAUST AND GENOCIDE
(formerly Wiener Library Institute of Contemporary History)

Wiener Library for the Study of the Holocaust and Genocide, 29 Russell Square, London WC1B 5DP
☎020 7636 7247
Fax 020 7436 6428
e-mail: library@wienerlibrary.co.uk
url: www.wienerlibrary.co.uk
Senior Librarian Ms Katharina Hübschmann
Director Ben Barkow

Specialism(s): Holocaust; Third Reich; Fascism; Modern German–Jewish history; Anti-semitism

WILLIAM SALT LIBRARY

William Salt Library, 19 Eastgate Street, Stafford ST16 2LZ
☎(01785) 278372
Fax (01785) 278414
e-mail: william.salt.library@staffordshire.gov.uk
url: www.staffordshire.gov.uk/salt
Librarian Ms Joanna Terry

Specialism(s): Staffordshire local history

DR WILLIAMS'S LIBRARY

Dr Williams's Library, 14 Gordon Square, London WC1H 0AR
☎020 7387 3727
e-mail: enquiries@dwlib.co.uk
url: www.dwlib.co.uk
Director of Dr Williams's Trust and Library D L Wykes BSc PhD FRHistS
Librarian Ms Fiona Turnbull
(The Congregational Library at 15 Gordon Square is administered by Dr Williams's Library, to which any application should be made. Other details are the same.)

Specialism(s): History and theology of religious dissent

THE WOMEN'S LIBRARY

The Women's Library, LSE Library, 10 Portugal Street, London WC2A 2HD
☎020 7955 7229
e-mail: library.enquiries@lse.ac.uk
url: www.library.lse.ac.uk
Academic Services Manager Martin Reid

Specialism(s): Women's history; Women's studies

WORKING CLASS MOVEMENT LIBRARY

Working Class Movement Library, Jubilee House, 51 The Crescent, Salford M5 4WX
☎0161 736 3601
Fax 0161 737 4115
e-mail: enquiries@wcml.org.uk
url: www.wcml.org.uk
Library Manager Lynette Cawthra MA DipLib MCLIP
Librarian Ms Jane Taylor MA DipLib MCLIP
Library Assistant Sam Ziesler BA MSc

Specialism(s): Labour history; Trade Unions; Communism; Socialism; Labour Party;
Independent Labour Party; Anarchism; Working class autobiography

YORK MINSTER

Historic Collections Team, York Minster, The Old Palace, Dean's Park, York YO1 7JQ
☎0844 939 0021 ext 2500
e-mail: library@yorkminster.org.uk
url: www.yorkminster.org; https://www.york.ac.uk/library
Special Collections and York Minster Librarian Ms Sarah Griffin MSc (e-mail:
sarahg@yorkminster.org)
Archivist Peter Young MA (e-mail: petery@yorkminster.org)
(Library open to the public Mon–Fri 9am–5pm, Archive Mon–Fri 1.30pm–5pm)

Specialism(s): History; Theology; Church history; Early printed books; Yorkshire history;
Stained glass; York Minster archives

ZOOLOGICAL SOCIETY OF LONDON

Library, Zoological Society of London, Regent's Park, London NW1 4RY
☎020 7449 6293
e-mail: library@zsl.org
url: www.zsl.org; http://library.zsl.org (library catalogue)
Librarian Ms A Sylph MSc MCLIP

Specialism(s): Zoology; Animal conservation

Selected Academic, National and Special Libraries in the Republic of Ireland

ARCHBISHOP MARSH'S LIBRARY see MARSH'S LIBRARY

CDETB CURRICULUM DEVELOPMENT UNIT
(formerly CDVEC)

CDETB Curriculum Development Unit, Library, McCann House, 99 Marlborough Road, Donnybrook, Dublin 4, Republic of Ireland
☎(00 353 1) 498 9512
Fax (00 353 1) 496 9087
url: www.curriculum.ie
Librarian Dr Eva Hornung DiplBibl MLIS ALAI FCLIP (e-mail: eva.hornung@cdu.cdetb.ie)

CENTRAL CATHOLIC LIBRARY

Central Catholic Library, 74 Merrion Square, Dublin 2, Republic of Ireland
☎(00 353 1) 676 1264 (enquiries and administration)
e-mail: catholiclibrary@imagine.ie
url: www.catholiclibrary.ie
Librarian Ms Teresa Whitington MA DLIS PhD

CHESTER BEATTY LIBRARY

Chester Beatty Library, Dublin Castle, Dublin 2, Republic of Ireland
☎(00 353 1) 407 0750
Fax (00 353 1) 407 0760
e-mail: info@cbl.ie
url: www.cbl.ie
Director and Librarian Ms Fionnuala Croke (e-mail: fcroke@cbl.ie)
Reference Librarian Ms Celine Ward BA MLIS (e-mail: cward@cbl.ie)

DUBLIN BUSINESS SCHOOL

Undergraduate Library, Dublin Business School, 13/14 Aungier Street, Dublin 2, Republic of Ireland
☎(00 353 1) 417 7572
Fax (00 353 1) 417 7543
e-mail: library@dbs.ie
url: http://library.dbs.ie
Head Librarian Ms Marie O'Neill BA GradDipBS GradDipLIS (00 353 1 417 7571; e-mail: marie.oneill@dbs.ie)
Deputy Librarian Ms Jane Buggle BA GradDipLIS MLIS (00 353 1 417 0667; e-mail: jane.buggle@dbs.ie)
Acquisitions Librarian Ms Marie O'Dwyer BEng GradDipLIS (00 353 1 417 7508; e-mail: marie.odwyer@dbs.ie)
Information Skills Librarian Ms Maria Rogers BA MLIS (00 353 1 417 0611; e-mail: maria.rogers@dbs.ie)

Research Librarian Alex Kouker BA MLIS (00 353 1 417 0612; e-mail: alexander.kouker@dbs.ie)

Postgraduate and Law Library, Dublin Business School, 19/22 Dame Street, Dublin 2, Republic of Ireland
☎(00 353 1) 417 8745 (Information Desk), (00 353 1) 417 7582 (Librarian's Office)
Postgraduate and Law Librarian Ms Joan Colvin DipLIS (00 353 1 417 7582; e-mail: joan.colvin@dbs.ie)

DUBLIN CITY UNIVERSITY

DCU Libraries, Dublin City University, Dublin 9, Republic of Ireland
☎(00 353 1) 700 5418 (enquiries); (00 353 1) 700 5212 (administration)
Fax (00 353 1) 700 5010
url: www.dcu.ie/~library/
Director of Library Services and Humanities Research Archive Centre
Christopher Pressler BA MA MSc FRSA (e-mail: christopher.pressler@dcu.ie)

DUBLIN INSTITUTE OF TECHNOLOGY

Central Services Unit, Dublin Institute of Technology, Rathmines Road, Dublin 6, Republic of Ireland
☎(00 353 1) 402 7800
e-mail: csu.library@dit.ie
url: www.dit.ie/library
Head of Library Services Dr Philip Cohen BA MSc PhD DipLib MCLIP
(00 353 1 402 3067; e-mail: philip.cohen@dit.ie)
Sub Librarian, Collection Development Ms Ann McSweeney BA DLIS MLIS
(00 353 1 402 7804; e-mail: ann.mcsweeney@dit.ie)
Sub Librarian, Systems Development Ms Ursula Gavin BA DLIS MLIS
(00 353 1 402 7805; e-mail: ursula.gavin@dit.ie)
College Librarian Ms Yvonne Desmond BA DLIS (00 353 1 402 7807; e-mail: yvonne.desmond@dit.ie)

Library, Dublin Institute of Technology, Bolton Street, Dublin 1, Republic of Ireland
☎(00 353 1) 402 3681
e-mail: bst.library@dit.ie
College Librarian Brian Gillespie BA DipLib (00 353 1 402 3682; e-mail: brian.gillespie@dit.ie)

Library, Dublin Institute of Technology, Kevin Street, Dublin 8, Republic of Ireland
☎(00 353 1) 402 4894 (general enquiries)
e-mail: kst.library@dit.ie
College Librarian Brendan Devlin BA DLIS MLIS MA (00 353 1 402 4631; e-mail: brendan.devlin@dit.ie)

Library, Dublin Institute of Technology, Cathal Brugha Street, Dublin 1, Republic of Ireland
☎(00 353 1) 402 4423/4 (enquiries and administration)
e-mail: cbs.library@dit.ie
College Librarian Ms Ann Wrigley BA DLIS (00 353 1 402 4128; e-mail: ann.wrigley@dit.ie)

Library, Dublin Institute of Technology, Rathdown House, Grangegorman, Dublin 7, Republic of Ireland
☎(00 353 1) 402 4108
e-mail: grg.library@dit.ie
College Librarian Ms Ann Wrigley BA DLIS (00 353 1 402 4128; e-mail: ann.wrigley@dit.ie)

Library, Dublin Institute of Technology, Aungier Street, Dublin 2, Republic of Ireland
☎(00 353 1) 402 3068/9
e-mail: ast.library@dit.ie
College Librarian Vacant

Music and Drama Library, Dublin Institute of Technology, Lower Rathmines Road, Dublin 6, Republic of Ireland
☎(00 353 1) 402 3461
e-mail: rmh.library@dit.ie
College Librarian Ms Ann Wrigley BA DLIS (00 353 1 402 4128; e-mail: ann.wrigley@dit.ie)

ENTERPRISE IRELAND

Market Research Centre, Enterprise Ireland, East Point Business Park, Dublin 3, Republic of Ireland
☎(00 353 1) 727 2324
e-mail: market.research@enterprise-ireland.com
url: www.enterprise-ireland.com/mrc
Head of Department Ms Deirdre McDonough
Information Specialist in Charge Ms Bernadette Mooney (00 353 1 727 2303; e-mail: bernadette.mooney@enterprise-ireland.com)

INSTITUTO CERVANTES

Library, Instituto Cervantes, Lincoln House, Lincoln Place, Dublin 2, Republic of Ireland
☎(00 353 1) 631 1515
Fax (00 353 1) 631 1599
e-mail: bibdub@cervantes.es
url: http://dublin.cervantes.es
Chief Librarian David Carrión

Specialism(s): Spanish culture, history, literature, language and teaching.

MARSH'S LIBRARY (formerly Archbishop Marsh's Library)

Marsh's Library, St Patrick's Close, Dublin 8, Republic of Ireland
☎(00 353 1) 454 3511 (enquiries and administration)
Fax (00 353 1) 454 3511
url: www.marshlibrary.ie
Keeper Dr Jason McElligott
(A well preserved library of the early Enlightenment (founded in 1707) with an important collection of Renaissance and early modern books)

NATIONAL ARCHIVES

National Archives, Bishop Street, Dublin 8, Republic of Ireland
☎(00 353 1) 407 2300
Fax (00 353 1) 407 2333
e-mail: mail@nationalarchives.ie
url: www.nationalarchives.ie
Acting Director Tom Quinlan (00 353 1 497 2385; e-mail: tquinlan@nationalarchives.ie)
(Formed by the amalgamation of the Public Record Office of Ireland and the State Paper
Office.)

NATIONAL COLLEGE OF ART AND DESIGN

The Edward Murphy Library, National College of Art and Design, 100 Thomas Street, Dublin 8, Republic of Ireland
☎(00 353 1) 636 4357
Fax (00 353 1) 636 4387
url: www.ncad.ie/library
Acting Librarian Ms Donna Romano BA MA MLIS (e-mail: romanod@staff.ncad.ie)

NATIONAL GALLERY OF IRELAND

Centre for the Study of Irish Art, National Gallery of Ireland, Merrion Square West, Dublin 2, Republic of Ireland
☎(00 353 1) 632 5517
Fax (00 353 1) 661 5372
e-mail: csia@ngi.ie
url: www.nationalgallery.ie
Administrator Donal Maguire
(By appointment)

Fine Art Library, National Gallery of Ireland, Merrion Square West, Dublin 2, Republic of
Ireland
☎(00 353 1) 663 3546 (direct)
Fax (00 353 1) 661 5372
e-mail: library@ngi.ie
url: www.nationalgallery.ie
Librarian Ms Andrea Lydon MA DLIS
Assistant Librarian Ms Catherine Sheridan BA HDipCompSci MLIS
(Opening hours 10–5 Mon–Fri. No appointment necessary)

NGI Archive, National Gallery of Ireland, Merrion Square West, Dublin 2, Republic of
Ireland
☎(00 353 1) 663 3508 (direct)
Fax (00 353 1) 661 5372
url: www.nationalgallery.ie
Archivist Ms Leah Benson MA HDipArch (e-mail: lbenson@ngi.ie)
(By appointment)

Yeats Archive, National Gallery of Ireland, Merrion Square West, Dublin 2, Republic of Ireland

☎(00 353 1) 632 3508
Fax (00 353 1) 661 5372
e-mail: yeats@ngi.ie
url: www.nationalgallery.ie
Archivist Ms Leah Benson MA HDipArch (e-mail: lbenson@ngi.ie)
(By appointment)

NATIONAL LIBRARY OF IRELAND

National Library of Ireland, Kildare Street, Dublin 2, Republic of Ireland
☎(00 353 1) 603 0200
Fax (00 353 1) 676 6690
e-mail: info@nli.ie
url: www.nli.ie
Acting Director Ms Catherine Fahy BA DipLIS
Keeper of Archival Collections Ms Colette O'Flaherty BA DipArchiv
Head of Public Services Ms Katherine McSharry
Head of Finance Ms Mary Neville
Head of Digital Library and Information Systems Ms Geraldine Wilson

National Photographic Archive

National Photographic Archive, Meeting House Square, Temple Bar, Dublin 2, Republic of
Ireland
☎(00 353 1) 603 0373
e-mail: npaoffice@nli.ie
url: www.nli.ie
Curator Ms Elizabeth M. Kirwan (e-mail: emkirwan@nli.ie)

NATIONAL UNIVERSITY OF IRELAND, GALWAY

**James Hardiman Library, National University of Ireland, Galway, University Road,
Galway, Republic of Ireland**
☎(00 353 91) 492540 (administration), 493005 (information point)
Fax (00 353 91) 522394; 494528 (interlibrary loans)
e-mail: library@nuigalway.ie
url: www.library.nuigalway.ie
University Librarian John Cox MA DipLib (00 353 91 493159; e-mail:
john.cox@nuigalway.ie)
Head of Organisational Development and Performance Peter Corrigan BA DipLIS
(00 353 91 492497; e-mail: peter.corrigan@nuigalway.ie)
Head of Information Access and Learning Services Ms Monica Crump BA MLIS
(00 353 91 493765; e-mail: monica.crump@nuigalway.ie)
Head of Customer Focus and Research Services Niall McSweeney BA HDipinEd
DipLib (00 353 91 493915; e-mail: niall.mcsweeney@nuigalway.ie)
Head of Staff Development and Service Environment Ms Ann Mitchell BA HDipEd
DipLIS (00 353 91 492738; e-mail: ann.mitchell@nuigalway.ie)
Head of Planning and Projects Ms Evelyn Bohan BComm (00 353 91 492403; e-mail:
evelyn.bohan@nuigalway.ie)

Branch library
Medical Library, National University of Ireland, Galway, Clinical Sciences Institute,
University Road, Galway, Republic of Ireland
☎(00 353 91) 493601
Fax (00 353 91) 494517
Assistant Librarian Ms Jane Mulligan BA(Hons) (00 353 91 495228)

NATIONAL UNIVERSITY OF IRELAND, MAYNOOTH

The Library, National University of Ireland, Maynooth, Co Kildare, Republic of Ireland
☎(00 353 1) 708 3884
Fax (00 353 1) 628 6008
e-mail: library.information@nuim.ie
url: http://library.nuim.ie
Librarian Cathal McCauley BA MLIS DipFM
Deputy Librarian Ms Helen Fallon MA DLIS
Senior Librarians Ms Mary Antonesa BA MLIS, Hugh Murphy MA DLIS

OIREACHTAS LIBRARY & RESEARCH SERVICE

Oireachtas Library & Research Service, Houses of the Oireachtas, Leinster House,
Kildare Street, Dublin 2, Republic of Ireland
☎(00 353 1) 618 3000 (switchboard)
Fax (00 353 1) 618 4109
e-mail: library.and.research@oireachtas.ie
url: www.oireachtas.ie
Head of Library and Research Services Ms Madelaine Dennison (00 353 1 618 4735;
e-mail: madelaine.dennison@oireachtas.ie)
Head of Research Ms Maria Fitzsimons (00 353 1 618 4734; e-mail:
maria.fitzsimons@oireachtas.ie)
Head of Collections John McDonough (00 353 1 618 4733; e-mail:
john.mcdonough@oireachtas.ie)

REPRESENTATIVE CHURCH BODY

Library, Representative Church Body, Braemor Park, Churchtown, Dublin 14, Republic
of Ireland
☎(00 353 1) 492 3979
Fax (00 353 1) 492 4770
e-mail: library@ireland.anglican.org
url: www.ireland.anglican.org/
Librarian & Archivist Dr Raymond Refaussé BA PhD (e-mail:
raymond.refausse@rcbdub.org)

ROYAL COLLEGE OF SURGEONS IN IRELAND

The Mercer Library, Royal College of Surgeons in Ireland, Mercer Street Lower, Dublin
2, Republic of Ireland

☎(00 353 1) 402 2407 (enquiries); 402 2411 (administration)
Fax (00 353 1) 402 2457
e-mail: library@rcsi.ie
url: www.rcsi.ie/library
Librarian Mrs Kate Kelly MSc DLIS AHIP (e-mail: katekelly@rcsi.ie))

Branch library
RCSI Library, Royal College of Surgeons in Ireland, Beaumont Hospital, Beaumont Road,
Dublin 9, Republic of Ireland
☎(00 353 1) 809 2531
Fax (00 353 1) 836 7396
e-mail: bhlibrary@rcsi.ie
Librarian Ms Breffni Smith MPhil DLIS (e-mail: breffnismith@rcsi.ie)

ROYAL DUBLIN SOCIETY

Library, Royal Dublin Society, Merrion Road, Ballsbridge, Dublin 4, Republic of Ireland
☎(00 353 1) 240 7274
Fax (00 353 1) 660 4014
e-mail: library@rds.ie
url: www.rds.ie/library
Library and Information Systems Manager Senan Healy BA MA MLIS (e-mail:
senan.healy@rds.ie)

ROYAL IRISH ACADEMY

Library, Royal Irish Academy, 19 Dawson Street, Dublin 2, Republic of Ireland
☎(00 353 1) 609 0620
Fax (00 353 1) 676 2346
e-mail: library@ria.ie
url: www.ria.ie
Librarian Ms Siobhán Fitzpatrick BA HDipEd DLIS (e-mail: s.fitzpatrick@ria.ie)
Deputy Librarian Dr Bernadette Cunningham MA DipLib PhD (e-mail:
b.cunningham@ria.ie)

TEAGASC (AGRICULTURE AND FOOD DEVELOPMENT AUTHORITY)

**Library, TEAGASC (Agriculture and Food Development Authority), Ashtown Food
Research Centre, Ashtown, Dublin 15, Republic of Ireland**
☎(00 353 1) 805 9500
Fax (00 353 1) 805 9550
url: www.teagasc.ie
Head Librarian Ms Maire Caffrey BSc DipLIS (e-mail: maire.caffrey@teagasc.ie)

Research libraries
Library, TEAGASC (Agriculture and Food Development Authority), Moorepark Food
Research Centre (dairy production, dairy products, cheese production), Fermoy, Co Cork,
Republic of Ireland

☎(00 353 25) 42222
Fax (00 353 25) 42340
Librarian Ms Siobhan Keating (e-mail: siobhan.keating@teagasc.ie)

Library, TEAGASC (Agriculture and Food Development Authority), Johnstown Castle
Agricultural Research Centre (environment), Wexford, Republic of Ireland
☎(00 353 53) 917 1200
Fax (00 353 53) 914 2213
Clerical Administrator Ms Sarah Lacey (e-mail: sarah.lacey@teagasc.ie)

Library, TEAGASC (Agriculture and Food Development Authority), Oak Park Research
Centre (crops production), Carlow, Republic of Ireland
☎(00 353 59) 917 0200
Fax (00 353 59) 914 2097
Librarian Ms Cheryl Austin

Library, TEAGASC (Agriculture and Food Development Authority), Grange Research
Centre (beef production), Dunsany, Co Meath, Republic of Ireland
☎(00 353 46) 906 1100 (switchboard); (00 353 46) 906 1151 (library)
Fax (00 353 46) 902 6154
Librarian Ms Ann Gilsenan (e-mail: ann.gilsenan@teagasc.ie)

TRINITY COLLEGE DUBLIN

Library, Trinity College Dublin, College Street, Dublin 2, Republic of Ireland
☎(00 353 1) 896 1127 (general enquiries); (00 353 1) 896 1661 (Librarian's office)
Fax (00 353 1) 896 3774
e-mail: librarian@tcd.ie
url: www.tcd.ie/library/
Librarian and College Archivist Ms Helen Shenton BA (e-mail: shentonh@tcd.ie)
Deputy Librarian Ms Jessie Kurtz BA BEd MLS (e-mail: jessie.kurtz@tcd.ie)

Departmental libraries
Hamilton Science and Technology Library, Trinity College Dublin, College Street, Dublin 2,
Republic of Ireland
☎(00 353 1) 896 4588
Fax (00 353 1) 896 3774
Sub-Librarian (Reading Room Services) Ms Kathryn Smith BSc MLIS (e-mail:
kathryn.smith@tcd.ie)

John Stearne Medical Library, Trinity College Dublin, St James's Hospital, James's Street,
Dublin 8, Republic of Ireland
☎(00 353 1) 896 2109
Fax (00 353 1) 453 6087
Medical Librarian David Mockler BSc DLIS (e-mail: mocklerd@tcd.ie)

UNIVERSITY COLLEGE CORK

The Boole Library, University College Cork, College Road, Cork, Republic of Ireland
☎(00 353 21) 490 2794

Fax (00 353 21) 427 3428
e-mail: library@ucc.ie
url: http://booleweb.ucc.ie
Director of Library Services Ms Colette McKenna (00 353 21 490 2492; e-mail:
cmckenna@ucc.ie)

Branch/department libraries
Boston Scientific Health Sciences Library, University College Cork, Brookfield Health
Sciences Complex, College Road, Cork, Republic of Ireland
☎(00 353 21) 490 1523
Fax (00 353 21) 490 1522
e-mail: brookfieldlibrary@ucc.ie
Therapies and Basic Sciences for Medicine Librarian Cathal Kerrigan (e-mail:
c.kerrigan@ucc.ie)
Nursing and Midwifery Librarian Ms Maura Flynn (e-mail: m.flynn@ucc.ie)

Cork University Hospital Library, University College Cork, Cork University Hospital,
Wilton, Cork, Republic of Ireland
☎(00 353 21) 490 2976
Fax (00 353 21) 434 5826
e-mail: CUH.Library@ucc.ie
Medical, Dental and Hospital Librarian Vacant

UNIVERSITY COLLEGE DUBLIN

**UCD James Joyce Library, University College Dublin, Belfield, Dublin 4, Republic of
Ireland**
☎(00 353 1) 716 7627 (enquiries), (00 353 1) 716 7694 (administration)
Fax (00 353 1) 716 7068
e-mail: library@ucd.ie
url: www.ucd.ie/library/
Librarian Dr John Howard (e-mail: john.b.howard@ucd.ie)
Associate Librarians Ms Marie Burke (e-mail: marie.burke@ucd.ie), Ms Carmel
O'Sullivan (e-mail: cosullivan@ucd.ie)

Site libraries
UCD Library, University College Dublin, Health Sciences Building, Belfield, Dublin 4,
Republic of Ireland
☎(00 353 1) 716 6588
Fax (00 353 1) 716 6451
Site Manager Ms Maeve Tannam (e-mail: maeve.tannam@ucd.ie)

UCD Library, University College Dublin, Veterinary Sciences Centre, Belfield, Dublin 4,
Republic of Ireland
☎(00 353 1) 716 6208
Fax (00 353 1) 716 6267
Site Manager Ms Maeve Tannam (e-mail: maeve.tannam@ucd.ie)

UCD Library, University College Dublin, Smurfit Graduate School of Business, Blackrock,
Dublin, Republic of Ireland

☎(00 353 1) 716 8069
Fax (00 353 1) 716 8011
Site Manager Brendan Stafford (e-mail: brendan.stafford@ucd.ie)

UCD Richview Library, University College Dublin, Richview, Clonskeagh, Dublin 14, Republic of Ireland
☎(00 353 1) 716 2727
Site Manager Ms Avril Patterson (e-mail: avril.patterson@ucd.ie)

UNIVERSITY OF LIMERICK

Library and Information Services, University of Limerick, Limerick, Republic of Ireland
☎(00 353 61) 202166 (enquiries); 202156 (administration)
Fax (00 353 61) 213090
e-mail: libinfo@ul.ie
url: www.ul.ie
Director, Library and Information Services Ms Gobnait O'Riordan MA DLIS

Schools and Departments of Information and Library Studies in the United Kingdom and the Republic of Ireland

This information is subject to change.
For a list of institutions that offer currently accredited courses, please visit the CILIP website, www.cilip.org.uk

ABERYSTWYTH UNIVERSITY

Department of Information Studies, Llanbadarn Fawr, Aberystwyth, Ceredigion SY23 3AS
☎(01970) 622188
e-mail: dis-dept@aber.ac.uk
url: www.dis.aber.ac.uk
Head of Department Dr Allen Foster BA MSc PhD FHEA

CITY UNIVERSITY LONDON

Department of Library and Information Science, Northampton Square, London EC1V 0HB
☎020 7040 8381
e-mail: enquiries@city.ac.uk
url: www.city.ac.uk/lis
Head of Department Dr Lyn Robinson (e-mail: lyn@soi.city.ac.uk)

UNIVERSITY COLLEGE DUBLIN

UCD School of Information and Library Studies, James Joyce Library Building, Belfield,
Dublin 4, Republic of Ireland
☎(00 353 1) 716 7055
Fax (00 353 1) 716 1161
e-mail: sils@ucd.ie
url: www.ucd.ie/sils
Head of School Dr Lee Komito MA PhD (e-mail: lee.komito@ucd.ie)

UNIVERSITY OF GLASGOW

Humanities Advanced Technologies & Information Institute (HATII), George Service
House, 11 University Gardens, Glasgow G12 8QQ
☎0141 330 5512
Fax 0141 330 3788
url: www.hatii.arts.gla.ac.uk
Course Director Prof Seamus Ross (e-mail: seamus.ross@glasgow.ac.uk)

LIVERPOOL JOHN MOORES UNIVERSITY

Information Systems and Public Relations, Liverpool Business School, Remonds
Building, Brownlow Hill, Liverpool L3 5UG
☎0151 231 3596/3427
Fax 0151 707 0423
url: www.ljmu.ac.uk
Principal Lecturer and Programme Leader Ms Janet Farrow MA BA MCLIP
(0151 231 3596; e-mail: a.j.farrow@ljmu.ac.uk)

UNIVERSITY COLLEGE LONDON

Department of Information Studies, Gower Street, London WC1E 6BT

☎020 7679 7204
Fax 020 7383 0557
e-mail: infostudies-enquiries@ucl.ac.uk
url: www.ucl.ac.uk/dis
Head of Department of Information Studies Dr Rob Miller

LOUGHBOROUGH UNIVERSITY

Information Management Discipline, School of Business and Economics, Ashby Road, Loughborough, Leics LEII 3TU
☎(01509) 223288
e-mail: sbereception@lboro.ac.uk
url: www.lboro.ac.uk/departments/sbe/research/business/groups/information-management/
Professor of Information Management Prof Graham Matthews BA DipLib PhD MCLIP
(e-mail: g.matthews@lboro.ac.uk)
Director of LISU (Library & Information Statistics Unit) Ms Claire Creaser BSc CStat
(e-mail: c.creaser@lboro.ac.uk)

MANCHESTER METROPOLITAN UNIVERSITY

Department of Languages, Information and Communications, Geoffrey Manton Building, Rosamond Street West, off Oxford Road, Manchester MI5 6LL
☎0161 247 6144
Fax 0161 247 6351
e-mail: hlssprogteam2@mmu.ac.uk
url: www2.mmu.ac.uk/infocomms
Head of Department Dr Derek Bousfield BA MA PhD
Professor of Information and Communications Prof Jenny Rowley BA MSc MSc DMS PhD FCLIP MBCS CEng MCMI

NORTHUMBRIA UNIVERSITY

Department of Mathematics and Information Sciences, Pandon Building, Camden Street, Newcastle upon Tyne NE2 IXE
☎0191 227 3766
Fax 0191 243 7630
e-mail: iSchool@northumbria
url: www.northumbria.ac.uk/sd/academic/ee/news/ischool
Head of Department Dr Gobinda Chowdhury BSc(Hons) MSc PhD FCLIP
Principal Lecturer in Information Science Dr Alison Pickard (e-mail: alison.pickard@northumbria.ac.uk)

ROBERT GORDON UNIVERSITY

Department of Information Management, Aberdeen Business School, Garthdee Road, Aberdeen ABIO 7QE
☎(01224) 262000 (University switchboard); (01224) 263800 (School Reception)
Fax (01224) 263838
e-mail: imopen@rgu.ac.uk
url: www.rgu.ac.uk/abs

Dean, Aberdeen Business School Prof Rita C Marcella MA DipEd DipLib PhD FCMI FCLIP (e-mail: r.c.marcella@rgu.ac.uk)
Professor in Information Management, Aberdeen Business School Prof Robert Newton MA PGDipLib PhD MCLIP (e-mail: r.newton@rgu.ac.uk)
Director of Research Institute, Aberdeen Business School Prof Dorothy A Williams BSc PGDipLib PhD (e-mail: d.williams@rgu.ac.uk)
Head of Department, Department of Information Management Prof Peter H Reid BA PhD (e-mail: p.reid@rgu.ac.uk)
Research Co-ordinator, Department of Information Management Dr Simon Burnett (e-mail: s.burnett@rgu.ac.uk)

THE UNIVERSITY OF SHEFFIELD

The Information School, Regent Court, 2ll Portobello Street, Sheffield SI 4DP
☎0114 222 2630 (dept/administration)
Fax 0114 222 2631
e-mail: is@shef.ac.uk
url: www.shef.ac.uk/is
Head of School and Professor of Higher Education Development Prof Philippa Levy BA(Hons) MA MA PhD FHEA (0114 222 2638; e-mail: p.levy@sheffield.ac.uk)

STRATHCLYDE UNIVERSITY

Department of Computer and Information Sciences, Livingstone Tower, 26 Richmond Street, Glasgow GI IXH
☎0141 548 3096 (direct); 0141 552 4400 (switchboard)
Fax 0141 548 4523
e-mail: pgi-enquiries@cis.strath.ac.uk
url: www.strath.ac.uk/cis
Head of Department Prof Ian Ruthven BSC(Hons) MSc PhD
Course Director David McMenemy BA MSc MCLIP FHEA

UNIVERSITY OF ULSTER

Library and Information Management, School of Education, Cromore Road, Coleraine BT52 ISA
☎028 7032 4719
e-mail: socsci@ulster.ac.uk
url: www.socsci.ulster.ac.uk/education/library.html
Course Director Dr Jessica Bates PhD PGCert PGDip MSc (e-mail: j.bates@ulster.ac.uk)

UNIVERSITY OF THE WEST OF ENGLAND, BRISTOL

Department of Computer Science and Creative Technologies, Bristol Institute of Technology, Frenchay Campus, Coldharbour Lane, Bristol BSI6 IQY
☎0117 328 4242
Fax 0117 328 3680
e-mail: bitgraduateschool@uwe.ac.uk

url: www.uwe.ac.uk/bit
Head of Department Dr David Coward PhD BSc CertEd(FoHE)
Programme Leader Paul Matthews (0117 328 3353)

The Regions of England

Public library authorities are arranged within the nine Government regions in England. (Upper Norwood Joint Library is included. This is not a public library authority but a service jointly managed by the London Boroughs of Croydon and Lambeth. However it has a separate entry.) Full entries for these public library authorities will be found in the English Public Libraries section.

East
Bedford
Cambridgeshire
Central Bedfordshire
Essex
Hertfordshire
Luton
Norfolk
Peterborough
Southend on Sea
Suffolk
Thurrock

East Midlands
Derby
Derbyshire
Leicester
Leicestershire
Lincolnshire
Northamptonshire
Nottingham
Nottinghamshire
Rutland

London
Barking and Dagenham
Barnet
Bexley
Brent
Bromley
Camden
City of London
Croydon
Ealing
Enfield
Greenwich
Hackney
Hammersmith and Fulham
Haringey
Harrow
Havering
Hillingdon
Hounslow
Islington
Kensington and Chelsea
Kingston upon Thames
Lambeth
Lewisham
Merton
Newham
Redbridge
Richmond upon Thames
Southwark
Sutton
Tower Hamlets
Upper Norwood Joint Library
Waltham Forest
Wandsworth
Westminster

North East
Darlington
Durham
Gateshead
Hartlepool
Middlesbrough
Newcastle upon Tyne
North Tyneside
Northumberland
Redcar and Cleveland
South Tyneside
Stockton-on-Tees
Sunderland

North West and Merseyside
Blackburn with Darwen
Blackpool
Bolton
Bury
Cheshire East
Cheshire West and Chester
Cumbria
Halton
Knowsley
Lancashire
Liverpool
Manchester
Oldham

Rochdale
St Helens
Salford
Sefton
Stockport
Tameside
Trafford
Warrington
Wigan
Wirral

South East

Bracknell Forest
Brighton and Hove
Buckinghamshire
East Sussex
Hampshire
Isle of Wight
Kent
Medway
Milton Keynes
Oxfordshire
Portsmouth
Reading
Slough
Southampton
Surrey
West Berkshire
West Sussex
Windsor and Maidenhead
Wokingham

South West

Bath and North East Somerset
Bournemouth
Bristol
Cornwall
Devon
Dorset
Gloucestershire
North Somerset

Plymouth
Poole
Somerset
South Gloucestershire
Swindon
Torbay
Wiltshire

West Midlands

Birmingham
Coventry
Dudley
Herefordshire
Sandwell
Shropshire
Solihull
Staffordshire
Stoke-on-Trent
Telford and Wrekin
Walsall
Warwickshire
Wolverhampton
Worcestershire

Yorkshire and The Humber

Barnsley
Bradford
Calderdale
Doncaster
East Riding of Yorkshire
Kingston upon Hull
Kirklees
Leeds
North East Lincolnshire
North Lincolnshire
North Yorkshire
Rotherham
Sheffield
Wakefield
York

Name and place index